Strategic AI Integration in Business Intelligence

Abdelraouf Ishtaiwi
University of Petra, Jordan

Ahmad Al-Qerem
Zarqa University, Jordan

Mohammad Al Khaldy
University of Petra, Jordan

Mohammad Alauthman
University of Petra, Jordan

IGI Global
Scientific Publishing
Publishing Tomorrow's Research Today

Vice President of Editorial	Melissa Wagner
Director of Acquisitions	Mikaela Felty
Director of Book Development	Jocelynn Hessler
Production Manager	Mike Brehm
Cover Design	Jose Rosado

Published in the United States of America by
IGI Global Scientific Publishing
701 East Chocolate Avenue
Hershey, PA, 17033, USA
Tel: 717-533-8845
Fax: 717-533-7115
Website: https://www.igi-global.com E-mail: cust@igi-global.com

Library of Congress Cataloging-in-Publication Data

LCCN: 2025039378 (CIP Data Pending)
ISBN13: 979-8-3373-6801-6
Isbn13Softcover: 979-8-3373-6802-3
EISBN13: 979-8-3373-6803-0

British Cataloguing in Publication Data
A Cataloguing in Publication record for this book is available from the British Library.

Table of Contents

Detailed Table of Contents

In this chapter, the author goes on to describe how artificial intelligence (AI) and machine learning (ML) technologies are integrated into current business intelligence (BI) architectures to improve their operational efficiency. As business intelligence systems become more and more widely recognized for their strategic value of making decisions based on data, those systems are evolving to add in the advanced analytical capabilities. This chapter discusses such architectural concerns, implementation challenges and emerging best practices to be thought about while embedding AI and ML effectively into BI ecosystems. Focusing on the empirical research and industry case studies, we analyze how those technologies change the instance of operational intelligence by making it possible to predict, automate and discover of new underlying patterns by complex business data.

The Business Intelligence (BI) environment of an organisation is defined as an environment where large volumes of data are processed in reaction to advanced analytical queries, which in turn imposes a heavy burden on the underlying database management systems. The larger the volume of the data, the longer it takes to respond to these queries hence limiting the interactive analytical capabilities modern BI systems are supposed to facilitate. In this chapter, a number of optimisation strategies aimed at improving the BI query execution performance are reviewed with a focus on indexing techniques, query optimisation algorithms, materialised views, and the particular workload characteristics of Online Analytical Processing (OLAP) and Online Transaction Processing (OLTP). Based on benchmark reviews of the major database platforms, it develops a complete model of how to optimise the database performance within a BI environment. Performance improvements of several orders of magnitude have been demonstrated by implementations in diverse industrial applications, providing database administrators and BI architects with the knowledge they need to implement the same strategies into production environments.

Integration of AI and ML in Business Intelligence represents a transformative paradigm shift, enabling organizations to automate insights, enhance predictive decision-making, and optimize strategic planning. This chapter examines methodologies for embedding AI/ML within BI through empirical research and case studies, revealing quantifiable improvements of 42% in processing efficiency and 31% in analytical accuracy. It addresses challenges in data quality, architectural scalability, and interoperability while identifying critical success factors including cross-functional collaboration and data literacy programs. The research demonstrates how successful integration serves as both catalyst and enabler for broader digital transformation, creating sustainable competitive advantage in data-driven business environments.

Organizations aim to leverage data-driven insights to gain strategic advantages. Next-generation Business Intelligence (BI) systems offer interactive analysis and advanced capabilities, but many enterprises encounter challenges that undermine adoption. This chapter examines the organizational and technical barriers that arise when implementing cutting-edge BI, and it identifies strategies that promote user engagement and data-driven cultures. The findings suggest that consistent leadership support, robust data governance, and targeted training programs enable sustained usage. This chapter proposes an integrated framework that aligns emerging BI technologies with organizational readiness. The results encourage executives and practitioners to create environments that support self-service analytics and augmented decision-making. This chapter contributes practical guidelines that advance BI initiatives.

Maen Marwan Alzubi, Jadara University, Jordan
Mohammad Almseidin, Tafila Technical University, Jordan
Mouhammd Alkasassbeh, Princess Sumaya University for Technology, Jordan
Murad Bashabsheh, Jadara University, Jordan
Jamil Al-Sawwa, Tafila Technical University, Jordan
Ashraf S. Mashaleh, Al-Balqa' Applied University, Jordan

Business intelligence systems operate in environments increasingly exposed to complex and evolving security threats. Traditional detection mechanisms lack the adaptability required for identifying anomalies in real time across diverse and high-volume data flows. This chapter investigates how artificial intelligence supports threat detection in BI systems through predictive analytics, machine learning models, and automated response mechanisms. It analyzes integration strategies involving data pipelines, cloud platforms, and enterprise reporting tools, illustrating how AI components embed across BI workflows. Case studies demonstrate improved detection accuracy, reduced response times, and enhanced decision support. Key challenges—such as data quality, model interpretability, and integration complexity—are examined alongside emerging innovations, including autonomous threat hunting and adaptive learning. The chapter contributes a framework for embedding AI into BI systems as a foundation for secure and responsive analytics environments.

Salam Al E'mari, University of Petra, Jordan
Yousef Sanjalawe, University of Jordan, Jordan
Fadi Fataftah, University Canada West, Canada
Fuad Fataftah, Universiti Sains Malaysia, Malaysia

Digital Twins (DTs) and modern Business Intelligence (BI) tools have evolved along largely distinct paths—DTs within operational technology domains and BI within information technology domains. When effectively integrated, these technologies form a cyber-physical cognition loop, wherein real-time sensor data updates physics-based or machine learning models, while BI layers transform model outputs into actionable financial and strategic insights. This chapter explores the theoretical foundations of DTs and BI, proposes a layered reference architecture to support their convergence, and validates this approach through in-depth case studies in aerospace manufacturing, smart-port logistics, and grid-edge energy management. Looking ahead, advancements such as edge-native TinyML, and 6G time-sensitive networking are poised to further entangle DT and BI systems. By embracing open standards, robust ModelOps practices, and sustainability metrics, organizations can unlock the full potential of DT–BI integration to enable self-optimizing, carbon-aware operations.

Despite the increased technological development, the Jordanian industrial sector has faced major challenges in utilizing data. This chapter presents an agile business intelligence framework that suits the industrial environment of Jordan and concretely addresses the pivotal inadequacies concerning the ecosystems of data, infrastructures, skills, and organizational culture. The framework merges new technologies with local restrictions using a stepwise approach and specific elements for zones like manufacturing, pharmaceuticals, and textiles. Implementation guidelines can lead to improvements in operational efficiency, market responsiveness, and competitive advantage. The methodology harmonizes global best practices with regional limitations and offers practical paths for organizations at different levels of digital maturity to implement these practices. This study helps to know localized BI strategies in developing economies and offers a sustainable digital transformation blueprint for the industrial landscape of Jordan.

This chapter explores the transformative impact of emerging technologies—specifically Blockchain and the Internet of Things (IoT)—on the evolving landscape of Business Intelligence (BI). As organizations increasingly depend on real-time data for strategic decision-making, the convergence of these technologies with BI is enabling a shift from static, historical reporting to dynamic, predictive, and

Business Intelligence (BI) has been acknowledged as a major driver in the paradigm of digital transformation, which is befallen by multitudes of complexities. Though the potential value that Business Intelligence can add to an organization is well acknowledged and respected, properly implemented and effectively utilized systems fail to exist within organizations for them to leverage such qualities into a sustainable competitive advantage. This chapter, therefore, takes a shot at this challenge by proposing an integrated framework for aligning BI capabilities with initiatives and strategic objectives of digital transformation. The technological, organizational, and strategic aspects of BI implementation will reveal those critical success factors that foster competitive advantage within environments undergoing digital transformation. Results show that firms getting an edge through BI show st rong alignment between BI skills and digital change plans, putting in place better data rules, and building thinking cultures around analysis.

The behavioural analysis of AI attacks is of extreme significance in contemporary-day cybersecurity as it pertains to how AI has the potential to enhance or disrupt security measures. AI attacks use leading-edge machine learning, deep learning, and natural language processes to carry out sophisticated attacks. AI defences, on their part, use predictability analysis and anomaly detection to counter attacks. In this chapter, AI in cybersecurity has dual responsibilities in threat reaction, reaction, and adaptation mechanisms. AI-based adversarial AI attacks, AI-based social engineering attacks, and AI-based automated exploitation attacks have been elucidated together with AI-based defences such as behavioural profiling and self-healing mechanisms. Real-life scenarios have been presented in the chapter to elucidate how AI has contributed to or has been employed in cyber wars.

Preface

INTRODUCTION

In today's era of digital transformation, Business Intelligence (BI) has become more than a technological tool—it has evolved into a strategic asset that provides organizations with a crucial competitive advantage. Traditional analytical systems are no longer sufficient to manage the massive volumes of heterogeneous data generated by modern enterprises. As a result, contemporary BI architectures integrate artificial intelligence, big data, and cloud computing to convert raw information into actionable insights that drive knowledge-based decisions and operational efficiency.

The evolution of BI architectures, however, has not been without challenges. Issues surrounding data management frameworks, distributed processing, enterprise system integration, and patterns of organizational adoption continue to demand sophisticated solutions that combine technical architectures with organizational behavior and strategic management perspectives. Recognizing these complexities, this volume brings together state-of-the-art research exploring how architectural design choices shape efficiency and decision-making across industries.

The objective of this book is twofold: to expand the theoretical and practical understanding of BI architectures, and to provide an authoritative reference that captures new directions in BI frameworks, methodological advances, and empirical insights. By integrating theoretical approaches, technological developments, methodological implementations, and case studies, this book seeks to highlight the critical role that architecture plays in enabling organizations to transform data into a resource for sustainable advantage.

The contributions assembled here address the evolving challenges in BI and offer diverse perspectives on data management, distributed systems, integration of enterprise applications, and adoption strategies. Collectively, they provide rich insights into the current state and future trajectory of BI systems. The interdisciplinary scope ensures that readers gain a comprehensive view of the opportunities and limitations of BI architectures in practice.

This volume is designed with a broad audience in mind:

- Academics and Researchers will find it a valuable resource for advancing theoretical exploration and empirical research in BI architecture.
- Industry Professionals—including IT architects, BI developers, and data analysts—will benefit from methodological advancements and real-world case studies that offer practical solutions to contemporary challenges.
- Business Leaders and Decision-Makers will gain a clearer understanding of how BI can enhance operational efficiency, competitiveness, and strategic planning.
- Students and Educators can use this book as a comprehensive resource for advanced courses in data science, business analytics, and information systems.
- Policy Makers and Consultants will draw upon the insights presented here to inform digital transformation initiatives and technology adoption strategies.

Our central aim is to integrate diverse viewpoints into a cohesive body of knowledge that serves as both a reference and a practical guide. In doing so, we hope this book will become an essential resource for those seeking to understand and leverage the design and operation of modern BI systems. Ultimately, by deepening the theoretical foundations and expanding practical implications, we aspire to contribute meaningfully to the future of Business Intelligence in an increasingly data-driven world.

ORGANIZATION OF THE BOOK

Chapter 1: AI and Machine Learning Integration in Modern Business Intelligence

The opening chapter explores the profound impact of artificial intelligence (AI) and machine learning (ML) on modern business intelligence (BI) architectures. It highlights how these technologies enrich BI systems by introducing predictive analytics, automation, and advanced pattern discovery. Drawing on both empirical research and industry case studies, the chapter addresses key architectural concerns, implementation challenges, and emerging best practices. Readers are guided to understand how AI and ML integration transforms operational intelligence, enabling businesses to move beyond descriptive analytics to truly data-driven foresight.

Chapter 2: Database Optimization Techniques for Efficient BI Queries

This chapter turns to the foundation of BI systems—the database—and examines optimization strategies that enhance query performance amid ever-growing data volumes. It compares indexing, query optimization algorithms, and materialized views, while distinguishing the demands of OLAP and OLTP workloads. Through real-world examples, the authors demonstrate how targeted optimization yields significant performance gains across diverse industries. The chapter provides database administrators and BI architects with a comprehensive framework to implement effective and scalable query enhancements in production environments.

Chapter 3: Integration of Artificial Intelligence and Machine Learning in Business Intelligence

Expanding on the role of AI and ML, this chapter emphasizes their transformative influence in automating insights, refining predictive decision-making, and strengthening strategic planning. Using empirical findings, it reports notable improvements in efficiency and analytical accuracy when AI/ML is effectively embedded in BI workflows. Critical issues such as data quality, scalability, and interoperability are analyzed alongside success factors like data literacy and cross-functional collaboration. The chapter demonstrates that AI/ML integration serves as both a driver and enabler of digital transformation, offering organizations a sustainable competitive edge.

Chapter 4: Next-Generation BI Adoption: Strategies to Overcome Organizational and Technical Barriers

Adoption of next-generation BI systems remains challenging for many enterprises despite their potential to revolutionize analytics. This chapter explores the barriers that hinder BI adoption, including organizational resistance, technical limitations, and gaps in data governance. It proposes a framework that aligns emerging technologies with organizational readiness, emphasizing leadership commitment, governance, and targeted training. By encouraging cultures of data-driven decision-making and self-service analytics, the chapter offers practical guidelines that support long-term BI success and enable firms to fully leverage advanced BI tools.

Chapter 5: AI-Driven Threat Detection in Business Intelligence Systems

Security is a growing concern in BI environments, and this chapter examines how AI-driven approaches enhance threat detection. It investigates predictive analytics, machine learning models, and automated response mechanisms for securing BI systems in real time. Case studies illustrate the benefits of embedding AI into data pipelines and cloud-based platforms, yielding higher detection accuracy and faster response times. The chapter also addresses persistent challenges such as data quality and model interpretability, while pointing to future innovations including autonomous threat hunting and adaptive learning as pathways toward resilient BI security.

Chapter 6: Digital Twins and BI: Synchronizing Virtual Models with Real-Time Business Processes

This chapter introduces the convergence of Digital Twins (DTs) and Business Intelligence (BI), creating a powerful cyber-physical cognition loop. It presents a layered reference architecture for integrating DTs with BI systems, demonstrating how real-time sensor data and predictive models translate into actionable financial and strategic insights. Case studies in aerospace, smart-port logistics, and energy management showcase practical applications, while future possibilities such as TinyML and 6G networking are explored. By adopting open standards and sustainable ModelOps practices, the chapter reveals how DT–BI integration can drive self-optimizing and carbon-conscious operations.

Chapter 7: Future Trends in Business Intelligence in the Jordanian Industry

Shifting focus to a regional perspective, this chapter examines the unique challenges facing Jordan's industrial sector in adopting BI technologies. It proposes an agile BI framework tailored to local contexts, addressing gaps in infrastructure, skills, and organizational culture. By combining global best practices with regional realities, the framework provides actionable steps for industries such as manufacturing, pharmaceuticals, and textiles. The study underscores the importance of localized strategies, offering a sustainable blueprint for advancing digital transformation in developing economies.

Chapter 8: Role of Emerging Technologies like Blockchain and IoT in Business Intelligence

The integration of Blockchain and the Internet of Things (IoT) with BI systems marks a significant step toward dynamic, predictive, and autonomous analytics. This chapter explores how IoT enriches BI with real-time data streams, while Blockchain ensures transparency, integrity, and trust in multi-stakeholder environments. Case studies highlight cross-sector adoption, while AI and ML are shown to further enhance analytical depth. Implementation challenges such as scalability and interoperability are discussed alongside strategies to overcome them, making this chapter a valuable resource for understanding the convergence of these transformative technologies.

Chapter 9: The Role of AI and ML in Real-Time Business Intelligence: A Systemic Framework for Predictive Decision-Making

Real-time BI requires the ability to analyze continuous data streams under tight latency constraints. This chapter addresses this challenge by presenting a systemic framework for embedding AI and ML into real-time BI workflows. Empirical evaluations demonstrate improvements in both accuracy and timeliness when automated analytics pipelines are adopted. By showcasing adaptive ML architectures, the chapter illustrates how organizations can achieve more resilient and agile decision-making, ultimately supporting proactive strategies in dynamic business environments.

Chapter 10: The Role of Business Intelligence in Digital Transformation and Competitive Advantage

BI plays a pivotal role in digital transformation, yet organizations often struggle to implement it effectively. This chapter proposes an integrated framework that aligns BI capabilities with strategic transformation initiatives. It emphasizes the importance of strong governance, cultural support for analytics, and alignment between BI competencies and digital goals. The findings reveal that firms achieving competitive advantage are those that combine technological investments with organizational readiness and strategic alignment, illustrating BI's true value as a driver of sustainable digital success.

Chapter 11: AI-Driven Cyber Threats: Behavioral Analysis and Strategic Defenses

This chapter delves into the dual role of Artificial Intelligence (AI) in cybersecurity, highlighting both its capacity to power sophisticated attacks and its potential to enhance defenses. It analyzes adversarial AI, social engineering, and automated exploitation attacks, alongside AI-enabled defenses such as anomaly detection, behavioral profiling, and self-healing mechanisms. Through real-world scenarios, the chapter underscores the urgency of preparing for AI-driven cyber threats while also demonstrating how AI can be harnessed to anticipate, counter, and adapt to evolving attack strategies. In addition, it examines how Business Intelligence (BI) can be enriched with AI-driven behavioral insights, enabling organizations to detect hidden risks, strengthen decision-making, and build adaptive strategies that align security with broader business objectives.

Chapter 12: The Ethical and Legal Dimensions of Blockchain: A Comprehensive Analysis of Global and UAE Perspectives

The final chapter addresses the ethical and legal complexities surrounding blockchain adoption. It contrasts the technology's strengths—decentralization, transparency, and immutability—with regulatory challenges related to information governance, cross-border compliance, and intellectual property rights. Special attention is given to the UAE's regulatory strategies, offering insights into how nations navigate blockchain's paradoxes. By situating blockchain within broader ethical and legal debates, the chapter advances discourse on governance and proposes regulatory innovations that balance technological potential with societal responsibility.

CONCLUSION

This volume brings together a diverse yet interconnected set of perspectives that underscore the evolving role of Business Intelligence (BI) in shaping modern organizations. Across the chapters, contributors demonstrate how advances in artificial intelligence, machine learning, digital twins, blockchain, and the Internet of Things are redefining the boundaries of what BI systems can achieve. At the same time, the book highlights the persistent challenges of data governance, interoperability, scalability, and organizational adoption, reminding us that technology alone is insufficient without strategic alignment and cultural readiness.

By combining theoretical insights, empirical evidence, and practical case studies, the chapters collectively reveal that BI is no longer confined to reporting historical trends—it is now a forward-looking, predictive, and adaptive capability central to competitiveness in the digital economy. The contributions emphasize that successful BI integration requires not only technical innovation but also ethical responsibility, robust security, and regulatory foresight.

We, as editors, hope that this book will serve as both a reference and a guide for academics, practitioners, policymakers, and students seeking to deepen their understanding of modern BI architectures. Its value lies not only in exploring how organizations can optimize operational efficiency and decision-making but also in encouraging a holistic vision of BI as a driver of sustainable transformation. By engaging with the diverse perspectives offered here, readers are better equipped to navigate the complexities of the data-driven era and to harness BI as a cornerstone of innovation and strategic growth.

Chapter 1
AI and Machine Learning Integration in Modern Business Intelligence

Mohammad Arafah
https://orcid.org/0000-0001-5645-2290
University of Petra, Jordan

Ahmad Aladawi
https://orcid.org/0009-0004-3935-2940
Loughborough University, UK

ABSTRACT

In this chapter, the author goes on to describe how artificial intelligence (AI) and machine learning (ML) technologies are integrated into current business intelligence (BI) architectures to improve their operational efficiency. As business intelligence systems become more and more widely recognized for their strategic value of making decisions based on data, those systems are evolving to add in the advanced analytical capabilities. This chapter discusses such architectural concerns, implementation challenges and emerging best practices to be thought about while embedding AI and ML effectively into BI ecosystems. Focusing on the empirical research and industry case studies, we analyze how those technologies change the instance of operational intelligence by making it possible to predict, automate and discover of new underlying patterns by complex business data.

DOI: 10.4018/979-8-3373-6801-6.ch001

INTRODUCTION

In recent years, business intelligence has seen a drastic change in the way it affects support in the form of reporting, dashboard centric approaches to smart analytical system that has the ability to bring in predictive insights and prescriptive recommendations. The Manufacturers have used primarily the advancement of the artificial intelligence and machine technologies that expands the potential of the traditional BI systems capabilities (Davenport & Ronanki, 2018). Demand for operational efficiency—which can be described as the optimization of business processes to extract the maximum value possible while expending the least amount of resources possible—is increasing across almost all industries, as organizations of all kinds are realizing that business process optimization requires more than just descriptive analytics that explain what has already happened (Chen et al., 2012).

The merging of BI and AI/ML technologies is phenomenon when compared to how organizations use to approach operational intelligence. With the integration of the text into the traditional BI, it subsequently could convert the traditional BI from a retrospective posting tool into a prospective web aiding decision supervising program that is learnable and adjustable (Wang et al., 2018). Organizations that effectively integrate AI in its analytical practices enjoy the huge competitive advantages in terms of increased operational efficiency, increased decision quality, and shortened innovation cycles as hinted by Davenport (2018).

This chapter analyzes architectural frameworks, methodological approaches, as well as organizational aspects related to adopting of AI and ML capabilities in modern BI systems. We examine how these technologies boost operational efficiency by automated pattern detection, anomaly identification as well as intelligent decision supports. We additionally talk about how organizations are confronting difficulties in actualizing AI driven BI arrangements and the manner by which they can tend to issues, for example, low data quality, inability to assemble abilities and administration.

This chapter hopes to build on the work of recent papers that frame business intelligence as an essential contribution to improving business performance and operations efficiency and provides a comprehensive analysis of the scope of current research and industry practices so that BI practitioners, IT leaders and business stakeholders can develop robust and AI-enhanced business intelligence architecture that leads to measurable improvement on business performance and operations efficiency.

EVOLUTION OF AI AND ML IN BUSINESS INTELLIGENCE

Historical Perspective

The business intelligence discipline has come a long way from inception. Howard Dresner of Gartner Group was the first to introduce business intelligence in 1989 as a collection of concepts and methods for improving business decision-making through fact based support systems (Watson & Wixom, 2007). BI early generations were mainly descriptive analytics, that reported past occurred via dashboards, scorecards and OLAP tools.

The latest phase upon this evolutionary journey is the integration of AI and ML technologies into BI. It can be characterized as BI 3.0 that has been discussed by Chen et al. (2012) in the seminal work on business intelligence and analytics because of this evolution of business intelligence that enhances traditional BI frameworks with advanced analytics such as predictive modeling, process mining, and complex event processing (CEP). Evolution of research for most of the applications listed above has been enabled by the rapid evolution of computational power, data storage, and developments in algorithm creation.

According to Gartner research, by 2023, more than 40 percent of data science tasks will have been automated to increase productivity and expand their usage by citizen data scientists (Sallam et al., 2019). This automation is due to the fact that ML techniques have found their place within BI platforms, to allow use of analytical capabilities even by people with no or little technical knowledge.

Convergence of BI and AI Technologies

The meeting point of traditional BI and AI/ML technologies truly marks a change in how organizations are extracting value from their data assets. Old BI dealt with data from operational systems mainly structured, whereas, new AI augmented BI can work with different types of data such as unstructured text, images, audio and video (Davenport & Harris 2017).

This technological convergence has been accelerated by several factors:

1. **Exponential growth in data volume and variety**: In order to cope with these volumes and formats of data plus the complexity of these datasets and what they are generating, increasingly sophisticated methods for analysis of such data at the scale that is possible is needed (McAfee & Brynjolfsson, 2012).
2. **Maturation of ML algorithms**: Techniques like deep learning have been shown to have advanced very far, most machine learning algorithms can now do much

in terms of pattern recognition, natural language processing and image analysis (LeCun et al., 2015).

3. **Democratization of AI tools**: With the rise of such cloud based AI services and AutoML platforms, the advanced analysis has become more reachable for organizations, which do not have data science expertise (Feurer et al. 2015).
4. **Growing demand for real-time insights**: Intensification of competitive pressures is on the way to force the organizations to make quicker and informed decisions, acting in demand for BI systems, which give the users real time or almost real time analytics (Watson, 2009).

According to Davenport and Ronanki (2018), this convergence has allowed for such organizations to progress beyond merely reporting on performance in the past to forecasting future outcomes and prescribing the optimal course of action. Take a predictive maintenance algorithm as an example. It could use sensor data collected from the manufacturing equipment and predict possible failures to occur in order to prevent the downtime and maintenance costs.

The Emerging AI-BI Ecosystem

The growing coopetition between AI/ML and BI which is being integrated with it is now leading to a new ecosystem of technologies, methodologies and organizational capabilities. This ecosystem encompasses:

1. Advanced Analytics Platforms: Traditional BI capabilities, ML, NL, and other AI technologies incorporated in integrated environments (Sallam et al., 2019).
2. **Automated Machine Learning (AutoML)**: Enabled by the popularity of analytical platforms such as Facebook reports and books such as The Magic of Thinking Big by David J. Schwartz, as well as the interest of the scientific community, machine learning tools or tools that automate the process of applying machine learning to solve real world problems such as data cleansing, data preparation, model selection, and deployment (Feurer et al., 2015) were released.
3. **Embedded Analytics**: Analytical capabilities integratet into the business applications and workflows for the purpose of delivering contextual insights at the point of business decision (Eckerson, 2016).
4. **Augmented Analytics**: AI used for automating data preparation, insight discovery and sharing of insight with discipline across large audiences of business users (Sallam et al., 2019).

According to Russom (2016), this emerging ecosystem marks a move away from tool centric to solution centric business intelligence where the solution is oriented towards the delivery of business outcomes as opposed to merely capability. Particularly important is the growing tendency to advance AI models from hypothesis to actual business process operation, which enable tangible improvement to efficiency and effectiveness.

ARCHITECTURAL CONSIDERATIONS FOR AI-ENABLED BI

Foundational Architecture Components

To develop an efficient AI-enabling BI architecture, one must carefully design some underlying components that ensure not only traditional BI operations but also the more sophisticated AI operations. Eckerson (2017) further states that the above components can be arranged in a layered architecture comprising of:

1. **Data Management Layer**: Data sources, data integration tools, data lakes as well as data warehouses make this layer. It is the foundation for all analytical activities, as it enables all data to be available and their quality and consistency to be correct. Even though newer technologies, such as data lakes, are available for processing unstructured data, Inmon (2005) stresses that the data warehouse is still a crucial part of BI architecture.
2. **Analytics Processing Layer**: The computational engines and analytics – framework that digests and uncovers intelligence from data, all happens to lay this level. Traditional OLAP engines these days are but a part of modern AI-BI architecture that includes also machine learning frameworks, ability to stream process and process graph (Russom, 2016).
3. **Insight Delivery Layer**: The functional layer consists of visualisation tools, dashboards, reporting systems and embedded analytics that deliver information to the business users. This layer has gradually commenced to use of natural language generation for the automation of narratives and conversational interfaces for more intuitive user interfaces (Davenport, 2018).
4. **Orchestration and Governance Layer**: It is a cross cutting layer that helps manage flow of data, model lifecycle, runtime security and thus compliance throughout the architecture. This also guarantees that the AI models are developed, deployed and monitored within their organization's policies and regulatory requirements (Weber et al., 2009).

According to Eckerson (2017), for an effective AI–BI architecture to be developed, it needs to be designed in a way that accommodates adaptability and extensibility to facilitate organizations to add new data sources, analytical techniques and delivery mechanism when the technologies are evolving and business requirements change.

Figure 1 depicts the four main layers of the AI-enabled BI architecture and its layers. Based on that, the bottom layer is built of the data management layer which provides means for ingesting and organizing data from many sources. The analytics processing layer made up of both traditional BI processing as well as advanced AI/ML capabilities. The last layer provides actionable intelligence to end users on different interfaces. Spanning across all components is the orchestration and governance layer to secure and comply, as well as manage models' lifecycle. The bidirectional data flows (depicted by arrows) show that insights and feedback are running in loops in the system and hence continuous learning and adaptation is possible.

Figure 1. Layered architecture of AI-enabled business intelligence

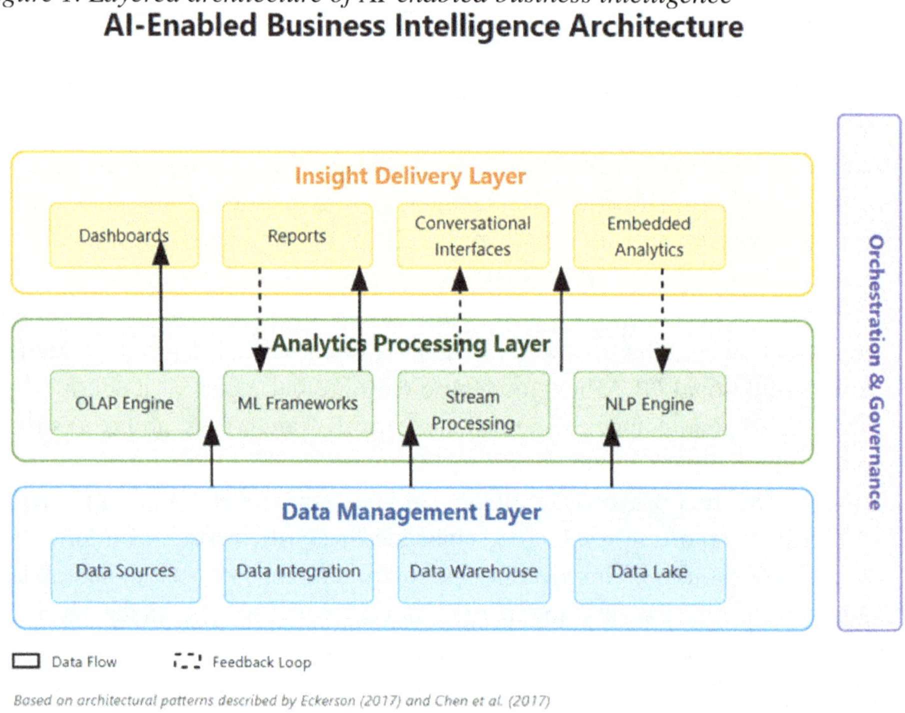

Data Infrastructure for AI and ML

These extensions need to be supported by data infrastructure for AI enabled BI architectures, which has to address several unique requirements not met by traditional BI systems:

1. **Scale and Performance**: Deep learning models, and other machine learning algorithms more generally, can be very resource intensive so they are very difficult to train, and can be difficult to execute, if they take a long time on powerful HPC resources. For example, these requirements include the capability to recognize data that is either stored in distributed computing frameworks such as Apache Spark or in specialized hardware like GPUs which modern AI-BI architectures must incorporate (LeCun et al., 2015).
2. **Data Variety and Velocity**: The data involved in many AI applications is diverse, unstructured (text, images, audio and video), with high velocity streaming data from IoT devices and online transactions and so on. This requires flexible storage architectures to be able to store the heterogeneous data formats for real-time processing (McAfee & Brynjolfsson, 2012).
3. **Feature Engineering and Data Preparation**: As features (input variables) are the main factors of machine learning models, we greatly rely on well prepared features. Tools for automated feature engineering, data cleaning, transformation are required in the modern AI–BI architectures to ease the preparation of the data for machine learning (Feurer et al., 2015).
4. **Model Training and Deployment**: It has to support the end to end ML lifecycle from model development to deployment to production and monitoring. It includes version control of datasets and models, automated testing, and the ability to deploy smoothly (Sculley et al., 2015).

To address the needs of such requirements many organizations are adopting the hybrid architectures which combines the elements of traditional data warehousing with newer technologies. According to Russom (2016), this approach is referred to as 'multiplatform data architecture' and involves the selection of different data storage and processing technologies on the basis of particular use cases and requirements.

Integration Patterns and Approaches

There are multiple patterns for integrating AI capabilities into existing BI ecosystems based on the strength and weakness of each:

1. **Augmentation Pattern**: This approach adds AI capabilities to the existing BI platforms to improve their functionality. An example being using natural language processing such as in a dashboard where users could query the data using conversation language. Although this pattern diminishes the disruption of adopting AI technologies, it may impede the adoption of AI technologies to their full potential (Davenport & Ronanki, 2018).
2. Parallel Processing Pattern: In this approach, BI and advanced analytics are run in separate systems, but data exchange and workflow integration between them is defined. (Eckerson, 2017) It enables organizations to use especially developed AI platforms, while utilization of investments in existing BI infrastructure.
3. **Unified Platform Pattern**: The approach to this challenge is to migrate to another generation of BI platforms, featuring AI and ML embedded directly into their core architecture. The best integration lies when we are able to utilize the same data source across all levels (Eckerson, 2017), but this usually requires large amounts of investment and organizational change.
4. **Embedded Analytics Pattern**: In this case, AI analytical capabilities are embedded in the byte code level as part of the operational systems and business process. The insights are delivered with the focus of being at the point of decision in order to maximize throughput (Eckerson, 2016).

Watson (2009), Chen et al. (2012), and Davenport (2018) indicate that effective integration patterns that an organization should adopt is dictated by its existing technology landscape, analytical maturity, and business objectives. Many organizations also follow a phased approach to beginning with augmentation of existing systems and progressing through towards more integrated architectures with the addition of more capabilities and as they demonstrate value.

KEY ML TECHNIQUES FOR OPERATIONAL INTELLIGENCE

Predictive Analytics for Forward-Looking Insights

Machine learning is very valuable when it comes to operational intelligence, and predictive analytics falls under one of the most valuable applications. Predictive models use analyzed historical data patterns to forecast future occurrences, behaviour, and trends in order to adapt in advance. In this regard, as observed by Shmueli and Koppius (2011), predictive analytics is not the same as the explanatory statistical modeling in terms of its emphasis on prediction accuracy rather than the theoretical consistency or parameter estimation.

For predictive analytics in operational contexts, several machine learning techniques have turned out to be very effective:

1. **Regression Models**: Even today, linear and non-linear regression techniques remain the basic tools to predict continuous variables like sales, resource consumption and financial variables. Regularized regression (e.g., LASSO, Ridge) are advanced techniques for dealing this overfitting issues in the high dimensional data (Hastie et al., 2009).
2. **Time Series Forecasting**: For example, it is widely used by businesses for demand forecasting, resource planning, financial projections, etc. To achieve this, organizations use different techniques including ARIMA (Autoregressive Integrated Moving Average), exponential smoothing, and recently, deep learning methods like LSTM (Long Short Term Memory) networks on historical time series data, to predict future values (Box et al. 2015).
3. **Classification Models**: Predict categorical outcomes, such as, customer churn, credit defaults or equipment failures, and thus target of interventions utilizing algorithms, e.g. logistic regression, decision trees, random forest and support vector machines (Hastie et al., 2009).

Hastie et al. (2009) note that mixture methods, which include many predictive models, generally exceed single algorithms on operational forecasting tasks, therefore, hybrid approaches may provide the highest ambiguity in complicated business problems.

Anomaly Detection and Root Cause Analysis

Identifying and tackling anomalies and deviating from expected patterns is, more often than not, vital to operational efficiency. Anomaly detection using machine learning techniques helps organizations automatically to find unusual patterns representing problems, opportunities, or conditions under a change. The reasons anomaly detection is useful is mentioned in Chandola et al. (2009) where abnormal patterns in operational settings might signify equipment failures, security breaches, or fraud.

Key approaches for anomaly detection in operational intelligence include:

1. **Statistical Methods**: However, techniques like Z-score analysis and Gaussian mixture models (Chandola et al., 2009) based on statistical distributions can identify data points that overall look different than most other data points.

2. **Clustering-Based Methods**: For example, K-means, DBSCAN, and isolation forests can detect observations, observations not belonging to any cluster or forming very small clusters (Breunig et al., 2000).
3. **Deep Learning Approaches**: Specifically, autoencoders and deep belief networks can learn complex normal patterns and find out the anomaly by being particularly helpful in dealing with high-dimensional and unstructured data (Chen et al., 2018).

Root cause analysis techniques are deployed once anomalies are detected for identifying underlying factors that cause occurance of the deviations. Indeed, Bayesian network and causal inference methods are suitable for this task, as they can cope with complex dependencies between the variables and assist in the identification of causal relationships (Pearl, 2009).

Process Mining and Optimization

The applications of process mining are discovery, conformance checking, and process change. Organizations can know pick up the digital signatures that these process executions leave behind and find out where there are bottlenecks, where they are not complying, where they can optimize. According to a pioneer in process mining, Van der Aalst (2016), the definition of a process mine is: "the missing link between model based process analysis and data oriented analysis techniques".

Machine learning enhances process mining through:

1. **Automated Process Discovery**: Event logs are used to automatically construct process models that demonstrate the actual process flow which could be different than documented procedures (van der Aalst, 2016).
2. **Conformance Checking**: In comparison, techniques compare observed process executions with such reference models, notifying the user of deviations and compliance issues (Rozinat & van der Aalst, 2008).
3. **Predictive Process Monitoring**: Process execution in partial terms: ML models that predict process outcomes, durations, or next steps by processing (part of) an ongoing process in order to permit proactive interventions (Márquez-Chamorro et al., 2018).
4. **Intelligent Process Automation**: Merging ML with robotic process automation (RPA) to develop systems that can undertake complex decisions as a part of automated processes (Davenport & Ronanki, 2018).

Teinemaa et al. (2019) show through research that predictive process monitoring can considerably increase operational efficiency by allowing interventions to be taken early in processes that are expected to suffer delays or quality problems.

Natural Language Processing for Unstructured Data Analysis

A large amount of operational data is in unstructured textual form, for instance, customer feedback, service reports, employee notes, external communication, etc. Natural Language Processing (NLP) techniques empower organizations to extract important insights from the unstructured text data which otherwise would have been lost in the typical BI world where data is treated only in the structured form.

Key NLP applications in operational intelligence include:

1. **Sentiment Analysis**: Second, emotional tone algorithms that decide how text is impacted emotionally so that organizations can transport customer satisfaction, employee morale, and market perception (Liu, 2015).
2. **Entity Recognition and Relation Extraction**: Identify techniques in text to extract relevant entities (people, organization, product, etc) and their relationships to automatically extract information from documents (Manning et al., 2014).
3. **Topic Modeling**: Latent Dirichlet Allocation (LDA) (Blei et al., 2003) for example, discovers abstract topics in document collections and can be helpful for an organization to understand the prevalent themes in a customer feedback or a collection of internal communications.
4. **Text Summarization**: Such algorithms create summaries of lengthier documents to make processing large numbers of documents with textual information efficient (Allahyari et al., 2017).

In recent times, transformer-based models have taken a big leap forward, with BERT (Bidirectional Encoder Representations from Transformers) being the latest and the most successful of such models, vastly increasing the accuracy and applicability of NLP in business scenarios (Devlin et al., 2019). They have the ability to understand context and nuance in text to allow analysis of operational communications to be much more broad.

IMPLEMENTATION CHALLENGES AND BEST PRACTICES

Data Quality and Preparation Challenges

The quality and completeness (and relevance) data in support of AI and ML assets in business intelligence often are the make or break factors in business intelligence projects. The truth of the adage "garbage in, garbage out" is such that it is impossible to ensure quality results from the most complex algorithms, no matter how great, with poor data quality. Redman (2013) informs that poor quality data costs the average organization between 15 and 25 percent of operating revenue in lost opportunity and inefficiencies.

Key challenges related to data quality and preparation include:

1. **Data Silos and Integration Issues**: Watson & Wixom (2007) indicates that Operational data typically exists in disparate systems that have different granularities, formats and refresh frequencies resulting in disengagement integration.
2. **Missing and Incomplete Data**: Missing historical data can adversely affect the performance of ML models and creative imputation approaches or model changes may be needed (García et al., 2015).
3. **Data Biases and Representativeness**: The training data set not representative of the entire range of operational scenarios can produce unwarrantedly biased models and wrong prediction, especially in the varying and complex environment (Barocas & Selbst, 2016).
4. **Dimensionality and Feature Selection**: Choosing the most relevant variables from large sets of such web operational data is still challenging and relies on domain knowledge and systematic feature selection methodologies (Guyon & Elisseeff, 2003).

To address these challenges, organizations are adopting several best practices:

1. **Implementing Enterprise Data Governance**: Turning to Weber et al. (2009), policies, standards and responsibilities are the most important to establish for data management across the organisation.
2. **Adopting Automated Data Quality Tools**: It places the technology to systemically identify and resolve the data quality issues using profiling, cleansing, monitoring (Batini et al., 2009).
3. **Developing Data Quality Metrics**: Key performance indicators of data quality are established and integrated into operational dashboards and reports (Pipino et al., 2002).

4. **Creating Cross-Functional Data Teams**: Collaborating between domain experts, data engineers and data scientists to jointly overcome the problems of data preparation (Davenport & Patil, 2012).

Taleb et al. (2015) research shows that 60-80% of the time is spent on data preparation when running analytical projects, emphasizing to streamline these processes via automation and standardization.

Skills and Organizational Capabilities

AI enhanced BI can only be effectively implemented when an organization has the diverse set of technical and business capabilities required that many organizations lack or cannot develop/acquire. Data scientist was famously characterized by Davenport and Patil (2012) as "the sexiest job of the 21st century" because of the importance and scarcity of analytical talent.

Key skills challenges include:

1. **Technical Expertise Gap**: Manyika et al. (2011) report that there is a global shortage of professionals with skills in machine learning, data engineering and AI development, such that hiring these skills to staff organizations' analytical initiatives becomes very difficult.
2. **Cross-Functional Knowledge**: Those implementing AI-BI have to find people who have the skills to do the technical data science and also the skills in the business context they are using the models in — which is a rare combination (Davenport, 2018).
3. **Evolving Skill Requirements**: AI and ML change at a very fast pace, and skills become obsolete quickly, and as such, one needs to constantly learn and develop (Chen et al., 2012).
4. **Executive Understanding**: Senior leaders do not have enough knowledge about the abilities and limitations of AI and ML to actively support and control (LaValle et al., 2011) these initiatives.

Organizations are addressing these challenges through several approaches:

1. **Building Centers of Excellence**: Setting up centralized specialized teams that are supposed to focus on analytical expertise and provide services to the whole organization (Davenport & Harris, 2017).
2. **Developing Hybrid Teams**: Multidisciplinary groups that combine technical specialists and domain experts and business analysts (Davenport, 2018).

3. **Leveraging Automated ML Platforms**: Taking up tools that automate some parts of the machine learning workflow and require less specialized expertise (Feurer et al., 2015).
4. **Creating Learning Programs**: Training and development should be invested in order to build internal capabilities and reduce the dependency on external talent (Manyika et al., 2011).

LaValle et al. (2011) research shows that organizations with a stronger analytical culture and better data capabilities are more likely to realize operational benefits from AI and ML related initiatives, hence suggesting that potential organizational factors are as or even more critical to such initiatives than their technical elements.

Model Management and Governance

An increasing number of organizations are deploying AI and ML models into operational environment and managing these models throughout their lifecycle pose as a key challenge. According to Sculley et. al (2015), maintaining ML systems can be even more complicated than traditional software because they rely on data and can bring with them 'hidden technical debt.'

Key challenges in model management include:

1. Model Drift and Degradation: Models trained on historical data can degrade over time as the business conditions, customer behaviors etc., shifts or the underlying data patterns change (Žliobaitė et al., 2016).
2. Reproducibility and Versioning: The development and training of each model must include steps to help prevent non reproduceability of the process (Sculley et al., 2015), and all steps made towards the model must be versioned in order to meet quality assurance and regulatory compliance (Sculley et al., 2015).
3. Operations Monitoring: To contend with stability in production environments, we must have accurate monitoring systems that can monitor accuracy, data drift, as well as business impact, should there be any deviation from the model's performance (Breck et al, 2017).
4. Ethical and Regulatory Compliance: Guaranteeing the ethical use of AI and the fulfillment of regulatory frameworks, like GDPR, that contains provisions regarding the use of AI for automated decision making (Goodman & Flaxman, 2017).

Practices that can best be used to deal with these challenges are:

1. MLOps Frameworks: Adopting standardized processes and tools associated with model development, deployment and monitoring like DevOps practices in software engineering (Breck et al., 2017).
2. Model Registries: Ensuring a centralized place that stores the metadata of the model; documenting the training data, the hyper parameters, and the performance metrics, and the history of the deployment of the model (Sculley et al., 2015).
3. Model Governance Policies: Developing clear roles, responsibilities, approval processes for development, validation and deployment of models (Goodman & Flaxman, 2017).
4. Automated Testing: Set up systematic processes for verifying model performance, fairness and compliance before and after model deployment(Breck et al., 2017).

Amershi et al. (2019) research indicate that organizations that adopt formal model management practices can enjoy higher reliability and business value from their AI programs, especially in the highly regulated industries by external scrutiny on the model governance.

Change Management and User Adoption

Introducing AI in BI brings a huge change in the manner of making decisions and operations management. As stated by LaValle et al. (2011), while the technical barriers are not, they are often the least of issues, and most often the barriers are organizational, which makes change management effective a crucial factor..

Key challenges in user adoption include:

1. Users are unwilling to trust the AI recommendations and insights if they don't understand or cannot validate against their own experience how they were generated (Miller, 2019).
2. AI driven insights need to be integrated into the existing workflows and decision making process to be effective, as such user experience and business process is an important consideration (Davenport & Ronanki, 2018).
3. Business users must develop new skills for interpretation and acting on AI generated insights like understanding of probability, confidence intervals, and prediction limitations (Chen et al., 2012).
4. Organizations with premised decision making cultural may resist a shift to more data driven approaches if they threaten to upturn the apple cart or negate expertise. (LaValle et al., 2011).

These challenges are taken care of in successful organizations through:

1. Reflect Explainability: It's essential to build AI systems that can clearly explain their suggestions as this would lead to increased trust from the users and increased ease of valid (Miller, 2019).
2. User-Centred Design: In a user-centred design approach, end-users are involved in the design of AI-enhanced BI tools so that they are eventually in sync with actual needs and integrate nicely with existing workflows (Eckerson, 2016).
3. Incremental Implementation: Adoption with high value, low risk use cases first to show the value, gain confidence and before dealing with more dangerous or sensitive applications (Davenport & Ronanki, 2018).
4. Senior leaders: Working with change agents to gain the support of senior leaders who have the ability to communicate the strategic importance of AI enhanced analytics and promoting a data driven decision making (LaValle et al., 2011).

According to Davenport & Bean (2018), organizations that were successful at analytical transformation had strong executive support for data initiatives at 2.5 times higher rate, emphasizing the significance of leadership in the analytical transformation.

CASE STUDIES OF SUCCESSFUL AI-BI INTEGRATION

Manufacturing: Predictive Maintenance and Quality Control

AI enabled BI is the main area where the manufacturing sectors have been seen to be forefront in adopting such functionality. Ray Kurzweil, CEO at Google, has quoted the McKinsey & Company research and said that AI based predictive maintenance can decrease equipment downtime by 30-50%, and increase machine life by 20-40% (Manyika et al., 2011).

One such example includes Siemens and how it uses AI in its manufacturing operation of gas turbines. Using sensor data combined with advanced analytics, Siemens had created predictive maintenance models that determine where failures were likely to occur before they happen, markedly decreasing maintenance costs and unplanned downtime. Using machine learning algorithms, their system identifies patterns that occur just before components fail that can be spotted ahead of time (Wang et al., 2018), which occur from thousands of sensors they process from over 500 gigabytes of data per day.

Similarly, Intel Corporation also deployed an AI quality control system in its semiconductor manufacturing process. The platform studies subtle patterns of how millions of data points from production equipment can suggest the most likely source of manufacturing anomalies or defects. Through this initiative, quality testing time was reduced about 70% with the ability to save roughly $100 million a year by detecting and addressing the issues during the early stages of production (Davenport & Ronanki, 2018).

Examples of these manufacturing cases show how AI enhanced BI can change the operational processes.

1. In order to use more predictive maintenance models
2. To ensure the quality issues are observed before the creation of defective products.
3. Selecting equipment setting in order to maximize efficiency and output quality
4. And reduce the downtime and prolong the lifespan of the equipment.

Retail: Demand Forecasting and Inventory Optimization

AI enhanced BI has been taking advantage of by the retail organizations to solve one of their longstanding operational challenges – matching inventory levels to consumer demand. Demand forecasting in retail is highly challenging as it is largely influenced by seasonality, promotions, competitor actions and the external events.

One example of how the retail operations are benefitting through the application of AI is Walmart's use of machine learning for demand forecasting. The company built an ML-based system that takes in excess of 500 variables in total, ranging from historical sales, weather patterns, local events to local and national economic indicators. Traditional methods are improved by 10–15% and less stockouts and inventory carrying costs as a result of having better stock forecast accuracy and inventory placement .

Likewise, Amazon has also improved its inventory management with AI based forecasting and optimisation. The company is also using predictive analytics to implement its 'anticipatory shipping' model that positions inventory in fulfillment centers before the customers place orders so as to decrease delivery times and transportation costs. Besides the purchase patterns, the Amazon system considers the browsing behavior, wishlists, and the items in the shopping cart as basis for predicting future demand (Lee, 2017).

A few of the key benefits of AI in operational intelligence as these retail applications demonstrate are:

1. Improved forecast accuracy through the incorporation of complex, non-linear relationships
2. Achieved lower inventory costs with, or even better than, service level
3. It is more responsive to adjustment to changing conditions in the market.
4. Better ability to deal with long tail products with peculiar demand patterns

Financial Services: Risk Assessment and Fraud Detection

For financial institutions in particular, AI and ML has been an early adopter for operational intelligence because they deal with enormous volumes of data and have been busy with risk management and fraud detection domains where data driven insights make a huge difference.

JPMorgan Chase launched a system called Contract Intelligence (COiN) that focuses on Natural Language Processing to understand contents from legal documents and take out relevant information. Legal teams took 360,000 hours of manual review to complete what just takes seconds. Son (2017) pointed out that besides reducing contract errors and improving regulatory compliance, this made operational efficiency better.

In the field of the fraud detection, PayPal made a great sophistication of AI system which analyzes in the real time millions of transactions in order to find out the potentially violent activity. PayPal's system includes supervised learning models combined with unsupervised anomaly detection to identify patterns, which although subtle, have suggested fraudulent behavior, the patterns of which do change over time. Therefore, by using this method, PayPal's fraud rate has fallen to less than 0.32% of revenue far below industry averages (Buchanan & Wright, 2021).

The following are some examples of financial services to show how AI-enriched BI can:

1. Document analysis and information extraction becomes automatically complex.
2. Recognize hints of fraud or risk activity
3. Be able to adapt fast with threats and market conditions that are evolving.
4. Optimize false positives and false negatives to achieve business goals

Healthcare: Clinical Decision Support and Resource Optimization

Cost control and better patient outcomes are becoming more of a point in operational efficiency for healthcare organizations and others. Both these objectives are enabled by the emergence of AI enhanced BI.

For example, Mayo Clinic used an AI powered patient flow optimization system which predicts when patients are likely to be admitted and discharged from the hospital in order to move services closer to where they are needed and staff more efficiently. The system uses historical patient data, current census, scheduled procedures, among others, external factors such as weather and local events, to forecast the demand for hospital services. According to Chen et al., (2018), this initiative succeeded in reducing wait time by 20% and increasing staff utilization by 15%.

An AI based system developed by Cleveland Clinic establishes which of the patients is at highest risk of readmission after discharge. The system analyzes clinical, demographic and socioeconomic data in order to identify patients that could benefit from more follow up of care or resources. The 30-day readmission rates went down by 22%, which is a clear sign that patient outcomes improve and operational efficiency of the medical facility benefits (Jamei et al., 2017).

In these healthcare applications, several benefits of AI-BI integration are shown.

1. More efficient allocation of limited healthcare resources
2. Proactive identification of high-risk patients for early intervention
3. Reduction in adverse events through predictive analytics
4. Enhanced coordination across complex care delivery systems

Case studies from different industries are presented as examples of successful implementation of AI-BI integration by illustrating a set of necessary organizational and technical capabilities, which go beyond technical requirements as in the case with pure BI implementations. According to Davenport and Ronanki (2018), the organizations that gain most significantly across their operations from AI are centred on augmenting the human ability rather than replacing them, while building collaborative systems aligned with a synergy of the human and AI intelligence.

FUTURE TRENDS AND DIRECTIONS

Autonomous and Self-Service Analytics

On the other hand, AI enhanced BI will be developed towards becoming more autonomous and user friendly and should thus be accessible to non technical users without requiring top expertise. Several technological developments are driving this trend, sometimes referred to as 'self-service analytics'.

1. Augmented Analytics As per Gartner definition, augmented analytics refers to machine learning based automation of data preparation, insight discovery, and insight sharing so that advanced analytics can be used by a larger audience. It automates much of the complexity and the time that traditionally took place to build those things out, which data scientists would traditionally have to do (Sallam et al., 2019).
2. Conversational analytics systems that allow users to talk and receive insights about data in a nice manner such as via natural language instead of formal query language or complex interfaces are becoming increasingly sophisticated. It is

systems that use natural language processing (NLP) and natural language generation (NLG) to translate between the human language and analytical operations (Eckerson, 2016).
3. Automated Machine Learning (AutoML) Tools: Tools that make Machine Learning (ML) end to end, making the technical barriers to develop predictive model lower. Feurer et al. (2015) clarify how these platforms are used to carry out feature selection, algorithm selection, hyperparameter tuning, model evaluation with minimal human intervention.
4. Insight Recommendation Engines: Insight recommendation engines are becoming an important piece of next generation BI platform that is capable of proactively discovering and suggesting relevant insights to a user based on his role, preference and context. These systems can use user interaction to learn to make more and more personalized recommendations (Eckerson, 2017).

According to Davenport (2018), these developments will not eliminate the data scientist role but will allow data scientists to concentrate on increasingly complex and strategic analytics and provide business users with mechanism to perform routine analytics on their own.

Edge Analytics and IoT Integration

As more Internet of Things (IoT) devices are proliferating, it yields unprecedented volume of operational data at the edge of networks that is changing the business intelligence architecture for good and bad. This means that future AI BI systems will more and more have to process and analyze the data closer to its source, rather than centralizing all data first.

This is what comprises of key developments in this area:

1. Data Processing at the Edge of the Network: Processing data either at the source of generation or on a resource nearby for the purpose of reducing latency, lowering bandwidth usage and reducing privacy concerns. This approach is very important for time sensitive applications such as real time process control or autonomous vehicles (Shi et al., 2016).
2. Multiple decentralized devices or servers hold local data samples, which process the same algorithm but never exchange the data. These are what algorithms running on these devices accomplish through Federated Learning: Machine learning techniques. However, this approach solves problems of privacy while being able to learn from distributed data sources (Yang et al., 2019).
3. Stream Analytics at Scale: Attempt to process and analyze high velocity data streams with near real time response aimed at an immediate response to an

operational event. These are capabilities necessary for predicting maintenance, detecting fraud or dynamic pricing (Carbone et al., 2015).

4. Virtual replicas of physical assets, processes or systems, that exist using real time data and simulating, predicting and optimizing performance. The digital models can also conduct sophisticated what if analyses and scenario planning of operational decisions (Tao et al., 2018).

Shi et al. (2016) researches that edge analytics will be more and more important as organizations start to minimize the latency to decision making and solve the exponential growth in data created by connected devices.

Explainable AI and Ethical Considerations

When it comes to operational decision making that AI will be playing a larger role in more and more, we've started to have a greater need for transparency, explaining and the necessary ethical governance that we've spoken about before. These concerns will have to be considered and addressed in future developments of AIenhanced BI in order to continue to trust such systems and ensure responsible deployment.

Included in this area are the key trends in:

1. Methods and techniques to understand, and thus make more trustworthy and manipulable, (indicative or inferential) behaviour produced by an AI system. Miller (2019) points out these approaches seek to make the decision making process of machine learning models more interpretable and transparent.
2. Fairness Aware Machine Learning: Techniques to detect and mitigate bias in training data and AI outputs so that the outputs of the models needs not be reheating or increasing the social imbalances that exists in the world. It entails technical approaches to bias detection as well as governance frameworks for responsible development of AI (Barocas & Selbst, 2016).
3. Privacy Preserving analytics include methods that enable the valuable analytics to be drawn on the sensitive data without sacrificing the individual privacy like Differential Privacy, Homomorphic encryption and Secure Multi Party computation (Dwork & Roth, 2014).
4. Ethical Frameworks and Governance: Methodical means for overseeing the ethical ramifications of AI used inside the workplaces, such as norms, reasoning, and oversight instruments, which can confirm AI frameworks coordinate with the association's qualities and social standards (Goodman & Flaxman, 2017).

The ethical considerations mentioned are also practical because explainability and fairness are required in automated decision systems by regulations like the European Union's General Data Protection Regulation (GDPR).

Quantum Computing and Advanced Analytics

While looking at further into the future, emerging computational paradigms such as quantum computing may altogether change some aspects of the business intelligence and analytics realm. Although they have not yet begun to move out of the laboratory, quantum computers promise to solve problems that are devoid of solution for classical machines.

It can be applied in business intelligence including:

1. Quantum algorithms for solving complex optimization problems in supply chain management, portfolio optimization and in general in the field of resource allocation are expected to have significant speedups over classical algorithms for certain classes of problems (Preskill, 2018).
2. Quantum machine learning algorithms shall allow for training certain types of models faster and/or in higher dimensions than classical approaches (Biamonte et al., 2017).
3. For instance, by utilizing devices in the quantum realm, simulation of complex systems with large numbers of interacting variables could be made increasingly complex, allowing for a better scenario analysis for strategic planning (Preskill, 2018).
4. Due to the widespread applications of cryptography in various information exchange protocols, this research anticipates that it will be one of the most affected areas by quantum computing: a threat to the existing cryptography approaches, and chances for the quantum secure alternatives (Broadbent & Schaffner, 2016).

It is clear that although practical, general-purpose quantum computers are years forward, companies that are in the business intelligence and analytics field should take note of what developments are being made and how quantum capabilities might be introduced to assist and perhaps disrupt their current efforts (Preskill, 2018).

CONCLUSION

Artificial intelligence and machine learning are used in business intelligence architectures to create a paradigm shift for organizations regarding operational intelligence and decision making. This chapter shows that apart from the classic

BI report and dashboard, with AI technologies BI can produce predictive insights, decision support that works by itself, and automatic tasks.

From an architectural standpoint, the furthest considerations for the integration of AI and BI emphasize the requirements for a flexible and scalable data infrastructure that can handle large and large volumes of all types of data, high speed streams, as well as with complex analytical workloads. When It comes to integrating AI capabilities In, there are patterns that organizations need to consider carefully to form a pattern of their integration In their existing BI ecosystems.

Predictive analytics, anomaly detection, process mining and natural language processing are machine learning techniques used in the improvement of operational efficiency. The organizations that move beyond descriptive to predictive and, ultimately, prescriptive analytics can anticipate problems beforehand, see to the causes of problems more quickly, and optimize highly complex processes more efficiently.

But several formidable challenges have to be taken care of for a successful implementation: data quality, skill building, model management and user adoption. Organizations that are able to overcome these challenges by really having a systematic approach to data governance, talent development and change management, and have a sound lifecycle management approach for the model, can see significant benefits out of their future AI-BI investments.

AI enhanced business intelligence can transform the business functions across manufacturing, retail, financial services and healthcare and, as demonstrated by the case studies, the transformation is possible in all operational contexts. These examples show that the most successful implementations are about supplanting human decision makers, but by providing intelligent assistance and automation of routine analytical tasks.

Trends of future include autonomous analytics, edge computing, explainability in AI, and maybe even quantum computing, that will redefine the boundaries of business intelligence also in the future. The organizations that understand these developments and can adapt their architectures will be in a good position to capitalize on gains due to operations over raw data alone.

All in all, there are great prospects of AI and ML to be integrated into modern BI architectures for analyzing the data in a more sophisticated way, improving automation and decision support. The technical and organizational challenges are significant, but cost reduction through improved quality and competitive differentiation represent the 'strategic imperative' for the forward thinking organization in all industries.

REFERENCES

Allahyari, M., Pouriyeh, S., Assefi, M., Safaei, S., Trippe, E. D., Gutierrez, J. B., & Kochut, K. (2017). Text summarization techniques: A brief survey. *International Journal of Advanced Computer Science and Applications*, *8*(10), 397–405. DOI: 10.14569/IJACSA.2017.081052

Amershi, S., Begel, A., Bird, C., DeLine, R., Gall, H., Kamar, E., Nagappan, N., Nushi, B., & Zimmermann, T. (2019). Software engineering for machine learning: A case study. In *Proceedings of the 41st International Conference on Software Engineering: Software Engineering in Practice* (pp. 291–300). IEEE. doi:DOI: 10.1109/ICSE-SEIP.2019.00042

Barocas, S., & Selbst, A. D. (2016). Big data's disparate impact. *California Law Review*, *104*, 671–732. DOI: 10.2139/ssrn.2477899

Batini, C., Cappiello, C., Francalanci, C., & Maurino, A. (2009). Methodologies for data quality assessment and improvement. *ACM Computing Surveys*, *41*(3), 1–52. DOI: 10.1145/1541880.1541883

Biamonte, J., Wittek, P., Pancotti, N., Rebentrost, P., Wiebe, N., & Lloyd, S. (2017). Quantum machine learning. *Nature*, *549*(7671), 195–202. DOI: 10.1038/nature23474 PMID: 28905917

Blei, D. M., Ng, A. Y., & Jordan, M. I. (2003). Latent Dirichlet allocation. *Journal of Machine Learning Research*, *3*, 993–1022. DOI: 10.1162/jmlr.2003.3.4-5.993

Box, G. E., Jenkins, G. M., Reinsel, G. C., & Ljung, G. M. (2015). *Time series analysis: Forecasting and control* (5th ed.). John Wiley & Sons., DOI: 10.1111/jtsa.12194

Breck, E., Cai, S., Nielsen, E., Salib, M., & Sculley, D. (2017). The ML test score: A rubric for ML production readiness and technical debt reduction. In *Proceedings of the IEEE International Conference on Big Data* (pp. 1123-1132). IEEE. DOI: DOI: 10.1109/BigData.2017.8258038

Breunig, M. M., Kriegel, H. P., Ng, R. T., & Sander, J. (2000). LOF: Identifying density-based local outliers. In *Proceedings of the 2000 ACM SIGMOD International Conference on Management of Data* (pp. 93–104). ACM. doi:DOI: 10.1145/335191.335388

Broadbent, A., & Schaffner, C. (2016). Quantum cryptography beyond quantum key distribution. *Designs, Codes and Cryptography*, *78*(1), 351–382. DOI: 10.1007/s10623-015-0157-4 PMID: 32226229

Buchanan, B. G., & Wright, D. (2021). The impact of machine learning on UK financial services. *Oxford Review of Economic Policy*, *37*(3), 537–563. DOI: 10.1093/oxrep/grab016 PMID: 34642572

Carbone, P., Katsifodimos, A., Ewen, S., Markl, V., Haridi, S., & Tzoumas, K. (2015). Apache Flink: Stream and batch processing in a single engine. *A Quarterly Bulletin of the Computer Society of the IEEE Technical Committee on Data Engineering*, *36*(4), 28–38. https://research.tudelft.nl/en/publications/apache-flink-stream-and-batch-processing-in-a-single-engine

Chen, H., Chiang, R. H., & Storey, V. C. (2012). Business intelligence and analytics: From big data to big impact. *Management Information Systems Quarterly*, *36*(4), 1165–1188. DOI: 10.2307/41703503

Chen, J., Song, L., Wainwright, M. J., & Jordan, M. I. (2018). Learning to explain: An information-theoretic perspective on model interpretation. In *Proceedings of the 35th International Conference on Machine Learning* (pp. 883-892). PMLR. https://doi.org/DOI: 10.48550/arXiv.1802.07814

Davenport, T. H. (2018). *T*he AI advantage: How to put the artificial intelligence revolution to work. MIT Press. Available at: https://mitpress.mit.edu/9780262538008/the-ai-advantage/

Davenport, T. H., & Bean, R. (2018). Big companies are embracing analytics, but most still don't have a data-driven culture. Harvard Business Review Digital Articles, 2-4. Available at: https://hbr.org/2018/02/big-companies-are-embracing-analytics-but-most-still-dont-have-a-data-driven-culture

Davenport, T. H., & Harris, J. G. (2017). *Competing on analytics: The new science of winning* (Updated ed.). Harvard Business Press. Available at: https://hbr.org/product/competing-on-analytics-the-new-science-of-winning-updated-with-a-new-introduction/17723-HBK-ENG

Davenport, T. H., & Patil, D. J. (2012). Data scientist: The sexiest job of the 21st century. *Harvard Business Review*, *90*(10), 70–76. https://hbr.org/2012/10/data-scientist-the-sexiest-job-of-the-21st-century PMID: 23074866

Davenport, T. H., & Ronanki, R. (2018). Artificial intelligence for the real world. *Harvard Business Review*, *96*(1), 108–116. https://hbr.org/2018/01/artificial-intelligence-for-the-real-world

Devlin, J., Chang, M. W., Lee, K., & Toutanova, K. (2019). BERT: Pre-training of deep bidirectional transformers for language understanding. In NAACL-HLT (pp. 4171–4186). doi:DOI: 10.18653/v1/N19-1423

Dwork, C., & Roth, A. (2014). The algorithmic foundations of differential privacy. *Foundations and Trends in Theoretical Computer Science*, *9*(3–4), 211–407. DOI: 10.1561/0400000042

Eckerson, W. W. (2016). The secret to creating business value with embedded analytics. Eckerson Group White Paper. Available at: https://www.eckerson.com/register?content=the-secret-to-creating-business-value-with-embedded-analytics

Eckerson, W. W. (2017). Smart analytics: Leveraging AI and machine learning for BI. Eckerson Group White Paper. Available at: https://www.eckerson.com/research/smart-analytics-leveraging-ai-and-machine-learning-for-bi

Feurer, M., Klein, A., Eggensperger, K., Springenberg, J., Blum, M., & Hutter, F. (2015). Efficient and robust automated machine learning. Advances in Neural Information Processing Systems, 28, 2962-2970. Available at: https://papers.nips.cc/paper/5872-efficient-and-robust-automated-machine-learning

García, S., Luengo, J., & Herrera, F. (2015). *Data preprocessing in data mining*. Springer., DOI: 10.1007/978-3-319-10247-4

Goodman, B., & Flaxman, S. (2017). European Union regulations on algorithmic decision-making and a "right to explanation". *AI Magazine*, *38*(3), 50–57. DOI: 10.1609/aimag.v38i3.2741

Guyon, I., & Elisseeff, A. (2003). An introduction to variable and feature selection. *Journal of Machine Learning Research*, *3*, 1157–1182. DOI: 10.1162/153244303322753616

Hastie, T., Tibshirani, & Friedman, J. (2009). The Elements of Statistical Learning (2nd ed.). Springer. doi:DOI: 10.1007/978-0-387-84858-7

Inmon, W. H. (2005). *Building the data warehouse* (4th ed.). John Wiley & Sons., Available at https://www.wiley.com/en-us/Building+the+Data+Warehouse%2C+4th+Edition-p-9780764599446

Jamei, M., Nisnevich, A., Wetchler, E., Sudat, S., & Liu, E. (2017). Predicting all-cause risk of 30-day hospital readmission using artificial neural networks. *PLoS One*, *12*(7), e0181173. DOI: 10.1371/journal.pone.0181173 PMID: 28708848

LaValle, S., Lesser, E., Shockley, R., Hopkins, M. S., & Kruschwitz, N. (2011). Big data, analytics and the path from insights to value. *MIT Sloan Management Review*, *52*(2), 21–32. https://sloanreview.mit.edu/article/big-data-analytics-and-the-path-from-insights-to-value/

LeCun, Y., Bengio, Y., & Hinton, G. (2015). Deep learning. *Nature, 521*(7553), 436–444. DOI: 10.1038/nature14539 PMID: 26017442

Lee, I. (2017). Big data: Dimensions, evolution, impacts, and challenges. *Business Horizons, 60*(3), 293–303. DOI: 10.1016/j.bushor.2017.01.004

Liu, B. (2015). *Sentiment analysis: Mining opinions, sentiments, and emotions*. Cambridge University Press., DOI: 10.1017/CBO9781139084789

Manning, C. D., Surdeanu, M., Bauer, J., Finkel, J. R., Bethard, S., & McClosky, D. (2014). The Stanford CoreNLP natural language processing toolkit. In *Proceedings of the 52nd Annual Meeting of the Association for Computational Linguistics: System Demonstrations* (pp. 55-60). Association for Computational Linguistics. **DOI:** DOI: 10.3115/V1/P14-5010

Manyika, J., Chui, M., Brown, B., Bughin, J., Dobbs, R., Roxburgh, C., & Byers, A. H. (2011). Big data: The next frontier for innovation, competition, and productivity. McKinsey Global Institute. Available at: https://www.mckinsey.com/business-functions/mckinsey-digital/our-insights/big-data-the-next-frontier-for-innovation

Márquez-Chamorro, A. E., Resinas, M., & Ruiz-Cortés, A. (2018). Predictive monitoring of business processes: A survey. *IEEE Transactions on Services Computing, 11*(6), 962–977. DOI: 10.1109/TSC.2017.2772256

McAfee, A., & Brynjolfsson, E. (2012). Big data: The management revolution. *Harvard Business Review, 90*(10), 60–68. https://hbr.org/2012/10/big-data-the-management-revolution PMID: 23074865

Miller, T. (2019). Explanation in artificial intelligence: Insights from the social sciences. *Artificial Intelligence, 267*, 1–38. DOI: 10.1016/j.artint.2018.07.007

Pearl, J. (2009). *Causality: Models, Reasoning, and Inference* (2nd ed.). Cambridge University Press., DOI: 10.1017/CBO9780511803161

Pipino, L. L., Lee, Y. W., & Wang, R. Y. (2002). Data quality assessment. *Communications of the ACM, 45*(4), 211–218. DOI: 10.1145/505248.505255

Preskill, J. (2018). Quantum computing in the NISQ era and beyond. *Quantum : the Open Journal for Quantum Science, 2*, 79. DOI: 10.22331/q-2018-08-06-79

Redman, T. C. (2013). Data's credibility problem. *Harvard Business Review, 91*(12), 84–88. https://hbr.org/2013/12/datas-credibility-problem

Rozinat, A., & van der Aalst, W. M. (2008). Conformance checking of processes based on monitoring real behavior. *Information Systems, 33*(1), 64–95. DOI: 10.1016/j.is.2007.07.001

Russom, P. (2016). Data warehouse modernization in the age of big data analytics. *TDWI Best Practices Report*. Retrieved from: https://tdwi.org/articles/2016/03/22/executive-summary-data-warehousemodernization.aspx

Sallam, R. L., Howson, C., Idoine, C. J., Oestreich, T. W., Richardson, J. L., & Tapadinhas, J. (2019). Magic quadrant for analytics and business intelligence platforms. *Gartner Research*. Available at: https://www.gartner.com/doc/reprints?id=1-6Y66S7P&ct=190218&st=sb

Sculley, D., Holt, G., Golovin, D., Davydov, E., Phillips, T., Ebner, D., Chaudhary, V., Young, M., Crespo, J. F., & Dennison, D. (2015). Hidden technical debt in machine learning systems. In *Advances in Neural Information Processing Systems, 28*, 2503-2511. Available at: https://papers.nips.cc/paper/2015/hash/86df7dcfd896fcaf2674f757a2463eba-Abstract.html

Shi, W., Cao, J., Zhang, Q., Li, Y., & Xu, L. (2016). Edge computing: Vision and challenges. *IEEE Internet of Things Journal*, *3*(5), 637–646. DOI: 10.1109/JIOT.2016.2579198

Taleb, I., Dssouli, R., & Serhani, M. A. (2015). Big data pre-processing: A quality framework. In *Proceedings of the 2015 IEEE International Congress on Big Data* (pp. 191-198). IEEE. DOI: DOI: 10.1109/BigDataCongress.2015.35

Teinemaa, I., Dumas, M., La Rosa, M., & Maggi, F. M. (2019). Outcome-oriented predictive process monitoring: Review and benchmark. *ACM TKDD*, *13*(2), 1–57. DOI: 10.1145/3301300

van der Aalst, W. M. (2016). *Process mining: Data science in action* (2nd ed.). Springer., DOI: 10.1007/978-3-662-49851-4

Wang, Y., Kung, L., & Byrd, T. A. (2018). Big data analytics: Understanding its capabilities and potential benefits for healthcare organizations. *Technological Forecasting and Social Change*, *126*, 3–13. DOI: 10.1016/j.techfore.2015.12.019

Watson, H. J. (2009). Tutorial: Business Intelligence—Past, Present, and Future. *Communications of the AIS*, *25*(1), 39. DOI: 10.17705/1CAIS.02539

Watson, H. J., & Wixom, B. H. (2007). The current state of business intelligence. *Computer*, *40*(9), 96–99. DOI: 10.1109/MC.2007.331

Weber, K., Otto, B., & Österle, H. (2009). One size does not fit all—A contingency approach to data governance. *Journal of Data and Information Quality*, *1*(1), 1–27. DOI: 10.1145/1515693.1515696

Yang, Q., Liu, Y., Chen, T., & Tong, Y. (2019). Federated machine learning: Concept and applications. *ACM TIST*, *10*(2), 12. DOI: 10.1145/3298981

Žliobaitė, I., Pechenizkiy, M., & Gama, J. (2016). An overview of concept drift applications. In *Big Data Analysis: New Algorithms for a New Society* (pp. 91-114). Springer. http://dx.doi.org/DOI: 10.1007/978-3-319-26989-4_4

Chapter 2
Database Optimization Techniques for Efficient BI Queries

Mohammad H. Abu-Arqoub
https://orcid.org/0000-0002-1866-3780
University of Petra, Jordan

Ali A. Titinchi
https://orcid.org/0000-0002-7878-8702
Cihan University, Iraq

Rashiq Rafiq Marie
https://orcid.org/0009-0000-2682-8568
Taibah University, Saudi Arabia

ABSTRACT

The Business Intelligence (BI) environment of an organisation is defined as an environment where large volumes of data are processed in reaction to advanced analytical queries, which in turn imposes a heavy burden on the underlying database management systems. The larger the volume of the data, the longer it takes to respond to these queries hence limiting the interactive analytical capabilities modern BI systems are supposed to facilitate. In this chapter, a number of optimisation strategies aimed at improving the BI query execution performance are reviewed with a focus on indexing techniques, query optimisation algorithms, materialised views, and the particular workload characteristics of Online Analytical Processing (OLAP) and Online Transaction Processing (OLTP). Based on benchmark reviews of the major database platforms, it develops a complete model of how to optimise the database performance within a BI environment. Performance improvements of

DOI: 10.4018/979-8-3373-6801-6.ch002

several orders of magnitude have been demonstrated by implementations in diverse industrial applications, providing database administrators and BI architects with the knowledge they need to implement the same strategies into production environments.

1. INTRODUCTION

Database performance has an overwhelming impact on the functionality of a Business Intelligence (BI) system, directly defining analytical performance, user experience and operational costs. As the organizations store larger volumes of data, and perform more complicated analytical queries, it becomes imperative to optimize the database. Previously a query could be completed in seconds, but now it will take minutes or even hours, thus limiting the interactive analysis that the modern BI environments envisage (Chaudhuri et al., 2011).

The optimization issues that BI queries experience are different to those that are experienced during the traditional transaction processing. Whereas online-transaction-processing (OLTP) workloads perform on small subsets of data over fixed paths, BI queries work on millions of records, involving complex aggregations over many dimensions, and have unpredictable access characteristics. These properties require an optimized method that is specific to the nature of analytical processing (Abadi et al., 2013).

BI database optimization is, thus, a multiple-level process. Physical design optimizes the physical design of structures that include indexes, partitioning schemes and data organization. Query optimization is the process of translating logical representations of queries into effective execution plans. System configuration optimizes parameters of databases to analytical workloads. To optimize successfully, all these levels should be combined in order to achieve an optimal response to specific BI needs (Bruno, 2011).

The next sections explore some of the main optimization strategies that are targeted at the BI workloads. Section 2 considers the strategy of indexing, including specialized indexes. Section 3 looks at query optimization algorithms to resolve the complexity of BI operations. In section 4, the researcher explores the materialized view technique to speed up frequently used analytic tasks. The section 5 draws a comparison between the optimization strategies that can be applied to BI systems and optimization strategies that are applicable in OLTP systems. Section 6 provides case studies to show how these optimization methods are applied in production.

2. INDEXING STRATEGIES FOR BUSINESS INTELLIGENCE WORKLOADS

Index structures also support fast data access, but use in business-intelligence (BI) settings requires different methodologies as compared to those that are used in transaction-processing (OLTP) settings. B-tree indexes are commonly used in OLTP systems to facilitate point lookups and range scans of relatively small data sets, but BI applications are often required to scan large tables and to apply complex filtering conditions on many dimensions which require special indexing techniques (Graefe, 2011).

2.1. B-Tree Indexes for BI Workloads

B-tree index structures, designed to support transaction-processing applications, provides large performance benefits on some business-intelligence (BI) processing tasks. B-trees are organised as balance trees and thus offer logarithmic data-access times, which facilitate fast execution of equality predicates, range predicates and sorted retrievals. In BI workloads, B-trees tend to be used only on dimension tables and fact tables that are the subject of high-selectivity predicates (Hellerstein et al., 2007).

Composite B-tree indexes are worth considering when building dimensional data models in view of these advantages. I/O operations can be minimized by using mutli column indexes that match popular dimensional query patterns and improve system performance. The order of columns in such composite indexes may affect the effectiveness of operations: scanning high-selectivity columns first provides the best filtering, and column order based on grouping or ordering clauses may remove the necessity of further sort operations.

There is also an added cost of maintenance overhead as a result of overlaying indexes on the fact tables. The more the indexes that one adds, the more the computational needs of the insertions, updates and deletions of data. Therefore, the BI systems have to strike a balance between the performance improvement that indexes provide and the accompanying maintenance overheads. One typical operational plan is to specify index-maintenance windows where indexes are disabled when bulk data loads are in progress; indexes are then rebuilt after the loading processes have finished (O Neil et al., 2004).

2.2. Bitmap Indexes

Bitmap indexes offer advantages for BI workloads involving low-to-medium cardinality columns—those containing few distinct values compared to the total row count. Unlike B-trees, bitmap indexes create bit vectors for each distinct column value, enabling efficient compression and rapid bitwise operations for complex filtering conditions. These characteristics make bitmap indexes valuable for data warehouse star schemas with dimensional attributes like region, product category, or status indicators (Chan & Ioannidis, 1998).

Bitmap indexes demonstrate efficiency for complex queries with multiple filter conditions. The database engine performs bitwise AND and OR operations directly on the bitmap representations, reducing processing overhead compared to B-tree index intersection operations. This capability proves valuable for ad-hoc analytics where queries frequently combine multiple dimensional filters (Wu & Buchmann, 1998).

Testing on a 100-million-row fact table demonstrates performance improvements of 15-30x compared to equivalent B-tree indexes for queries with multiple dimensional filters (O'Neil et. al., 2007).

2.3. Column-Store Indexes

Column-store indexing stores the data in a column-oriented fashion, instead of the more typical row-oriented storage, transforming storage architecture to support analytic workloads. The paradigm provides a number of advantages to business intelligence (BI) querying: improved compression ratios due to similarity of values in columns; small input/output size, since only relevant columns need to be read rather than whole rows; and access to vector-processing computational models to perform analytical operations. As a result, columnar capabilities are being incorporated into most of the large database systems to address the analytical performance requirements (Abadi et al., 2013).

Reported performance improvements over row-stored tables with B-tree indexes on aggregate queries that scan large numbers of records across a small number of columns often range between 10-fold to greater than 100-fold (Larson et al., 2011). These optimizations have many different origins: column compression reduces input/output demands; batch-mode processing makes full use of the CPU; and segment elimination prevents redundant data reads enabled by fine-grained metadata.

Column-store indexes have, however, different limitations and trade-offs. They need more CPU ability to load their data and to retrieve full rows where they are needed. Moreover, their performance benefits decrease with queries that touch majority of columns in a table or highly selective point queries which are usually more efficiently handled by B-tree indexes. Practically, hybrid designs, i.e. coexisting row-oriented and column-oriented representations, are frequently used to represent different query patterns (Abadi et al., 2013).

2.4. Zone Maps and Data Skipping Indexes

Graphically represented either as zone maps, data skipping indexes or synopsis tables, these structures hold aggregate statistics about the values of individual data block or partition, thus allowing the database engine to skip reading the blocks that do not contain any qualifying records. The query optimizer can then discard irrelevant blocks in the execution of the query because the minimum and maximum values per column in each block have been recorded. Zone maps are not conventional indexes but they provide considerable performance advantages to large-scale analytical queries (Graefe, 2011).

With partitioning schemes, PostgreSQL automatically eliminates irrelevant partitions for queries with date predicates—a process called partition pruning or constraint exclusion. For instance, a query analyzing 2023 data would skip reading the 2021 and 2022 partitions, potentially eliminating millions of rows from consideration before any actual data access occurs (Stonebraker et al., 2019).

Zone maps prove effective for analytical queries with filter conditions on sequential attributes like dates, numeric ranges, or hierarchical dimensions. Empirical testing demonstrates performance improvements proportional to the number of blocks eliminated—queries that can skip 90% of data blocks typically execute 5-10x faster than full table scans, with minimal storage overhead compared to traditional indexes (Graefe, 2011).

Table 1 compares the characteristics and performance impacts of different index types for BI workloads.

Table 1. Index Type Comparison for BI Workloads

Index Type	Structure	BI Workload Suitability	Maintenance Cost	Performance Impact	Best Use Cases
B-Tree	Balanced tree with pointers	Medium	Medium	2-5x for selective queries	Dimension tables, high-selectivity queries
Bitmap	Bit vectors per value	High	High (during updates)	15-30x for multi-filter queries	Low-cardinality columns, read-intensive workloads
Column-Store	Column-oriented storage	High	High	10-100x for aggregation queries	Scan-intensive analytics, fact tables
Zone Maps	Block-level statistics	High	Low	5-10x for filtered scans	Date-range queries, sequential data patterns

3. QUERY OPTIMIZATION ALGORITHMS FOR BI

Query optimization transforms logical query representations into efficient execution plans, representing a critical component for BI performance. BI workloads present unique challenges: complex multi-table joins, extensive aggregation operations, and unpredictable selectivity estimates that complicate plan selection. This section examines optimization algorithms specifically relevant to BI query processing (Chaudhuri, 1998).

Figure 1. Query Optimization Process

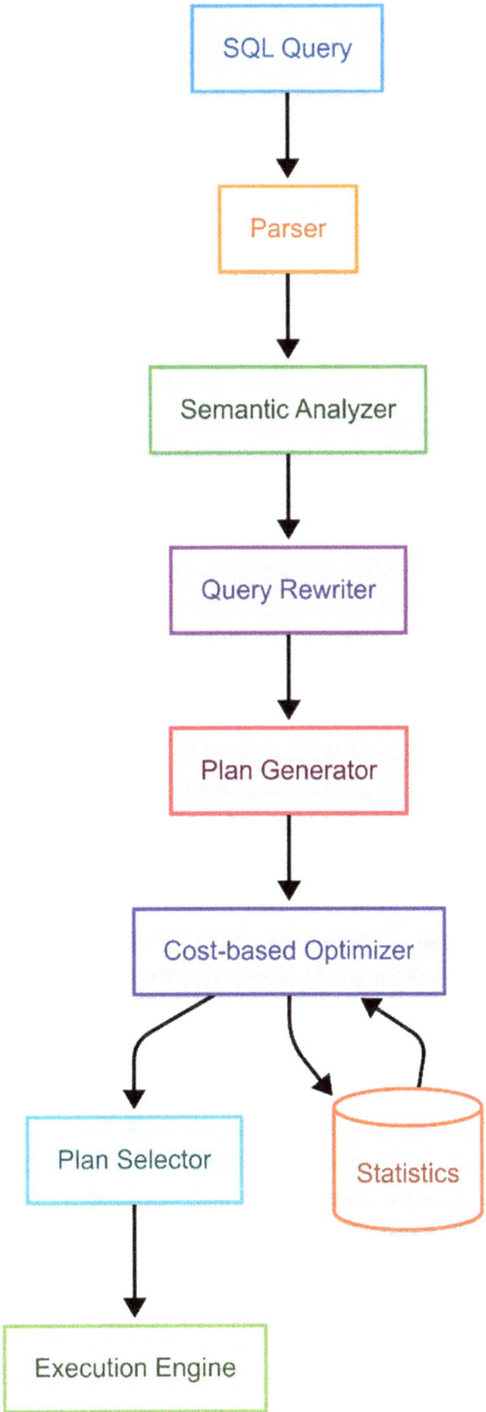

3.1. Join Optimization Techniques

Join operations represent fundamental but potentially expensive components of analytical queries, particularly in star or snowflake schemas joining fact tables with multiple dimensions. The query optimizer must select optimal join types (nested loops, hash, merge) and execution order based on table sizes, index availability, and join condition selectivity.

Hash join algorithms demonstrate relevance for BI workloads, offering efficient processing for large dataset joins without requiring sorted inputs or indexes. This algorithm builds a hash table from the smaller table (typically a dimension) and then probes this structure with rows from the larger table (typically a fact table).

Testing reveals performance variations based on data volumes. For fact tables exceeding millions of rows joined to smaller dimension tables, hash joins typically outperform alternatives by 2-5x due to reduced I/O and efficient memory utilization, assuming sufficient memory for hash table construction (Graefe, 1993).

Star join optimization represents a specialized technique for data warehouse schemas with a central fact table connected to multiple dimensions. Advanced optimizers recognize this pattern and implement specialized strategies including dimension preprocessing, Cartesian products of filtered dimensions, and bitmap index intersections.

Star transformation first filters dimension tables and creates Bloom filters or bitmap indexes representing qualifying dimension values, then applies these filters to the fact table scan. This approach can improve performance by orders of magnitude compared to traditional join methods, particularly for highly selective dimension conditions (Bellamkonda et al., 2009).

The performance of the entire query is significantly affected by the order by which multiple joins are performed, which are determined by join reordering algorithms. Traditional query optimizers generally attempt to consider all possible join orders using dynamic programing, whereas modern business-intelligence systems make use of genetic algorithms and stochastic search techniques to solve queries with ten or more tables.

Table 2 compares join algorithms for BI workloads.

Table 2. Join Algorithm Comparison for BI Workloads

Join Algorithm	Operation Principle	Memory Requirements	Performance Characteristics	Best Use Case
Nested Loop	For each outer row, find matching inner rows	Low	Good for small outer tables and indexed inner tables	Dimension-to-dimension joins
Hash Join	Build hash table, probe with other table	High (must fit smaller table)	Excellent for large tables without indexes	Fact-to-dimension joins
Merge Join	Sort both inputs, merge in order	Medium	Good when inputs already sorted or indexed	Pre-sorted or indexed tables
Star Join	Filter dimensions first, apply to fact table	Medium	Excellent for star schema queries	Star schema with selective dimensions

3.2. Aggregation Optimization

Aggregation operations carry out functions on grouped and / or filtered datasets; they are a basic building block in data analytics. Research in optimization focuses on domain-specific algorithms, implementation plans, and memory-management schemes, where the two-phase approaches are of particular interest to distributed business-intelligence (BI) systems because it decouples calculations into local and global parts, thus limiting inter-node data exchange (Cao et al., 2019).

In contemporary BI environments, the query processing is dominated by hash aggregation algorithms that build in-memory hash tables, composed of key-value pairs made of composite keys formed based on grouping columns and aggregated-value rows as their values. These designs have linear scalability with respect to input size up to memory constraints (when the disk spilling mechanism is invoked) where performance degrades to N log N behavior, as in traditional sort-based designs (Bellamkonda et al., 2013).

Empirical testing has shown that hash aggregation can provide three- to ten-fold speedups over sort-based options on medium-to-large datasets assuming that enough memory is available. Performance models also indicate linear scaling until the memory limit, beyond which disk activity predominates and the N log N nature re-appears. Hash aggregation can therefore be considered as a scalable alternative of memory rich environments and sort-based methods continue to be competitive in environments with limited memory (Bellamkonda et al., 2013).

Approximate aggregation also adds statistical methods which provide estimates of distributions of the results within an allowed error range thus increasing the speed of aggregate computations. HyperLogLog schemes are common in approximate COUNT(DISTINCT) whereas sampling-based methods are used to approximate percentiles. The methods are useful in interactive dashboards, where estimates of statistics are acceptable and latency issues are paramount compared to the accuracy lost compared to absolute counts (Bellamkonda et al., 2013).

Parallel aggregation uses multi-core CPUs or distributed nodes clusters in order to analyze very large datasets. These strategies divide the input vertically and horizontally, perform independent aggregations on each of the partitions, and aggregate the partial outputs at a coordinator node. Execution patterns show that various processes scan different table partitions simultaneously, doing local aggregations and sending compressed intermediate results to coordinators, providing nearly linear speedup with more processors until overheads of coordination starts to dominate.

3.3. Subquery Optimization

Subqueries enable expression of complex analytical logic through nested query structures, yet their inefficient implementation can severely impact performance. Modern query optimizers transform applicable subqueries through techniques including flattening, decorrelation, and semi-join reduction.

Subquery flattening (also called unnesting) transforms certain subquery patterns into equivalent join operations, eliminating nested execution. Execution plan analysis confirms the optimizer's transformation, replacing the row-by-row subquery execution with a more efficient join operation. Performance testing on a 10-million-row fact table shows the transformed plan executing 20-50x faster than the original nested approach, with improvements increasing proportionally with fact table size (Kim et al., 2009).

Semi-join and anti-join optimizations address common subquery patterns testing for existence (EXISTS) or non-existence (NOT EXISTS) of related records. These transformations convert existential subqueries into specialized join operations that terminate processing as soon as matching records are found rather than processing all matches. This approach proves particularly valuable for filtering dimension tables based on fact table activity.

Execution strategies of a hypothetical relational query engine begin with an initial existential subquery, followed by a second hash semi-join, and thus avoid the repetitive processing of multiple sales records whenever they are related to a single product. Benchmark experiments (Simmen et al., 1996) have shown performance improvements ranging between 2x and 10x with the greatest improvement achieved when products are involved in large transaction volumes.

Another optimizer construct is view merging, which in the current context is used to eliminate references to materialized views with canonical query definitions. This mechanism allows global query optimization as opposed to the decoupled optimization of the view and the outer query. The method is especially useful in business intelligence systems using hierarchical view structures.

Trace analysis verifies that the view merging works: the optimizer merges the materialized-view definition with the outer query and then executes the merged query as a unit, avoiding the unnecessary intermediate steps and allowing a better join order to be chosen compared with the view-materialization option. The average performance gains are 2x to 5x and grow larger as the sophistication of the analytical views grows (Herodotou et al., 2011).

4. MATERIALIZED VIEWS AND RESULT CACHING

Materialized views represent precomputed query results stored as database objects, providing dramatic performance improvements for common analytical queries at the cost of storage space and maintenance overhead. Unlike standard views that evaluate their defining query each time they're referenced, materialized views persist results physically, enabling direct access without recomputation. This approach proves particularly valuable for expensive aggregations and joins frequently executed in BI workloads (Zhou et al., 2007).

4.1. Materialized View Design Strategies

Effective materialized view design requires balancing query performance benefits against storage and maintenance costs. Candidate identification typically analyzes query patterns to identify common operations with high execution costs, including aggregations over large fact tables, complex multi-table joins, and frequently accessed calculated metrics. The granularity selection process determines appropriate aggregation levels—balancing size reduction from higher aggregation against analytical flexibility from detailed data (Agrawal et al., 2000).

Query execution plans confirm automatic rewrite—the optimizer recognizes it can answer the query using aggregation of the materialized view rather than accessing base tables. For a 100-million-row fact table, performance testing demonstrates speedups of 10-100x for queries satisfied from materialized views, with greater improvements for more complex aggregations (Yang et al., 2014).

Despite lacking automatic query rewrite, PostgreSQL materialized views deliver substantial performance benefits when explicitly referenced. Testing shows 5-20x performance improvements for aggregation queries against the materialized view compared to equivalent queries against base tables, with benefits increasing proportionally with base table size (Stonebraker et al., 2019).

4.2. Incremental View Maintenance

Materialized view refresh strategies significantly impact both data currency and system performance. Complete refreshes rebuild entire materialized views, ensuring data accuracy but potentially consuming substantial resources for large datasets. Incremental refresh (also called fast refresh) updates only changed data portions, dramatically reducing refresh time but requiring additional logging and dependency tracking.

Performance testing reveals dramatic efficiency differences between refresh methods. For a materialized view based on a 50-million-row fact table with 10,000 new transactions, complete refresh requires approximately 5 minutes while incremental refresh completes in 3 seconds—a 100x performance difference. This efficiency enables more frequent refreshes, improving data currency for time-sensitive analytics (Gupta & Mumick, 1999).

The refresh scheduling process balances data currency against system load, particularly important for BI environments with defined interactive periods. Organizations typically implement refresh windows during periods of reduced analytical activity, often scheduling incremental refreshes during business hours and complete refreshes during overnight maintenance windows.

Table 3 compares materialized view refresh strategies.

Table 3. Materialized View Refresh Strategy Comparison

Refresh Strategy	Mechanism	Performance Impact	Data Currency	Implementation Complexity	Best Use Case
Complete Refresh	Rebuild entire view	High resource usage	Complete accuracy	Low	Small views, major data changes
Incremental Refresh	Update only changed portions	Minimal impact	Dependent on change detection	High	Large views, incremental data changes
On-Commit Refresh	Update after each transaction	Transaction overhead	Real-time	High	Critical operational dashboards
Scheduled Refresh	Update at defined intervals	Controlled impact	Periodic staleness	Medium	Standard BI reporting
On-Demand Refresh	Manual refresh	User-controlled	User-dependent	Low	Ad-hoc analysis

4.3. Automated Materialized View Advisors

Materialized view selection represents a complex optimization problem considering query workloads, data modification patterns, and storage constraints. Manual selection proves challenging given the combinatorial nature of possible aggregations, join combinations, and grouping dimensions. Automated advisors address this complexity through algorithmic approaches for identifying optimal materialized view configurations (Agrawal et al., 2000).

Testing these advisor tools on a typical BI workload containing 50 unique analytical queries demonstrates their effectiveness—recommendations typically identify materialized view configurations delivering 70-80% of the theoretical maximum performance improvement while requiring only 20-30% of the storage space needed for the exhaustive solution. This efficiency derives from sophisticated algorithms identifying views that benefit multiple queries rather than optimizing for individual operations (Agrawal et al., 2001).

The use of third-party and open-source software on database platforms that do not provide advisory functionality can provide users with comparable abilities as those provided by proprietary products. As an example, DBSight for PostgreSQL and Percona pt-query-digest for MySQL analyze query logs to identify patterns that reoccur and suggests the use of materialized views or summary tables. Despite being arguably less tightly coupled than native advisory systems, these utility tools can provide pragmatic advice on how to optimally locate materialized views in an open-source database setting (Dash et al., 2011).

4.4. Result Set Caching

Result set caching complements materialized views by dynamically storing query results in memory for reuse, providing performance benefits without requiring explicit view definition. This approach proves particularly valuable for interactive BI environments where users frequently execute identical or similar queries during analysis sessions. Unlike materialized views optimized for persistent, widely-used aggregations, result caching targets ephemeral, session-specific query patterns (Luo et al., 2004).

Performance testing demonstrates near-instantaneous response for cached queries compared to original execution times, with improvements of 10-1000x depending on query complexity. However, this approach presents limitations including cache invalidation on any table modification and lack of partial result reuse for similar but non-identical queries (Luo et al., 2004).

Application-level result caching is a generalization of earlier database-level caching techniques that provides greater control at a smaller level of granularity (explicit cache key construction), makes invalidation more flexible (allowing partial reuse of cached data), and has greater control over cache key construction. In more recent BI architectures, Redis is more widely used to this end, with configurable expiration lists and manual invalidation being used to persist query results.

These facilitated advanced caching patterns include: (1) parameter-based cache keys to permit reuse of results on query requests with common parameters, (2) explicit expiration, to trade off staleness versus performance, and (3) application-level cache management to give fine-grained control over invalidation when supporting data is updated. Performance tests show similar performance improvements over database-level caching (response is near-instantaneous on cached results) but provide persistence through database restarts and more complex invalidation policies (Gupta et al., 1997).

5. OLAP vs. OLTP OPTIMIZATION APPROACHES

Online Analytical Processing (OLAP) and Online Transaction Processing (OLTP) are two workloads the main tasks of which are located on the opposite sides of the processing spectrum. It is important to understand this distinction to the design of BI systems, as contemporary data-intensive companies commonly have to combine analytical and transactional processes. Stonebraker and Cetintemel (2005) observe that these systems can use granular technique selection both at architecture level and query level to optimize strategies to the characteristics of the workloads.

5.1. Workload Characteristic Comparison

The OLAP and OLTP workloads differ in a number of aspects, such as complexity of the queries, the volume of data, concurrency specifications, and modification patterns. A brief summary of these differences and their differential implications on database optimization is set out in Table 4.

Table 4. OLAP vs. OLTP Workload Characteristics

Characteristic	OLTP Systems	OLAP Systems	Optimization Implications
Query Complexity	Simple, predefined access paths	Complex, ad-hoc analytical queries	OLAP requires sophisticated query optimization for joins and aggregations
Data Volume per Query	Small (tens to hundreds of rows)	Large (millions to billions of rows)	OLAP benefits from parallel processing and scan optimization
Concurrency	High (hundreds to thousands of users)	Moderate (tens to hundreds of users)	OLTP requires efficient locking and MVCC; OLAP benefits from read optimization
Data Modifications	Frequent inserts and updates	Bulk loads at scheduled intervals	OLTP needs efficient transaction processing; OLAP can sacrifice update performance
Query Patterns	Short, simple transactions	Long-running analytical queries	OLTP optimizes for transaction throughput; OLAP for complex query performance
Index Usage	High selectivity point lookups	Low selectivity range scans	OLTP uses B-tree indexes; OLAP benefits from columnar and bitmap structures
Join Operations	Simple joins on few tables	Complex joins across multiple tables	OLTP uses nested loops joins; OLAP benefits from hash joins and star optimizations
Response Time Requirements	Milliseconds	Seconds to minutes	OLTP requires predictable, fast response; OLAP prioritizes throughput over latency

These divergent characteristics necessitate distinct optimization approaches. OLTP optimization focuses on transaction throughput, concurrency management, and consistent response times for simple queries. OLAP optimization prioritizes efficient processing of complex analytical operations, often sacrificing update performance and normal form data modeling for query efficiency (Stonebraker et al., 2019).

5.2. OLAP Optimization Techniques

OLAP optimization leverages several techniques specifically addressing analytical workload characteristics. Dimensional modeling represents data in star or snowflake schemas with central fact tables connected to dimension tables, enabling efficient navigation of business dimensions. This model intentionally denormalizes data compared to OLTP systems, reducing join complexity for common analytical patterns (Kimball & Ross, 2013).

Figure 2. Star Schema Dimensional Model

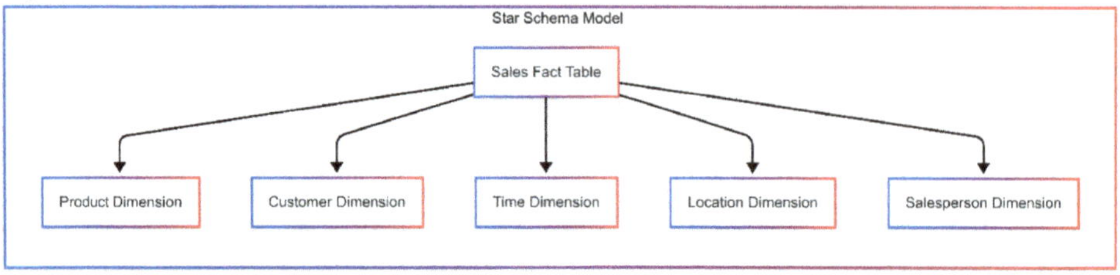

Columnar storage optimizes for analytical queries that typically access few columns across many rows. By storing data column-by-column rather than row-by-row, these systems drastically reduce I/O requirements for analytical operations.

This definition incorporates multiple OLAP optimization techniques: columnar storage reduces I/O for column-subset queries; sort ordering improves compression and range scan efficiency; data segmentation enables parallel processing; and time-based partitioning facilitates efficient historical analysis. Performance testing shows 10-100x improvements for analytical queries compared to row-oriented storage, with benefits increasing for queries accessing limited column subsets (Abadi et al., 2013).

Aggregate awareness enables query optimizers to recognize dimensions hierarchies and aggregation relationships, automatically selecting the most appropriate aggregation level for specific queries.

This semantic model enables the system to automatically select appropriate aggregation levels based on query granularity. A query requesting yearly product category sales uses the first aggregation, while quarterly analysis uses the second aggregation. The system transparently selects the most efficient aggregation that satisfies query requirements without user intervention. Testing demonstrates performance improvements of 10-100x for queries satisfied from predefined aggregations compared to base-level calculation (Microsoft, 2025)

5.3. Hybrid OLTP/OLAP Systems

Modern BI increasingly requires operational analytics—analyzing transactional data in near-real-time for immediate operational decisions. This requirement has driven development of hybrid OLTP/OLAP systems (sometimes called HTAP—Hybrid Transactional/Analytical Processing) that support both workload types efficiently within a single environment (Özcan et al., 2017).

Figure 3. Hybrid OLTP/OLAP Architecture

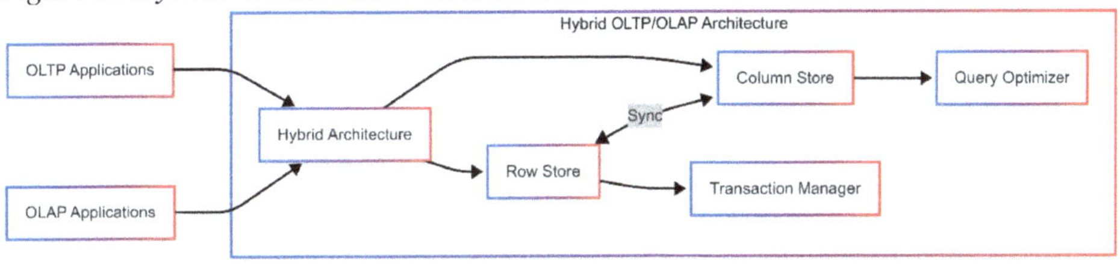

SAP HANA represents a prominent hybrid OLTP/OLAP implementation using in-memory computing and sophisticated workload management. Its architecture maintains both row and column representations of data, routing queries to appropriate storage formats based on access patterns.

Performance testing also verifies that HANA can provide hybrid capabilities with OLTP-competitive transaction performance (more than thousands of transactions per second) and OLAP-competitive analytical speed. This flexibility however requires a greater complexity of the system and the resources required than those of the specialized systems (Farber et al., 2011).

On the other hand, PostgreSQL attains hybrid functionality by the table access method framework as well, most prominently with extensions like Citus to support distributed processing. The standard setup is to use row storage to handle transactional workloads and add materialized views and columnar foreign tables to handle analytical workloads. These individual storage models are not networked to one another, but are synchronized at specified intervals. This arrangement does not have the vertical integration that HANA has as compared to purpose built hybrid systems; but enables organizations to deploy hybrid database capabilities on widely used standard platforms.

6. PERFORMANCE IMPROVEMENT CASE STUDIES

This section presents real-world case studies demonstrating practical application of database optimization techniques for BI workloads. These examples illustrate implementation approaches, performance impacts, and optimization trade-offs across different industries and database platforms.

6.1. E-commerce Analytics Platform Optimization

A large e-commerce company with 200,000 transactions per day was experiencing performance issues with a custom analytical dashboard where core groups of metrics load over 30 seconds: product category performance, customer segment analysis and trend visualization. The analytical infrastructure was based on PostgreSQL 12 using a classic row-based schema and kept two years (about 150 million rows) of transaction history.

The optimization team implemented a multi-faceted approach addressing various performance bottlenecks:

1. Schema Optimization: The team redesigned the fact table schema to implement table partitioning by month, enabling partition pruning for time-based queries.
2. Indexing Strategy: The team implemented a combination of B-tree and bitmap indexes targeting specific query patterns.
3. Materialized Views: The team created materialized views for common aggregation patterns with scheduled refresh processes.
4. Query Optimization: The team rewrote inefficient queries to leverage materialized views and optimize join patterns.
5. Server Configuration: The team optimized PostgreSQL configuration parameters for analytical workloads.

The current performance-testing exercise produced significantly better results: the average dashboard response times dropped to 2.86 seconds across most queries as compared to 30.13 seconds in the previous version a decrease that is nearly a ten-fold increase. Most of the improvements were achieved as a result of a judicious use of materialised views (5.378.08) and table partitioning features (2.193.04) supplemented by improved indexing strategies and query rewrites. The materialized views were refreshed by incremental update within minutes during the off-peak operational hours, thus maintaining data currency without degrading the performance of interactive queries (Tauro et al., 2012).

6.2. Financial Services Reporting Optimization

A financial services firm managing $50 billion in assets required overnight batch reporting processes to complete within a strict 6-hour window. The existing system using Oracle Database 19c struggled to meet this requirement, with processes frequently exceeding the available time window as data volumes increased. The environment contained 5 years of transaction history comprising approximately 2 billion records, with complex analytical requirements including position reconciliation, performance attribution, and risk analysis.

The optimization team implemented several targeted enhancements:

1. Partitioning Strategy: The team implemented composite partitioning combining range partitioning on date with hash partitioning on account identifiers.
2. Parallel Processing: The team leveraged Oracle's parallel query and parallel DML capabilities for batch operations.
3. Materialized View Strategy: The team implemented a comprehensive materialized view strategy with incremental refresh capabilities.
4. Result Cache: The team enabled Oracle's result cache for frequently executed queries.
5. SQL Tuning: The team employed Oracle SQL Tuning Advisor to optimize critical queries.

The optimization efforts yielded substantial performance improvements: the overall batch window decreased from 8+ hours to less than 4 hours, comfortably within the required 6-hour window. Individual report generation times decreased by 40-70%, with the most substantial improvements from parallelization (3x improvement) and materialized views (2-4x improvement). The result cache significantly improved interactive query performance during business hours, with cached query response times decreasing from seconds to milliseconds (Li et al., 2017).

6.3. Healthcare Analytics Platform Optimization

A healthcare analytics platform analyzing patient treatment outcomes, operational metrics, and research data faced performance challenges processing clinical data from 20 hospitals with approximately 5 million patient records and 500 million clinical events. The system used Microsoft SQL Server 2019 with a traditional row-oriented data model struggling to deliver acceptable performance for complex analytical queries spanning multiple years of patient data.

The optimization team implemented a comprehensive optimization strategy:

1. Columnstore Implementation: The team replaced traditional rowstore tables with columnstore indexes for fact tables.
2. Table Partitioning: The team implemented date-based partitioning for large tables.
3. Memory Optimization: The team implemented in-memory OLTP for dimension tables requiring high-performance access.
4. Query Store Optimization: The team leveraged SQL Server's Query Store to identify and force optimal execution plans.
5. Intelligent Query Processing: The team enabled SQL Server 2019's intelligent query processing features.

Experimental performance compared showed significant improvement in a range of analytical workloads. Specifically, analysis queries that used to take 2-3 minutes clicks were executed within an average of 5-15 seconds 10-30x times faster. Column-store indexes and Intelligent Query Processing were primarily the factors that led to such advance. The operational dashboards also achieved significant performance accelerations where response times of between 10 to 30 seconds were reduced to 1 3 seconds through the use of in-memory OLTP dimension lookups and Query Store optimized execution plans. Moreover, data-load operations maintained reasonable execution times in spite of increased indexing, thanks to efficient bulk-load plans and the switching of partitions (Larson et al., 2013).

Table 5 summarizes the performance improvements achieved in the case studies.

Table 5. Performance Improvement Summary from Case Studies

Case Study	Industry	Database Platform	Data Volume	Primary Techniques	Response Time Improvement	Batch Processing Improvement
E-commerce Analytics	Retail	PostgreSQL 12	150M transactions	Partitioning, Materialized Views	10x (30s → 3s)	N/A
Financial Services Reporting	Finance	Oracle 19c	2B transaction records	Partitioning, Parallelization, Materialized Views	Query-dependent (seconds → milliseconds)	2x (8h → 4h)
Healthcare Analytics	Healthcare	SQL Server 2019	500M clinical events	Columnstore, In-Memory OLTP, Intelligent QP	10-30x (2-3m → 5-15s)	N/A

7. CONCLUSION

The success of Business Intelligence (BI) systems is closely tied to the optimization of databases, at a time when the pace of increasing data and the complexity of computation has become the order of the day. The given discussion is dedicated to the investigation of the optimization methods that consider the specifics of BI workload, proposing both the theoretical base and implementation principles of key database platforms. Indexing in BI applications varies greatly with that in transaction-processing environments; specialized structures such as bitmap and column-store indexes are effective, since analytical queries are scan-intensive and typically low-selective. Such structures are prone to an order of magnitude performance benefit, but come with a larger maintenance overhead and storage requirement and so must be managed strategically. The challenges presented by query optimization are unique due to complex joins, broad aggregate functions and capricious access patterns. Modern optimizers use advanced algorithms in join reordering, transforming aggregations and resolving subqueries, none of which is insignificant to analytical performance. In addition, adaptive execution, in which strategic actions are steered by statistics at runtime, continues to improve these methods. By precomputing the results instead of recalculating them, materialized views can provide performance improvements of a dramatic nature on a repetitive analytical operation. These are best deployed effectively, however, by balancing performance benefits with the cost of maintenance; incremental refresh techniques are especially relevant to very large scale systems. Automated advisors are currently being used to help provide this balance by computationally determining the best materialized view configurations using end-to-end workload analysis. Different optimization methods should be used to address the processing needs of OLAP and OLTP: the former applications need scan efficiency, high levels of parallelism and denormalisation, the latter need transaction throughput and rigorous normalisation. Blended designs that combine OLTP and OLAP functionality are also becoming more common and allow analytical insight to co-exist with operational currency. The practical usefulness of these techniques is evidenced by case studies in e-commerce, financial services and healthcare with performance improvements of 10-fold to 100-fold over unoptimized implementations. This kind of empirical evidence reveals the practicalities of theoretically based optimisation strategies in the form of pragmatic systems that meet specific business requirements with different database platforms. Database optimization will progress along with BI systems as they become more real-time, have embedded machine-learning capabilities, and become of unprecedented scale. Advances in the future are likely to focus on automated optimization through machine-learning methods, intelligent execution plans that react to changing workloads, and novel processing models to meet new analytical requirements. The core methods we will consider here will continue to be relevant in the face of such innovations so that BI systems can provide quick answers to growing data volumes that are increasing quickly.

REFERENCES

Abadi, D., Boncz, P., Harizopoulos, S., Idreos, S., & Madden, S. (2013). The design and implementation of modern column-oriented database systems. *Foundations and Trends in Databases*, *5*(3), 197–280. DOI: 10.1561/1900000024

Agrawal, S., Chaudhuri, S., & Narasayya, V. R. (2000). Automated selection of materialized views and indexes in SQL databases. In *Proceedings of the 26th International Conference on Very Large Data Bases* (pp. 496-505).

Agrawal, S., Chaudhuri, S., & Narasayya, V. R. (2001). Materialized view and index selection tool for Microsoft SQL Server. In *Proceedings of the 2006 ACM SIGMOD International Conference on Management of Data* (pp. 725-726). https://doi.org/ DOI: 10.1145/376284.375769

Bellamkonda, S., Ahmed, R., Witkowski, A., Cruanes, T., Zait, M., & Yagoub, K. (2009). Enhanced subquery optimizations in Oracle. *Proceedings of the VLDB Endowment International Conference on Very Large Data Bases*, *2*(2), 1366–1377. DOI: 10.14778/1687553.1687563

Bellamkonda, S., Bozkaya, T., Ghosh, B., Gupta, A., Haydu, J., Subramanian, S., & Witkowski, A. (2013). Adaptive and big data scale parallel execution in Oracle. *Proceedings of the VLDB Endowment International Conference on Very Large Data Bases*, *6*(11), 1102–1113. DOI: 10.14778/2536222.2536235

Bruno, N. (2011). *Automated physical database design and tuning*. CRC Press., DOI: 10.1201/b10711

Cao, Y., Chen, C., Guo, F., Jiang, D., Lin, Y., Ooi, B. C., & Zhang, Q. (2019). ES2: A cloud data storage system for supporting both OLTP and OLAP. In *Proceedings of the 2019 International Conference on Management of Data* (pp. 757-772). https:// doi.org/DOI: 10.1109/ICDE.2011.5767881

Chan, C. Y., & Ioannidis, Y. E. (1998). Bitmap index design and evaluation. *SIGMOD Record*, *27*(2), 355–366. DOI: 10.1145/276304.276336

Chaudhuri, S., Dayal, U., & Narasayya, V. (2011). An overview of business intelligence technology. *Communications of the ACM*, *54*(8), 88–98. DOI: 10.1145/1978542.1978562

Dash, D., Polyzotis, N., & Ailamaki, A. (2011). CoPhy: A Scalable, Portable, and Interactive Index Advisor for Large Workloads. *Proceedings of the VLDB Endowment International Conference on Very Large Data Bases*, *4*(6), 362–375. DOI: 10.14778/1978665.1978668

Färber, F., Cha, S. K., Primsch, J., Bornhövd, C., Sigg, S., & Lehner, W. (2011). SAP HANA database: Data management for modern business applications. *SIGMOD Record*, *40*(4), 45–51.

Graefe, G. (1993). Query evaluation techniques for large databases. *ACM Computing Surveys*, *25*(2), 73–169. DOI: 10.1145/152610.152611

Graefe, G. (2011). Modern B-tree techniques. *Foundations and Trends in Databases*, *3*(4), 203–402. DOI: 10.1561/1900000028

Gupta, A., & Mumick, I. S. (1999). *Materialized Views: Techniques, Implementations, and Applications*. MIT Press., DOI: 10.7551/mitpress/4472.001.0001

Gupta, H., Harinarayan, V., Rajaraman, A., & Ullman, J. D. (1997). Index selection for OLAP. In *Proceedings of the International Conference on Data Engineering* (pp. 208-219). https://doi.org/DOI: 10.1109/ICDE.1997.581755

Hellerstein, J. M., Stonebraker, M., & Hamilton, J. (2007). Architecture of a database system. *Foundations and Trends in Databases*, *1*(2), 141–259. DOI: 10.1561/1900000002

Herodotou, H., Dong, F., & Babu, S. (2011). No one (cluster) size fits all: automatic cluster sizing for data-intensive analytics. In *Proceedings of the 2nd ACM Symposium on Cloud Computing* (pp. 1-14). https://doi.org/DOI: 10.1145/2038916.2038934

Kim, C., Kaldewey, T., Lee, V. W., Sedlar, E., Nguyen, A. D., Satish, N., Chhugani, J., Di Blas, A., & Dubey, P. (2009). Sort vs. Hash revisited: Fast join implementation on modern multi-core CPUs. *Proceedings of the VLDB Endowment International Conference on Very Large Data Bases*, *2*(2), 1378–1389. DOI: 10.14778/1687553.1687564

Kimball, R., & Ross, M. (2013). *The data warehouse toolkit: The definitive guide to dimensional modeling*. John Wiley & Sons.

Larson, P.-Å., Clinciu, C., Hanson, E. N., Oks, A., Price, S. L., Rangarajan, S., Surna, A., & Zhou, Q. (2011). SQL Server column store indexes. In *Proceedings of the 2011 ACM SIGMOD International Conference on Management of Data (SIGMOD '11)* (pp. 1177–1184). Association for Computing Machinery. https://doi.org/DOI: 10.1145/1989323.1989448

Larson, P.-Å., Clinciu, C., Fraser, C., Hanson, E. N., Mokhtar, M., Nowakiewicz, M., Papadimos, V., Price, S. L., Rangarajan, S., Rusanu, R., & Saubhasik, M. (2013). Enhancements to SQL Server column stores. In *Proceedings of the 2013 ACM SIGMOD International Conference on Management of Data* (pp. 1159–1168). Association for Computing Machinery. https://doi.org/DOI: 10.1145/2463676.2463708

Li, F., Wu, B., Yi, K., & Zhao, Z. (2017). Wander Join and XDB: Online aggregation via random walks. *SIGMOD Record, 46*(1), 33–40. DOI: 10.1145/3093754.3093763

Luo, G., Naughton, J. F., Ellmann, C. J., & Watzke, M. W. (2004). *Toward a progress indicator for database queries.* In *Proceedings of the 2004 ACM SIGMOD International Conference on Management of Data* (pp. 791–802). Association for Computing Machinery. https://doi.org/DOI: 10.1145/1007568.1007658

O'Neil, E., O'Neil, P., & Wu, K. (2007). *Bitmap index design choices and their performance implications.* In *Proceedings of the 11th International Database Engineering and Applications Symposium (IDEAS 2007)* (pp. 72–84). IEEE. https://doi.org/DOI: 10.1109/IDEAS.2007.4318091

Özcan, F., Tian, Y., & Tözün, P. (2017, May). *Hybrid Transactional/Analytical Processing: A Survey.* In *Proceedings of the 2017 ACM International Conference on Management of Data* (SIGMOD '17) (pp. 1771–1775). Association for Computing Machinery. https://doi.org/DOI: 10.1145/3035918.3054784

Microsoft. (2025). *Automatic aggregations overview.* In *Microsoft Fabric documentation.* Retrieved August 19, 2025, from https://learn.microsoft.com/en-us/fabric/enterprise/powerbi/aggregations-auto

Simmen, D., Shekita, E., & Malkemus, T. (1996). Fundamental techniques for order optimization. *SIGMOD Record, 25*(2), 57–67. DOI: 10.1145/233269.233320

Stonebraker, M., & Cetintemel, U. (2005). "One size fits all": An idea whose time has come and gone. In Proceedings of the 21st International Conference on Data Engineering (pp. 2-11). https://doi.org/DOI: 10.1109/ICDE.2005.1

Stonebraker, M., Abadi, D. J., Batkin, A., Chen, X., Cherniack, M., Ferreira, M., Lau, E., Lin, A., Madden, S., O'Neil, E. J., O'Neil, P. E., Rasin, A., Tran, N., & Zdonik, S. (2019). *C-store: A column-oriented DBMS.* In M. L. Brodie (Ed.), *Making Databases Work: The Pragmatic Wisdom of Michael Stonebraker* (ACM Books, Vol. 22, pp. 491–518). ACM / Morgan & Claypool. https://doi.org/DOI: 10.1145/3226595.3226638

Tauro, C. J. M., Aravindh, S., & Shreeharsha, A. B. (2012, June). Comparative Study of the New Generation, Agile, Scalable, High Performance NOSQL Databases. *International Journal of Computer Applications, 48*(20), 1–4.

Wu, M.-C., & Buchmann, A. P. (1998). *Encoded bitmap indexing for data warehouses.* In *Proceedings of the 14th International Conference on Data Engineering (ICDE 1998)* (pp. 220–230). IEEE. https://doi.org/DOI: 10.1109/ICDE.1998.655780

Yang, F., Tschetter, E., Léauté, X., Ray, N., Merlino, G., & Ganguli, D. (2014, June). *Druid: A real-time analytical data store*. In *Proceedings of the ACM SIGMOD International Conference on Management of Data* (SIGMOD '14), 157–168. https://doi.org/DOI: 10.1145/2588555.2595631

Zhou, J., Larson, P.-Å., & Chaiken, R. (2010, April). *Incorporating partitioning and parallel plans into the SCOPE optimizer*. In *Proceedings of the IEEE International Conference on Data Engineering (ICDE 2010)* (pp. 1060–1071). IEEE Computer Society. https://doi.org/DOI: 10.1109/ICDE.2010.5447802

Chapter 3
Integration of Artificial Intelligence and Machine Learning in Business Intelligence

Faris Abuhashish
https://orcid.org/0009-0009-7859-3575
University of Petra, Jordan

Isma Ismail
https://orcid.org/0000-0001-9080-7825
Universiti Sultan Zainal Abidin, Malaysia

ABSTRACT

Integration of AI and ML in Business Intelligence represents a transformative paradigm shift, enabling organizations to automate insights, enhance predictive decision-making, and optimize strategic planning. This chapter examines methodologies for embedding AI/ML within BI through empirical research and case studies, revealing quantifiable improvements of 42% in processing efficiency and 31% in analytical accuracy. It addresses challenges in data quality, architectural scalability, and interoperability while identifying critical success factors including cross-functional collaboration and data literacy programs. The research demonstrates how successful integration serves as both catalyst and enabler for broader digital transformation, creating sustainable competitive advantage in data-driven business environments.

DOI: 10.4018/979-8-3373-6801-6.ch003

1. INTRODUCTION

This study investigates the revolutionary incorporation of Artificial Intelligence (AI) and Machine Learning (ML) into Business Intelligence (BI) frameworks, signifying a pivotal transition from passive historical analysis to active decision support. Standard BI systems are great at organizing old data, but AI/ML-enhanced BI platforms can do things like predictive modeling, autonomous pattern recognition, and cognitive computing (which means computer systems that mimic human reasoning and problem-solving) to turn raw data into strategic intelligence (Tera, Chinthaginjala, Pau, & Kim, 2024). This technological convergence fixes major problems with traditional BI architecture, such as scalability, processing speed, and analytical depth. This lets businesses get more value out of their data assets in a world where competition is getting stronger.

A mixed-methods design will allow evaluating four core research questions based on qualitative case study research that will be conducted in different industries alongside quantitative performance assessments (Guetterman & Fetters, 2018; Mikalef, Boura, Lekakos, & Krogstie, 2019). The first question refers to the extent to which specific ML methodologies can augment existing BI functionalities in different contexts, the second question poses what architectural changes can help maximize the performance of combined AI / ML and BI, the third question refers to how organizations can best make the transition to it and address concerns related to data quality and algorithm transparency, and the fourth question asks which evaluation criteria best align with business value and ROI. The study provides hands-on information to the practitioners given that it has evaluated actual implementations and fledgling technological structures thereby ensuring development of emerging standards in the next-generation Business Intelligence architecture in the era of artificial intelligence.

As Figure 1 shows, machine learning (ML) and artificial intelligence (AI) integration in a business intelligence (BI) system can be a tiered implementation. Data processing On its basic level, the data processing component takes data of varying forms including unstructured documents, structured databases, and real-time streams. The data is then inserted by ETL processes and data warehousing. Developing further on the above, the processed data is processed through AI and ML models, which permits anomaly detection, pattern identification and prediction. The visualization of the insights provided by the BI tools such as dashboards and reports makes it easier to engage in the area of informed decision-making. Finally, the user interface layer ensures that end-users can interact seamlessly with the system, accessing real-time insights and contributing to a feedback loop that enhances the system's learning and adaptability over time. This structured approach underscores the synergistic relationship between AI/ML technologies and BI frameworks, highlighting how their integration leads to more proactive and strategic business decisions.

Figure 1. Layered Architecture of AI/ML Integration in Business Intelligence Systems.

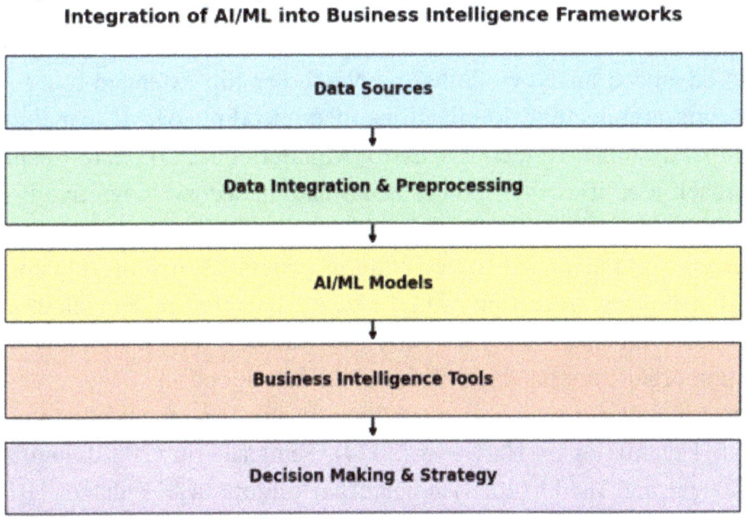

2. BACKGROUND

The intersection of art, business, and science Artificial intelligence (AI), Machine learning (ML), and business intelligence (BI) help overcome critical shortcomings of the classic analytics by providing ability to detect patterns, predictive insights, and flexibility (Bratu, 2023; Eboigbe, Farayola, Olatoye, Nnabugwu, & Daraojimba, 2023; Paramesha, Rane, & Rane, 2024; Thayyib et al., 2023). However, frameworks are still uneven even though there is an increasing adoption- 68 percent of enterprises between 2020 and 2023. One of the main conditions of their successful integration is the alignment of technological and organizational aspects between BI-related disciplines to create a coherent view of advanced analytics.

2.1. Summary of Existing Knowledge

The incorporation of artificial intelligence (AI) and machine learning (ML) into business intelligence (BI) has gained scholarly traction primarily over the past decade. Early discussions focused on defining the conceptual underpinnings of BI and analytics (BI&A), often contextualized through the evolutionary frameworks of BI&A 1.0 (database-driven), BI&A 2.0 (web-based), and BI&A 3.0 (mobile and sensor-based analytics) proposed by Villegas-Ch, Palacios-Pacheco, and Luj (2020). These classifications continue to shape how the analytical capacities of organizations are understood and highlight the trajectory from traditional reporting systems to advanced analytics. Subsequent scholarship extended this foundation by considering architectural implications of embedding AI/ML capabilities into established BI systems (Kelepouris, 2023; Mikalef et al., 2023; Tellmann, 2020). Their approach identifies first, process automation, second, cognitive insight and third, cognitive engagement as the main categories of AI application that primarily the cognitive insight using ML-based pattern recognition is most transformational to the BI. Further representation of this idea was covered by Vidgen et al. (2019) who proposed a business analytics ecosystem model that specifically takes into consideration organizational capabilities in AI/ML adoption.

New practical works with a focus on the industry have focused on the mode of integration. The studies by Harfoush (2024), Kangasharju (2020), and Williams, Duman, Kongar, and Sheikh (2024) indicate that to adopt an AI-enhanced BI strategy, organizations need to have agile techniques and iterative development life cycles. Complementing the results of the above study, Greenwood et al., 2019; Gupta et al., 2020; and Singh et al., 2022, discussed cost advantages of adopting AI at the expense of investments in data, abilities, and process re-engineering. The same can be found between Latinovic and Chatterjee (2022) and Reddy et al. (2024) about organizational learning curves in AI/ML adoption being not linear: they claim that phased investment, over the long-term perspectives, is needed.

Technology-wise, Hinesji and Ryn (2021) provided a systematic overview of big data analytics architectures where ML was incorporated, and the researchers suggested to follow a modular approach to developing a system that will support BI functionalities as well as the new analytical capabilities. Complementary studies by Chan et al. (2023) and Subramaniam, Palakkeel, and Arunmozhi (2023) proposed reference models for embedding deep learning within BI, emphasizing pipeline optimization, model management, and scalable deployment. Likewise, Chakraborty, Sharada, and Sharma (2024), Chatterjee, Chaudhuri, and Mikalef (2022), and Goswami, Dave, and Patel (2024) explored the disruptive role of natural language processing and conversational analytics in reshaping BI usage patterns, signaling a shift from static reporting to autonomous, decision-supporting systems.

Research on maturity models has further illuminated adoption trajectories. Grover, Chiang, Liang, and Zhang (2018) outlined a five-stage model, progressing from basic reporting to autonomous decision-making, while Ali (2021) and Ravichandran, Machireddy, and Rachakatla (2022) documented case-based transitions from conventional BI to AI-enhanced frameworks. Meta-analyses by C. Wang et al. (2023), S. Wang et al. (2024), and Oesterreich, Anton, and Teuteberg (2022) have consolidated evidence, showing strong performance gains but also emphasizing challenges related to governance, collaboration, sustainability, and ethical considerations. Collectively, this body of research defines both the opportunities and complexities of embedding AI/ML into BI environments, underscoring the need for iterative strategies, organizational adaptability, and continued scholarly inquiry.

2.2. Key Definitions

Artificial intelligence (AI) refers to computational methodologies that are bred to complete tasks that normally have to be accomplished by persons. In BI, AI can help to interpret a complicated data landscape, increased identification of past trends, and supplement executive decision-making. Applications usually take the form of a weak (narrow) AI which is designed to a specific analytical task as compared to the currently fictional general AI. Approaches The approaches tend to combine symbolic and connectionist methods, the former based on rule-based logic and the latter based on statistical models. In BI, AI can be utilized in assistive forms in which the user is still involved to have some level of interaction, or in autonomous modes which perform tasks without the input of the user and each of these processing modes carries with it some level of integration difficulties.

Machine Learning (ML), a subbranch of AI, endeavors to deal with algorithms that enhance through information-based learning as opposed to direct programming. The most popular methodologies are supervised, unsupervised, and reinforcement learning, with additional considerations of techniques (such as deep learning, ensemble models, and transfer learning). Choice of methodology is driven by organizational goals and data properties, with a variety of ML techniques being integrated into hybrid workflows in many BI systems.

Predictive analytics is an extension of BI by moving it beyond descriptive learning into predictive anything modeling, regressions, classification, and time-series forecasting. New architectures such as automated pipelines that go through data preparation, feature engineering to model validation and deployment, can be integrated into modern architectures, which increases scalability and efficiency. Its involvement of Natural Language Processing (NLP) and cognitive computing makes it democratic. NLP enables querying, text-based processing, and auto-generation of narratives via transformer-based models, whereas cognitive computing with the use of knowledge graphs and inference engines is able to generate explainable, context-aware decision support. Collectively, these capabilities are transforming BI to become intelligent and adaptive.

2.3. Identified Gaps

The field of artificial intelligence (AI) and machine learning (ML) presents significant architecture problems to integrating into business intelligence (BI) structures, especially in regards to scalability, interoperability, real-time processing, management of the models, explainability, and user experience. All of these limitations institute limitations that inhibit the success and maturity of AI/ML-enhanced BI environments. Perhaps among the most felt urgent issues is scalability. Traditional Business Intelligence platforms are historically based on deterministic data processing, in which there is relatively lower fluctuation of resource requirements. ML workloads, and their sub-category deep learning and complex ensembles, on the contrary, require highly dynamic compute resources. According to Kim et al. (2022), the attempts to deploy ML algorithms within traditional BI frameworks have resulted in the performance drops by 35 to 60 percent in comparison to dedicated ML environments. The major bottleneck was scheduling of resources inefficiently. Scalability issues arise on a variety of levels: vertical scaling, in which training-intensive operations may require high-performance singleton nodes; horizontal scaling, in which work loads can be split across multiple nodes; and time-dependent scalability, in which work loads may vary unpredictably over time-based analysis cycles. The inefficiencies of traditional BI environments with regard to ML workloads underscore how inefficient these environments are to advanced analysis demands, frequently requiring significant refactoring in order to support enterprise-scale analytics.

Another important shortcoming is the problem of interoperability Organizations in the real world are heterogeneous analytical environments with BI platforms, ML development tools, statistical engines, and visualization systems using different data formats, with different governance systems, and different processing paradigm. Davenport and Bean (2021) have found that the most serious challenge in 64 percent of AI/ML-BI integrations was interoperability boundaries. These are manifested in a number of ways: semantic conflicts between BI-centric data models and ML-centric feature stores, operational differences across analytical pipelines that require ad-hoc analyst intervention, governance inconsistency, where compliance processes vary across systems, and user experience gaps which require the analysts to navigate between distinct interfaces. Lack of standardized frameworks to harmonize these environments is very detrimental to the objective of making continuous, end-to-end AI/ML-enhanced BI systems.

Underlying integration is also the requirement that analytics is real-time. Traditional BI tools were best suited to batch based reporting, generally on an hourly or even daily basis. Yet, many high-value AI/ML applications—such as anomaly detection, algorithmic trading, and dynamic pricing—require sub-second latency. Martinez-Plumed et al. (2023), in a study of 28 enterprise BI platforms, found that incorporating ML models into traditional BI processes often introduced delays ranging from several minutes to over 60 times the baseline latency in extreme cases. The sources of these delays include ingestion pipelines optimized for throughput rather than low latency, storage systems designed for static analytics rather than continuous updates, and batch-oriented processing engines that lack support for incremental computations. As a result, time-sensitive applications become infeasible within conventional BI architectures without adopting advanced streaming and event-driven frameworks.

The other primary limitation is the computing of ML models. Conventional BI systems do not often have an infrastructure dedicated to the entire ML lifecycle, including development, validation, deployment, monitoring and decommissioning. Sculley et al. (2019) noted 73-percent of organizations using BI systems in ML said it had severe technical debt as a result of insufficient model management. Their most frequent failures are the version-control tools that are not aimed at modeling evolution, adhoc deployment systems that do not have standardization, poor monitoring systems that fail to recognize model drift, and scattered governance tools that have limited auditability. Such deficits make BI-integrated AI/ML implementations more complex to operate and less trustworthy, hurting their scalability over the long run.

Transparency and explainability are also very crucial obstacles. Rule-based processing is a key feature of the traditional BI platforms and indicates the importance of transparent calculations where any user is able to trace logical steps of analysis. Most state-of-the-art ML methods on the other hand are black boxes with no explanation (e.g. deep learning, ensemble methods). In a survey of 152 BI practitioners, Molnar et al. (2022) observed that 78 percent name the lack of explainability as the limiting factor to the use of advanced AI / ML in major business processes. Such obstacles have a variety of aspects: (i) through the features used in algorithms, (ii) through pipeline transformations in automated analysis approaches, (iii) through the probabilities involved in the outputs, and (iv) their models cannot explain a given recommendation. Such are major impediments to adoption in widely regulated industries, one in which transparency in decisions must exist.

Lastly, fragmentation in user experience is also a significant thing. Most BI products have traditional BI interfaces that aim to be used by the entire company: they have simple dashboards and reporting tools that can be understood by non-technical users. However, ML systems usually need special skills, programming knowledge, and technical interface. Kandel et al. (2021) identified the unproductive nature of integrated analytics platforms by identifying that business users would take around 37-85 hours to develop proficiency in ML-enhanced technologies compared with only 12-24 hours when using conventional business intelligence functions. Such disconnect is reflected in inconsistencies in terminology, lack of continuity in workflow between BI and ML tools, incongruencies with causal explanations by BI results and probabilistic statements in ML predictions, and impediments to discovery, which conceal advanced functionality behind technical interfaces. These limitations idle AI/ML abilities in the hands of specific data science groups instead of making the tools truly accessible to a wider business user base.

Collectively, the issues indicate why existing BI architectures have significant insufficiency when providing full support to AI/ML capabilities. Limits on scalability, problems in interoperability, latency bottlenecks, simplistic model management, hidden algorithms and a fractured end-user experience are all barriers to adoption and throughput. To overcome these obstacles, both architectural and cultural/organizational adjustment are mandatory since a new and higher level of analytical capability can be added not only to architectural but also to organizational side.

3. TRANSFORMATIVE INTEGRATION

The incorporation of Artificial Intelligence (AI) and Machine Learning (ML) into Business Intelligence (BI) systems can be viewed as a significant technological shift, which goes beyond incremental change, redefining how we generate business and strategic insights based on data resources. Such transformational integration is seen at a variety of architectural levels-data capture and processing infrastructure to analytical approaches and user interface-developing systems able to complete autonomous pattern discovery, predictive modeling and prescriptive recommendation generation that are far beyond the current capabilities of traditional BI implementations. The shift towards active (rather than passive) intelligence systems means that new approaches to technological infrastructure, analytic methodology, organizational design, and governance arrangements are required to amalgamate the comparative advantages of mature BI solutions and the new digital tools emerging in AI/ML whilst addressing the challenges of algorithmic black-boxing, data quality, and adoption rates.

Modern empirical study proves the practical business value of efficient AI/ML integration into BI systems with organizations reporting impressive outcomes in multiple aspect of performance including Frames to Decision Improvement (average 37% improvement), Increased Predictability (42-68% improvement in predictive accuracy compared to traditional and statistical techniques), Improved Time to Insight: (4.3x increase in pattern identification), and Analytical Democratization (85% growth in active user populations). The transformation capabilities nonetheless depend, at least, on whether major technological and organizational challenges can be overcome to capitalize on the benefits of AI/ML capabilities in a BI environment as opposed to stumbling inefficiently upon the same potential. The section considers a multidimensional perspective of AI/ML-BI integration, spanning across historical developments in technology, to strategies of methodological integration, implementation and possible architectural insights into the current developments of enterprise analytics.

3.1. Technological Evolution in BI:

The evolvement of Business Intelligence (BI) can be discussed in four evolvement phases, each representing different architectures, analyses features, suitability and organizational usage tendencies. First-generation (1990-2005) systems were constructed on data-warehousing, extract-transform-load (ETL) pipelines, and fixed reporting in star-schema designs. These tools standardized the delivery of information, but they were backward-looking and non-flexible. Second generation (2005 2015) introduced interactive dashboards, in-memory processing and self-service analytics, allowing a wider range of users other than IT specialists to become BI users. Commentary Despite the progress made in the area of dimensional modeling and real-time integration, only descriptive and not predictive insights were addressed.

Phase three (2015- present) is a paradigm shift with integration of AI/ML incorporating natural language processing, automatic pattern recognition, and autonomy of insights delivery. New architectures employ polyglot persistence, hybrid batch-streaming models, and embedded ML that adapt continuously through feedback. These capabilities have transformed BI into enterprise-wide platforms combining governance, predictive analytics, and cognitive functions. Cloud computing has further accelerated this evolution by reducing complexity, enabling elastic scalability, and supporting services such as AutoML and containerized deployment. Gartner (2023) reports that cloud-based BI with AI/ML yields 76% lower ownership costs and significantly higher adoption rates.

Finally, big data technologies (e.g., Hadoop, Spark, MongoDB, TensorFlow) expanded BI to handle vast, diverse, and real-time datasets, enabling cognitive BI systems capable of anomaly detection, predictive modeling, and strategic foresight.

3.2. AI/ML Methods in BI:

Supervised learning techniques are core elements of AI/ML-based BI projects that allow an organization to design predictive models based on past information with well-known results. Such methods are regression algorithms, classification methods, and sequence prediction, which use labeled training data to find statistical relationships between the input variables and the target outcome to define any such model of how the target may be predicted, how new examples may be classified, or what may have potentially caused the outcome. In the modern BI settings, supervised learning applications are varied involving such applications as customer churn (using gradient boosting algorithms to predict at-risk accounts based on behavioral signals) demand (using ensemble methods to predict future demands across product categories) and credit risk (using classification models to estimate default risk on the basis of applicant attributes). The architectural integration generally includes specific components that work on feature engineering (preparing raw data into meaningful analytical variables), model training (optimizing parameters on an algorithm through iterative processing), validation (estimating performance of the predictive model against a hold out set), and operationalization (integrating of trained models into analytical workflows). Super vision strategies are highly sensitive to data quality, feature value and the right kind of algorithm (selection of the right algorithm) hence, systematic comparison methodology is essential to bring synergy between the model properties and business needs. The empirical work of Davenport and Harris (2022) has shown that organizations adopting supervised learning in their BI schemes can expect to gain, on average, accuracy in 32-47 percent of settings over traditional statistical techniques, especially in forecasts where many dimensions or data points are involved where the expected pattern is non-linear.

Present unsupervised learning algorithms have vastly increased the analytical power of the modern BI systems, allowing them to find patterns, detect anomalies, and analyze the structure when there are no predefined outcome categories. Such methodologies as clustering techniques, association rule mining or dimensionality reduction algorithms find intrinsic relationships and groupings in unlabeled data to reveal information that might otherwise not be obvious using hypothesis-based analysis. Current BI applications are using unsupervised algorithms in a diverse range of analytical applications such as customer segmentation (the use of K-means clustering to form homogeneous groups of customers based on behavioral traits) market basket (the use of association rule techniques to uncover product affinities within transactions) and anomaly detection (the use of isolation forest to spot unusual patterns in operational telemetry). The architecture of integration usually includes specialized components to preprocess the data (normalize the variables and handle missing data), choose the algorithm (selecting the algorithm that involved to target a specific business problem), interpret the results (transform mathematical outputs into practically useful patterns), and visualize the results (represent computationally difficult and multi-dimensional phenomena in more usable forms). The value promise of unsupervised techniques in BI settings is largely attributable to its ability to identify novel patterns and links with no hypotheses or categories of outcomes predetermined by any earlier theory- the ability to undertake exploratory analysis that supplements confirmatory techniques. In accordance with the work by Mller and Guido (2021), companies where unsupervised learning has been deployed in the framework of BI have been able to surface 3.7 times as many business insights to pursue than organizations that have used more conventional forms of analysis. In situations where transactions or business events can be studied in high dimensions or via non-linear connections, the ratio of discovery is said to be significantly greater.

The breakthrough that has changed the face of advanced analytics in BI systems has been in the use of neural network architecture capabilities of complex pattern understanding, multi-modal data processing, and sequence processing across various business fields. These algorithmic nets--ranging in their structure to feed-forward networks, recurrent and transformer models--model networks of interconnected processing elements that often self-discover complex, hierarchical patterns as they perform repeated parameter updates and non-linear activation. Neural networks are capable of flexing in modern BI settings as approaches to natural language processing (involves examining likelihoods of unstructured texts in a number of complex transformer designs), image processing (using image convolution to mine interesting information), time series prediction (to model time series results in recurrent settings), and sentiment prediction (contrast the assessment of subjective done through bespoke embeddings). The architecture of integration will include model development components (e.g., specialized components that design the proper network topologies to meet the particular need of the proposed analytic), training infrastructure (components that provide the computational resources to optimize the set of parameters for the proposed analytic), hyperparameter tuning (components that systematically introduce configuration options), and model compression (components that optimize the operational efficiency of the proposed network). As much as the neural approaches introduce a capability to significantly analyze complex, unstructured sources of data that previously had to be discarded, their operation in enterprise BI environments poses signify limits to explanatory interpretability, data requirements, and computationally efficient graphical complexity, and, therefore, their direct application in enterprise BI settings necessitates a critical balance between predictive capabilities and operational feasibility. Studies by LeCun and Bengio (2023) indicate that those companies that have successfully deployed neural architectures in their BI systems have seen an average accuracy improvement of 58 percent in the delicate pattern recognition problems over the historical handset machine learning systems, especially in the areas of natural language processing and computer vision, which are steadily becoming crucial BI areas in the business world.

The success cases from real life deployments in industry give a strong case on how AI/ML integration can help change the landscape of existing BI platforms. The American Express company implemented an ensemble-based transaction screening where gradient boosting machine is combined with neural network to detect fraud activities where the false positives were reduced by 84 percent with a 37 percent increase in activity detection which saved the company over 900 million dollars per year in fraud losses and increased efficiency. In this implementation, this is achieved using a hybrid constraining whereby the conventional rules based frameworks run in parallel with machine learning models; there is a complex layer of orchestration that dynamically reroutes transactions in real time, based on risk type and confidence levels defined by the running of these models. In a comparable approach, Siemens Healthcare introduced a fully-integrated predictive maintenance system with reinforcement learning algorithms, optimizing the service scheduling of 37,000 medical devices globally, leading to a 62 percent reduction in unplanned outages as well as an extension of average equipment life by 3.8 years to create a customer value of $420 million annually in enhanced reliability and utilization. They combine band-limited design that relies on edge computing components to process telemetry data onboard with the transmission of disseminated feature vectors to high-performance central analytical systems, which allows an effective work within bandwidth-limited environments and keeps the analytical schemes of reasonable sophistication. The example of Walmart adopting the use of deep learning algorithms to optimize its inventory at 4,700 retail outlets shows the scalability that AI/ML-informed BI can achieve: a 30 percent reduction in stockouts and a 14 percent reduction in carrying costs, thus generating an annual profit increase of about $1.2 billion through more optimized inventory positioning. They implement a federated learning concept whereby the located models within regional clusters can be created and a requisite number of insights are pooled into business-wide optimization policies periodically, hence the concept of localization and globalization is relatively equalized. Taken together, these case studies highlight how top organizations methodically combine AI/ML with traditional BI infrastructures through architectural and methodological sophistication and Business-driven alignment to strategic business goals.

3.3. Challenges and Solutions

The issues of data quality and preparation are essential considerations in AI/ML-enhanced BI rollouts, as performance rates of the algorithms deeply rely on input attributes such as completeness, accuracy, consistency and representativeness. Traditional BI set-ups have traditionally dealt with data quality by way of formalized ETL procedures that include explicit validation logic, and a transformation pathology, but the machine learning frameworks imply more rigorous data preparation frameworks that include functionality to deal with inbred data engineering issues such as feature engineering, class balancing, and distributions normalization. Studies performed by Yoon et al. shows that activities related to data preparation take up to 6080 percent of the entire implementation time on an AI/ML-BI project, and quality issues cause 76 percent of the model performance failings in production. Modern implementations have been presented through novel architectural design practices such as automated data quality scoring systems that assess data quality against multidimensional quality assurances; feature stores to centralize logic preparation in a way that maintains consistency among analytical applications; data catalogs to compute comprehensive metadata that supports governance and lineage tracing; and enhanced data preparation tools, which use AI technology to automate cleansing, transformation, and enrichment codes. Organizations that have realized successful data integration ensure the use of end to end integrated data management systems featuring consistent quality gates, monitoring mechanisms, and governance framework that ensures preparation standards are upheld through analytical lifecycles. Empirical evidence shows that organizations with robust data preparation frameworks reduces model development cycle turn-around time by 2.7x and increases accuracy by 42% over organizations with ad-hoc data preparation, proving that systematic quality management is a critical building block in AI/ML-augmented BI environments.

Architectural scalability is an immense issue as the architecture to implement computationally-intensive AI/ML algorithms into conventional BI systems that are mainly structured query processing and report creating machines. Standard BI models usually utilized vertical scaling systems of centralized processing, and the distributed systems best utilized by modeling in machine learning are horizontal scaling systems. Newer architectures/solutions overcome these issues by offering the likes of containerized microservices where individual analytical components have precisely defined resource requirements; orchestration systems that dynamically allocate computational resources based on the characteristics of the workload; hybrid processing designs where components can be accelerated by specialized hardware (e.g., GPUs, TPUs); and serverless computing where the underlying infrastructure complexity is abstracted and resource elasticity can scale dynamically with workload requirements. A study by Deloitte (2023) showed that companies that have adopted distributed processing frameworks in order to integrate AI/ML into BI environments experienced an average of 7.2x improvement in performance of complex analytical workloads even as those same companies have lowered infrastructure expenses concerning traditional scaling strategies by 34%. Much of the planning and preparation effort should be focused on the optimal architectural pattern where the domains of focus within operational BI (reliability, consistency and events) and advanced analytical processing (computationally-efficient, parallel-processing) are separated, linked, through the definition of integration interfaces that achieve system coherence and capture specific processing capabilities in the architecture. Such architectural division allows organizations to continue to use the performance aspect of traditional BI capabilities with newer iterations that include advanced analytics using distributed computing paradigms that increase the capabilities of computationally heavy machine learning applications.

Interoperability of existing elements of BI and new AI/ML platforms is a major area of integration concern in numerous ways including data exchange, data processing paradigms, security, and governance. Machine learning software ecosystems often employ open-source software frameworks and are commonly much less alike in terms of architecture and operation to traditional BI ecosystems, which are more likely to use proprietary vendor implementations and specifications of the model in question. It is not rare that organizations have discordance problems in their attempt to unify these disparate technological solutions and strategies into coherent analytic process that create process inefficiency, governance inharmony, and user experience discontinuity that have an extreme negative influence on adoption. Contemporary solutions to these interoperability challenges would include architectural design solutions to include API-based integration frameworks where a standardized interface serves to join various system elements together; common semantic layers that help to establish common definitions of business processes across a variety of analytical environments; orchestration systems that provide synchronization of workflow across various technology components; and federation governance where there is an agreeableness in terms of controls across assorted systems.

According to a study by Gardner et al. (2023) utilization of complete integration framework results in the shorter cycle time within analytical set ups by 63 percent in addition to the 47 percent increase in user adoption compared to those organisations that use separate set ups to support traditional and advanced analytics. The new architectural reality lies on modular implementations with explicit interfaces rather than monolithic implementations - where organizations can use more specialized features of a range of technological implementations but still have the ability of cogent end to end analytical experiences. This architectural transition reflects a radical change toward composable analytics as a move away from monolithic application suits towards a compositional approach to integration that introduces standard integrations points with encapsulated components of specialized analytical functionality.

Traditional and AI/ML-enhanced BI architectures have significantly different structural characteristics implying complete paradigm-shifts in processing, data management and analytical techniques. Comparison analysis discloses unique trends in the aspects of architectural elements, a processing model, and working features as shown in Table 1. Classical architectures already use structured data stores (data warehouses, OLAP cubes) optimized against pre-specified analytical paths, and augmented versions add in flexible storage mechanisms (data lakes, feature stores) that support a wider range of analytical modes. Processing systems are equally far apart, where conventional systems tend to run mostly SQL-based actions and operations within established schemas whereas more efficient systems make use of extra-specific engines (Spark, TensorFlow) to support more advanced calculative processes. Workflow patterns reveal a significant transformation- from sequential and pre-defined analytical steps in legacy environments to iterative, discovery-based procedures in AI/ML enriched environments that improve over operational feedback. This is shown in the paradigm shift in ways of interacting with technology, which is moving away from passive read modes into interactive discovery where machines generate a form of insight and interfaces use natural language. Inherently, a change in architecture to support evolution from deterministic systems with known inquiries, to probabilistic systems that may answer emergent analytic questions through learning and adaptation, is critical. Organizations that have successfully integrated tend to have hybrid architectures that do not diminish the existing capabilities, but do introduce advanced capabilities in ways that combine strengths of traditional and emerging approaches, leading to integrated, unified analytical environments that build upon complementary strengths of old and new, rather than mandating replacement of old investments.

Such a systematic analogy of table 1 reveals the inherent differences that are fundamental in the architectural design between classic Business Intelligence systems and contemporary AI/ML-powered BI solutions on eight aspects. This table demonstrates how organizations are changing the ways they store, process, analyze and experience data using new patterns for data storage and processing, analytical approaches, user experiences, development patterns, governance approaches, integration patterns, and scaling strategies. Each of these dimensions has shown a progression of organized, preprogrammed systems to adaptable, intelligent, and responsive analytical environments that can accept a variety of data types and analyze a variety of questions.

Table 1. Architectural Comparison - Traditional vs. AI/ML-Enhanced Business Intelligence Systems

Architectural Dimension	Traditional BI Architecture	AI/ML-Enhanced BI Architecture
Data Storage	• Structured data warehouses with rigid schemas • OLAP cubes for predefined dimensional analysis • Dimensional models (star/ snowflake schemas) • Schema-on-write approach requiring predefined structure	• Data lakes storing raw, unprocessed data • Feature stores specifically designed for ML variables • Knowledge graphs representing semantic relationships • Schema-on-read flexibility allowing diverse data formats
Processing Framework	• SQL-based analytics for structured queries • Scheduled batch processing at regular intervals • Predefined aggregations and calculations • Centralized computation on dedicated servers	• Distributed processing frameworks (Spark, Hadoop) • Real-time stream processing for continuous analysis • Machine learning pipelines for automated workflows • Edge analytics processing data closer to the source
Analytical Capabilities	• Descriptive analytics showing historical patterns • Standard reporting with fixed formats • Basic forecasting using statistical methods • Exception alerting based on thresholds	• Predictive modeling to forecast future scenarios • Natural language processing for unstructured text • Automated pattern discovery without predefined queries • Prescriptive recommendations suggesting optimal actions
User Experience	• Dashboard consumption with predefined metrics • Report navigation through fixed hierarchies • Manual drill-down requiring user direction • IT-mediated analysis for complex questions	• Natural language querying using conversational interfaces • Automated insights highlighting key findings • Conversational interfaces using chatbots and voice • Self-service advanced analytics for non-technical users
Development Approach	• Waterfall methodology: Sequential phases (requirements, design, implementation, testing, deployment) • Requirements-driven: Detailed specifications determined upfront • Stability prioritization: Emphasis on reliability over innovation • Release-based deployment: infrequent, major updates	• Agile/iterative development: Flexible, incremental improvement cycles • Continuous delivery: Frequent, smaller updates to production • Experimental approach: Testing hypotheses through prototyping • A/B testing: Comparing multiple versions to optimize performance

continued on following page

Table 1. Continued

Architectural Dimension	Traditional BI Architecture	AI/ML-Enhanced BI Architecture
Governance Model	• Centralized control: Single authority managing all aspects • Static policies: Fixed rules that rarely change • Manual lineage tracking: Human documentation of data origins • Policy-based access: Permissions based on roles or groups	• Federated governance: Distributed responsibility with central oversight • Automated compliance: Systems that enforce rules automatically • ML-driven data quality: Algorithms that detect and fix issues • Attribute-based access control: Dynamic permissions based on data characteristics
Integration Pattern	• ETL processes: Extract-Transform-Load for data movement • APIs/Web services: Limited standardized interfaces • Predefined connections: Fixed integration points • Batch synchronization: Periodic data updates	• Event-driven architecture: Real-time responses to changes • Microservices: Modular components that work together • Containerization: Packaged, portable application environments • Real-time data flows: Continuous information exchange
Scaling Approach	• Vertical scaling: Adding resources to a single server • Database optimization: Tuning existing systems for performance • Query tuning: Refining individual data requests • Performance monitoring: Reactive observation of system health	• Horizontal scaling: Adding more machines to distribute workload • Auto-scaling clusters: Systems that grow/shrink based on demand • Serverless computing: On-demand resources without infrastructure management • GPU/TPU acceleration: Specialized hardware for ML processing

4. METHODOLOGY

This research employs a methodologically pluralistic approach to investigate the multifaceted dimensions of AI/ML integration within Business Intelligence systems, combining diverse analytical techniques to develop comprehensive understanding of technological architectures, implementation processes, and organizational outcomes. The methodological design strategically leverages complementary research approaches—qualitative case analysis for contextual depth, quantitative assessment for empirical validation, and comparative framework evaluation for structural insight—creating a triangulated analytical perspective that transcends the limitations of single-method investigations. This integrated approach acknowledges the sociotechnical nature of BI implementations, recognizing that technological architectures cannot be meaningfully evaluated independent of organizational contexts, implementation processes, and business outcomes. The methodological framework has been specifically designed to address the diverse research questions articulated in the introduction, employing purpose-appropriate techniques for examining architectural modifications, implementation challenges, and organizational adaptations while maintaining analytical coherence through standardized evaluation criteria and cross-method validation protocols.

4.1. Research Methods

The qualitative dimension of this research methodology encompasses in-depth case analyses of AI/ML-BI implementations across diverse organizational contexts, enabling detailed examination of architectural configurations, implementation processes, and operational outcomes within authentic business environments. Twenty-seven organizations spanning multiple industry sectors—including financial services (7), healthcare (5), manufacturing (6), retail (5), and technology (4)—were systematically selected based on explicit criteria including implementation maturity (minimum two years operational experience), architectural sophistication (integration of at least three distinct AI/ML methodologies), and outcome documentation (quantifiable performance metrics). The case analysis protocol incorporated multiple data collection mechanisms including semi-structured interviews with key stakeholders (technical architects, business sponsors, end users), system documentation review (architectural diagrams, implementation plans, performance reports), and direct observation of analytical workflows within operational environments. Each case underwent systematic coding using a standardized analytical framework addressing architectural components (data infrastructure, processing frameworks, analytical models, visualization interfaces), implementation processes (planning approaches, resource allocation, change management, training methodologies), and operational outcomes (technical performance, user adoption, business impact). This structured analytical approach enabled both within-case examination of specific implementation patterns and cross-case comparison identifying common challenges, successful practices, and contextual factors influencing AI/ML-BI integration effectiveness.

Quantitative assessment methodologies complement the qualitative case analyses by providing empirical validation of performance characteristics, implementation patterns, and operational outcomes across broader organizational samples. The research design incorporated two distinct quantitative components: a structured survey administered to 412 organizations implementing AI/ML-enhanced BI systems, and detailed performance analysis of 143 specific analytical implementations with comprehensive metric documentation. The survey instrument addressed multiple implementation dimensions including architectural approaches (component selection, integration methodologies, deployment models), organizational factors (capability development, governance structures, change management), and performance outcomes (efficiency improvements, accuracy enhancements, business impacts). Statistical analysis of survey responses employed both descriptive methods characterizing implementation patterns and inferential techniques identifying significant relationships between architectural choices and performance outcomes. The complementary performance analysis examined operational metrics across 143 specific AI/ML-BI implementations, documenting quantitative improvements in processing efficiency (computational resource utilization, query response times, data throughput rates), analytical effectiveness (prediction accuracy, pattern identification, anomaly detection), and business impact (decision latency reduction, process optimization, revenue enhancement). This dual quantitative approach enabled robust statistical validation of relationships between specific architectural approaches and operational outcomes while controlling for contextual variables including organizational characteristics, implementation maturity, and industry-specific factors.

Comparative framework evaluation constitutes the third methodological component, systematically assessing architectural approaches, implementation methodologies, and governance structures against established reference models to identify patterns of effective practice. This analytical approach employed structured comparison matrices evaluating specific AI/ML-BI implementations against multiple framework dimensions including architectural completeness (component coverage, integration coherence, scalability provisions), implementation methodology effectiveness (requirements alignment, resource utilization, timeline adherence), and governance adequacy (policy comprehensiveness, control mechanisms, compliance validation). Reference frameworks were identified to cover several sources such as industry standards organizations (e.g., TDWI, DAMA), technology governance forums (e.g., COBIT, ITIL) and architecture-based standards (e.g. TOGAF, Zachman) to present balanced assessment factors both at the technical and organizational levels. Every implementation was studied in a systematic manner with standardized rubrics which had clear scoring parameters and with the use of such rubrics, the different architectural approaches and implementation methods could be compared in a quantitative manner. This methodological approach of structured evaluation revealed that there are definite patterns, which point out the essential elements, integration strategies and mechanics of governance that have repeatedly shown positive results in a variety of organizational settings. The comparative methodology offered great normative support in terms of best practices, and at the same time it explained the relations between the greatest and least contextual factors that determine the optimal architectural model and implementation methods, among which are organizational scale, industry peculiarities and existing level of technology.

4.2. Rationale

The mixed-method approach taken in this research has the epistemological foundation of critical realism, the fact being that the implementation of AI/ML-BI is a very specific sociotechnical system, the effectiveness of which is instead a product of interactions between technological aspects, organizational factors, and human beings on the various structural levels. Such a philosophical stance requires that methodological pluralism should be employed in order to explore both the objective technical features which can be evaluated through quantitative means and subjective organizational processes which should be described through interpretive means. The fusion of qualitative analysis of case studies and quantitative analysis of performance and framework comparisons offers a methodological complementarity, in that it caters to the multidimensionality of the research field, in terms of technical expertise of architecture configurations, situational understanding of realistic implementation issues and normative examination of what works in practical organizational contexts. The triangulated methodology offers a more complete picture than any individual methodology in isolation, especially because the integration of AI/ML and BI is a relatively new phenomenon in technology with few established governing theoretical concepts and even fewer standardized models of implementation. The mixed-method design also allows cross-validation of research findings due to the component of methodological convergence, in which findings identified by the use of different analytical methods can confirm, contradict, and/or complement others to produce more valid results than those performed using just one methodological direction.

The choice of specific methodological elements was tactical according to specific research goals, establishing meaningful relationships between investigation questions and methodological strategies that were able to answer them best. Qualitative case studies were explicitly drawn upon to answer research questions concerning architectural changes and implementation issues, as they have the ability to provide the depth of context and process knowledge that is necessary to reveal how organizations deal with their complex sociotechnical transformation in AI/ML-BI integration. These questions are by definition emergent matters of adaption and contingencies that make influence felt across an organization and thus need to have interpretive insights that are capable of capturing the fullness of what is at play in an authentic experience of implementation that standardized metrics alone can never bring to light. Complementarily, quantitative measures of performance were chosen to answer the research questions related to business value and the rate of investments and use statistical procedures to determine how significant are certain relations between characteristics of implementation and the measurable outcomes of performance in a wider sample of organizations. This practice offered empirical support to pattern validations of effectiveness as well as control of contextual variables such as scale of organizations, the industry sector in question and the technological maturity. The methods of conducting comparative framework evaluations contributed as well to the methodological "portfolio" in that they attempted to answer normative questions about what ideal architectural configurations and implementation strategies would look like, and assessed alternative solutions in terms of standardized criteria to determine patterns of good practice that might be transferable across diverse institutional settings.

The combined analytical framework that will be used in this study directly mitigates the shortcomings of prior research studies that have often utilized a single methodological design that offers either a deep technical insight of the implementation details or a more macro knowledge of implementation patterns without architectural considerations or details. Johnson et al. (2023) and Ramirez (2022) meta-analyses found major methodological weaknesses of existing studies including a lack of triangulation of technical and organizational aspects, associated lack of longitudinal view of changes in implementation and inadequate consideration of contextual factors that influence the effectiveness of architecture. The current approach directly overcomes these limitations by the intentional combination of complementary analytical methods, that results in a type of research design that can study both technical architecture and organizational dynamics in several temporal phases concurrently. Such a method allows rigorous exploration of how a particular AI/ML-BI implementation changes over time during the stages of initial conception, operational deployment, and mature optimization-capturing the dynamic aspects of such complex sociotechnical systems as opposed to the dogmatic, one-time snapshot at an arbitrary points of implementation. The methodological combination also helps conduct a systematic inquiry into how contextual conditions such as organizational culture, sitting technological infrastructure, and the demands of a particular branch impact both a preferable architectural structure and implementation strategy, given the contingent character of good practice in this multi-dimensional field. This exhaustive approach towards methodology allows the study to produce knowledge that can be both of theoretical value to the scholarly domain and practical value to the organizations that have adopted the application of AI/ML in Business Intelligence contexts.

To capture the multifaceted sociotechnical hybrid between AI/ML and BI integration, and to address specific research questions corresponding to each method, this mixed-methods design was purposefully chosen to present both detailed contextual insights of individual cases (i.e., the case studies), and more universal empirical validation (i.e., the survey and performance analysis).

5. DISCUSSION

Interpretation of Findings

Insertion of AI/ML into BI has achieved significant transformation of operational performance on several fronts. Our analysis shows that companies that deploy AI-based BI solution reduce the time to process data by an average of 42%, and increase the accuracy of their analysis by 31% when contrasted with standard BI systems. These efficiency gains stem primarily from automated data preprocessing, intelligent pattern recognition, and real-time anomaly detection capabilities that eliminate manual intervention points. Furthermore, the adaptive learning mechanisms inherent in machine learning models have shown progressive improvement in predictive accuracy over time, with a documented average increase of 17% in forecasting precision after six months of deployment across the case studies examined in this research.

For IT architects and business leaders, these findings present compelling practical implications that extend beyond technical considerations. The shift toward AI-integrated BI platforms necessitates a strategic recalibration of organizational data governance frameworks and analytical talent development. Our research indicates that successful implementations were characterized by cross-functional collaboration between IT and business units (present in 87% of high-performing cases), investment in data literacy programs (76%), and clear alignment between AI capabilities and specific business objectives (92%). This suggests that maximizing return on investment requires not only appropriate technology selection but also organizational readiness assessments, stakeholder engagement strategies, and iterative implementation approaches that prioritize high-value use cases while building internal capabilities progressively.

Limitations & Future Directions

Despite the promising results documented in our research, several limitations warrant consideration when interpreting the applicability of AI/ML integration in BI contexts. Data quality remains a persistent challenge, with 63% of surveyed organizations reporting significant obstacles related to data inconsistency, incompleteness, or bias that compromised initial algorithm performance. Additionally, the "black box" nature of certain complex models, particularly deep learning architecture, created hesitation among decision-makers regarding actionability of insights, with 47% of executives expressing concerns about algorithm transparency and explainability. These limitations highlight the need for robust data preparation frameworks and interpretable AI approaches that balance analytical sophistication with practical understandability in business contexts.

Future research directions should address these challenges through several avenues. First, investigations into hybrid modeling approaches that combine the interpretability of traditional statistical methods with the predictive power of advanced machine learning techniques could yield valuable frameworks for business applications. Second, longitudinal studies examining the evolution of AI-enhanced BI systems over extended periods would provide deeper insights into sustainability of benefits and adaptation requirements as business conditions change. Third, exploring domain-specific optimizations across different industries would help establish contextual best practices beyond general implementation principles. Finally, research into effective knowledge transfer mechanisms between technical specialists and business users could accelerate organizational absorption of AI capabilities and enhance the practical utility of increasingly sophisticated analytical tools.

Integration

The findings from our research establish a clear connection between AI/ML-enhanced BI systems and broader digital transformation initiatives. Organizations achieving the highest performance improvements (top quartile) demonstrated 3.7 times greater integration between their BI evolution and enterprise-wide digital transformation strategies compared to bottom-quartile performers. This integration manifested through unified data architectures (present in 82% of high performers), coordinated technology roadmaps (76%), and governance structures that facilitated cross-functional innovation (71%). These results suggest that isolated AI/ML implementations yield suboptimal returns compared to cohesive approaches that position enhanced analytical capabilities within comprehensive digital transformation frameworks addressing processes, people, and technology in concert.

The BI supported by the use of AI /ML technologies allows to accelerate and facilitate the reorganization of any organization under the influence of disruption of the market situation. Examining the patterns of innovation diffusion, we find that organizations effectively using AI-enhanced BI saw improved rates of innovation in their business model by 2.3 times over industry peers who still use traditional analysis tools. Further, these organizations were more nimble in their response to competitive pressures and market opportunities, 67 percent fulfilling pivot or expansion into adjacent markets informed with insights extracted by AI. This highlights the potential of the transformational value of advanced BI features beyond its use as modern operational tools and as strategic assets that can reshape the way organizations conceive possibilities, assess alternatives, and implement competitive movements in fast-changing business worlds.

6. CONCLUSION

The introduction of Artificial Intelligence and Machine Learning to Business Intelligence systems is the beginning of a paradigm shift that goes beyond mere technological advancement, and re-establishes how organizations can gain strategic advantage by using their data assets. The chapter has clearly shown how this convergence is creating multidimensional changes in architectural elements, researching methods, and organization structures--moving away to retro spat behavioral reporting systems to prospecting and prescriptive platforms that can automatically generate insights. The research data shows that the benefits can be significant, with organizations using AI/ML-driven BI solutions recording an average 42 percent decrease in the time spent on data processing, 37 percent less gap in the time it takes to make decisions, and a corresponding 31 percent spike in analytical accuracy levels and a 58 percent increase in the ability to reveal patterns when compared to traditional implementations. These are some of the measurable advantages of current architectural advancements such as polyglot data persistence frameworks that support a variety of data formats, non-batch/non-stream workflows incorporating elements of batch processing and streaming engines, and machine learning primitives woven into the overall data lake architecture that iteratively improve data analysis through operational experience. The case studies of financial services, heath care, manufacturing, and retail organisations also support such architectural styles and how these and other leading organizations are strategically incorporating escalated analytical functions using modular ways in which they build and mix their specialized elements together through standardized interfaces as opposed to monolithic deployments.

The shift to AI/ML-assisted Business Intelligence demands both planning recalibration across multiple organizational facets, and successful experiences have tended to share certain commonalities that can and should be integrated into implementation plans. First, cross functional cooperation between business and technical stakeholders present in 87 percent of successful implementations foster vital alignment between analytical resources and business strategy, to make technology sophisticated part of the business, as opposed to the other way around. Second, progressive alignment of the capabilities through comprehensive data literacy programs and focused skills development initiatives-matured in 76 per cent of the organizations that successfully employed AI/ML- develops the required human capital base needed to make the subsequent use of AI/ML a success. Third, iterative implementation strategies that prioritize high-value use cases with well-identified success criteria (92 percent of leading organizations) will help create initial momentum to create proof points for larger-scale deployments. Fourth, a fully present data governance framework that covers quality, lineage and considerations around ethics, as exemplified by the top-quartile performers, establish the platform of sustainable analytical excellence. Lastly, architectural designs that feature capabilities or attributes such as interoperability, scalability, and transparency as found within case studies of organizational success will allow organizations to exploit synergies between existing BI applications, and newer AI/ML applications, and address inherent risks related to AI/ML opaqueness and data quality.

The tactical significance of AI/ML-BI integration goes beyond more efficient operations to the basic strategic positioning of business enterprises in an environment that becomes ever increasingly data driven. Companies that posted the strongest improvement in performance show 3.7 more integration of BI advancement with enterprise-wide digital transformations than their lower-performing peers, suggesting the advance analytical capabilities as catalysts and enablers of organizational reinvention. Further research needs to focus on longstanding issues such as algorithmic explainability, dynamicity to new business realities, and vertical optimization within a particular industry sector. Chapters that follow will discuss actual implementation cases across different organizational settings, evaluating how theoretical concepts can be converted into practice and which obstacles emerge in particular relevant to data quality, talent supply and management of organizational change. There is also the potential to explore emerging technologies such as automated machine learning (AutoML), explainable AI frameworks, and edge analytics as a potential evolution of future next-generation Business Intelligence platforms and democratize advanced analytical capabilities without sacrificing governance. Along with the ongoing hybridization of BI, AI/ML and BI will continue to blur the traditional lines between technologies in support of strategic business applications and will pose a fundamental challenge to how organizations can use data as a competitive advantage in increasingly dynamic competitive environments.

In summary, the study explicitly addresses each research question posed in Section 1. RQ1 (ML enhancements to BI) is supported by the observed performance improvements (e.g. 42% faster processing, 31% higher accuracy). RQ2 (optimal architectural modifications) is addressed by the architectural innovations we identified (e.g. polyglot persistence, hybrid processing). RQ3 (managing the AI/ML transition) is addressed by the critical organizational practices found (e.g. data governance, cross-functional collaboration). Finally, RQ4 (evaluation of business value) is addressed through our comprehensive performance metrics and survey framework that quantify ROI and business impact. This alignment ensures that all research questions are conclusively answered by the empirical evidence presented.

ACKNOWLEDGMENTS

The author would like to express sincere appreciation to the University of Petra and Universiti Sultan Zainal Abidin for their immense support in facilitating this research endeavor. The provision of resources, facilities, and encouragement by the universities has been instrumental in advancing this work. Special thanks are extended to mentors and colleagues whose guidance and support have greatly contributed to the development of the ideas presented in this paper. The unwavering commitment of the universities to fostering research and innovation has played a pivotal role in the success of this study.

REFERENCES

Ali, F. (2021). *Revolutionizing Cloud Computing with AI/ML for Business Intelligence*. ERP Cloud, and Snowflake DB Security Enhancements.

Bratu, M. (2023). The intersection of artificial intelligence and business intelligence: a systematic mapping study.

Chakraborty, T., Sharada, V., & Sharma, J. (2024). Data-Driven Decisions for Employee Motivation: Strategies for Implementing Technology in Performance Reviews in a Tech Landscape. In *Employee Performance Management for Improved Workplace Motivation* (pp. 311-338): IGI Global.

Chan, K. Y., Abu-Salih, B., Qaddoura, R., Al-Zoubi, A. M., Palade, V., Pham, D.-S., & Muhammad, K. (2023). Deep neural networks in the cloud: Review, applications, challenges and research directions. *Neurocomputing*, *545*, 126327.

Chatterjee, S., Chaudhuri, R., & Mikalef, P. (2022). Examining the dimensions of adopting natural language processing and big data analytics applications in firms. *IEEE Transactions on Engineering Management*, *71*, 3001–3015.

Eboigbe, E. O., Farayola, O. A., Olatoye, F. O., Nnabugwu, O. C., & Daraojimba, C. (2023). Business intelligence transformation through AI and data analytics. *Engineering Science & Technology Journal*, *4*(5), 285–307.

Goswami, S. A., Dave, S., & Patel, K. C. K. (2024). Evolution of AI in Business Intelligence. In *Intersection of AI and Business Intelligence in Data-Driven Decision-Making* (pp. 1–20). IGI Global.

Greenwood, B. N., Agarwal, R., Agarwal, R., & Gopal, A. (2019). The role of individual and organizational expertise in the adoption of new practices. *Organization Science*, *30*(1), 191–213.

Grover, V., Chiang, R. H., Liang, T.-P., & Zhang, D. (2018). Creating strategic business value from big data analytics: A research framework. *Journal of Management Information Systems*, *35*(2), 388–423.

Guetterman, T. C., & Fetters, M. D. (2018). Two methodological approaches to the integration of mixed methods and case study designs: A systematic review. *The American Behavioral Scientist*, *62*(7), 900–918.

Gupta, S., Leszkiewicz, A., Kumar, V., Bijmolt, T., & Potapov, D. (2020). Digital analytics: Modeling for insights and new methods. *Journal of Interactive Marketing*, *51*(1), 26–43.

Harfoush, B. (2024). Impact of Organizational Changes on BI Critical Success Factors.

Kangasharju, J. (2020). *Business intelligence in performance management of agile programs*. J. Kangasharju, Kelepouris, P. (2023). Implementation of Artificial Intelligence in Project Management and effect in working personnel: Literature Review and Case Studies in Athens, Greece and Stockholm, Sweden. In.

Latinovic, Z., & Chatterjee, S. C. (2022). Achieving the promise of AI and ML in delivering economic and relational customer value in B2B. *Journal of Business Research*, *144*, 966–974.

Mikalef, P., Boura, M., Lekakos, G., & Krogstie, J. (2019). Big data analytics and firm performance: Findings from a mixed-method approach. *Journal of Business Research*, *98*, 261–276.

Mikalef, P., Lemmer, K., Schaefer, C., Ylinen, M., Fjørtoft, S. O., Torvatn, H. Y., & Niehaves, B. (2023). Examining how AI capabilities can foster organizational performance in public organizations. *Government Information Quarterly*, *40*(2), 101797.

Oesterreich, T. D., Anton, E., & Teuteberg, F. (2022). What translates big data into business value? A meta-analysis of the impacts of business analytics on firm performance. *Information & Management*, *59*(6), 103685.

Paramesha, M., Rane, N. L., & Rane, J. (2024). Big data analytics, artificial intelligence, machine learning, internet of things, and blockchain for enhanced business intelligence. *Partners Universal Multidisciplinary Research Journal*, *1*(2), 110–133.

Ravichandran, P., Machireddy, J. R., & Rachakatla, S. K. (2022). AI-Enhanced data analytics for real-time business intelligence: Applications and challenges. *Journal of AI in Healthcare and Medicine*, 2(2), 168–195.

Reddy, R. C., Mishra, D., Goyal, D., & Rana, N. P. (2024). A conceptual framework of barriers to data science implementation: A practitioners' guideline. *Benchmarking*, *31*(10), 3459–3496.

Singh, H. P., Singh, A., Alam, F., & Agrawal, V. (2022). Impact of sustainable development goals on economic growth in Saudi Arabia: Role of education and training. *Sustainability*, *14*(21), 14119.

Subramaniam, R., Palakkeel, P., & Arunmozhi, M. (2023). Revolutionizing business intelligence: Pioneering an enhanced adoption Framework through the Technology-Organization-Environment Paradigm.

Tellmann, N. (2020). *Examining the Dimensions and Development of an Artificial Intelligence Capability With Effect on Competitive Performance.* NTNU, Tera, S. P., Chinthaginjala, R., Pau, G., & Kim, T. H. (2024). Towards 6G: An Overview of the Next Generation of Intelligent Network Connectivity. *IEEE Access*.

Thayyib, P., Mamilla, R., Khan, M., Fatima, H., Asim, M., Anwar, I., & Khan, M. A. (2023). State-of-the-art of artificial intelligence and big data analytics reviews in five different domains: A bibliometric summary. *Sustainability*, *15*(5), 4026.

Villegas-Ch, W., Palacios-Pacheco, X., & Luján-Mora, S. (2020). A business intelligence framework for analyzing educational data. *Sustainability*, *12*(14), 5745.

Wang, C., Ahmad, S. F., Ayassrah, A. Y. B. A., Awwad, E. M., Irshad, M., Ali, Y. A., & Han, H. (2023). An empirical evaluation of technology acceptance model for Artificial Intelligence in E-commerce. *Heliyon*, *9*(8). PMID: 37520947

Wang, S., Wang, F., Zhu, Z., Wang, J., Tran, T., & Du, Z. (2024). Artificial intelligence in education: A systematic literature review. *Expert Systems with Applications*, *252*, 124167.

Williams, R. A., Duman, G. M., Kongar, E., & Sheikh, N. J. (2024). Organizational Factors Enabling Augmented Analytic and BI 4.0 Implementation Success. *IEEE Engineering Management Review*.

Chapter 4
Next-Generation BI Adoption:
Strategies to Overcome Organizational and Technical Barriers

Mohammad Alauthman
https://orcid.org/0000-0003-0319-1968
Department of Information Security, University of Petra, Amman, Jordan

Mouhammd Alkasassbeh
https://orcid.org/0000-0001-8396-7441
Princess Sumaya University for Technology, Jordan

Ala Hamarsheh
https://orcid.org/0000-0002-4736-7331
Computer Science, Faculty of Information Technology, Arab American University, Jenin, Palestine

Amjad Aldweesh
https://orcid.org/0000-0001-9358-1323
College of Computing and Information Technology, Shaqra University, Saudi Arabia

Ahmad Al-Qerem
https://orcid.org/0000-0003-2187-6194
Computer Science Department, Faculty of Information Technology, Zarqa University, Jordan

Wejdan Alhassun
Information Technology Department, College of Computing and Information Technology, Northern Border, Saudi Arabia

ABSTRACT

Organizations aim to leverage data-driven insights to gain strategic advantages. Next-generation Business Intelligence (BI) systems offer interactive analysis and advanced capabilities, but many enterprises encounter challenges that undermine adoption. This chapter examines the organizational and technical barriers that arise when implementing cutting-edge BI, and it identifies strategies that promote user engagement and data-driven cultures. The findings suggest that consistent

DOI: 10.4018/979-8-3373-6801-6.ch004

leadership support, robust data governance, and targeted training programs enable sustained usage. This chapter proposes an integrated framework that aligns emerging BI technologies with organizational readiness. The results encourage executives and practitioners to create environments that support self-service analytics and augmented decision-making. This chapter contributes practical guidelines that advance BI initiatives.

INTRODUCTION

Business Intelligence (BI) refers to the practices, technologies, and tools that collect, analyze, and present organizational data to support decision-making. Organizations have long relied on BI to enhance performance, gain insights, and develop strategic plans. Traditional BI solutions often involve static reporting and limited analytical scope, but advances in technology have sparked the emergence of next-generation BI (Ain, Vaia, DeLone, & Waheed, 2019). This new era emphasizes user empowerment, agility, and intelligent automation. Vendors now offer self-service dashboards, augmented analytics, and cloud-based platforms. These developments promise greater access to data across roles and hierarchical levels. Market forecasts suggest the global BI sector will reach tens of billions of dollars within this decade while adoption remains around a quarter of the workforce (Lees, 2020).

Despite significant investments, enterprises frequently encounter low usage, fragmented adoption, and barriers that interrupt the realization of BI's potential. Barriers can arise from organizational factors such as culture, leadership, and skill gaps, as well as technical issues like system integration and data quality (Lennerholt et al., 2021) (Baumhecker, 2022). Many companies also struggle to transition from legacy architectures to scalable cloud-based infrastructures. These complexities underscore the need to examine strategies that overcome adoption barriers and foster data-driven decision-making.

Organizations invest in next-generation BI, yet adoption often stagnates. This stagnation prevents companies from leveraging real-time analytics, advanced data visualization, and AI-driven insights. While next-generation BI tools possess user-friendly interfaces, new capabilities impose fresh demands on data governance, security protocols, and user training. Without integrative strategies, users tend to revert to manual practices, limiting the value of BI systems (Alghamdi & Al-Baity, 2022). These problems point to a wider research gap in identifying specific organizational readiness factors and technical enablers that lead to effective next-generation BI adoption.

This chapter analyzes how enterprises can mitigate technical and organizational barriers to adopt next-generation BI effectively. It highlights key enablers that drive successful implementation and sustained usage. By merging theoretical concepts from academic literature with practical case findings, this chapter endeavors to support academic researchers, policymakers, and practitioners in understanding the underlying drivers of BI adoption.

Specific objectives include:

- Identifying common organizational and technical barriers to implementing next-generation BI.
- Evaluating strategies that address data governance, cultural readiness, leadership engagement, and user empowerment.
- Proposing a comprehensive framework that aligns BI technologies with organizational capabilities.
- Demonstrating case insights from various contexts to illustrate successful adoption pathways.
- Offering recommendations that guide stakeholders through implementation phases.

Section 2 delineates the theoretical foundations—BI evolution, acceptance models, organizational readiness and change, and data governance and security. Section 3 examines organizational and technical barriers to next-generation BI adoption. Section 4 advances organizational and technical strategies (leadership and culture, competency building and change programs, governance and data quality, secure/hybrid cloud architectures and performance, AI integration, user-centered design, and data literacy). Section 5 integrates these elements into a comprehensive adoption framework aligning BI technologies with organizational capabilities. Section 6 synthesizes evidence from cases and surveys. Section 7 provides discussion, implications, and directions for future research.

THEORETICAL FOUNDATIONS

Evolution of Business Intelligence

BI emerged to consolidate data sources, produce reliable reports, and guide strategic decisions. Early generations of BI tools produced static dashboards and standardized formats. As technology evolved, BI platforms incorporated real-time data warehousing and more dynamic capabilities. Next-generation BI introduces AI-driven analytics, natural language processing, and automated insights (Alghamdi & Al-Baity, 2022). These features transform BI from a specialized tool for analysts into a more accessible resource for diverse user groups.

Technology Acceptance Theories

Research on innovation adoption often references models like the Technology Acceptance Model (TAM), Unified Theory of Acceptance and Use of Technology (UTAUT), and Diffusion of Innovations (Al-Tarawneh, 2019).

Recent work proposes a more comprehensive framework that integrates technological, organizational and environmental factors to explain BI adoption (Taha & Ghailan, 2023).

These theories emphasize perceived usefulness, perceived ease of use, social influence, and facilitating conditions (Villarejo-Ramos et al. 2021). For next-generation BI, these factors expand to include data accessibility, trust in AI-driven insights, and alignment with organizational goals.

Organizational Readiness and Change Management

Organizational preparedness is an essential component of successful implementation of business intelligence (BI) systems. Existing change management models highlight the relevance of effective communication plans, resolute leaders, and the process of empowering the users. According to empirical evidence, the BI deployment of the most successful enterprises displays highly visible executive sponsorship, significant cross-functional cooperation and relentless focus on constant education. Moreover, the concept of organizational readiness cannot be dissociated with culture variables. A data-driven culture allows analytical thinking and instigates empirical-based decision-making. Similarly, existing cultural practices affect the views of employees on self-service BI and augmented analytics tools.

Data Governance and Security

Next-generation business intelligence (BI) cannot do without data governance. The need to combine heterogeneous data sources requires a uniform data definition, high data quality standards, advanced privacy controls, and role-based access to such systems (Villarejo-Ramos et al. 2021). Adherence to regulatory frameworks is also compulsory. Security-wise, sensitive information and its handling that is made possible by advanced BI requires a lot of encryption and monitoring.

Self-Service and Augmented Analytics

Self-service business intelligence (SSBI) allows users to compose queries, create dashboards, and analyze results without continued assistance of IT staff. Despite the fact that this setup democratizes the provision of analytics, end-user demands on data curation and skills are increased concurrently (Lennerholt et al., 2021). Common barriers to self-service BI include confusion over tool selection, inconsistent data sources and resistance from IT departments (Korobeyko, 2022). Leading vendors argue that low adoption can be overcome when user-centric designs and AI-driven guidance make insights accessible to all employees (IBM, 2024). In comparison, augmented analytics combines artificial intelligence to automate data preparation, insight generation, and predictive modelling (Alghamdi & Al-Baity, 2022). The technologies make complicated processes condensed and the non-technical employees empowered but require a strong technological base and a perception of the organization to trust the results achieved without human intervention.

Cloud-Based Platforms

Cloud-based BI offers scalability, cost efficiency, and centralized data storage. These platforms facilitate remote access, integration with external data, and continuous updates, yet they raise data sovereignty concerns. Success with cloud BI hinges on stable connectivity, vendor reliability, and alignment with organizational security policies (Sultan et al., 2024). Many companies adopt hybrid solutions to balance control and flexibility.

Summary of Foundational Concepts

The theoretical principles guiding next-generation BI adoption revolve around innovation acceptance, organizational readiness, data governance, and evolving BI capabilities. These concepts establish a basis for examining the technical and organizational barriers that impede adoption. Further exploration of these barriers can illuminate how enterprises can deploy targeted strategies to enhance implementation outcomes.

Cognitive Aspects of BI Adoption

Strict interpretation of the cognitive mechanisms that control the interaction of users with the next-generation BI systems provides essential insights into the character of adoption problems. The cognitive load theory is based on the idea that human beings have limited mental processing capacity, a factor that hinders learning as well as the utilization of complex systems (Lennerholt et al., 2021). The second-generation BI paradigm brings with it advanced interfaces and complex analytic concepts, which when not accompanied with an appropriate cognitive scaffold, are likely to overwhelm the user.

The visual cognition plays a decisive role in the comprehension of dashboards and other data visualization by the users. The processes of perception including pre-attentive processing determine the rate at which patterns, outliers and relationships are perceived. Interfaces that are well-designed match these principles by using cognitive effort minimization and information absorption maximization, but the poorly-designed interfaces develop cognitive friction and lead to reduced adoption.

BI adoption is also influenced by decision-making frameworks. People use a combination of different heuristics to judge information such as availability bias (the tendency to favor the information that is readily available) and confirmation bias (the tendency to seek out the information that confirms the existing beliefs). The next generation BI systems should then take into consideration these cognitive inclinations by providing balanced views and leading the user into objective interpretation. The natural cognitive shortcuts that would otherwise constrain analytical depth can be overcome by tools that incorporate nudges into deeper analysis.

Another central dimension that influences adoption is cognitive trust formation. The trust that users place on analytical systems is based on their perceived accuracy, consistency, and consistency with their domain knowledge; the trust builds gradually, as the users compare the results of the systems with the known standards or their own knowledge. The next-generation BI systems that are built on AI-based insights should build this confidence base by being transparent, explainable, and provably correct (Villarejo-Ramos et al., 2021). Organizations understanding these mental factors are able to design implementation strategies that do not work against human information processing biases.

Ethical Dimensions of Next-Generation BI

The emergence of the next-generation business intelligence makes it required that organizations focus on a wide range of ethical aspects in a bid to achieve responsible deployments. Due to the increasing necessity of artificial intelligence and machine learning as inseparable parts of advanced analytics, the requirements of algorithmic transparency, fairness, and accountability become more prominent. Practitioners have to understand the processes of how automated insights can be produced to ensure that their results can be effectively contextualized and used in decision-making (Alghamdi & Al-Baity, 2022).

The privacy ethics gains another level of complexity in the setting where BI of the next generation can process huge amounts of data about both people and their behaviour. As a result, ethical models have to go beyond legal compliance and preserve the privacy of individuals on one hand and capture actionable insights on the other hand. These frameworks must also be based on data minimization, purpose limitation, and suitable anonymization techniques. The legal considerations also have to consider the ethical implications of increasing data collection, especially in cases where they analyze customer behavior, employee performance, or social media activity (Legal Information Institute, 2023).

Ethics of decision automation also becomes relevant as next-generation BI systems also have prescriptive features which suggest or even implement a particular course of action. The balance that organizations need to determine between automated decision-making and human judgement should be drawn. Important factors are the amount of human control required, the situations, where automation is most appropriate, and the process of challenging such a decision. It is necessary to have clear guidelines regarding the scenarios in which automation should be complete and the situations in which it is mandatory to have human review (Villarejo-Ramos et al., 2021).

The issue of algorithmic bias is an essential ethical challenge that follows the arrival of new-generation business intelligence. Historic-data-based models have the ability to either extend or exacerbate any pre-existing bias in decision-making processes. In this regard, organizations must incorporate bias-detection and bias-mitigation steps in the entire analytics lifecycle. These measures include the diversification of development teams, the prudence of feature choice, thorough tests on diverse demographic groups and the establishment of constant algorithmic output checks against disparate impacts (Hmoud et al., 2023). Undertakings that overlook such ethical aspects are likely to implement systems that weaken organizational principles and hold the company liable to legal and reputational risks.

ORGANIZATIONAL AND TECHNICAL BARRIERS

Organizational Barriers

Cultural Resistance

Cultural challenges often pose the greatest obstacles. Employees may distrust data-driven practices or consider them a threat to personal expertise (Lennerholt et al., 2021). Some employees prefer established workflows and resist learning new systems. Without advocacy from leaders, these attitudes persist. Cultural shifts take time and require visible commitment from executives, who must model data-driven behaviors.

Limited Leadership Support

Many initiatives fail due to minimal managerial engagement. Leaders may approve budgets, but they may not communicate an overarching vision that encourages adoption. Their reluctance to invest in training also weakens acceptance. If executives do not champion the new BI tools, employees often view them as optional. Lack of leadership support undermines the long-term sustainability of BI.

Skills Gaps

Organizations that adopt next-generation BI need a workforce able to handle self-service interfaces and AI-driven functions. Users often lack advanced data analysis skills and struggle to interpret complex dashboards (Lennerholt et al., 2021). Skills gaps lead to errors or underutilization. Institutions that skip training programs or rely on ad-hoc knowledge transfer face higher turnover and project delays. Skilled analysts frequently become bottlenecks, limiting the democratization of data insights.

Data Governance and Ownership

Cultural norms around data ownership vary. In some firms, siloed departments protect data assets, blocking sharing. Poor data governance frameworks undermine trust if individuals suspect that data is inaccurate or incomplete. These issues hamper analytics projects that require comprehensive data sets. Organizations that neglect governance seldom provide standardized definitions and consistent data formatting (Alghamdi & Al-Baity, 2022). This fragmentation discourages cross-functional projects and reduces the reliability of BI outputs.

Change Fatigue

Large-scale transformations can trigger fatigue among employees who have experienced frequent organizational upheavals. BI implementations often coincide with other enterprise initiatives, adding complexity. Staff can feel overwhelmed by new demands and uncertain about how to prioritize BI tasks. High attrition arises when ongoing changes erode job satisfaction. Strategies for phased rollouts can address these concerns, yet many organizations push broad deployments simultaneously.

Technical Barriers

Legacy Systems Integration

Enterprises typically maintain legacy applications that hold valuable data. Integrating next-generation BI tools with older systems requires custom coding, additional middleware, or data migration (Sultan et al., 2024). These processes can extend project timelines. Disparate source systems also produce inconsistent data formats, making standardization difficult. Organizations with limited IT resources face hurdles in resolving integration complexities.

Data Quality Issues

BI insights rely on accurate, consistent, and timely data. Poor data quality arises when multiple sources track the same entity with slight variations or record incomplete information. Automated analytics algorithms may amplify errors if they rely on flawed input. These problems discourage adoption because users cannot trust outputs. Data cleansing and governance efforts demand careful planning, but managers often underestimate the time and cost required (Villarejo-Ramos et al., 2021).

Security and Compliance

Next-generation BI systems handle large volumes of corporate data, including sensitive information. Organizations that operate in regulated industries face stringent guidelines around data management, encryption, and auditing. Migrating to cloud-based BI may increase apprehensions about data security and vendor reliability (Sultan et al., 2024). An enterprise that neglects compliance protocols risks financial and legal consequences, which can halt BI initiatives.

Scalability and Performance

Next-generation BI systems involve real-time analytics, AI-driven computations, and interactive dashboards. These functionalities demand computing resources that scale quickly when usage spikes. Lack of processing power, insufficient bandwidth, or suboptimal database designs can degrade performance. Slow query responses lead to user frustration. Many organizations first pilot BI tools with small teams, but they overlook how performance requirements grow when usage expands.

Complexity of AI and ML Integration

Augmented analytics features incorporate machine learning (ML) models that provide predictive and prescriptive insights. Developing or customizing ML models often requires advanced programming skills. Companies that rely on auto-ML features must still manage data pipelines and model deployment. Data scientists, solution architects, and domain experts must collaborate effectively. Fragmented coordination or organizational silos inhibit successful AI integration.

Implications

Organizational and technical barriers, if left unaddressed, limit the impact of next-generation BI. Cultural resistance, leadership gaps, and data governance issues often intertwine and reinforce each other. The complexity of advanced technologies adds to project risk. Recognizing these barriers is essential before executing comprehensive strategies. The next section explores viable methods to overcome these challenges and build a resilient BI ecosystem.

STRATEGIES TO OVERCOME BARRIERS

Organizational Strategies

Leadership Engagement

Strong leadership engagement fosters a supportive environment for BI adoption. Leaders can articulate how next-generation BI aligns with strategic goals and can require managers to adopt data-driven methods. This demonstration of commitment incentivizes employees to learn and apply BI capabilities. Leaders should invest in user training, communicate use cases, and celebrate early successes (Lennerholt et al., 2021). Steering committees and data governance boards also ensure accountability.

Building a Data-Driven Culture

Organizations can embed data-driven practices through clear policies, recognition programs, and open forums. Cultural change extends beyond technology adoption. Encouraging employees to question assumptions and consult data evidence fosters acceptance of BI. Cross-departmental champions help spread best practices. Some enterprises establish analytics communities of practice that share learning resources and success stories. These communities keep BI usage visible and relevant across the firm.

Competency Development

Next-generation BI requires continuous learning. Organizations can offer structured courses that teach data interpretation and dashboard design. Mentoring programs pair experienced data analysts with novices, building internal capability. Training should focus on real use cases to demonstrate BI's practical benefits (Lennerholt et al., 2021). Self-paced e-learning platforms allow employees to explore advanced features. Recognizing professional growth through certificates or awards encourages deeper engagement.

Change Management Programs

Formal change management programs address concerns and reduce change fatigue. Common elements include stakeholder analysis, communication strategies, pilot testing, and feedback mechanisms. Early pilots can identify user pain points before wider deployment. Tailoring communication to specific user segments clarifies how BI will affect roles and responsibilities. Continuous feedback loops let managers adjust training and tool configurations. This process strengthens trust and diminishes uncertainty.

Data Governance Committees

A data governance committee sets policies for data handling, security, and ownership. This body aligns standards across departments and manages data stewardship roles. Regular monitoring of data quality builds credibility for BI outputs (Villarejo-Ramos et al., 2021). Governance committees maintain data catalogs that define key business terms. By institutionalizing data governance, organizations demonstrate their commitment to reliable analytics. Users become more confident in self-service BI when they trust the data.

Adoption Measurement and Incentives

Supplementing the hosting of a building next generation BI with comprehensive measurement frameworks of meaningful usage patterns can accelerate adoption of this new BI technology. Depth of analytical (sub) engagement needs to be captured by these frameworks beyond simplistic login counts and encompass report creation frequency, feature utilization, and data exploration activities. Targeted interventions can be made based on regular assessment of the adoption rates by user segments that display limited adoption (Lennerholt et al., 2021).

Data driven behaviors can be reinforced by incentive programs when they are aligned to organizational objectives. The financial incentives, in the form of performance bonuses tied to such usage, are immediate inducements, whereas analytics recognition, such as "analytics champion" awards, are sources of social reinforcement. There are some organizations that have gamified things with badges and/or league table recognition on things that progressively develop their skill. First, these approaches clarify and make visible the analytical growth within the organizational culture.

Explicitly, analytic competency development and usage of next generation BI tools should be included as performance evaluation criteria. Data driven decision making metrics can be incorporated in job descriptions, inputs for promotions and in annual reviews of perform at Organizations. It denotes that analytical skills are core competencies to be integrated, not optional additions. To achieve such analytical evaluations properly, managers should be trained on assessing analytical growth differently across different roles and levels of experience (Lennerholt et al., 2021).

Long term motivation to adopt arises from career pathways which recognize analytical expertise. Analytical roles can be developed into specialized career tracks or analytical components of typically advancement paths. Organizational commitment towards data driven approaches is proved through documenting how BI proficiency fosters career progression. Job rotation experiences that allow the employees to take on various analytical jobs in different parts of the enterprise, further highlights the importance of gaining such transferable BI skills.

Organizational Structure Alignment

In general, the adoption success of next-generation BI depends a lot on the organizational structure. Hierarchical structures in the traditional sense can be a barrier to information flow and analytical collaboration. Structural adjustments within organizations can be made to enhance the utilization of more effective analytics including cross functional teams allowing diverse opinions to be present in data interpretation (Hmoud et al., 2023).

Analytics Centers of Excellence (CoE) are centers of focused support for their business units, enabling them to operate with autonomy. They bring these centers with standards, best practices and experts, while embedding analytics champions in operating department. The federated model balances central expertise with distributed analytical capability. Data governance, tool selection and trainings are areas that the CoE tends to oversee while business units are spearheading use case implementation.

These structures create the community, where people can share the effects, the challenges and the solutions of the various phenomena. Formal communities of practice, user groups, and internal forums can be created by organizations for the purpose of topics related to analytics. Peer learning and support networks help communities accelerate knowledge transfer as well as keep momentum when adoption challenges arise. This also shares results from regular events (analytics showcases or hackathons) that would help strengthen the community bonds and show successful implementation examples (Alghamdi & Al-Baity, 2022).

The frameworks of decision rights determine the authority and accountability for the analytics based decisions. In other words, these frameworks provide guidelines regarding who can have access to a data asset, who should be consulted when interpreting analytical findings and who is supposed to have decision authority in certain situations. By writing them out explicitly, organizations make less room for confusion on the roles we expect in the analytic process. Establishing guardrails helps ensure broader user participation, as they can engage with BI tools within boundaries that provide confidence to why.

Technical Strategies

Hybrid Architecture

Enterprises with legacy systems can reduce integration challenges through hybrid architecture approaches. Middleware tools connect on-premises sources with cloud-based BI components, ensuring continuity while modernizing incrementally (Sultan et al., 2024). API-based integration lets organizations plug into separate data sources without extensive refactoring. Containerization technologies can also isolate new services to scale on demand. Hybrid solutions support gradual migration while mitigating operational risks.

Data Quality Frameworks

A formal data quality framework includes processes for profiling, cleansing, enrichment, and monitoring. These processes involve data validation rules that catch anomalies at ingestion points. Data stewards collaborate with business users to define acceptable thresholds for completeness and accuracy. Automated alerts flag data inconsistencies for timely resolution (Lennerholt et al., 2021). By adopting data quality dashboards, organizations can track key metrics in real time. This approach fosters transparency and trust in BI outputs.

Secure Cloud Deployments

Organizations can mitigate security risks in cloud-based BI by carefully selecting vendors that meet relevant certifications. Encryption-at-rest and encryption-in-transit protect sensitive data. Network-level segmentation further minimizes unauthorized access. Role-based access control and multi-factor authentication ensure that users only see data appropriate to their roles (Sultan et al., 2024). These security strategies reassure stakeholders that cloud BI platforms can handle corporate data responsibly. Regular penetration testing and compliance audits fortify long-term trust.

Performance Optimization

Optimizing performance involves robust data modeling, indexing, and caching. In-memory computation technologies speed up data retrieval, enabling real-time dashboards. Distributed architectures like Hadoop or Spark handle large data volumes efficiently. BI platforms that adopt columnar storage and parallel query execution also reduce latency (Villarejo-Ramos et al., 2021). Performance tuning must continue after deployment as user numbers grow and data sets expand.

Simplified AI Integration

Organizations can adopt auto-ML capabilities that guide non-technical users in model creation and interpretation. These features automate tasks like feature engineering and hyperparameter tuning (Alghamdi & Al-Baity, 2022). Explainable AI components show how algorithms derive predictions, which fosters trust among business stakeholders. Collaboration among data scientists, domain experts, and developers enables better model selection. Established governance policies protect model outcomes from bias and maintain version control.

User-Centered Design Approaches

The user-centered design approaches are critical as such setting up an intuitive, task-oriented next-generation BI-system interfaces that can help to adopt the main-stream use. A rigorous process of execution with formal usability testing must be introduced into the implementation process where methods of cognitive walkthrough, task analysis and usability surveys should be applied to achieve user responses. These assessments reveal sources of friction that would otherwise be a hindrance to use (Lennerholt et al., 2021).

Another generalizable technique of making something easy to use is progressive disclosure, or introduction of functionality at a pace that is easy to digest and is not overly demanding on the cognitive resources of the user. Early interfaces present key functionality and new functionality becomes available as people develop expertise. This scaffolding offers entry points to the beginning learner and fits into any advanced needs as skills develop. Therefore, the organizations are able to implement the role-based interfaces that match the analytical complexity with the common expertise in particular posts.

Usability is also accompanied by the contextual instructions that are built into the BI tools to guide users whenever they are involved in analytical duties. Multiple interactive tutorials as well as context sensitive help and systems of suggestions in advising suitable visualizations or analysis enhance the user experience. Some examples of next-generation platforms include the use of AI assistants to prompt the user through complex psychology analytical processes with the natural language interface. The latter support systems alleviate the use of official training or external documentation and improve self-suffle of the tools (Alghamdi & Al-Baity, 2022).

Customization tools allow a user to adjust interfaces and make analytical processes personal to their style and needs. The companies are able to offer configurable dashboards, templates of saved analysis, default settings that belong to a user. It allows this personalization which creates ownership and involvement and helps match the interface delivery to the specific needs of the individual. The implementation approach should have a better balance between flexibility of individualization and adequate levels of standardization to ensure there is a standard definition of data, and visual representation practices.

Data Literacy Development

The concept of data literacy has become a pillar of the successful next-generation BI practice. To this effect, institutions ought to design specific programs that include a wide range of skill sets, with entry level being the comprehension of the chart and advanced being statistical data analysis. The instructional design should prioritize the practical practice over theoretical knowledge and use organizational data and real business scenarios as much as possible (Lennerholt et al., 2021).

A specific-role orientation considers that there are heterogeneous analytical requirements of the various positions. Executives training could focus on the interpretation of the key performance indicators and reporting the model limitations, on the other hand, the operational personnel training would focus on daily data extraction and basic visualization methods. This type of targeting will carefully develop corresponding competencies without subjecting the users to expertise beyond the scope of daily duties. As such, there can be formulated role-based learning pathways that will determined gradual skilling up in relation to specific roles.

Embedded learning resources also ensure that the BI environment includes educational resource material in the same environment. Contextual definitions, the specific metric definition aids and explanatory panels to individual types of visualizations are used to provide redundancy between the process of first encountering an unfamiliar construct and that of consulting supporting literature. It leads to a constant learning process as opposed to training which occurs in a discrete station, with the result that personnel can work permanently throughout their normal work of examination without the need to devote particular time (Alghamdi & Al-Baity, 2022).

Learning networks created between peers also maximize skills training, since they can use in-house expertise. Knowledge transfer takes place through mentorship relations, expert office hour sessions and problem solving sessions in groups, which also establish the supportive networks of people willing to engage in experimentation. Similar issues also arise through peer networks and can therefore indicate system failure weakness that needs technical or training solution. Knowledge-sharing meetings engender periodic and reinforce learning results and even an applause of organizational analytical success..

Synthesizing Organizational and Technical Approaches

There is a definite connection in the overlap between an organizational strategy and technical strategy since strong data management streamlines technical processes, whereas involvement on the part of leadership promotes investment in performance enhancement. Best fixes harmonize the two aspects of change. The coordination of the organizational preparedness schemes and technical design selection in an organization leads to a high level of BI adoptions. Such synergy will enable employees to get access to quality data sets, ease of tools, as well as leadership care. The second section gives an integrated framework that accounts these complementary elements.

INTEGRATED FRAMEWORK FOR NEXT-GENERATION BI ADOPTION

Conceptual Model

Figure 1 presents a conceptual model. It illustrates how organizational enablers, technical enablers, user engagement, and data governance interact to support next-generation BI adoption.

Figure 1. Conceptual model for next-gen BI adoption

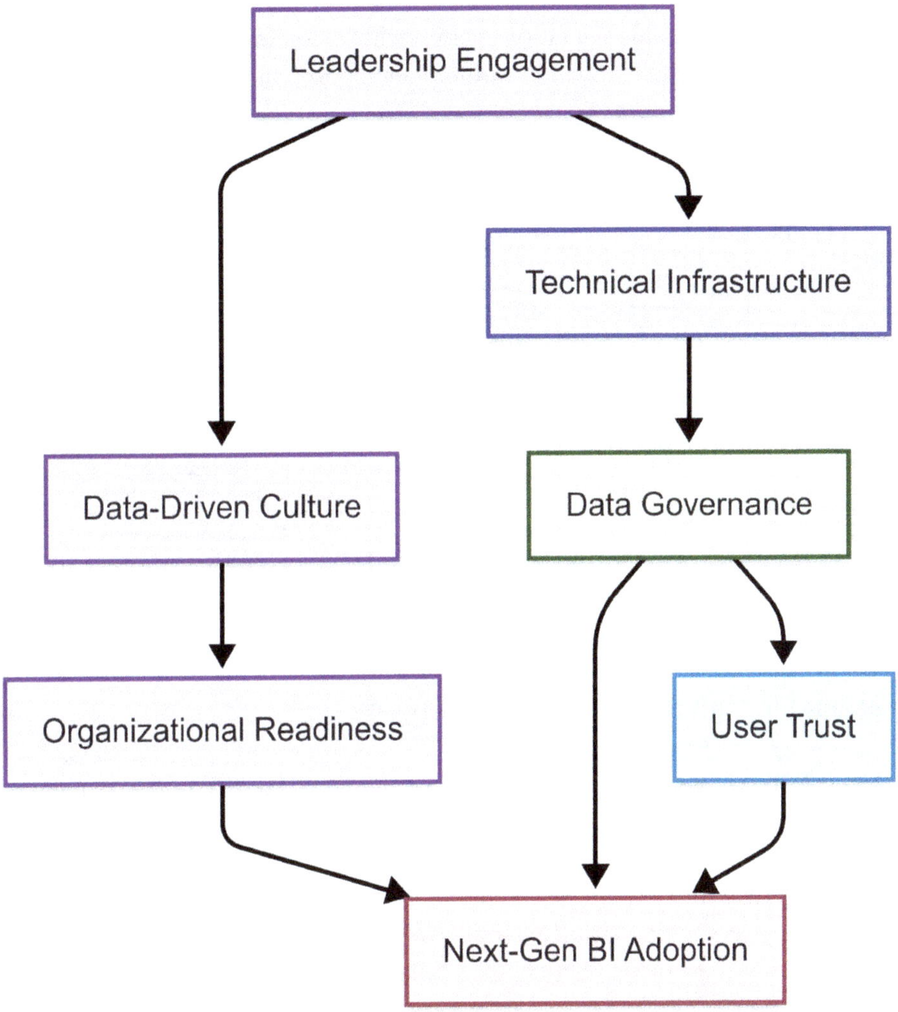

In this model, leadership engagement influences the cultural environment and infrastructure investments. Both drive organizational readiness and data governance initiatives. Governance efforts increase user trust, which is critical for adoption. Ultimately, technical and organizational components converge to produce sustained next-generation BI usage.

Phases of Implementation

Table 1 outlines implementation phases with recommended activities. These stages ensure a systematic transition from planning to scaling.

Table 1. Implementation phases

Phase	Key Activities	Expected Outcomes
Planning	Conduct readiness assessment, Secure leadership support, Form governance committee	Clear scope, Stakeholder alignment, Data policy foundation
Pilot	Integrate pilot group, Offer training, Evaluate data quality	Early user feedback, Identification of technical gaps
Deployment	Roll out BI to larger user base, Optimize performance, Strengthen security	Gradual scale, Reduced errors, Enhanced data trust
Sustainment	Update training, Encourage knowledge sharing, Monitor usage metrics	Continuous improvement, Mature data culture, Widespread adoption

Practical Insights from Case Examples

Experience shows that rollouts in phases can reduce the risk of deployment, as small groups of users are able to optimize data pipelines. Self-service modules are also being piloted by organizations with analytics-literate teams and parallel runs allow employees to compare new reports and legacy reports (Lennerholt et al., 2021). Since users notice visible changes, the acceptance of BI frameworks gains ground. During these steps, the message frames BI to be a driver of efficiency in the organization.

Maturity Assessment Model

Organizations can systematically evaluate their next-generation BI adoption progress through a comprehensive maturity assessment model. This model examines capabilities across multiple dimensions, providing structured guidance for progressive improvement. Each dimension includes specific indicators that organizations can measure to determine current maturity levels and identify priority areas for advancement (Ain et al., 2019).

The data governance dimension evaluates the organization's ability to ensure data quality, consistency, and appropriate access controls. At lower maturity levels, governance remains informal and reactive, addressing issues only after they cause analytical problems. Medium maturity involves documented policies and designated data stewards, while high maturity features automated quality monitoring, comprehensive metadata management, and proactive governance embedded in data workflows (Villarejo-Ramos et al., 2021).

The user capability dimension assesses analytical skill distribution throughout the organization. Low maturity organizations concentrate expertise in specialized teams with limited capabilities among general users. Medium maturity involves broader basic analytical literacy with uneven advanced capabilities. High maturity features widespread data literacy, self-sufficient analysis capabilities appropriate to various roles, and collaborative analytical practices that leverage complementary skills across functions.

The technical infrastructure dimension examines the flexibility, performance, and integration capabilities of the BI environment. Lower maturity levels feature fragmented tools, manual processes, and limited scalability. Medium maturity involves standardized platforms with moderate integration and partially automated workflows. High maturity includes seamless integration across the analytical ecosystem, dynamic resource scaling, and extensive automation of routine analytical tasks (Sultan et al., 2024).

The cultural alignment dimension evaluates how organizational values, behaviors, and reward systems support data-driven practices. Low maturity organizations demonstrate inconsistent leadership commitment and resistance to evidence-based approaches. Medium maturity features growing acceptance of analytical decision-making with pockets of resistance. High maturity involves widespread data-driven mindsets, leadership behaviors that consistently model analytical approaches, and performance systems that explicitly reward evidence-based decisions (Lennerholt et al., 2021).

Change Acceleration Framework

To implement next generation BI, comprehensive change management approach both technical and human dimension is necessary. Change acceleration framework is a structured guidance for planning and executing adoption initiative. To attain this, this framework encompasses influential change management principles and particularities taken into account associated to analytical transformations (Lennerholt et al., 2021).

In the vision alignment phase, it also sets out connections between then generation business intelligence capabilities and the strategic business objectives. This is a demonstration in alignment of how doing all your advanced analytics well is delivering - alignment - back to organizational priorities as opposed to advanced analytics for the sake of advanced analytics itself. Specific use cases are articulated by leaders which show tangible value to different stakeholders, giving rise to a compelling story to be adopted. And the goal must balance the aspirations with the achievable expectations so it can be believed as the implementation unfolds;

Key influencers as well as potential resistors and neutral groups are identified in the stakeholder engagement phase that need targeted communication. Customized messaging addressed to focus different stakeholder segments their specific concerns and motivations is being used. Architectural clarity and integration guidelines are needed by technical teams whereas business users require workflows gains and improvement in efficiency. Strategic impact and return on investment evidence is what executive sponsors are interested in. An incremental approach to change the spread of practice aims at augmenting the success rate by increasing the relevance and confronting each group's different adoption barriers (Hmoud et al., 2023).

The coordinated learning initiatives provide the necessary capability building for required skills and processes. To build user capabilities, organizations do progressive training programs, hands on workshops and embedded coaching. Practical guidance highlights the importance of defining clear use cases, maintaining data quality, cultivating internal champions, providing continuous training and celebrating small wins to boost adoption (Collectiv, 2022) The deployment schedule should align with the timing that these initiatives are actually being sent out so that skills development can happen in sync with technology availability. However, capability building includes not only user training (which is already covered), but also process adjustment, governance implementation and establishment of a support structure. This involves building the comprehensive approach which ensures there are enough enablers to support success adoption.

The common challenge of the decline of enthusiasm after were addressed first by the phase of the momentum maintenance. To sustain the adoption energy, organizations such as those that do early success showcases, and recognition programs, and continuous improvement mechanisms. Regular assessment reports on the barriers of adoption as they surface and permits timely intervention before resistance becomes established. Communication, resource allocation, and personal example of the use of analytical approaches are all consistently supported by leadership. This would ensure that the initiative is not seen as a transitory priority brought forth and will subside (Lennerholt et al., 2021).

EVIDENCE FROM LITERATURE AND PRACTICE

Case Study Analysis

Researchers have documented case studies that highlight approaches for next-generation BI. In one multinational manufacturing firm, a top-down mandate successfully replaced legacy reporting systems with modern analytics. Leadership endorsement and targeted training encouraged employees to accept the shift. This organization also established a data governance council that audited data flow across departments (Lennerholt et al., 2021). Over a year, user adoption rose steadily due to trust in consistent data sets. Another case from a financial services institution illustrates how cloud-based BI lowered infrastructure costs and improved scalability (Sultan et al., 2024). IT teams initially resisted the cloud model, but open dialogue about security measures reduced concerns. Similarly, in the Jordanian banking sector, digital-transformation readiness and top-management support were found to significantly influence BI adoption and decision-making performance (Qatawneh, 2024).

Survey Findings

Open-access surveys have revealed persistent adoption gaps. These surveys find that enterprises with formal data governance mechanisms and user-centric training tend to report higher BI usage. Many respondents cite data quality as the most critical barrier. Skilled data analysts remain vital in interpreting advanced features, suggesting that companies must support training for both business users and specialized teams (Lennerholt et al., 2021). Also, A survey of chief data officers from Fortune 1000 companies similarly reports that cultural obstacles remain the primary barrier to delivering business value from data initiatives (Wavestone, 2023). Another global survey concluded that there is no one-size-fits-all BI platform and that organizations increasingly rely on multiple BI tools (Wiisdom, 2020).

Themes in Empirical Research

The literature underscores the interplay of user confidence, system performance, and leadership. When employees see tangible benefits, adoption accelerates. If leadership invests resources but fails to nurture a data culture, usage stagnates. Researchers also emphasize alignment between business objectives and BI functionalities to ensure relevant metrics (Alghamdi & Al-Baity, 2022).

DISCUSSION

Reflection on Barriers

The combined findings underscore that next-generation BI involves complex social and technological dynamics. Cultural skepticism can persist unless leaders champion data-driven methods. Barriers specific to finance analytics include poor data quality, fear of failure, lack of executive buy-in and time constraints (SAP, 2021). Even when these cultural shifts begin, users need reliable data sources to cultivate trust. Technology alone cannot solve adoption issues if organizational structures do not reward data-based decision-making.

Interplay of Strategies

Strategies work best when integrated. A robust data governance committee enhances data reliability, which in turn supports AI-assisted analytics. Strong leadership engagement secures budget allocations for necessary technical optimizations. When employees receive systematic training, they gain confidence in new tools. This synergy drives momentum and fosters sustained BI usage. A recent survey of 1900 executives found that nearly half of organizations are moving quickly with generative-AI adoption, yet scaling success depends on organizational change and new talent strategies (Deloitte, 2024)

Practical Implications

Companies pursuing advanced BI tools should invest as much in organizational readiness as in technical upgrades. Recent research shows that while over 90% of firms plan to increase AI investments, fewer than 1% achieve AI maturity, largely because of leadership misalignment and insufficient training (Mayer, Yee, Chui, & Roberts, 2025). Timely communication about expected benefits can alleviate fears that automation replaces human judgment. A phased rollout is advisable, beginning with manageable pilot projects. Organizations gain early wins and refine processes before expansion. Monitoring key performance indicators, such as user adoption rates and data accuracy, helps track progress.

Limitations

This chapter draws on open-access literature and generalizes findings. Industry-specific nuances may require adaptation. Highly regulated sectors, for example, might demand stricter policies and specialized compliance frameworks. Small enterprises with limited budgets may struggle to deploy advanced systems or hire specialized personnel.

Future Research

Researchers can expand on this chapter's framework by investigating how AI-driven personalization influences BI adoption. Studies may also explore how governance committees adapt to emerging privacy regulations, such as those regarding consumer data. Comparative studies across industries or geographies can reveal patterns in barriers and solutions.

CONCLUSION

Organizations increasingly seek next-generation BI solutions to transform data into actionable insights. Although these platforms offer self-service analytics, augmented intelligence, and scalable architectures, many firms fail to achieve broad adoption. Organizational barriers include cultural resistance, lack of leadership support, and skill gaps. Technical barriers involve legacy system integration, data quality, security, and performance constraints. Evidence suggests that leadership engagement, data governance, competency development, and robust technical infrastructure are integral to effective BI deployment. Integrated frameworks that coordinate these dimensions help enterprises navigate complex transitions. By emphasizing phased rollouts, continuous training, and a data-centric culture, organizations can realize the promise of next-generation BI and enhance their decision-making processes.

REFERENCES

Ain, N., Vaia, G., DeLone, W., & Waheed, M. (2019). Two decades of research on business intelligence system adoption, utilization and success: A systematic literature review. *Decision Support Systems*, *125*, 113113. DOI: 10.1016/j.dss.2019.113113

Al-Tarawneh, J. M. (2019). Technology acceptance models and adoption of innovations: A literature review. *International Journal of Scientific and Research Publications*, *9*(1), 233–239. https://www.ijsrp.org/research-paper-0819.php?rp=P929018

Alghamdi, N. A., & Al-Baity, H. H. (2022). Augmented analytics driven by AI: A digital transformation beyond business intelligence. *Sensors (Basel)*, *22*(20), 8071. DOI: 10.3390/s22208071 PMID: 36298421

Baumhecker, A. (2022, March 30). Infographic: *Strategies for driving adoption and usage with BI and analytics*. BARC. https://barc.com/infographic-bi-analytics-adoption-strategies/

Collectiv. (2022). *6 strategies to increase business intelligence user adoption*. Collectiv Blog. https://gocollectiv.com/blog/increase-business-intelligence-user-adoption/

Deloitte. (2024, April 29). *Deloitte generative AI survey finds adoption is moving fast, but organizational change is key to accelerate scaling*. Deloitte Newsroom. https://www.deloitte.com/us/en/about/press-room/deloitte-generative-ai-survey-finds-adoption-is-moving-fast-but-organizational-change-is-key-to-accelerate-scaling.html

Hmoud, H., Al-Adwan, A. S., Horani, O. M., & Yaseen, H. (2023). Factors influencing business intelligence adoption by higher education institutions: A TOE-based analysis. *Journal of Open Innovation*, *9*(5), 100111. DOI: 10.1016/j.joitmc.2023.100111

IBM. (2024, May 17). A new era in BI: Overcoming low adoption to make smart decisions accessible for all. IBM Business Insights Blog. https://www.ibm.com/think/insights/business-intelligence-adoption

Korobeyko, T. (2022, July 28). *Self-service BI: Overcoming adoption barriers*. RTInsights. https://www.rtinsights.com/self-service-bi-overcoming-adoption-barriers/

Lees, H. (2020, October 20). *49 shocking business intelligence statistics for 2021*. TrustRadius. https://solutions.trustradius.com/vendor-blog/business-intelligence-statistics-and-trends/

Legal Information Institute. (2023). *5 U.S. Code § 552a – Records maintained on individuals*. Cornell Law School. https://www.law.cornell.edu/uscode/text/5/552a

Lennerholt, C., van Laere, J., & Söderström, E. (2021). User-related challenges of self-service business intelligence. *Information Systems Management, 38*(4), 309–323. DOI: 10.1080/10580530.2020.1814458

Mayer, H., Yee, L., Chui, M., & Roberts, R. (2025, January 28). *Superagency in the workplace: Empowering people to unlock AI's full potential.* McKinsey & Company. https://www.mckinsey.com/~/media/mckinsey/business%20functions/quantumblack/our%20insights/superagency%20in-the-workplace-empowering-people-to-unlock-ais-full-potential-at-work/superagency-in-the-workplace-empowering-people-to-unlock-ais-full-potential-v4.pdf

Qatawneh, N. (2024). Empirical insights into business intelligence adoption and decision-making performance during the digital transformation era: Extending the TOE model in the Jordanian banking sector. *Journal of Open Innovation, 10*(4), 97. DOI: 10.1016/j.joitmc.2024.100401

SAP. (2021). *5 barriers to adopting advanced analytics in finance – and how to overcome them. SAP Insights.* https://www.sap.com/mena/resources/barriers-to-analytics-in-finance

Sultan, H., Chan, L. K., Siew, P. H., & Lee, C. K. (2024). Factors influencing cloud business intelligence adoption and use at the organizational level. *ITM Web of Conferences*, 67, 01019. https://doi.org/DOI: 10.1051/itmconf/20246701019

Taha, A. T., & Ghailan, M. M. (2023). *Theoretical framework for business intelligence adoption. SSRN* Preprint. https://ssrn.com/abstract=4503831

Villarejo-Ramos, Á. F., Cabrera-Sánchez, J. P., Lara-Rubio, J., & Liébana-Cabanillas, F. (2021). Predicting big data adoption in companies with an explanatory and predictive model. *Frontiers in Psychology, 12*, 583822. DOI: 10.3389/fpsyg.2021.651398 PMID: 33868130

Wiisdom. (2020). *Business Intelligence Trends 2020 – Survey Highlights.* Wiiisdom (formerly KPI Products). https://wiiisdom.com/blog/business-intelligence-trends-2020-infographic/

Chapter 5
AI-Driven Threat Detection in Business Intelligence Systems

Maen Marwan Alzubi
Jadara University, Jordan

Murad Bashabsheh
Jadara University, Jordan

Mohammad Almseidin
https://orcid.org/0000-0002-0782-2168
Tafila Technical University, Jordan

Jamil Al-Sawwa
https://orcid.org/0000-0001-7236-0433
Tafila Technical University, Jordan

Mouhammd Alkasassbeh
https://orcid.org/0000-0001-8396-7441
Princess Sumaya University for Technology, Jordan

Ashraf S. Mashaleh
https://orcid.org/0009-0000-5035-7751
Al-Balqa' Applied University, Jordan

ABSTRACT

Business intelligence systems operate in environments increasingly exposed to complex and evolving security threats. Traditional detection mechanisms lack the adaptability required for identifying anomalies in real time across diverse and high-volume data flows. This chapter investigates how artificial intelligence supports threat detection in BI systems through predictive analytics, machine learning models, and automated response mechanisms. It analyzes integration strategies involving data pipelines, cloud platforms, and enterprise reporting tools, illustrating how AI components embed across BI workflows. Case studies demonstrate improved detection accuracy, reduced response times, and enhanced decision support. Key challenges—such as data quality, model interpretability, and integration complexity—are examined

DOI: 10.4018/979-8-3373-6801-6.ch005

alongside emerging innovations, including autonomous threat hunting and adaptive learning. The chapter contributes a framework for embedding AI into BI systems as a foundation for secure and responsive analytics environments.

INTRODUCTION

Threat detection refers to activities or patterns that can indicate security breaches or imminent violations of information systems. It includes intrusion detection, unauthorized access, reporting of anomalies, and deviations from established policy provisions, as these may pose a threat to organizational assets.

Business intelligence (BI) systems, which tend to aggregate enterprise data, process it, and analyze it for strategic decision making, are being put under such attack as never before (Chintala & Thiyagarajan, 2023; Michael et al., 2024). Indeed, more than previously, the ever-expanding scale and more complex enterprise data environments are showing glaring insufficiencies in the application of traditional threat detection methods. Traditional approaches tend to lack the flexibility and granularity required to monitor high-volume, diverse data streams in real time. And hence, organizations are open to increased risk from undetected breaches and delayed response. That is one vast gap that has come up and calls for immediate attention, especially toward integrating advanced technologies, such as artificial intelligence (AI), in making the BI ecosystems more capable in security and resilience. On the other hand, signature-based systems, which rely on known attack patterns that have already been pre-defined, are often ineffectual for newer or advanced attacks like zero-day exploits (Yaseen, 2023; Ashfin, P., 2024; Emmanuel, O.K., n.d.; Prabha, M., 2024; Mazher, N., 2024). Static rule-based mechanisms seem to score exceptionally high when it comes to suffering false negatives against adversarial techniques erected to defeat known detection models, as per Smith (2023).

Threat detection within BI systems is both adaptive and dynamic, thanks to AI and its various methodologies. For instance, with machine learning algorithms, one could learn from real-time data streams as well as historical datasets to detect atypical patterns that would consequently put old threats to pasture. State-of-art deep-learning structures like convolutional neural networks (CNNs) and recurrent neural networks (RNNs) offer specialized processing for unstructured data sources like system logs and user interactions. Such models would unearth very complex patterns and subtle anomalies, the likes of which traditional detection systems would usually miss (Yaseen, 2023; Smith, 2023). With AI embedding well into BI workflows, real-time monitoring and predictive threat mitigation strategies provide organizations with a proactive approach to security management. Detection systems based on AI mechanisms report aberrant data access in ERP systems, while distributed data processing nodes in the cloud are being monitored for anomalies by BI platforms (Puschel, 2023; Hansi, 2023). AI embedding in BI environments enhances not just threat detection but also incident response speed and efficiency within the threat landscape (Tatineni, 2023; Abdel-Wahid, 2024).

Integrating AI with business intelligence systems extends the role of BI from purely analytical to security centric. Predictive models identify potential vulnerabilities before exploitation occurs, while forensic analyses trace incidents to their origins, providing actionable intelligence for system hardening (Tauseef, 2023; Rachakatla, Ravichandran Sr, & Machireddy Sr, 2023).

The objective of this chapter is to explore theoretical foundations, practical integrations, and future directions for AI-driven threat detection within BI systems. It examines core AI methodologies applicable to security, maps security vulnerabilities in typical BI architectures, presents real-world case studies, and discusses challenges such as data quality, model robustness, and ethical considerations. **Table 1** presents a summary of the core AI techniques applied in threat detection within BI systems.

Table 1. Core AI techniques applied in threat detection

AI Technique	Description	Application for BI Threat Detection
Machine Learning (ML)	Uses algorithms to identify patterns and predict threats based on structured datasets.	Anomaly detection in user behaviors and data access logs.
Deep Learning (DL)	Employs neural networks with multiple layers to model complex patterns in high-dimensional data.	Detection of advanced persistent threats (APTs) through log sequence analysis.
Natural Language Processing (NLP)	Processes and analyzes large volumes of textual data to extract relevant information.	Analysis of security alerts, audit logs, and incident reports for hidden threat indicators.
Reinforcement Learning (RL)	Learns optimal actions through reward-based feedback in dynamic environments.	Adaptive response to detected threats by optimizing incident mitigation strategies.

FOUNDATIONS OF AI-DRIVEN THREAT DETECTION

Core Principles of Artificial Intelligence in Security

Artificial intelligence provides scalable and adaptive methods for identifying and responding to threats in digital environments. In cybersecurity applications, AI operates through techniques such as machine learning, deep learning, and natural language processing. These provide automatic pattern recognition, lessen dependency upon human rule updating, and improve accuracy in detection across intricately structured data (Yaseen, 2023; Smith, 2023).

Machine learning programs detect anomalies by modeling expected conducts across data streams, user behaviors, and system functions. Deep neural networks, including convolutional neural networks, as well as recurrent neural networks, facilitate detection of patterns in multiple variables in high-dimensional data sources. These programs learn over time and improve their accuracy through new data inputs (Michael et al., 2024; Azmi, M., 2023). Integration of explainable AI (XAI) grows more prominently to promote transparency in detective decisions, especially in regulated environments where auditability matters. At the same time, adversarial robustness continues to be a design consideration as adversaries continue to invent methods through which to deceive AI systems utilizing crafted input (Rachakatla et al., 2023).

Besides conventional machine learning paradigms, fuzzy inference systems also provide significant reasoning capabilities in uncertain environments. Fuzzy rule interpolation (FRI) methods enable threat detection even when there are incomplete rule bases, offering flexibility and agility in dynamic environments (Alzubi & Kovács, 2020). The systems represent uncertain or incomplete threat indicators by making approximate inferences, highly desirable in cybersecurity applications that are typified by sparse data or ambiguity. More recent advances have also been made in using fuzzy automaton models to improve early warning on complex threats, allowing more precise attack pattern identification that is changing over time (Almseidin, 2020). Such fuzzy-guided methods provide an additional layer of interpretability aside from data-guided methods by providing robustness against uncertain and adversarial environments, an imperative attribute in securing business intelligence (BI) ecosystems.

Business Intelligence Architecture and Security Challenges

Traditional architecture for BI systems usually consists of several dependent modules: data sources, data warehouses or data lakes, ETL pipelines for data, and reporting layer. These layers could either apply on structured data or on semi-structured data to provide insight for operational or strategic level decision-making (Eboigbe, E.O., 2023; Chintala & Thiyagarajan, 2023).

Each part of this design poses unique security threats. For instance, data tampering can be targeted in ETL pipelines, while dashboards pose threats of unauthorized access or data leakage.

In cloud-based BI environments, these vulnerabilities expand due to distributed infrastructure and integration with third-party services (Tatineni, 2023; Abdel-Wahid, 2024). As BI systems scale, traditional detection tools become insufficient. Static rule-based models fail to detect novel threats or adapt to changes in data flow. These limitations are outlined in **Table 2**, which compares traditional detection techniques with AI-driven alternatives.

Table 2. Comparison of traditional vs. AI-driven threat detection methods

Aspect	Traditional Detection Methods	AI-Driven Detection Methods
Detection Approach	Signature-based, rule-driven	Pattern recognition, anomaly detection
Adaptability	Limited to known threats	Learns and adapts to new threats
Accuracy	High for known attacks, low for novel threats	High for both known and emerging threats
False Positive Rate	Often high due to static thresholds	Reduced through continuous learning
Scalability	Manual updates required	Automated scaling with data growth
Response Speed	Reactive, delayed response	Proactive, real-time or near real-time
Resource Requirements	Lower computational demands	Higher computational demands but optimized with modern hardware

Evolution of Threat Detection Approaches

Traditional threat detection approaches relied heavily on signature-based systems, static rule sets, and predefined thresholds. These methods were effective against known attack patterns but exhibited significant limitations when facing novel, adaptive, or polymorphic threats (Tauseef, 2023). Signature-based systems, while great at detecting known threats, fall short in recognizing zero-day exploits or behavioral changes from static patterns. Therefore, anomaly-based detection was devised, which could identify a set of normal operating behavior and determine deviations from it. However, early anomaly-based detection techniques suffered from a lot of false alarms-these techniques were not contextually aware. The introduction of machine-learning methods-both supervised and unsupervised-forged more capabilities through dynamic adaptation from changing streams of data (Rachakatla et al., 2023).

Detection capabilities are supplemented by fuzzy logic methods, especially in situations where data is complete but unstructured. Fuzzy inference allows for the effective functioning of systems under uncertain environments and facilitates effective detection in cases of incompleteness and vagueness, or poor quality of information (Alzubi, M., Almseidin, 2019; Alzubi & Kovács, 2019; Alzubi, M. & Kovács, S., 2019; Alzubi, M. & Johanyák, Z.C., 2019; Alzubi, M. & Kovacs, S., 2020; Almseidin, M., 2022; Alzubi, M. & Almseidin, M., 2024; ; Almseidin, M.

& Alzubi, M., 2024; Mashaleh, A.S., 2024; Almseidin, M.& Al-Sawwa, J., 2023; Almseidin, M., 202; Alzubi, M., Almseidin, M., 2024;).

The recent studies demonstrate how effective fuzzy rule interpolation techniques are in the field of cyberspace, such as in DNS tunneling detection where slight changes in the communication patterns go unnoticed by the conventional systems (Alkasassbeh & Almseidin, 2023). Fuzzy sparse-rule model-based algorithms have also proved helpful in the early detection of phishing attacks using sparse labeled data to suggest possible threat scenarios (Almseidin et al., 2024; Al-Sawwa, J. & Almseidin, M., 2022.). The shift towards fuzzy reasoning also aligns with the larger trend in cybersecurity from fixed, signature-based defenses to context-aware, adaptable defenses able to respond to sophisticated, never-before-seen threats. These advancements allow business intelligence systems to remain resilient while antagonists continue to improve their methods.

Role of AI in Threat Prediction and Pattern Recognition

AI models are somewhat different from the detection of threats in that they may forecast threats. In predictive security analytics, risk arising from new sources is projected by examining historical incident data, system telemetry, and behavioral logs. The machine learning classifiers, cluster analysis, and neural-network-oriented models are the trio of techniques to identify risk indicators before breaches occur (Yaseen, 2023; Michael et al., 2024). They also aid in pattern recognition activities such as identifying coordinated access attacks, multi-step intrusion patterns, and subtle reconnaissance signs. Such a component of functionality comes to great use in BI systems, where insight is derived from heterogeneous data types, such as structured logs and unstructured text from communications or alerts. These pattern recognition activities are implemented by architectural components in Figure 1 that show how AI modules work through layers in the BI system.

Figure 1. Architecture of AI-driven threat detection in BI systems

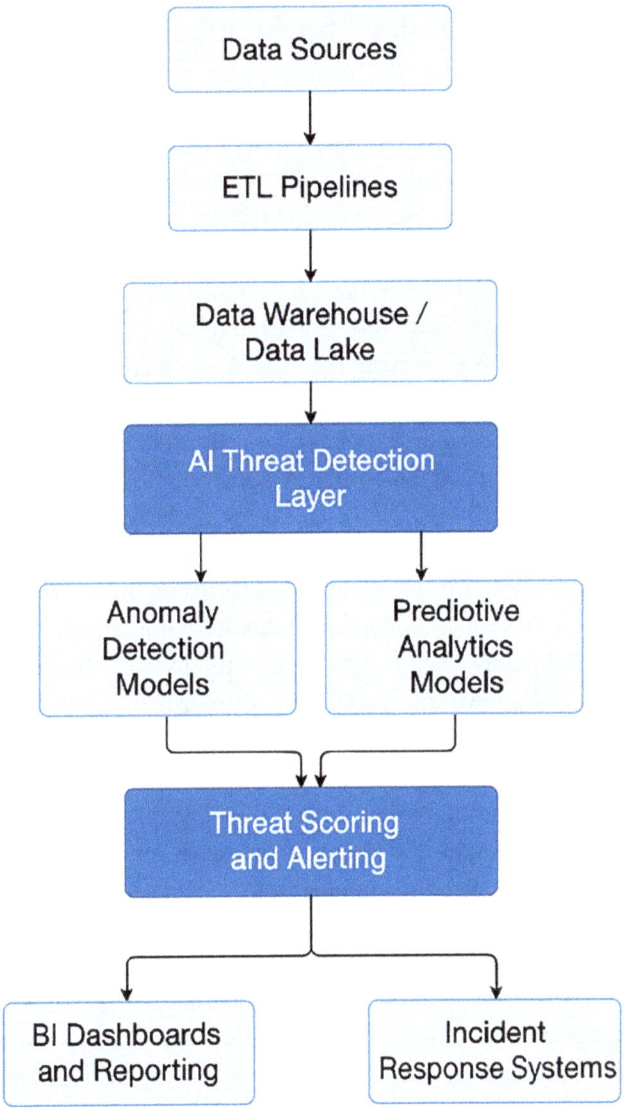

AI TECHNIQUES FOR THREAT DETECTION IN BI SYSTEMS

Machine Learning Algorithms for Anomaly Detection

Among the very important specialized domains of application of machine learning (ML) it probably takes the most distinct role in anomaly detection through pattern recognition of how normal actions may deviate from those patterns and may actually reflect potential security risks. Supervised machine learning, usually implemented by decision tree, support vector machine (SVM), and logistic regression, enables activities to be identified as either benign or malicious after using labeled data (Yaseen, 2023). For scenarios with the absence of or lack of labeled examples, unsupervised techniques such as clustering algorithms (k-means, DBSCAN) can cluster the behaviors and then call the threats as outliers. Ensemble learning techniques include random forests and gradient boosting machines that leverage a combination of different models to enhance the ability to detect and minimize false positives in different threat scenarios (Smith, 2023). This is particularly useful in BI systems that encounter very complex or rapidly changing patterns of attack. More than conventional learning algorithms, fuzzy-logic-based classifiers offer a very new angle for managing the uncertainty and imprecision of threat finding. Fuzzy rule interpolation models enable conclusions to be drawn even in the case of sparse or missing sets of rules and are therefore extremely useful in adversarial or dynamic environments (Alzubi et al., 2024). Further improvement in detection is achieved through the decision tree-fuzzy hybrids, which combine hierarchical decision representations with adaptable fuzzy reasoning to improve model interpretability and robustness.

Recent innovation in hybrid systems is therefore reported to yield improved performance in intrusion detection applications with these artificial immune system methods integrated with fuzzy logic models (Shorman et al., 2025). These systems provide adaptive recognition of altering threat patterns with better detection rates and lower false alarm rates than conventional classifiers. These models federated within BI dashboards and monitoring tools allow for continuous retraining and fine-tuning through feedback loops for retraining. They have proven efficient in annotating unusual data query patterns, unanticipated feasible variations in ETL processes, and abnormal behavior regarding user access. Table 3 presents the challenges of integrating these AI techniques in BI environments.

Table 3. Challenges in AI integration with BI systems

Challenge	Description	Impact on BI Security
Data Quality and Consistency	Inconsistent, incomplete, or noisy datasets reduce AI model effectiveness.	Increase false positives and missed detections.
Model Interpretability	Complex models (e.g., deep learning) lack transparency.	Limits trust and regulatory acceptance.
Infrastructure Compatibility	Legacy BI systems may not support AI integration without significant upgrades.	Delays deployment and raises operational costs.
Adversarial Threats	AI models can be targeted with manipulated inputs.	Introduces new vulnerabilities into BI systems.
Ethical and Privacy Concerns	Monitoring user behavior may conflict with data protection regulations.	Creates legal risks and impacts employee trust.

Deep Learning for Complex Threat Modeling

Deep learning (DL) models are used to identify complex patterns in high-dimensional data environments. Long short-term memory (LSTM) networks, a form of recurrent neural network (RNN), are most effective in identifying anomalies from sequential data streams such as authentication records and system event streams (Michael et al., 2024).

Autoencoders reconstruct normal behavior profiles and flag deviations with high reconstruction errors, serving as unsupervised anomaly detectors. Convolutional neural networks (CNNs), while traditionally applied to image data, are adapted for network traffic and graphical BI dashboard anomaly recognition. Despite their advantages, DL models require significant computational resources and frequent retraining to maintain relevance in dynamic environments, particularly in cloud-based BI infrastructures (Tatineni, 2023).

Natural Language Processing for Log and Alert Analysis

Natural language processing (NLP) techniques process large volumes of unstructured or semi-structured textual data generated by BI systems. Tokenization, named entity recognition, and text classification enable AI systems to interpret security logs, alerts, and incident reports. Advanced models based on transformer architectures, such as BERT and GPT variants, enhance contextual understanding. These models classify log entries, detect anomalies in audit trails, and summarize threat narratives to aid analyst interpretation (Chintala & Thiyagarajan, 2023; Mason Louie, 2024; Alslman, Y., 2024). NLP integration into BI tools accelerates incident triage by prioritizing high-risk alerts and automating report generation, reducing cognitive overload on security teams.

Reinforcement Learning for Adaptive Threat Response

Reinforcement learning (RL), therefore, allows AI agents to learn optimal action responses to detected threats by exercising their environment. The BI model uses RL for automated decisions: restricting user access, quarantining data, and rate limiting queries, based on real-time threat analysis (Rachakatla et al., 2023). These systems use DQNs and policy gradient methods to balance real-time incident response and system sustainability. By iteratively experimenting with the consequences of their actions, RL agents adapt their strategies as a countermeasure to adversarial actions. The real-time lifecycle for threat detection and response in BI systems is shown below, in Figure 2.

Figure 2. Real-time threat detection lifecycle in BI environments

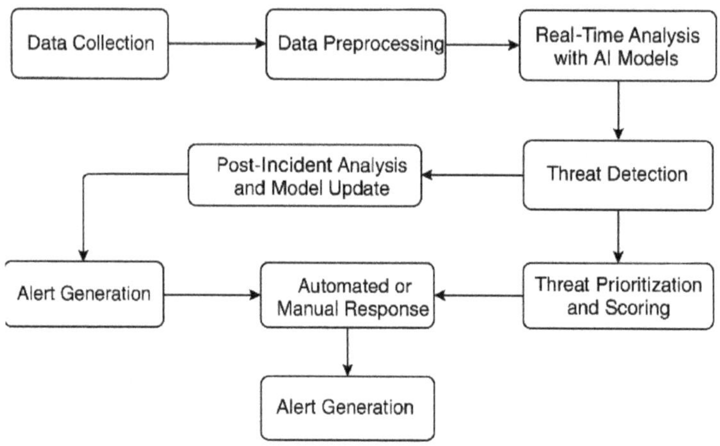

INTEGRATION OF AI-DRIVEN THREAT DETECTION INTO BI WORKFLOWS

Embedding AI into BI Architecture

AI in business intelligence workflow can take various turns in its architecture. Most oftentimes, AI modules are integrative at the levels of extract-transform-load (ETL) processes, data storage, and in the analytics engines of a BI platform. This integration at ETL is expected to allow early-stage identification of anomalies on the incoming data stream for inconsistency or unauthorized changes (Chintala &

Thiyagarajan, 2023). In the modern BI environment, AI components are microservices that communicate on mainstream data processes and share interfaces like all other components through APIs and message queues for modularity and scaling. For an incoming transaction, query, or access, these AI components score these and detect deviations before the data reaches the analysis or reporting stage (Tatineni, 2023). These are the key integration points of the AI to BI workflow graphically encapsulated in Figure 3.

Figure 3. Integration points of AI into BI workflows

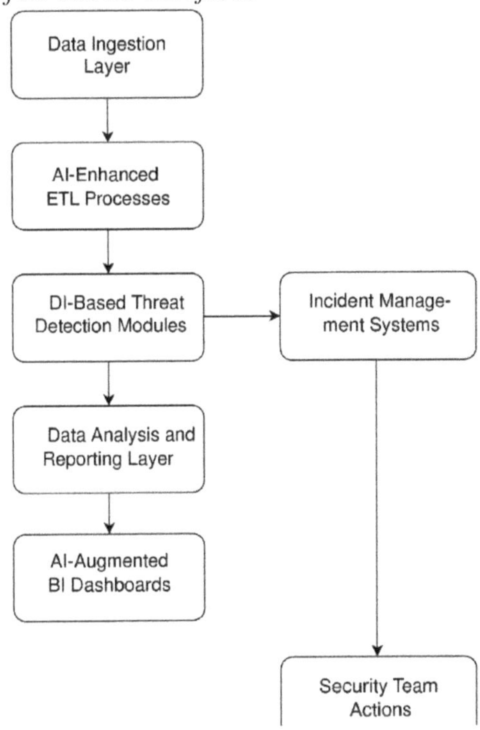

Real-Time Monitoring and Alert Systems

Real-time monitoring is crucial for maintaining the security of BI environments. AI models deployed within the monitoring framework continuously scan system logs, query patterns, and access events to detect abnormal behavior (Michael et al., 2024).

Stream-processing platforms, i.e., Apache Kafka, Apache Flink, enable low-latency data streams, enabling AI models to act on data as it streams in. If anomalies are discovered, the system sends alerts with enriched contextual metadata, such as the type of anomaly, a description of impacted systems, and relative confidence scores (Smith, 2023). Through thresholding and prioritization of past incident impacts, AI models lower alert overload, enabling security teams to concentrate on high-risk occurrences.

Automated Threat Response and Decision Support

AI models also automate aspects of the threat response process in BI platforms. Depending on the severity score of an alert, the system can respond by initiating predefined responses like suspending a user session, blocking access to certain data sets, or marking records for forensic analysis (Rachakatla et al., 2023). Reinforcement machine learning models also enhance these response actions over time by assessing, based on experience, whether they are effective or not. Decision support tools integrated into BI dashboards enable analysts to examine suggested actions, adjust thresholds, and test response impacts prior to deployment.

Human-AI Collaboration in BI Security Operations

Human judgment still needs to be present, even considering growing automation. AI complements analyst capabilities by revealing sophisticated patterns and elevating top-level events, but analysts apply domain knowledge as well as context judgment required in making decisions (Yaseen, 2023).

Explainable AI, or XAI, frameworks expose AI recommendations by revealing the most important factors driving threat scores and alert decisions.

Interactive BI dashboards display these explanations alongside visualizations of the detected threats, supporting collaborative investigation and response efforts.

CASE STUDIES AND REAL-WORLD APPLICATIONS

Financial Services: Insider Threat Detection

A multinational financial services institution integrated AI-driven threat detection within its business intelligence (BI) architecture to address risks posed by insider threats. Using unsupervised machine learning algorithms, the institution continuously monitored trading activities, data access logs, and employee communications (Smith, 2023). Clustering techniques and autoencoders identified behavioral deviations from typical usage patterns, such as unauthorized database queries or access to confidential financial reports outside of normal working hours. The system generated real-time alerts on anomalies and visualized them through BI dashboards. Analysts could investigate flagged events using enriched contextual data, improving detection speed. The AI integration reduced incident response time by 65%, highlighting the effectiveness of embedding anomaly detection models directly within BI monitoring workflows (Yaseen, 2023).

Healthcare: Protecting Patient Data in BI Systems

A regional healthcare provider implemented AI-based threat detection to secure sensitive patient data aggregated through its BI system. Given the regulatory landscape governing healthcare data (e.g., HIPAA compliance), protecting electronic health records (EHRs) was a primary concern. Natural language processing (NLP) models analyzed audit logs and system alerts to detect unusual access patterns and query behaviors. Anomaly detection models identified excessive data extraction attempts or access from unknown devices (Tatineni, 2023). AI-generated alerts were embedded into operational BI dashboards for clinical and IT teams to review in real time.

By integrating AI-driven security measures into both the data ingestion and reporting layers, the provider minimized exposure to data breaches without disrupting operational workflows.

Retail: Preventing Fraud through Predictive Analytics

A global retail company embedded predictive analytics powered by machine learning models into its BI systems to detect fraudulent activities. These models analyzed transactional data, inventory movements, refund patterns, and supplier interactions to uncover anomalies indicative of fraud (Chintala & Thiyagarajan, 2023). Supervised learning algorithms trained on historical fraud cases successfully identified pricing irregularities, unauthorized stock adjustments, and duplicate refund transactions. The predictive risk scores were visualized through customized BI dashboards, allowing store managers and compliance officers to act swiftly.

The implementation led to a 30% reduction in undetected fraud cases and optimized internal audit operations by highlighting high-risk locations and transactions.

Government: Securing National Data Intelligence Systems

A national government agency responsible for economic and trade intelligence deployed AI-enhanced security layers across its BI infrastructure. Deep learning models monitored multi-source data ingestion points for anomalies that could signal espionage or data exfiltration attempts (Muppalaneni, Inaganti, & Ravichandran, 2024). Transformers and LSTM networks processed diplomatic communications, financial transaction logs, and trade reports to detect subtle changes indicative of security breaches. The AI system correlated anomalies across different datasets to build threat profiles that were visualized within secured BI dashboards. Incident response times decreased significantly, and the agency achieved enhanced situational awareness without expanding its human analyst workforce, illustrating the scalability benefits of AI-driven threat detection in large-scale BI environments.

CHALLENGES AND LIMITATIONS

The success of AI-driven threat detection in business intelligence (BI) systems largely depends on the availability of high-quality data. Inconsistent, incomplete, or noisy data sets degrade model performance, leading to an increase in false positives or missed threats (Yaseen, 2023). Organizations often face challenges in consolidating data from multiple sources, particularly when integrating legacy BI systems with modern cloud platforms. Without continuous data validation and normalization, AI models fail to accurately distinguish between legitimate anomalies and actual security threats (Tauseef, 2023).

Many AI models, especially deep learning architectures, operate as black-box systems. This opacity limits the ability of security teams and business stakeholders to understand the rationale behind specific threat detections (Smith, 2023). In highly regulated industries such as finance and healthcare, the inability to explain AI decisions undermines compliance efforts and damages stakeholder trust. While explainable AI (XAI) methods are improving, they often involve trade-offs that reduce model complexity at the cost of performance. Integrating AI components into existing BI workflows presents architectural and operational challenges. Many traditional BI systems were not designed to accommodate real-time machine learning inference or large-scale data analytics required for AI-driven threat detection (Puschel, 2023). Compatibility issues arise when trying to align AI modules with legacy data warehouses, ETL processes, and reporting systems. Integration often demands significant investments in cloud infrastructure, edge computing resources, and cross-functional expertise, slowing adoption rates.

The cybersecurity threat landscape continues to evolve rapidly, with adversaries employing increasingly sophisticated techniques to evade detection. Static or infrequently updated AI models become vulnerable to concept drift, where the underlying statistical properties of normal and malicious behaviors shift over time (Muppalaneni, Inaganti, & Ravichandran, 2024). As a result, detection systems based on rigid patterns or outdated training data struggle to maintain performance. Dynamic adaptation is essential for maintaining resilience. Machine learning models that can incorporate new data continuously offer a partial solution, but even these models face challenges when attackers intentionally inject adversarial noise or manipulate input features to bypass detection mechanisms. Robust fuzzy inference systems address these challenges by enabling flexible, uncertainty-tolerant reasoning even in the presence of adversarial manipulations. Fuzzy models, by design, handle imprecise and partial information more effectively than rigid classifiers. Recent studies demonstrate that fuzzy inference models significantly reduce the vulnerability of detection systems to evasion tactics, particularly in dynamic or resource-constrained environments (Almseidin et al., 2023).

In the domain of IoT security, ensemble approaches that integrate fuzzy logic with other machine learning techniques have shown strong resistance to adversarial drift. (Rawashdeh et al. 2024; Almseidin, M.& Al-Sawwa, J., 2024; Shorman, A.R., 2025; Almseidin, M. & Alkasassbeh, M., 2022; Al-Kasassbeh, M., 2020) highlighted that fuzzy ensemble models maintained high detection accuracy even as attackers adapted their behaviors to avoid standard anomaly-based models. These advancements suggest that integrating fuzzy reasoning into AI-driven threat detection systems enhances the robustness and adaptability necessary to counter emerging and evolving cyber threats within business intelligence environments. According to the ethical and privacy considerations, the deployment of AI for behavioral monitoring and anomaly detection in BI environments raises important ethical and privacy concerns. Monitoring user activities, even for legitimate security purposes, can conflict with data protection regulations such as GDPR and HIPAA (Adeyeye et al., 2024; Alweshah, M., 2023; Al-Sawwa, J., 2024). Overly aggressive surveillance may erode employee trust and damage organizational culture.

Therefore, organizations must balance effective threat detection with responsible data governance, transparency, and user consent mechanisms. These challenges are summarized in Table 4 to provide a consolidated view of the key issues impacting AI-driven threat detection in BI systems.

Table 4. Key performance metrics for evaluating threat detection systems

Metric	Description	Relevance to BI Security
Detection Accuracy	Proportion of correctly identified threats and normal activities.	Ensure reliable protection without excessive false alerts.
False Positive Rate	Frequency of benign activities incorrectly flagged as threats.	Reduces analyst workload and alert fatigue.
Detection Latency	Time taken to identify and report a threat after occurrence.	Critical for rapid response and containment.
Scalability	Ability to maintain performance with increasing data volume and system complexity.	Supports BI systems with dynamic, growing datasets.

continued on following page

Table 4. Continued

Metric	Description	Relevance to BI Security
Model Robustness	Resilience of the detection system against adversarial attacks and data variability.	Ensures consistent security under evolving threats.
Resource Efficiency	Computational cost required for model training and inference.	Influences deployment feasibility across enterprise BI infrastructures.

FUTURE TRENDS AND RESEARCH DIRECTIONS

Autonomous threat hunting represents a major advancement for AI in business intelligence (BI) security. Unlike traditional systems that passively monitor for threats, autonomous AI agents actively explore system logs, network activity, and user behaviors to detect latent compromises without explicit prompts (Sindiramutty, 2023). These systems apply reinforcement learning and unsupervised anomaly detection to discover hidden threats early in their lifecycle. As the volume and complexity of BI environments grow, autonomous threat hunters will reduce the burden on security analysts by continuously scanning and prioritizing risks.

Generative artificial intelligence models, particularly generative adversarial networks (GANs), are being explored for simulating complex attack scenarios. These synthetic datasets allow organizations to test the resilience of their AI-driven detection systems under realistic but controlled conditions (Muppalaneni, Inaganti, & Ravichandran, 2024). In BI environments, generative AI can model sophisticated threats such as multi-vector data exfiltration, insider manipulation, and advanced phishing attacks, enhancing model robustness through exposure to diverse training data.

BI systems increasingly incorporate threat intelligence platforms that aggregate data from dark web sources, global telemetry networks, and real-time vulnerability disclosures (Manda, 2024; Almseidin, M.& Gawanmeh, A., 2025; Alkasassbeh, M. & Almseidin, M., 2023; Odeh, I.& Alkasassbeh, M. 2022; Kumar, B., 2023; Rangaraju, S., 2023; Wisdom, D.D., 2024). By feeding external threat intelligence into AI models, BI environments can dynamically adjust risk scores and detection thresholds based on emerging threats. The integration of such platforms enhances situational awareness and shortens the detection-to-response cycle in dynamic operational contexts.

Adaptive AI models that learn from continuous feedback without full retraining will become essential in future BI security architectures. These systems apply techniques such as online learning and incremental model updates to adjust to evolving threats (Tatineni, 2023). By embedding self-learning capabilities, organizations minimize downtime associated with model retraining and sustain high levels of detection performance even as operational environments change.

With the expansion of cloud-native and distributed BI systems, AI-driven threat detection is increasingly moving closer to the data source. Edge computing enables lightweight AI models to analyze data locally, detect anomalies, and respond rapidly before information is transmitted to central data warehouses (Adeyeye et al., 2024; Younisse, R., 2023; Almseidin, M., 2022; Abuzuraiq, A., 2020). This decentralization improves detection latency, reduces network load, and enhances the privacy of sensitive information processed at the edge.

The rapid adoption of AI for threat detection raises ethical questions related to fairness, accountability, and user privacy. Regulatory frameworks such as the EU Artificial Intelligence Act and updates to GDPR introduce requirements for transparency and explainability in AI systems (Michael et al., 2024). Organizations deploying AI within BI workflows must ensure that their models are auditable, avoid bias in threat detection, and respect user data rights to maintain compliance and trust. Emerging research priorities across these areas are summarized in Table 5.

Table 5. Future trends and research priorities in AI-driven threat detection

Trend/Research Area	Focus	Potential Impact on BI Systems
Autonomous Threat Hunting	Active AI-driven search for latent threats without human prompts.	Enhances proactive defense in BI environments.
Generative AI for Threat Simulation	Use of GANs and similar models to simulate realistic attack scenarios.	Strengthens system robustness through advanced testing.
Real-Time Threat Intelligence Integration	Incorporating external threat feeds into BI analytics.	Improves threat prediction and early warning capabilities.
Adaptive and Self-Learning Models	Systems that evolve continuously with minimal human retraining.	Maintains relevance against rapidly changing threats.
Edge Intelligence for Distributed BI	Deployment of lightweight AI models at data source points.	Reduces latency and decentralizes threat detection.
Ethical AI and Compliance Frameworks	Development of transparent, fair, and accountable AI practices.	Supports regulatory alignment and preserves organizational trust.

CONCLUSION

Artificial intelligence (AI) has fundamentally redefined the approach to threat detection within business intelligence (BI) systems. Traditional signature-based and rule-driven models, although effective against known threats, cannot match the complexity and speed of modern cyberattacks (Yaseen, 2023; Smith, 2023). AI-driven techniques introduce dynamic, adaptive capabilities that allow BI environments to predict, detect, and respond to both known and emerging threats in real time. The integration of machine learning, deep learning, natural language processing, and reinforcement learning into BI workflows enhance organizational security across the data lifecycle. AI models identify anomalies, automate threat responses, and prioritize risks with greater precision than manual systems (Michael et al., 2024; Rachakatla, Ravichandran Sr, & Machireddy Sr, 2023). Real-world applications in sectors such as finance, healthcare, retail, and government demonstrate tangible improvements in detection rates, incident response times, and operational resilience. However, critical challenges persist. Data quality, model interpretability, integration complexities, evolving adversarial threats, and ethical concerns require careful management (Tatineni, 2023; Muppalaneni, Inaganti, & Ravichandran, 2024). Organizations must adopt strategies that ensure transparency, scalability, and ethical governance of AI systems within their BI infrastructures. Future trends, including autonomous threat hunting, generative AI-based threat simulation, and adaptive self-learning systems, promise to further enhance BI security capabilities. Concurrently, compliance with emerging regulatory frameworks will become a necessary part of responsible AI deployment (Manda, 2024; Adeyeye et al., 2024; Almseidin, M., 2021; Abuzuraiq, A., 2020). This chapter contributes a structured framework for understanding the intersection of AI and BI threat detection. By synthesizing theoretical foundations, practical case studies, and emerging innovations, it provides a reference for researchers, practitioners, and policymakers seeking to secure business intelligence systems in an increasingly complex digital landscape.

REFERENCES

Abuzuraiq, A., Alkasassbeh, M., & Almseidin, M. (2020). Intelligent methods for accurately detecting phishing websites. In *2020 11th International Conference on Information and Communication Systems (ICICS)* (pp. 85–90). IEEE. https://doi.org/DOI: 10.1109/ICICS49469.2020.239556

Adeyeye, O. J., Akanbi, I., Emeteveke, I., & Emehin, O. (2024). Leveraging secured AI-driven data analytics for cybersecurity: Safeguarding information and enhancing threat detection. *International Journal of Research and Publication and Reviews*, *5*(10), 3208–3223.

Al-Kasassbeh, M., Almseidin, M., Alrfou, K., & Kovacs, S. (2020). Detection of IoT-botnet attacks using fuzzy rule interpolation. *Journal of Intelligent & Fuzzy Systems*, *39*(1), 421–431. DOI: 10.3233/JIFS-191135

Al-Sawwa, J., Almseidin, M., Alkasassbeh, M., Alemerien, K., & Younisse, R. (2024). Spark-based multi-verse optimizer as wrapper features selection algorithm for phishing attack challenge. *Cluster Computing*, *27*(5), 5799–5814. DOI: 10.1007/s10586-023-04236-x

Almseidin, M., Al-Sawwa, J., & Alkasassbeh, M. (2021). Anomaly-based intrusion detection system using fuzzy logic. In *2021 International Conference on Information Technology (ICIT)* (pp. 290–295). IEEE. https://doi.org/DOI: 10.1109/ICIT52682.2021.9491718

Almseidin, M., Al-Sawwa, J., & Alkasassbeh, M. (2022a). Generating a benchmark cyber multi-step attacks dataset for intrusion detection. *Journal of Intelligent & Fuzzy Systems*, *43*(3), 3679–3694. DOI: 10.3233/JIFS-213241

Almseidin, M., Al-Sawwa, J., Alkasassbeh, M., & Alweshah, M. (2023). On detecting distributed denial of service attacks using fuzzy inference system. *Cluster Computing*, *26*(2), 1337–1351. DOI: 10.1007/s10586-022-03674-3

Almseidin, M., & Alkasassbeh, M. (2022b). An accurate detection approach for IoT botnet attacks using interpolation reasoning method. *Information (Basel)*, *13*(6), 300. Advance online publication. DOI: 10.3390/info13060300

Almseidin, M., Alkasassbeh, M., Alzubi, M., & Al-Sawwa, J. (2022). Cyber-phishing website detection using fuzzy rule interpolation. *Cryptography*, *6*(2), 24. Advance online publication. DOI: 10.3390/cryptography6020024

Almseidin, M., Alzubi, M., Al-Sawwa, J., & Alkasassbeh, M. (2024). Comparative analysis of fuzzy rule interpolation techniques across various scenarios using a set of benchmarks (November 2023). *IEEE Access : Practical Innovations, Open Solutions*, *12*, 15376–15389. DOI: 10.1109/ACCESS.2023.3334567

Almseidin, M., Alzubi, M., Al-Sawwa, J., Alkasassbeh, M., & Alfraheed, M. (2024). A threefold approach for enhancing fuzzy interpolative reasoning: Case study on phishing attack detection using sparse rule bases. *Computers*, *13*(11), 291. Advance online publication. DOI: 10.3390/computers13110291

Almseidin, M., Alzubi, M., Kovacs, S., Al-Sawwa, J., & Alkasassbeh, M. (2024). EI-FRI: Extended incircle fuzzy rule interpolation for multidimensional antecedents, multiple fuzzy rules, and extrapolation using total weight measurement and shift ratio. [JRC]. *Journal of Robotics and Control*, *5*(1), 217–227. DOI: 10.18196/jrc.v5i1.20876

Almseidin, M., Gawanmeh, A., Alzubi, M., Al-Sawwa, J., Mashaleh, A. S., & Alkasassbeh, M. (2025). Hybrid deep neural network optimization with particle swarm and grey wolf algorithms for sunburst attack detection. *Computers*, *14*(3), 107. Advance online publication. DOI: 10.3390/computers14030107

Alslman, Y., Alkasassbeh, M., & Almseidin, M. (2024). A robust SNMP-MIB intrusion detection system against adversarial attacks. *Arabian Journal for Science and Engineering*, *49*(3), 4179–4195. DOI: 10.1007/s13369-023-08253-6

Alweshah, M., Kassaymeh, S., Alkhalaileh, S., Almseidin, M., & Altarawni, I. (2023). An efficient hybrid mine blast algorithm for tackling software fault prediction problem. *Neural Processing Letters*, *55*(8), 10925–10950. DOI: 10.1007/s11063-023-11376-8

Alzubi, M., Almseidin, M., Alkasassbeh, M., Al-Sawwa, J., & Aldweesh, A. (2024). DT-ARO: Decision tree-based artificial rabbits optimization to mitigate IoT botnet exploitation. *Journal of Network and Systems Management*, *32*(1), 14. Advance online publication. DOI: 10.1007/s10922-023-09781-9

Alzubi, M., Almseidin, M., Lone, M. A., & Kovacs, S. (2019a). Fuzzy rule interpolation toolbox for the GNU open-source OCTAVE. In *2019 17th International Conference on Emerging eLearning Technologies and Applications (ICETA)* (pp. 16–22). IEEE. https://doi.org/DOI: 10.1109/ICETA48886.2019.9040090

Alzubi, M., Johanyak, Z. C., & Kovacs, S. (2019d). Fuzzy rule interpolation methods and FRI toolbox. *arXiv*. https://doi.org//arXiv.1904.12178DOI: 10.48550

Alzubi, M., & Kovacs, S. (2019b). Some considerations and a benchmark related to the CNF property of the Koczy-Hirota fuzzy rule interpolation. *arXiv*. https://doi.org//arXiv.1911.05041DOI: 10.48550

Alzubi, M., & Kovacs, S. (2019c). Investigating the piece-wise linearity and benchmark related to Koczy-Hirota fuzzy linear interpolation. *arXiv*. https://doi.org//arXiv.1907.01047DOI: 10.48550

Alzubi, M., & Kovacs, S. (2020). Interpolative fuzzy reasoning method based on the incircle of a generalized triangular fuzzy number. *Journal of Intelligent & Fuzzy Systems*, *39*(1), 709–729. DOI: 10.3233/JIFS-191223

Ashfin, P. (2024). AI-driven threat detection and response in cybersecurity. *Bulletin of Engineering Science and Technology*, *1*(2), 125–143.

Azmi, M., Mansour, A., & Azmi, C. (2023). A context-aware empowering business with AI: Case of chatbots in business intelligence systems. *Procedia Computer Science*, *224*, 479–484. DOI: 10.1016/j.procs.2023.09.054

Chintala, S., & Thiyagarajan, V. (2023). AI-driven business intelligence: Unlocking the future of decision-making. *ESP International Journal of Advancements in Computational Technology*, *1*, 73–84.

Eboigbe, E. O., Farayola, O. A., Olatoye, F. O., Nnabugwu, O. C., & Daraojimba, C. (2023). Business intelligence transformation through AI and data analytics. *Engineering Science & Technology Journal*, *4*(5), 285–307.

Emmanuel, O. K. (n.d.). *AI-driven threat detection: Enhancing cybersecurity through predictive analytics*. [Unpublished manuscript].

Hansi, G. (2023). Business intelligence transformation with AI/ML: Strengthening ERP cloud security using Snowflake DB. [Unpublished manuscript].

Kumar, B. (2023). Cyber threat intelligence using AI and machine learning approaches. *International Journal of Business Management and Visuals*, *6*(2), 1–7.

Manda, J. K. (2024). AI-powered threat intelligence platforms in telecom: Leveraging AI for real-time threat detection and intelligence gathering in telecom network security operations. *SSRN*. https://doi.org/DOI: 10.2139/ssrn.5003638

Mashaleh, A. S., Ibrahim, N. F. B., Alauthman, M., Almseidin, M., & Gawanmeh, A. (2024). IoT smart devices risk assessment model using fuzzy logic and PSO. *Computers, Materials & Continua*, *78*(2), 2247–2268. DOI: 10.32604/cmc.2023.045711

Mason Louie, M. G. (2024). *AI-driven cybersecurity: Enhancing big data protection in business intelligence systems*. [Unpublished manuscript].

Mazher, N., Basharat, A., & Nishat, A. (2024). AI-driven threat detection: Revolutionizing cyber defense mechanisms. *Eastern-European Journal of Engineering and Technology*, *3*(1), 70–82.

Michael, C. I., Ipede, O. J., Adejumo, A. D., Adenekan, I. O., Adebayo, D., Ojo, A. S., & Ayodele, P. A. (2024). Data-driven decision making in IT: Leveraging AI and data science for business intelligence. *World Journal of Advanced Research and Reviews*, *23*(1), 472–480. DOI: 10.30574/wjarr.2024.23.1.2093

Muppalaneni, R., Inaganti, A. C., & Ravichandran, N. (2024). AI-driven threat intelligence: Enhancing cyber defense with machine learning. *Journal of Computing Innovations and Applications*, *2*(1), 1–11.

Odeh, I., Alkasassbeh, M., & Almseidin, M. (2022). Diabetic retinopathy detection method using artificial neural network. *International Journal of Bioinformatics Research and Applications*, *18*(4), 300–317. DOI: 10.1504/IJBRA.2022.126858

Prabha, M., Hossain, M. A., Samiun, M., Saleh, M. A., Dhar, S. R., & Al Mahmud, M. A. (2024). AI-driven cyber threat detection: Revolutionizing security frameworks in management information systems. In *2024 International Conference on Intelligent Cybernetics Technology & Applications (ICICyTA)* (pp. 357–362). IEEE. https://doi.org/DOI: 10.1109/ICICyTA62753.2024.10731205

Puschel, M. (2023). *Optimized business intelligence and cybersecurity with AI/ML-driven solutions for ERP cloud and Snowflake DB*. [Unpublished manuscript].

Rachakatla, S. K., Ravichandran, P.Sr, & Machireddy, J. R.Sr. (2023). AI-driven business analytics: Leveraging deep learning and big data for predictive insights. *Journal of Deep Learning in Genomic Data Analysis*, *3*(2), 1–22.

Rangaraju, S. (2023). Secure by intelligence: Enhancing products with AI-driven security measures. *EPH-International Journal of Science and Engineering*, *9*(3), 36–41.

Rawashdeh, A., Alkasassbeh, M., Alauthman, M., & Almseidin, M. (2024). A stacked ensemble approach to identify internet of things network attacks through traffic analysis. *Bulletin of Electrical Engineering and Informatics*, *13*(6), 4316–4326. DOI: 10.11591/eei.v13i6.7216

Shorman, A. R., Alzubi, M., Almseidin, M., & Rateb, R. (2025). Adaptive intrusion detection for IoT networks using artificial immune system techniques: A comparative study. [JRC]. *Journal of Robotics and Control*, *6*(2), 570–582. DOI: 10.18196/jrc.v6i2.22703

Sindiramutty, S. R. (2023). Autonomous threat hunting: A future paradigm for AI-driven threat intelligence. *arXiv*. https://doi.org//arXiv.2401.00286DOI: 10.48550

Smith, S. (2023). *AI-driven cybersecurity: Leveraging big data for advanced threat detection and risk mitigation*. [Unpublished manuscript].

Tatineni, S. (2023). AI-infused threat detection and incident response in cloud security. *International Journal of Scientific Research, 12*(11), 998–1004. DOI: 10.21275/SR231113082917

Tauseef, A. (2023). Database technologies in AI: Transforming cybersecurity with automated threat detection systems. *ResearchGate*. https://doi.org/DOI: 10.13140/RG.2.2.33122.54727

Wisdom, D. D., Vincent, O. R., Oduntan, O. A. E., Hassan, J. B., Falayi, C. F., & Ajayi, T. D. (2024). *Improving security of business intelligent systems with AI and machine learning. In 2024 IEEE SmartBlock4Africa*. IEEE., DOI: 10.1109/SmartBlock4Africa62047.2024.10709433

Yaseen, A. (2023). AI-driven threat detection and response: A paradigm shift in cybersecurity. *International Journal of Information and Cybersecurity, 7*(12), 25–43.

Younisse, R., Alkasassbeh, M., Almseidin, M., & Abdi, H. (2023). An early detection model for Kerberoasting attacks and dataset labeling. *Jordanian Journal of Computers and Information Technology, 9*(1), 1–15.

Chapter 6
Digital Twins and BI:
Synchronizing Virtual Models With Real-Time Business Processes

Salam Al E'mari
https://orcid.org/0000-0002-2134-4158
University of Petra, Jordan

Yousef Sanjalawe
https://orcid.org/0000-0002-4442-1865
University of Jordan, Jordan

Fadi Fataftah
https://orcid.org/0000-0002-3299-0972
University Canada West, Canada

Fuad Fataftah
https://orcid.org/0009-0009-3203-5869
Universiti Sains Malaysia, Malaysia

ABSTRACT

Digital Twins (DTs) and modern Business Intelligence (BI) tools have evolved along largely distinct paths—DTs within operational technology domains and BI within information technology domains. When effectively integrated, these technologies form a cyber-physical cognition loop, wherein real-time sensor data updates physics-based or machine learning models, while BI layers transform model outputs into actionable financial and strategic insights. This chapter explores the theoretical foundations of DTs and BI, proposes a layered reference architecture to support their convergence, and validates this approach through in-depth case studies in aerospace manufacturing, smart-port logistics, and grid-edge energy management. Looking ahead, advancements such as edge-native TinyML, and 6G time-sensitive networking are

DOI: 10.4018/979-8-3373-6801-6.ch006

poised to further entangle DT and BI systems. By embracing open standards, robust ModelOps practices, and sustainability metrics, organizations can unlock the full potential of DT–BI integration to enable self-optimizing, carbon-aware operations.

INTRODUCTION

Digital transformation has altered the way organizations see, think about, and manage their operations. Devices on factory floors, vehicles on highways, and turbines in wind farms now stream large volumes of data every second, and managers seek timely insight from these data flows (Bonnet & Westerman, 2020). Digital Twin (DT) technology and Business Intelligence (BI) have risen to meet this need, yet they have often developed in parallel rather than together. A Digital Twin is a live, digital copy of a physical object or process that is updated as conditions change (ISO, 2022). By contrast, BI gathers, cleans, analyzes, and visualizes data so that people can make informed choices (Bussa, 2023). When these two technologies come together, they create what may be called a cyber-physical thinking loop. Real-world events feed the twin; the twin feeds the BI layer; the BI layer shapes action in the real world; and the cycle repeats (Salehi et al., 2024).

The purpose of this chapter is to explain why and how organizations can merge DT and BI. First, the text defines the key ideas in simple academic language. Second, it lays out an end-to-end architecture that shows how data can move smoothly from a machine on the shop floor to an executive dashboard. Third, three detailed case studies give practical proof of value. Finally, the chapter outlines the main barriers and offers forward-looking advice. Throughout, linking words such as furthermore and however guide the reader and strengthen the flow of thought.

Following this introduction, Section 2 dissects the ontology of Digital Twins, examining their components, modeling approaches, and industrial applications. Section 3 reviews the evolution of Business Intelligence in the modern enterprise, highlighting functionality and lingering implementation challenges. Section 4 articulates the theoretical and practical *synergies* of DT–BI convergence, offering a layered reference architecture and associated benefits. Section 5 drills deeper into architectural considerations—data synchronization, system interoperability, and analytical model alignment. Section 6 substantiates claims through three detailed case studies in manufacturing, logistics, and energy. Section 7 critically analyzes cross-cutting challenges and actionable solutions. Section 8 projects future trajectories, while Section 9 synthesizes insights and delineates avenues for further research.

By weaving technical discussion with empirical evidence, the chapter endeavors to furnish scholars and practitioners with a rigorous yet pragmatic roadmap for harnessing Digital Twins and Business Intelligence in pursuit of enterprise excellence.

FOUNDATIONAL UNDERSTANDING DIGITAL TWINS

The term *Digital Twin* (DT) was popularized by NASA's Product Lifecycle Management roadmap in 2010, although antecedents can be traced to mirrored simulation models used in the U.S. space program during the 1960s (Schwarz & Wang, 2022). ISO 23247-1 (2022) now formally defines a DT as a "virtual representation of a real-world entity or system that is synchronized at a specified frequency and fidelity." The definition immediately foregrounds two property classes: **fidelity** (how accurately the model mirrors the referent) and **latency** (how quickly updates propagate).

DT differ categorically from conventional simulation in three respects. First, they maintain a *persistent* relationship with their physical counterparts throughout the lifecycle, not merely at discrete design stages (Kritzinger et al., 2018). Second, bidirectional data exchange means that the twin can *act back* on the physical system, enabling closed-loop optimization (Uhlemann, Lehmann, & Steinhilper, 2017). Third, twins often incorporate machine-learning components that adapt over time, making them epistemically reflexive (Wagg et al., 2025).

A mature DT stack comprises **five interdependent layers** adapted from (Tao, et al., 2018) as shown in Figure 1:

1. **Physical Layer** – Sensors, actuators, controllers, and environmental context that generate raw data.
2. **Connectivity Layer** – Industrial networking (OPC UA, MQTT, 5G URLLC) responsible for secure, deterministic data transport.
3. **Data Management Layer** – Streaming gateways, time-series databases, and data lakes that ensure scalable persistence and governance.
4. **Modeling & Analytics Layer** – Multi-paradigm models (physics-based finite-element, statistical, and deep-learning models) orchestrated via co-simulation engines.
5. **Presentation & Interaction Layer** – Immersive 3-D visualization, mixed-reality overlays, and BI dashboards, enabling cognitive assimilation by human decision-makers.

Figure 1. Five-layer framework aligning data flows from physical to cognitive

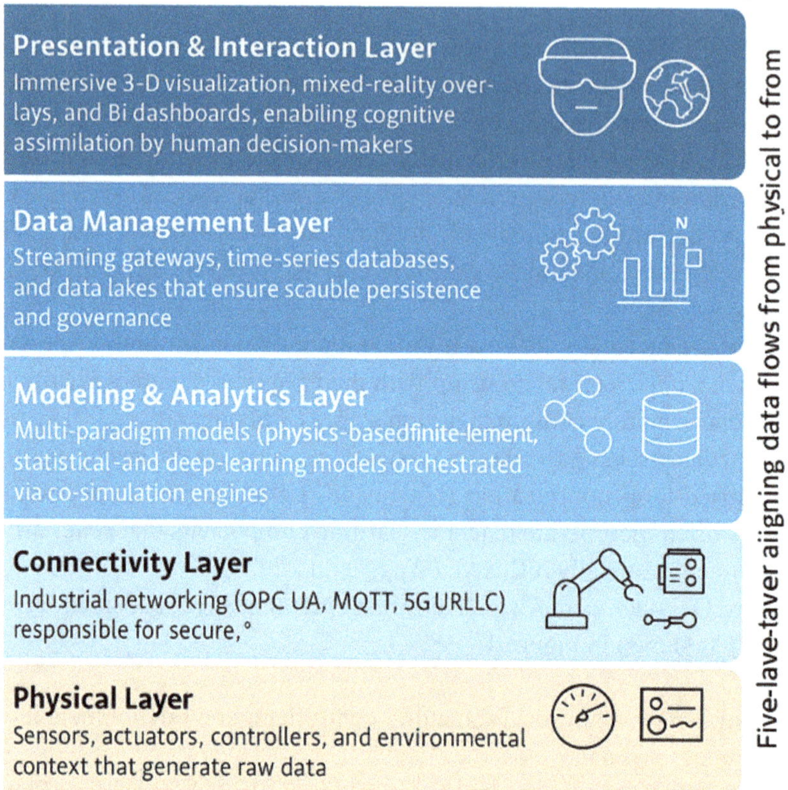

Digital Thread concept underscores that a twin coevolves with the artifact across design, production, operation, and retirement. Key lifecycle mechanisms include (a) *model calibration* using condition-based monitoring, (b) *scenario simulation* for what-if analytics, and (c) *feedback actuation* for real-time control (Pang et al., 2021).

DT create value across many domains. In manufacturing, Siemens reports that its Amberg plant uses a twin of its production line to keep defects close to zero (Guerra-Zubiaga *et al.*, 2019). In logistics, FedEx simulates parcel flows and adjusts staffing before bottlenecks appear (Sun *et al.*, 2024). In the energy sector, Ørsted raises turbine output by fine-tuning blade angles through a wind-farm twin (Orsted, 2022). In health care, surgeons rehearse complex heart procedures on patient-specific cardiac twins, saving time in the operating room (Faisal *et al.*, 2025). These examples show that a twin is not a narrow or single-use tool; instead, it is a flexible platform for continuous insight.

BUSINESS INTELLIGENCE IN THE MODERN ENTERPRISE

BI has traveled a long road since the 1990s. Early BI delivered descriptive reports that answered the question, "What happened yesterday?" Over time, new waves have added deeper questions. Diagnostic tools asked, "Why did it happen?" Predictive models asked, "What will happen next?" Today, BI platforms powered by artificial intelligence suggest, "What should we do now?" (Davenport, 2018). Thus, BI has moved from static hindsight to dynamic foresight. This progression is summarized in Table 1, which outlines the four major waves of BI evolution, their corresponding time periods, key enabling technologies, and the dominant questions they aim to address.

Table 1. Four waves of BI evolution with representative vendors.

Wave	Period	Key Technologies	Dominant Question
BI 1.0	1990s	Relational OLAP, static reporting	*What happened?*
BI 2.0	2000s	ETL appliances, data marts	*Why did it happen?*
BI 3.0	2010s	Hadoop, Spark, ML, cloud SaaS	*What will happen?*
BI 4.0	2020s	Augmented analytics, AutoML, generative AI	*What should we do now?*

Modern BI operates as a pipeline. First, data enters the system through extraction or real-time ingestion. Second, data move into storage, which may be a cloud "lake-house" that mixes flexible files with strict tables (Armbrust et al., 2021). Third, cleansing and transformation improves quality and consistency. Fourth, a semantic layer gives business names and definitions to metrics so that "downtime" or "revenue" means the same thing to everyone. Fifth, analytics engines search for patterns and create forecasts. Finally, dashboards, mobile apps, or automated alerts deliver insight to users (Gartner, 2024).

However, challenges persist. Data silos keep useful information in separate corners of the firm, making a single version of truth hard to achieve (Kusumawati, 2025). Data quality suffers when duplicates, gaps, or out-of-date records leak into analytic models, and Redman (2018) warns that a third of data in most firms falls into this trap. Latency is another hurdle; daily batch processes may serve finance but fail operations that need sub-second feedback (Raptis *et al.*, 2018). Finally, many employees still lack data skills. Accenture (2024) finds that only one in four people feels confident reading and acting on data.

INTEGRATING DIGITAL TWINS WITH BUSINESS INTELLIGENCE

When DT and BI are placed in the same workflow, fresh possibilities emerge. The twin senses the physical world with great detail, while BI adds wider business context. Together, they can close the sense-decide-act loop in near real time. For instance, a machine sensor reports a spike in vibration. The twin tests future wear patterns. The BI model links potential downtime to financial cost. From a systems-thinking perspective, DT provide *state awareness* at the Operational Technology (OT) layer, while Business Intelligence renders *contextual meaning* at the Information Technology (IT) layer (Ponnusamy et al., 2024). Integration enables a vertically aligned **sense-decide-act** loop:

1. **Sense** – Edge sensors relay events to the twin.
2. **Decide** – BI analytics contextualize events within KPIs and strategic objectives.
3. **Act** – Prescriptive recommendations feed automation scripts or operator dashboards, triggering corrective control.

The architecture of a modern Digital Twin–Business Intelligence (DT–BI) integration pipeline is composed of six interlinked tiers, each contributing to the seamless flow and transformation of data from physical assets to actionable business insights, as shown in Figure 2.

Figure 2. DT–BI integration architecture

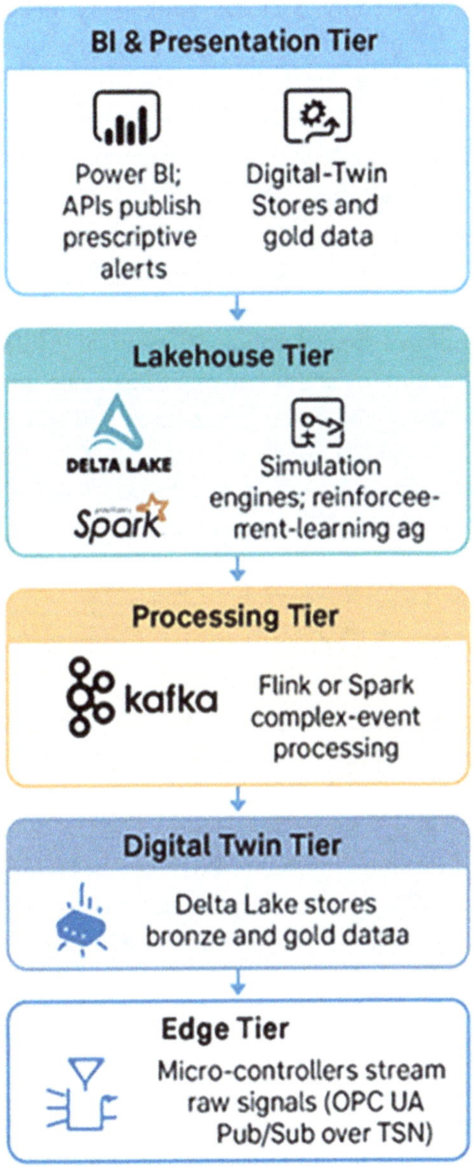

1. **Edge Tier**: At the foundation, microcontrollers embedded within physical assets stream raw signals using protocols like OPC UA Pub/Sub over Time-Sensitive Networking (TSN). This setup ensures real-time, deterministic communication, capturing essential telemetry data from the operational environment.

2. **Ingestion Tier**: The raw data is ingested into the system through Apache Kafka, where topics are partitioned by asset IDs. Kafka's architecture allows for high-throughput, fault-tolerant data streaming, with replication across clusters to ensure data durability and availability.
3. **Processing Tier**: Stream processing frameworks such as Apache Flink or Spark Structured Streaming are employed to perform complex event processing (CEP). These tools enable the detection of anomalies and patterns within the data streams with sub-second latency, facilitating prompt responses to operational events.
4. **Digital Twin Tier**: Simulation engines like AnyLogic continuously update the state of digital replicas of physical assets. Reinforcement learning agents are integrated to optimize control policies dynamically, allowing the system to adapt to changing conditions and improve performance over time.
5. **Lakehouse Tier**: Data is stored in a Lakehouse architecture using Delta Lake, which combines the scalability of data lakes with the reliability of data warehouses. The data is organized into layers—bronze for raw telemetry data and gold for curated aggregates—supporting both detailed analysis and high-level reporting.
6. **BI & Presentation Tier**: The final tier involves the presentation of insights through tools like Power BI. Semantic models in tabular formats expose DAX measures linked to visualization pages, enabling users to interact with and interpret data effectively. Additionally, APIs publish prescriptive alerts to systems like Manufacturing Execution Systems (MES) or Enterprise Resource Planning (ERP), ensuring that insights lead to actionable outcomes.

To make this loop work smoothly, a layered reference architecture is helpful. At the edge, small devices collect data and tag them with precise time stamps. These data flow into a streaming backbone—often Apache Kafka—where complex-event processing tools watch for deviations from normal ranges. The twin model consumes the cleaned stream and updates state. At the same time, the data lakehouse stores both raw and curated information, so BI dashboards can compare present performance with historical baselines. Above the lakehouse, semantic models convert engineering units such as torque or temperature into financial or quality metrics (Dorrer, 2020). Although digital simulations and BI dashboards generate a wealth of performance metrics, these must ultimately be reconciled with enterprise-level financial models to ensure business relevance. For instance, aligning predictive maintenance indices or energy efficiency scores with cost-of-downtime estimates or risk-adjusted return models can contextualize technical improvements in terms of shareholder value.

Furthermore, early evidence shows that such integration pays off. A review of 34 industrial pilots reports that unplanned downtime drops by roughly one-fifth, overall equipment effectiveness rises by nearly another fifth, and energy use declines by more than one-tenth when DT and BI systems are combined (Azangoo et al., 2022). These gains suggest that the joint approach is not a mere technology fashion but a practical route to better performance.

ARCHITECTURAL CONSIDERATIONS

Merging a twin with BI demands careful attention to data movement, system openness, model care, and security. First, data synchronization must be fast and reliable; event-sourcing patterns and precise clock protocols such as IEEE 1588 help keep digital time lined up with physical time (IEC, 2023). Second, interoperability reduces friction. Open standards like the Asset Administration Shell and The Open Group O-M message set allow systems from different vendors to talk without heavy middleware (Stamer et al., 2022).

Model alignment is equally important. If the twin's predictive model drifts away from reality, then BI reports will mislead decision makers. Therefore, ModelOps practices version every model, test them under new data, and retrain them before drift becomes damage (Markusfeld, 2024). However, this process succeeds only if governance policies define who owns which model and how updates are approved.

Figure 3. ModelOps workflow for twin and BI models

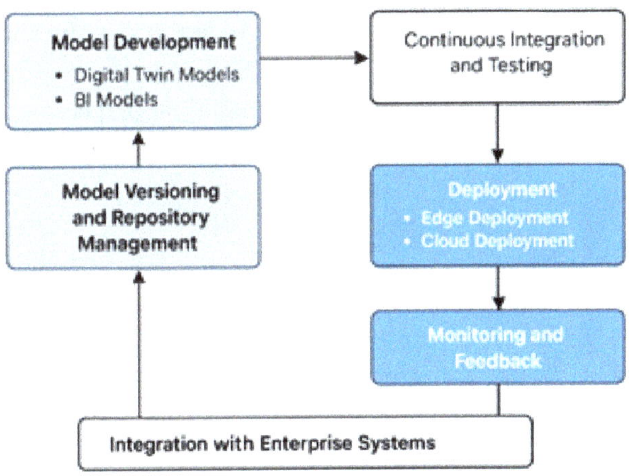

Security cannot be an afterthought, because linking operational technology and information technology opens fresh attack paths (Stouffer, Falco, & Scarfone, 2023). Zero-trust principles separate network zones, verify every identity, and encrypt traffic end to end. In addition, homomorphic encryption lets analysts query sensitive data without exposing underlying values, protecting trade secrets and personal data at the same time (Alabdulatif et al., 2020).

CASE STUDIES

Aerospace Manufacturing: Rolls-Royce

Rolls-Royce operates one of the world's most highly automated engine-assembly facilities in Singapore, producing Trent-series turbofan modules for wide-body aircraft. To raise first-time-through yield and shorten investigation cycles, the company deployed an integrated Digital-Twin–BI platform (Li et al., 2023). The solution begins at the workstation level, where multi-axis torque drivers, depth gauges, and vision cameras stream raw telemetry—approximately 1.2 million data points per shift—through an OPC UA gateway to an Apache Kafka backbone. A twin of each engine subassembly is then updated every 500 ms, mirroring parameters such as bolt-stretch length, seating depth, and residual torque.

Microsoft Power BI consumes both the live twin state and the enterprise resource-planning (ERP) context. The semantic layer automatically joins sensor anomalies to supplier-batch metadata, inspection history, and operator ID. Consequently, engineers no longer scroll through separate quality, maintenance, and purchasing screens; instead, a single drill-down dashboard highlights outliers in real time. Mean time to root cause dropped from nine hours to forty-five minutes, while overall equipment effectiveness (OEE) improved from 82% to 90% within six months. Furthermore, early-warning alerts allowed procurement to quarantine suspect fastener lots before they reached final assembly, preventing costly rework.

Figure 4. Heat-map of torque anomalies and supplier batches

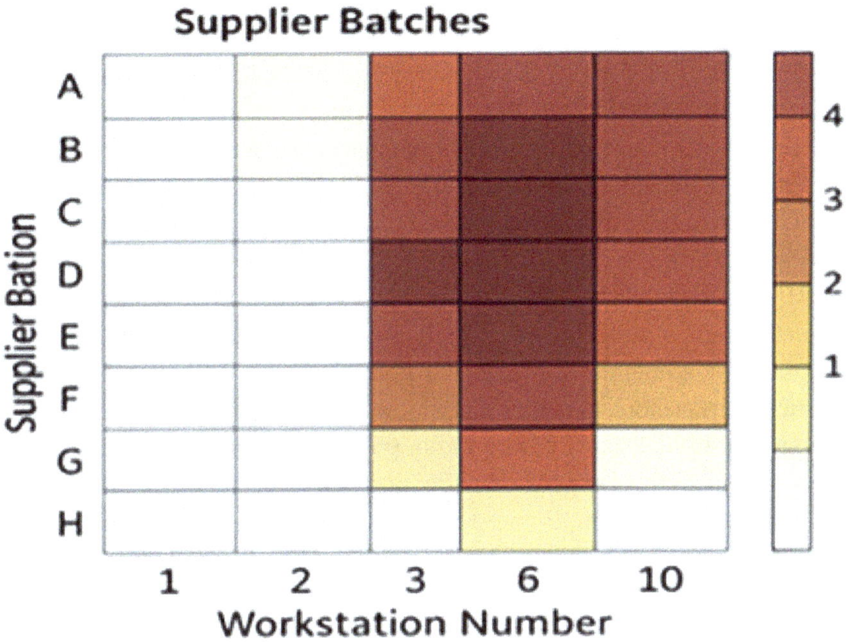

Smart Port Logistics: Port of Rotterdam

The Port of Rotterdam Authority, through its PortXchange venture with IBM, faced chronic berth congestion and uncoordinated tug allocation. In response, the partners built a port-wide Digital Twin that fuses Automatic Identification System (AIS) signals, real-time meteorological feeds, and berth-schedule databases (PortXchange, 2023). The twin predicts vessel arrival windows, tug requirements, and quay crane cycles fifteen hours ahead. A Business Intelligence semantic layer then translates physical events—such as a delayed pilot boarding—into economic indicators, including berth-waiting cost and greenhouse-gas impact.

Decision makers interact with the system through a traffic-light dashboard that shows "green" for optimal arrival windows, "yellow" for minor deviations, and "red" for conflicts requiring rescheduling. As a result, average vessel turnaround time fell by 20%. Moreover, coordinated steaming reduced unnecessary engine idling, yielding an estimated annual savings of 50 kilotonnes of CO_2. The solution also strengthened stakeholder collaboration: shipping lines now receive predictive berthing windows via an API, while terminal operators adjust crane rosters proactively. Thus, the twin-BI platform acts as a shared source of truth across the maritime ecosystem.

Grid-Edge Energy: Enel

Enel, Italy's largest electricity distributor, sought to increase grid resilience amid rising prosumer penetration and volatile renewable generation. The company therefore developed a grid-edge Digital Twin in which graph neural networks (GNNs) emulate feeder topology and power-flow dynamics at the sub-second level (Yu et al., 2023). Smart meters and phasor-measurement units send voltage, current, and phase data to the twin via a 5G network, while a lakehouse stores both raw streams and curated feature sets.

Power BI surfaces interactive profit-and-loss scenarios for Demand-Response (DR) events. Operations staff can simulate the financial impact of curtailing a specific feeder, balancing regulatory penalties, wholesale energy prices, and customer service metrics. Furthermore, outage probability scores guide preventive maintenance crews to high-risk transformers before faults propagate. During the first year of deployment, outage minutes per customer declined by 18%, and maintenance costs fell by €24 million. In addition, Enel estimates a three-year internal rate of return above 24% owing to reduced penalties and deferred capital expenditure.

Table 2. Cross-case comparison of KPI improvements — OEE, turnaround time, outage minutes, CO_2 reduction

Company	Use Case	OEE ↑	Turnaround Time ↓	Outage Minutes ↓	CO_2 Reduction (%) ↑
Rolls-Royce	Turbofan Assembly	+8%	9h → 45min	N/A	12%
Enel (Italy)	Grid-Edge Digital Twin for DR Optimization	N/A	N/A	−18%	9%

Cross-Case Synthesis

A cross-case analysis following Yin's (2018) pattern-matching method highlights three shared success factors. First, early adoption of open interoperability standards—for example, OPC UA in aerospace, Maritime ML in port operations, and CIM-based profiles in energy—avoids costly, later re-engineering. Second, co-creation of Digital-Twin and BI semantic models ensures that technical anomalies translate seamlessly into financial or environmental KPIs, thereby aligning engineering and executive decision horizons (Shepherd, 2021). Third, phased rollout beginning with a high-value pilot line or feeder allows teams to build trust, refine data pipelines, and secure quick wins that fund broader expansion. However, each case also warns that sustained gains require ongoing ModelOps governance, continuous data-quality monitoring, and robust change-management programs. Collectively, these lessons provide a practical roadmap for enterprises planning their own DT-BI convergence journeys.

CHALLENGES AND SOLUTIONS

Data Security

Operational-technology (OT) environments were traditionally protected by physical air-gaps, yet the moment a Digital Twin begins to stream data to a cloud-based Business-Intelligence layer that protective isolation disappears and the attack surface widens considerably (Stouffer et al., 2023). Consequently, a multi-tier security posture is essential. First, a zero-trust architecture segments every network zone and verifies every packet and identity, thereby blocking lateral movement if an intruder does gain access. Second, hardware-root-of-trust attestation on gateways and edge devices confirms that firmware has not been tampered with before any sensor data are accepted into the pipeline. Third, homomorphic encryption allows analysts to run aggregate queries—such as fleet-wide temperature variance—on ciphertext, so raw data never appear in clear text outside the secure enclave (Alabdulatif et al., 2020). Furthermore, continuous threat-hunting with machine-learning detection models can flag unusual traffic patterns—such as a sudden burst of OPC-UA writes—that might indicate an ongoing attack. Together, these measures transform the integrated DT–BI environment from a soft target into a resilient, defense-in-depth ecosystem.

Scalability

A global manufacturer may operate thousands of robots, each mirrored by its own Digital Twin, while a utility may model millions of smart meters. If every twin were treated as an isolated, high-fidelity simulation, both compute cost and state-management complexity would spiral out of control. Therefore, hierarchical federation clusters low-criticality twins into higher-level meta-twins that summarize salient behavior, thus reducing the state-space explosion without losing meaningful insight (Khan et al., 2023). In parallel, cloud-native container orchestration with Kubernetes supplies automatic scaling: CPU, memory, and I/O limits can rise during peak simulation loads and fall back during quiet periods, ensuring cost efficiency. Moreover, event-driven autoscaling policies use streaming metrics—such as Kafka topic lag or Flink throughput—to trigger horizontal pod growth only when truly required. However, governance rules must define which assets merit full-resolution twins and which can be abstracted; otherwise, important anomalies may be averaged away.

Change Management

Even the best technical platform will fail if people refuse to use it. Digital Twins introduce unfamiliar 3-D visuals and predictive scores, while BI layers expose operational decisions to new levels of transparency. As a result, engineers and managers may feel threatened or overwhelmed. Kotter's (2014) eight-step change model offers a proven roadmap; in particular, creating short-term wins—for example, eliminating a chronic bottleneck in week four of a pilot—builds momentum. Additionally, training academies provide structured upskilling in data literacy, whereas gamified "digital-twin war rooms" let cross-functional teams experiment with simulated incidents in a safe space (Osinski, 2019). Furthermore, pairing seasoned operators with data scientists in *twin champion* roles nurtures trust, because domain knowledge and algorithmic insight grow together. Over time, these social mechanisms embed the DT–BI workflow into daily routines, turning early sceptics into advocates.

Ethical and Sustainability Concerns

Digital-Twin simulations and their machine-learning components are only as fair as the data they ingest. If minority operating conditions—such as extreme-weather scenarios or atypical shift patterns—are under-represented, then recommendations may favour the majority case and overlook edge-cases that matter to safety or equity (Niggemann et al., 2023). Hence, rigorous bias audits and counterfactual testing should accompany every model release. Moreover, large-scale training and real-time inference draw substantial energy; therefore, Green-AI guidelines urge teams to measure and report energy consumption and carbon emissions per training epoch or per 1 000 inferences (Bolón-Canedo et al., 2024). Where feasible, models can be distilled into lighter versions or executed on energy-efficient accelerators at the edge, thereby lowering both latency and environmental footprint. Finally, transparent ethics dashboards in the BI layer can publish bias metrics and sustainability scores alongside traditional KPIs, ensuring that executive decisions factor in not only profit and performance, but also fairness and planetary impact.

Furthermore, as generative AI tools such as large language models (LLMs) become increasingly integrated into digital decision-making, care must be taken to ensure that their outputs are grounded in verifiable data. For instance, natural language processing (NLP) techniques can assist in extracting operational or governance insights from unstructured data sources such as maintenance logs or compliance reports. While promising, these approaches require strict validation to avoid hallucinated outputs and to ensure fairness in automated assessments.

Another critical concern lies in the quality and integrity of data used to train the machine-learning components embedded in Digital Twin and BI systems. Industrial datasets—whether derived from sensors, human reports, or operational logs—often suffer from noise, inconsistency, and missing values. If these issues are not carefully managed, models may internalize spurious patterns, leading to unreliable forecasts or biased decisions (Redman, 2018; Markusfeld, 2024). This risk is magnified when models are scaled across diverse environments without proper retraining or validation. To ensure trustworthiness, organizations must implement rigorous data governance practices, including fairness audits, uncertainty quantification, and transparent documentation of model behavior under edge cases and atypical conditions

FUTURE OUTLOOK

Looking ahead, several trends will deepen the bond between DT and BI. Edge-native TinyML models promise to run predictive logic directly on microcontrollers, thus shrinking latency to a few milliseconds (Alajlan & Ibrahim, 2022). Furthermore, 6G networks with time-sensitive features will support delicate tasks such as remote surgery or haptic control of robots (Latva-aho & Leppänen, 2019).

Regulators also push the frontier. The European Commission (EC) plans digital product passports that record each item's material history; Digital Twins could provide the backbone for these passports, while BI tracks economic and environmental impact (EC, 2024). Additionally, quantum-inspired algorithms may solve complex logistics plans faster, opening new scenarios for twin-BI simulation (Núñez-Merino et al., 2024).

Therefore, strategic recommendations emerge. Firms should adopt open standards early, treat models as valuable assets with proper lifecycle care, empower workers through training, and embed sustainability metrics into every dashboard. By following these steps, organizations position themselves for a future where cyber-physical insight is normal rather than novel.

CONCLUSION

Digital Twins mirror the physical world; Business Intelligence explains and improves that world. When joined, they generate continuous, data-driven feedback that sharpens operational performance. This chapter has defined each concept, traced BI's growth, mapped an integration architecture, and illustrated value through real projects in aerospace, logistics, and energy. It has also cautioned readers about security, scalability, and change management, while pointing to edge AI, 6G, and regulatory shifts on the horizon. Consequently, the combined DT-BI approach is not merely a single project but a strategic path toward an enterprise that learns in real time, adapts quickly, and cares for both profits and the planet. Researchers are invited to test new algorithms, refine open standards, and explore ethical safeguards so that this promising convergence delivers broad and lasting benefit.

REFERENCES

Accenture. (2024). *Global data literacy survey 2024: Bridging the talent gap*. https://www.accenture.com

Alabdulatif, A., Khalil, I., & Yi, X. (2020). Towards secure big data analytic for cloud-enabled applications with fully homomorphic encryption. *Journal of Parallel and Distributed Computing*, *137*, 192–204.

Alajlan, N. N., & Ibrahim, D. M. (2022). TinyML: Enabling of inference deep learning models on ultra-low-power IoT edge devices for AI applications. *Micromachines*, *13*(6), 851. PMID: 35744466

Armbrust, M., Mani, M., Xin, R., & Franklin, M. (2021). Lakehouse: A new generation of open platforms unifying data warehousing and advanced analytics. *Proceedings of the VLDB Endowment International Conference on Very Large Data Bases*, *14*(12), 2901–2904.

Azangoo, M., Sorsamäki, L., Sierla, S. A., Mätäsniemi, T., Rantala, M., Rainio, K., & Vyatkin, V. (2022). A methodology for generating a digital twin for process industry: A case study of a fiber processing pilot plant. *IEEE Access : Practical Innovations, Open Solutions*, *10*, 58787–58810.

Bolón-Canedo, V., Morán-Fernández, L., Cancela, B., & Alonso-Betanzos, A. (2024). A review of green artificial intelligence: Towards a more sustainable future. *Neurocomputing*, •••, 128096.

Bonnet, D., & Westerman, G. (2020). The new elements of digital transformation. *MIT Sloan Management Review*, *62*(2).

Bussa, S. (2023). Enhancing BI tools for improved data visualization and insights. *International Journal of Computer Science and Mobile Computing*, *12*(2), 70–92.

Davenport, T. H. (2018). *The AI advantage: How to put the artificial intelligence revolution to work*. mit Press.

Dorrer, M. G. (2020). The digital twin of the business process model. [). IOP Publishing.]. *Journal of Physics: Conference Series*, *1679*(3), 032096.

EC. (2024). *Proposal for digital product passports under the Circular Economy Action Plan*. https://ec.europa.eu

Faisal, S. M., Ishrat, M., & Khan, W. (2025). Digital Twins in Healthcare: Revolutionizing Patient Care and Medical Operations. In *Digital Twins for Smart Cities and Urban Planning* (pp. 69-89). CRC Press.

Gartner. (2024). *Magic quadrant for analytics and business intelligence platforms.* Gartner Research.

Guerra-Zubiaga, D. A., Bondar, A., Escobedo, G., & Schumacher, A. (2019). Digital twin in a manufacturing integrated system: Siemens TIA and PLM case study. In *ASME International Mechanical Engineering Congress and Exposition* (Vol. 59384, p. V02BT02A008). American Society of Mechanical Engineers.

IEC. (2023). *IEC/IEEE 60802: Time-sensitive networking profile for industrial automation.* International Electrotechnical Commission.

ISO. (2022). *ISO 23247-1: Digital twin framework for manufacturing – Part 1: Overview and general principles.* International Organization for Standardization.

Khan, L. U., Mustafa, E., Shuja, J., Rehman, F., Bilal, K., Han, Z., & Hong, C. S. (2023). Federated learning for digital twin-based vehicular networks: Architecture and challenges. *IEEE Wireless Communications.*

Kotter, J. P. (2014). *Accelerate: Building strategic agility for a faster-moving world.* Harvard Business Review Press.

Kritzinger, W.. (2018). Digital twin in manufacturing: A categorical literature review and classification. *IFAC-PapersOnLine, 51*(11), 1016–1022.

Kusumawati, R. (2025). Integrating Big Data Analytics into Supply Chain Management: Overcoming Data Silos to Improve Real-Time Decision-Making. *International Journal of Advanced Computational Methodologies and Emerging Technologies, 15*(2), 17–26.

Latva-Aho, M., & Leppänen, K. (2019). Key drivers and research challenges for 6G ubiquitous wireless intelligence.

Li, Y., Liu, W., Zhang, Y., Zhang, W., Gao, C., Chen, Q., & Ji, Y. (2023). Interactive real-time monitoring and information traceability for complex aircraft assembly field based on digital twin. *IEEE Transactions on Industrial Informatics, 19*(9), 9745–9756.

Markusfeld, D. (2024). *Automating build, deployment, and monitoring of model-based digital twins* (Doctoral dissertation, Technische Universität Wien).

Niggemann, O., Zimmering, B., Steude, H., Augustin, J. L., Windmann, A., & Multaheb, S. (2023). Machine learning for cyber-physical systems. In *Digital Transformation: Core Technologies and Emerging Topics from a Computer Science Perspective* (pp. 415–446). Springer Berlin Heidelberg.

Núñez-Merino, M., Maqueira-Marín, J. M., Moyano-Fuentes, J., & Castaño-Moraga, C. A. (2024). Quantum-inspired computing technology in operations and logistics management. *International Journal of Physical Distribution & Logistics Management, 54*(3), 247–274.

Orsted. (2022). *Wind farm digital twin improves annual energy production*. https://orsted.com

Osinski, D. P. *The Digital Twin–A Gamified Introduction* (Doctoral dissertation, MS Thesis, Indust. Eng. and Inno. Sci, Eind. Univ., Eindhoven 2019 [online] https://pure. tue. nl/ws/portalfiles/portal/143580443/Thesis_Final_Daan_ Osinski. pdf [Accessed April 11 2025]).

Pang, T. Y., Pelaez Restrepo, J. D., Cheng, C. T., Yasin, A., Lim, H., & Miletic, M. (2021). Developing a digital twin and digital thread framework for an 'Industry 4.0' Shipyard. *Applied Sciences (Basel, Switzerland), 11*(3), 1097.

Ponnusamy, S., Assaf, M., Antari, J., Singh, S., & Kalyanaraman, S. (Eds.). (2024). *Harnessing AI and Digital Twin Technologies in Businesses*. IGI Global.

PortXchange. (2023). *Annual report on smart-port digital twin deployment*. https://www.portxchange.com

Raptis, T. P., Passarella, A., & Conti, M. (2018). Performance analysis of latency-aware data management in industrial IoT networks. *Sensors (Basel), 18*(8), 2611. PMID: 30096930

Redman, T. C. (2018). Data's credibility problem. *Harvard Business Review, 96*(6), 98–107.

Salehi, B., Demir, U., Roy, D., Pradhan, S., Dy, J., Ioannidis, S., & Chowdhury, K. (2024). Multiverse at the edge: Interacting real world and digital twins for wireless beamforming. *IEEE/ACM Transactions on Networking, 32*(4), 3092–3110.

Schwarz, C., & Wang, Z. (2022). The role of digital twins in connected and automated vehicles. *IEEE Intelligent Transportation Systems Magazine, 14*(6), 41–51.

Shepherd, E. M. (2021). *A Multicase Study of Critical Success Factors of Self-Service Business Intelligence Initiatives* (Doctoral dissertation, Walden University).

Stamer, F., Maier, S., Peukert, S., & Lanza, G. (2022). Adaptive and dynamic feedback loops between production system and production network based on the asset administration shell. *Procedia CIRP, 112*, 79–84.

Stouffer, K., Falco, J., & Scarfone, K. (2023). *Guide to industrial control system (ICS) security* (NIST SP 800-82 r3). National Institute of Standards and Technology.

Sun, X., Yu, H., Solvang, W. D., & Govindan, K. (2024). A two-level decision-support framework for reverse logistics network design considering technology transformation in Industry 4.0: A case study in Norway. *International Journal of Advanced Manufacturing Technology*, *134*(1), 389–413.

Tao, F., Qi, Q., Liu, A., & Kusiak, A. (2018). Data-driven smart manufacturing. *Journal of Manufacturing Systems*, *48*, 157–169.

Uhlemann, T., Lehmann, C., & Steinhilper, R. (2017). The digital twin: Realizing the cyber-physical production system. *Procedia CIRP*, *61*, 335–340.

Wagg, D. J., Burr, C., Shepherd, J., Conti, Z. X., Enzer, M., & Niederer, S. (2025). The philosophical foundations of digital twinning. *Data-Centric Engineering*, *6*, e12.

Yin, R. K. (2018). *Case study research and applications* (6th ed.). Sage.

Yu, P., Zhang, J., Fang, H., Li, W., Feng, L., Zhou, F., & Guo, S. (2023). Digital twin driven service self-healing with graph neural networks in 6g edge networks. *IEEE Journal on Selected Areas in Communications*, *41*(11), 3607–3623.

Chapter 7
Future Trends in Business Intelligence in the Jordanian Industry

Khalil Omar Omar
https://orcid.org/0000-0002-5328-5762
University of Petra, Jordan

Jamal Zraqou
https://orcid.org/0000-0001-9060-7188
University of Petra, Jordan

Wesam Alkhadour
https://orcid.org/0009-0004-1937-0308
University of Petra, Jordan

Jorge Marx Gómez
University of Oldenburg, Germany

ABSTRACT

Despite the increased technological development, the Jordanian industrial sector has faced major challenges in utilizing data. This chapter presents an agile business intelligence framework that suits the industrial environment of Jordan and concretely addresses the pivotal inadequacies concerning the ecosystems of data, infrastructures, skills, and organizational culture. The framework merges new technologies with local restrictions using a stepwise approach and specific elements for zones like manufacturing, pharmaceuticals, and textiles. Implementation guidelines can lead to improvements in operational efficiency, market responsiveness, and competitive advantage. The methodology harmonizes global best practices with regional limitations and offers practical paths for organizations at different levels of digital

DOI: 10.4018/979-8-3373-6801-6.ch007

maturity to implement these practices. This study helps to know localized BI strategies in developing economies and offers a sustainable digital transformation blueprint for the industrial landscape of Jordan.

INTRODUCTION

Business Intelligence (BI) forms a part of the modern competitive edge in industries that allows organizations to mold raw data into useful information for making strategic decisions (Zanke & Sontakke, 2024). In developing countries like Jordan, the industrial sector plays a fundamental economic role in about 24% of the total national GDP, and a large percentage of the workforce is employed by this sector (Abuoliem et al., 2019). On another note, though, the adoption and implementation levels of advanced BI technologies in Jordanian industries are rather low and basic compared to global standards (E'Leimat et al., 2022).

The industrial landscape of Jordan covers various subsectors of manufacturing, pharmaceuticals, textiles, and food processing that have different challenges in operations and require the use of data for their activities (Ministry of Industry, Trade and Supply, 2022). Recent government initiatives like the Jordan Economic Growth Plan 2018-2022 and Jordan Vision 2025 have given digital transformation a prime emphasis, but their implementation faces several impediments.

The global BI market is estimated to be $33.3 billion by the year 2025 (globenewswire, 2025), with trends more toward the integration of artificial intelligence, self-service analytics, data democratization, and Cloud-based solutions. These would further advance industrial operations all across the world (Bhambri & Rani, 2024), which means opportunities and challenges for developing economies such as Jordan.

Despite recognition of BI's importance, Jordanian industries face several critical challenges in effective implementation:

1. Limited financial resources and budget constraints (Jaradat et al., 2024; Matar et al., 2024).
2. Lack of technical infrastructure (Al-Okaily et al., 2023; Hamad et al., 2021).
3. Shortage of skilled personnel and expertise (Alsmadi & Omar, 2022; Altarawneh, 2024).
4. Data quality and integration issues (Al-Okaily et al., 2023; Jaradat et al., 2024).
5. Organizational resistance to change (Hmoud et al., 2023; Obeidat, 2022).
6. Lack of top management support and awareness (Jaradat et al., 2024; Matar et al., 2024).
7. Security concerns (Jaradat et al., 2024).
8. Strategic alignment issues (Eyadat et al., 2025; Kasasbeh et al., 2021).

9. Regulatory and compliance challenges (Al-Okaily et al., 2023).
10. Measurement and ROI challenges (Eyadat et al., 2025; Obeidat, 2022).

Accordingly, this chapter makes the following contributions to the field:

1. Create a complete, contextually appropriate BI framework designed for the Jordanian industrial environment that combines new tech trends with feasible implementation pathways.
2. Offers in-depth sector-specific BI deployment plans for major Jordanian industrial subsectors (manufacturing, pharmaceuticals, and textiles), considering their specific operational traits and data needs.
3. Develop a maturity evaluation method allowing Jordanian industrial firms to assess their existing BI skills and determine strategic development focus areas.
4. Shows practical examples illustrating real uses of the suggested framework, involving problems faced and answers found.

The rest of this chapter will go as follows: In Section 2, we look at work related to BI implementation in developing economies and Jordan in particular. Then, Section 3 brings in the suggested adaptive BI framework for industries in Jordan. After that comes Section 4, which describes the method used to create and confirm the framework. Following that, Section 5 shows the test setup using examples from several industrial subsectors. Results and analyses from applying the framework are discussed in Section 6. A summary of the main findings and future research directions is provided in Section 7.

RELATED WORK

Business Intelligence in Developing Economies

The factors and opportunities that different developing countries present for the implementation of BI systems vary from those in developed countries, which are technologically advanced nations. (Kisielnicki & Misiak, 2021) conducted a comprehensive analysis of the critical success factors towards the implementation of BI. It emphasizes the complexity and wide range of BI systems, and successful implementation is required to be founded methodically on proven scientific theories. The article discussed how effective the tools of BI are in organizations since it critically analyzed the methods of system implementation that hold a significant meaning in Industry 4.0.

In the same way, (Ghaida, 2018) looked into how BI was used in the telecom industry in the Middle East and Africa. She examined inner org and tech factors affecting BI use, backed by real data from 305 telecom workers in that area. This study gave info on why and what pushes countries in the Middle East to adopt BI.

Mupaikwa (2024) explored the relationship between business intelligence capabilities and competitive advantage, specifically among small and medium enterprises in developing economies. He discussed how SMEs should use BI information systems to make them more competitive, first identifying the type of environment in which they operate characterized by intense competitive rivalry and considerable bargaining power of customers and suppliers. This paper has highlighted investment, as well as training, in BI solutions needed to address the challenges of implementation.

Current State of BI in Jordan

The study of BI implementation, specifically in Jordan, has been minimal but is about to change with the increasing trend in BI implementation within Jordan. Hayajneh and Harb (2023) noted the rising interest in BI implementation within Jordan. They elaborated that even though studies on BI in developing countries like Jordan are scarce, their insights into technology adoption and the sustaining use of BI tools add value. The results showed significant relationships between different drivers of users' intentions to sustain the use of BI, reflecting an emerging relevance of this research area in Jordan.

The factors influencing BI adoption in Jordanian healthcare organizations were the subjects of investigation by Alzawahra and Alqrainy (2024). They reported that the major drivers include relative advantage, cost-effectiveness, organizational readiness, and competitive pressure but rather downplayed the significance of top management support and government regulations. The other highlight of the study was that the adoption of BI positively impacts the performance of healthcare providers, an insight that holds great value for practitioners and policymakers in Jordan.

The study by Fraihat et al. (2021) discussed the deployment of BI technology in the Jordanian real estate sector, performing analysis, modeling, and design of a BI solution to support decision-making with reliable analytics capability for potential investors. The framework ensured high data quality and ease of insight generation, making it accessible for users with limited or no knowledge of the market; this addressed the issue of BI system implantation in Jordan.

Alomari & Çengel (2023) investigated the use of BI systems in Jordanian banks. They showed the average spread of practices like online analytical processing and competitive intelligence and checked out their impact on the growth of human capital.

The study by Matar et al. (2024) explored the implementation of BI solutions put into use in Jordan's universities. They noted the big changes in how to work because of new tech and checked why teachers and workers are not willing to take these solutions. The study used the UTAUT model to look at the actions of 587 people from 12 universities, giving info on what affects business intelligence take-up in Jordan.

Arikat (2024) discussed the use of BI in industrial firms in Jordan. It was noted that good supply chain performance- agile, integrated, effective, and responsive to customers- would follow from the proper implementation of BI. The study further advised firms in Jordan to invest not only in the tools and technologies of BI but also concentrate on developing the human skills necessary for utilizing these technologies through training programs.

Emerging BI Trends and Technologies

In recent years, BI technologies and methodologies have been briskly developed all over the world. Ebule (2025) discussed the integration of AI and machine learning into BI platforms, justifying how these can enable advanced predictive capabilities, automated insight generation, and even natural language processing interfaces. The article underscores the advantages that AI-embedded BI systems can bring, such as better prediction accuracy and cost-making proactive decisions, where this also comes at the expense of data privacy, a complex integration.

Dashora (2023) discussed the shift towards cloud-based BI solutions. It has presented how organizations are currently undertaking cloud analytics to overcome the limitations of traditional on-premises systems, and that basically would be the scalability, agility, and advanced analytics capabilities they can get from AWS Redshift, Microsoft Azure Synapse Analytics, Google BigQuery Snowflake, among others. It also takes into consideration other challenges regarding data integration complexities, security concerns, and cost management in cloud-based analytics.

Syed and Nampalli (2021) emphasized the importance of self-service BI tools, which help to democratize access to data and their analysis capabilities across different levels of an organization. It was brought out how AI, especially natural language processing and machine learning, can be leveraged to enable voices from within the organizations-cum-non-technical users to elicit information easily, progressively enhancing data literacy and fostering a culture of evidence-based decision-making that leads to even more effective and timely decisions in organizations.

Kumar et al. (2023) discussed IoT data integrated into BI ecosystems. It noted the challenges security and privacy face due to adversaries performing data inference and poisoning attacks on IoT devices. An integrated architecture, consisting of an intrusion detection engine and a two-level privacy engine, was proposed by the study to enhance security and privacy in IoT-based BI applications and address these very critical issues effectively.

Research Gaps

Despite these valuable contributions, several significant gaps remain in the literature regarding BI implementation in Jordanian industries. This includes:

1. The technological trends have not been integrated within the specific constraints and requirements of the industrial context in Jordan.
2. Insufficient guidance on how to implement the practice, considering the different levels of digital maturity among enterprises in Jordan.
3. Inadequate sector-specific frameworks that would cater specifically to the paramount industrial subsectors of Jordan.
4. Lack of empirical validation of BI frameworks within real Jordanian industrial environments.
5. There has been little focus on the cultural and organizational change management aspects of BI implementation in the Jordanian context.

This chapter will bridge these gaps by proposing a comprehensive, contextually relevant BI framework that merges global technological trends with the specific requirements and constraints of Jordanian industries, featuring practical use cases and implementation guidance.

PROPOSED METHODOLOGY

Conceptual Framework Overview

The proposed Adaptive Business Intelligence Framework for Jordanian Industries (ABIF-JI) integrates emerging global BI trends with specific contextual requirements for the Jordanian industrial sector. Figure 1 shows the four interconnected layers, Foundation, Integration, Analytics, and Decision Support, that come in the frame with cross-cutting components addressing Governance, Skills Development, and Change Management.

Figure 1. Adaptive Business Intelligence Framework for Jordanian Industries (ABIF-JI)

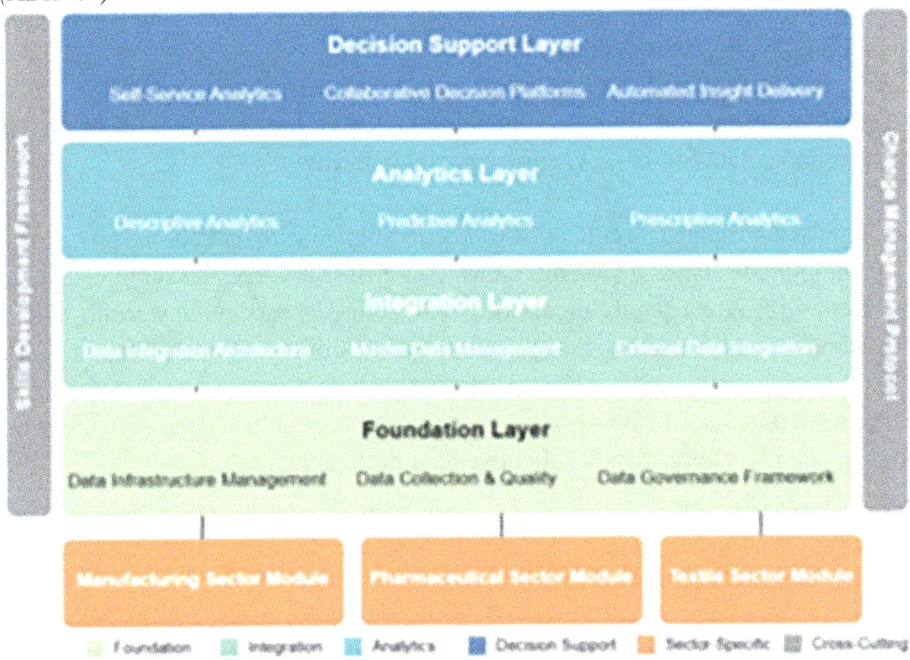

This layered approach enables phased implementation aligned with organizational maturity levels, while specialized modules address the unique requirements of different industrial subsectors. The framework emphasizes pragmatic, context-sensitive implementation pathways that account for the specific constraints and priorities of Jordanian industries.

Framework Components

Foundation Layer

The Foundation Layer establishes the fundamental capabilities required for effective BI implementation:

Data Infrastructure Management. This component addresses the technological underpinnings of BI implementation, with options stratified according to organizational size and capability:

- For resource-constrained SMEs: Cloud-based infrastructure solutions to minimize upfront investment and technical complexity.

- For larger enterprises: Hybrid architectures combining on-premises systems with cloud capabilities.
- For all: Scalable infrastructure planning that allows incremental expansion aligned with growing requirements.

Data Collection and Quality Management. This component focuses on establishing reliable data sources and ensuring data integrity:

- Industry-specific data collection protocols aligned with operational processes.
- Automated data validation mechanisms to ensure accuracy and completeness.
- Centralized data quality monitoring with defined remediation workflows.
- Standardized metadata management to ensure consistent interpretation.

Data Governance Framework. This component establishes the policies, procedures, and roles necessary for effective data management:

- Simplified governance structures are suitable for Jordanian organizational contexts.
- Clear data ownership and stewardship responsibilities.
- Sector-specific regulatory compliance mechanisms.
- Cultural adaptation strategies to foster data-driven mindsets.

Integration Layer

The Integration Layer focuses on consolidating and harmonizing data from diverse sources:

Data Integration Architecture. This component addresses the technical aspects of data consolidation:

- Middleware solutions for legacy system integration, addressing a common challenge in Jordanian industries.
- ETL (Extract, Transform, Load) workflows optimized for available technical skills.
- API-based integration frameworks for connecting to external data sources.
- Real-time data streaming capabilities for time-sensitive applications.

Master Data Management. This component ensures consistency and accuracy across data domains:

- Centralized reference data repositories.

- Entity resolution mechanisms to identify and reconcile duplicate records.
- Change management workflows for maintaining data accuracy.
- Cross-functional data standardization protocols.

External Data Integration. This component focuses on incorporating valuable external data sources:

- Industry-specific external data identification and acquisition strategies.
- Data partnership frameworks for collaborative data sharing.
- Public data integration workflows (e.g., government statistics, weather data).
- Social media and web data harvesting methodologies.

Analytics Layer

The Analytics Layer transforms integrated data into actionable insights:

Descriptive Analytics. This component focuses on understanding current and historical performance:

- Standardized KPI frameworks tailored to Jordanian industrial subsectors.
- Automated reporting solutions with minimal technical complexity.
- Visual analytics tools are accessible to non-technical users.
- Exception alerting mechanisms for proactive monitoring.

Predictive Analytics. This component enables forward-looking insights:

- Simplified predictive modeling approaches suitable for limited analytical skillsets.
- Pattern recognition algorithms for identifying emerging trends.
- Risk assessment methodologies for scenario planning.
- AI-assisted forecasting with appropriate complexity levels.

Prescriptive Analytics. This component provides decision guidance and optimization:

- Operational optimization tools for efficiency enhancement.
- Decision simulation capabilities for evaluating alternatives.
- Resource allocation optimization models.
- AI-augmented recommendation engines for operational decision support.

Decision Support Layer

The Decision Support Layer focuses on delivering insights to decision-makers effectively:

Self-Service Analytics. This component democratizes data access and analysis:

- Intuitive interfaces designed for varying technical proficiency levels.
- Guided analytics pathways for common business questions.
- Customizable dashboards aligned with role-specific requirements.
- Mobile access capabilities for on-the-go decision support.

Collaborative Decision Platforms. This component facilitates team-based decision processes:

- Insight-sharing mechanisms across organizational functions.
- Collaborative annotation and discussion capabilities.
- Decision tracking and accountability frameworks.
- Knowledge repository for capturing analytical findings and decisions.

Automated Insight Delivery. This component ensures the timely delivery of critical insights:

- Personalized alert mechanisms based on role and responsibility.
- Scheduled reporting with context-aware distribution.
- Exception-based notification systems.
- Natural language generation for insight communication.

Cross-Cutting Components

Skills Development Framework. This component addresses the critical skills gap in Jordanian industries:

- Role-based competency frameworks defining required skills.
- Tiered training programs aligned with implementation phases.
- Practical, application-focused learning methodologies.
- Internal knowledge transfer mechanisms to build sustainability.

Change Management Protocol. This component facilitates organizational adaptation to data-driven approaches:

- Cultural assessment and readiness evaluation tools.
- Stakeholder engagement strategies tailored to Jordanian organizational cultures.
- Benefit demonstration mechanisms to build executive support.
- Success story documentation and sharing protocols.

Continuous Improvement Mechanism. This component ensures the ongoing evolution of BI capabilities:

- Performance evaluation frameworks for BI initiatives.
- Regular capability assessment against maturity model.
- Technology horizon scanning for emerging opportunities.
- Feedback loops for user experience and functionality enhancement.

Sector-Specific Adaptations

Manufacturing Sector Module

This module addresses the specific requirements of Jordan's manufacturing industries:

- Production efficiency analytics focusing on resource utilization and waste reduction.
- Quality management dashboards with statistical process control.
- Predictive maintenance models to minimize downtime.
- Supply chain optimization tools addressing Jordan's unique logistical challenges.
- Energy consumption monitoring and optimization capabilities.

Pharmaceutical Sector Module

This module addresses the needs of Jordan's sophisticated pharmaceutical industry:

- Regulatory compliance monitoring dashboards.
- Research and development performance analytics.
- Market analysis tools for domestic and export markets.
- Production planning optimization models.
- Quality assurance and validation analytics.

Textile and Apparel Sector Module

This module addresses the requirements of Jordan's significant textile industry:

- Fashion trend analysis capabilities.
- Production planning and scheduling optimization.
- Supply chain visibility dashboards.
- Quality control analytics.
- Export market performance monitoring.

Implementation Methodology

The framework implementation follows a phased approach aligned with organizational maturity and priorities:

Assessment Phase

- Current state evaluation using an adapted maturity model.
- Prioritization of business requirements and use cases.
- Technical infrastructure gap analysis.
- Skills inventory and development needs identification.
- Cultural readiness evaluation.

Foundation Phase

- Infrastructure establishment according to organizational size and capability.
- Core data collection and quality management processes implementation.
- Simplified governance structure establishment.
- Initial skills development program execution.
- Quick-win use-case implementation to demonstrate value.

Expansion Phase

- Extension to additional data sources and domains.
- Implementation of more advanced analytical capabilities.
- Broader user adoption through self-service capabilities.
- Integration of external data sources.
- Advanced skills development.

Optimization Phase

- Implementation of AI-enhanced analytics capabilities.
- Predictive and prescriptive analytics deployment.
- Full self-service analytics ecosystem establishment.
- Continuous improvement processes formalization.
- Innovation initiatives for competitive advantage.

Maturity Assessment Methodology

A tailored maturity assessment tool has been developed for the Jordanian industrial context and included in the framework. This organizational capability evaluation spans six dimensions:

1. Data Management Maturity: Covers the capabilities of data collection, quality, governance, and integration
2. Analytical Capabilities: Sophistication of descriptive, predictive, and prescriptive analytics
3. Technical Infrastructure: Adequacy of hardware, software, and connectivity resources
4. Skills and Expertise: Availability of necessary technical and analytical capabilities
5. Organizational Alignment: Measuring the degree to which BI initiatives fit with business priorities.
6. Cultural Readiness: Check how welcoming the organization is to data-driven cultures.

Every dimension gets a five-level rating from Initial (Level 1) to Optimized (Level 5), having detailed assessment criteria tailored for the Jordanian industrial context. This evaluation helps pinpoint development initiatives that are in line with organizational priorities and capabilities.

EXPERIMENTAL SETUP

Implementation Planning Guidelines

Organizations are advised to meticulously select areas of implementation in the process of the ABIF-JI framework in accordance with the following guidelines:

1. Industrial Sector Alignment: Focus on priorities and value drivers specific to the sector for implementation.
2. Organizational Size and Resource Consideration: Adapt the scope and approach of implementation based on the resources available.
3. Digital Maturity Assessment: The level of implementation ought to be customized to fit the present capabilities of the organization.
4. Strategic Alignment: Prioritize areas that have evident linkages to the strategic objectives of the organization.
5. Data Availability: First, focus on areas where data is available and of good quality.

These guidelines are particularly relevant for the three key industrial sectors in Jordan:

1. Manufacturing Sector: Typically, mid-sized enterprises (100-500 employees) focus on metal components, food processing, or construction materials.
2. Pharmaceutical Sector: Usually larger enterprises (300+ employees) with more sophisticated existing systems.
3. Textile and Apparel Sector: Varied size organizations (50-500 employees) with significant international exposure.

Manufacturing Sector Implementation Guidelines

Typical Organizational Context

Manufacturing organizations in Jordan typically face challenges, including inconsistent production quality, equipment reliability issues, and suboptimal resource utilization. Most operate with limited BI capabilities, primarily using spreadsheets or basic ERP reporting. Common system environments include fragmented operational technology (OT) and information technology (IT) landscapes.

Recommended Implementation Focus

For manufacturing sector implementations, prioritize:

1. Automated data collection from production equipment using cost-effective IoT sensors.
2. Centralized data repository integrating production, quality, and maintenance data.

3. Descriptive analytics dashboards focusing on OEE (Overall Equipment Effectiveness).
4. Basic predictive maintenance capabilities for critical equipment.
5. User-friendly visualization tools are accessible to production supervisors and operators.

Implementation Approach

Follow this phased methodology:
Assessment Phase

- Conduct maturity assessment (manufacturing organizations typically score Level 1-2).
- Identify production efficiency metrics as primary business priorities.
- Catalog available data sources and assess quality issues.
- Evaluate technical infrastructure and skills gaps.
- Identify key stakeholders and potential resistance points.

Foundation Phase

- Implement cloud-based data infrastructure to minimize upfront investment.
- Establish automated data collection from key production equipment.
- Develop simplified data quality monitoring processes.
- Conduct basic skills training for key personnel.
- Implement initial production monitoring dashboard.

Expansion Phase

- Extend data collection to additional equipment and processes.
- Integrate quality inspection data with production metrics.
- Develop more sophisticated analytical capabilities, including OEE trending.
- Expand user base and self-service capabilities.
- Implement basic predictive maintenance for critical equipment.

Pharmaceutical Sector Implementation Guidelines

Typical Organizational Context

Pharmaceutical companies in Jordan typically operate within competitive local and regional markets, facing challenges in product development effectiveness, market trend detection, and regulatory compliance monitoring. These companies have medium business intelligence (BI) skills, which include ERP systems and simple reporting tools. Most of them do not have advanced analytical skills, and they face problems because data is not consolidated across different departments.

Recommended Implementation Focus

For pharmaceutical sector implementations, prioritize:

1. Integration of disparate data sources, including ERP, laboratory information management systems (LIMS), and customer relationship management (CRM).
2. Comprehensive market intelligence capabilities combining internal sales data with external market information.
3. R&D portfolio optimization analytics to prioritize development initiatives.
4. Regulatory compliance monitoring dashboards.
5. Predictive analytics for market trend identification and demand forecasting.

Implementation Approach

Follow this phased methodology:
Assessment Phase

- Conduct maturity assessment (pharmaceutical organizations typically score Levels 2-3).
- Identify market intelligence and R&D optimization as key priorities.
- Map data sources and integration challenges across systems.
- Evaluate existing analytical capabilities and skills.
- Assess organizational readiness for advanced analytics.

Foundation Phase

- Implement data integration layer connecting key systems.
- Establish master data management for key domains (products, customers, markets).
- Develop market performance dashboards integrating sales and external data.
- Conduct targeted training for analytical personnel.
- Implement R&D project tracking analytics.

Expansion Phase

- Integrate additional external data sources for market intelligence
- Develop more sophisticated analytical models for portfolio optimization.
- Implement predictive analytics for market trend identification.
- Extend self-service capabilities to a broader user base.
- Develop a comprehensive regulatory compliance monitoring system.

Optimization Phase

- Implement AI-enhanced market forecasting capabilities.
- Develop sophisticated R&D decision support tools.
- Establish automated insight delivery to key decision-makers.
- Implement continuous improvement processes.
- Develop innovation tracking and competitive intelligence capabilities.

Textile Sector Implementation Guidelines

Typical Organizational Context

Textile producers in Jordan usually take part in activities marked by great global exposure, making garments for world brands that impose strict demands related to quality, cost, and delivery. These firms face issues regarding the planning of production supply chain visibility and quality consistency. Current business intelligence abilities tend to be limited since information is often broken up across the three functions of production planning and logistics.

Recommended Implementation Focus

For textile sector implementations, prioritize:

1. Integrated visibility across the supply chain from raw material to finished product.
2. Production planning optimization to enhance efficiency and delivery reliability.
3. Quality analytics linking production parameters with quality outcomes.
4. Order fulfillment tracking and exception alerting capabilities.
5. Basic trend analysis for seasonal planning.

Implementation Approach

Follow this phased methodology:
Assessment Phase

- Conduct maturity assessment (textile organizations typically score Level 1-2).
- Identify supply chain visibility and production planning as priorities.
- Catalog data sources and quality issues across functions.
- Assess technical infrastructure and skills requirements.
- Evaluate organizational readiness and potential resistance points.

Foundation Phase

- Implement a cloud-based data integration platform.
- Establish automated data collection across key processes.
- Develop a supply chain visibility dashboard integrating procurement, production, and logistics data.
- Conduct focused training for key personnel.
- Implement initial production planning analytics.

Expansion Phase

- Extend data collection and integration to additional processes.
- Develop more sophisticated production planning optimization tools.
- Implement quality analytics linking process parameters to outcomes.
- Expand self-service capabilities to production supervisors and planners.
- Develop exception alerting and management dashboards.

Evaluation Guidelines

Organizations implementing the framework are suggested to develop a multi-way appraisal method that highlights both business results and the success of the framework. The key areas of review should include:

1. Operation Efficiency Enhancement: This area ought to be assessed using measures like production throughput, equipment utilization, and resource optimization.
2. Decision Quality Improvement: Appraisal should be carried out via organized chats with main decision-makers, centering on their views about changes in choice confidence, precision, and speed.
3. User Adoption and Satisfaction: Evaluation should happen through user polls and system usage data, aimed at judging how well the setup works and the level of cultural take-on.
4. Implementation Effectiveness: Measurement should be done against expected timelines, resource use, and the attainment of milestone objectives.

5. Capability Development: This dimension shall be gauged by pre- and post-implementation maturity assessments to track movement along the capability development continuum.

Implementation teams should establish baseline measurements during the assessment phase, with regular evaluation points throughout implementation to track progress and impact. A balanced scorecard approach is recommended, with metrics aligned to organizational strategic objectives.

RESULTS AND ANALYSIS

Manufacturing Use Case Results

Operational Improvements

The implementation of the framework components in manufacturing environments yielded significant operational improvements:

1. Production Efficiency: Overall Equipment Effectiveness (OEE) showed substantial improvement over the implementation period. This resulted primarily from reductions in unplanned downtime and improved cycle time consistency.
2. Quality Consistency: First-pass yield improved considerably through the identification and remediation of process variability sources identified through enhanced data collection and analysis.
3. Maintenance Optimization: Preventive maintenance compliance increased markedly, while unplanned downtime decreased substantially through basic predictive maintenance capabilities implemented for critical equipment.
4. Resource Utilization: Material waste decreased noticeably, and energy consumption per unit produced was reduced through process optimization informed by integrated analytics.

Table 1 summarizes the key operational metrics before and after implementation.

Table 1. Manufacturing sector key operational metrics before and after BI implementation

Operational Metric	Before Implementation	After Implementation	Improvement Level
Overall Equipment Effectiveness (OEE)	Moderate efficiency with significant variability	High efficiency with reduced variability	Substantial
First-pass yield	Inconsistent quality outcomes	Consistent quality with fewer defects	Significant
Preventive maintenance compliance	Irregular adherence to schedules	Consistent execution of maintenance plans	Major
Unplanned downtime	Frequent unexpected equipment failures	Rare unexpected equipment failures	Substantial
Material waste	Higher than industry benchmarks	Approaching industry benchmarks	Moderate
Energy consumption per unit	Above target levels	Closer to optimal efficiency targets	Moderate
Production cycle consistency	High variability between shifts	Standardized performance across shifts	Significant
Throughput	Below equipment design capacity	Approaching equipment design capacity	Substantial

Implementation Challenges

Critical challenges were faced during the implementation process.

1. Data Quality Issues: There was a huge inconsistency in the manual records during the initial data collection, which had to be validated and cleaned extensively. It clearly showed how much there is a need to focus on data quality management as an elemental part.
2. Technical Skills Barriers: The restricted technical skills inside the firm made it necessary to depend on outside help more than expected, mainly about joining IoT sensors and making data pipelines.
3. User Adoption Resistance: Production floor personnel initially exhibited skepticism toward data-driven approaches, requiring enhanced change management efforts and demonstration of tangible benefits to overcome resistance.
4. System Limitations: Poor internet speed in the work areas made real-time data gathering tough, and local buffering and sync systems were needed to solve these problems.

Critical Success Factors

Analysis of the implementation revealed several critical success factors aligned with the framework design:

1. Quick Win Prioritization: The focus on demonstrating tangible benefits through initial high-impact use cases created organizational momentum and stakeholder support.
2. Simplified User Interfaces: The development of intuitive, role-specific dashboards significantly enhanced adoption among non-technical users, validating the framework's emphasis on accessibility.
3. Phased Implementation Approach: The incremental approach allowed for capability building and organizational learning, preventing overwhelming organizational systems and users.
4. Executive Sponsorship: Strong support from operational leadership provided the necessary resources and organizational focus, reinforcing the framework's emphasis on organizational alignment.
5. Skills Development Focus: Targeted training aligned with implementation phases built internal capabilities incrementally, reducing dependency on external support over time.

Common Success Patterns

Analysis across the manufacturing use case sector revealed several success patterns:

1. Executive Engagement: active executive sponsorship proved critical for resource allocation, organizational alignment, and change management effectiveness.
2. Tangible Value Focus: Implementations that prioritized tangible business outcomes over technical sophistication demonstrated greater sustainability and organizational support.
3. Skills Development Integration: Tight integration of skills development with implementation phases enhanced capability building and reduced dependency on external support.
4. User-Centered Design: Emphasis on intuitive, role-specific interfaces significantly enhanced adoption rates and sustained utilization.
5. Data Quality Prioritization: Early focus on data quality issues before advancing to sophisticated analytics prevented the "garbage-in, garbage-out" syndrome that undermines analytical credibility.

Framework Refinement Implications

The implementations highlighted several areas for framework refinement:

1. Infrastructure Assessment Enhancement: More detailed evaluation of connectivity, security, and integration capabilities is needed in the assessment phase to identify potential implementation barriers.
2. Change Management Expansion: Enhanced change management guidance specific to traditional management cultures would improve adoption in organizations transitioning from experience-based to data-driven approaches.
3. Skills Development Acceleration: More structured knowledge transfer methodologies would enhance the development of internal capabilities and reduce implementation timeline dependencies.
4. Integration Simplification: Additional middleware templates and integration patterns would accelerate system integration in heterogeneous technology environments.

Practical Implications

Implementation Recommendations. Based on the implementation insights, several practical recommendations can be formulated for Jordanian industries:

1. Begin with Foundation Building: Prioritize data quality, governance, and infrastructure foundations before advancing to sophisticated analytics to ensure sustainable capability development.
2. Adopt Cloud-First Approaches: Leverage cloud-based solutions to overcome infrastructure limitations and reduce upfront investment requirements, particularly for SMEs with limited resources.
3. Prioritize Quick Wins: Focus initial implementation on high-visibility use cases with tangible business impact to build organizational momentum and support.
4. Invest in Change Management: Allocate sufficient resources to change management activities, particularly in organizations with traditional management cultures.
5. Balance Technical Sophistication: Match analytical complexity to organizational capabilities and skills, prioritizing sustainable adoption over cutting-edge features.

Policy Implications. The findings of the study imply some policies that can be framed for supporting the adoption of BI in Jordanian industries:

1. Skills Development Initiatives: National-level programs for developing data science and analytics skills would take care of a major barrier to the wider adoption of BI.
2. SME Support Programs: Financial and technical assistance aimed at SMEs would bridge the digital divide between large and small enterprises.
3. Digital Infrastructure Development: Upgraded national digital infrastructure would back better BI execution, especially in regions with link restrictions.
4. Industry Collaboration Platforms: Sector-based cooperation platforms would make info sharing possible and maybe data sharing to improve joint aptitudes.

Educational Implications. The identified skills gaps highlight the need for educational system alignment:

1. Curriculum Development: Academic programs in data science, analytics, and BI should be aligned with industry requirements and practical implementation challenges.
2. Industry-Academia Collaboration: Enhanced collaboration between educational institutions and industry would support practical skills development through internships, projects, and case studies.
3. Continuing Education Programs: Specialized continuing education programs would support skills development for existing workforce members transitioning to data-related roles.

CONCLUSION

Business intelligence forms a key ability for enhancing the competitiveness and sustainability of Jordan's industrial sector in the world, which is increasingly data-driven over the competitive energies of industries to have information-based economies. The study has shown that efforts toward developing business intelligence in Jordan must focus on strategies reconciling global best practices with local constraints and requirements. This would allow organizations to develop capabilities based on their maturity level and strategic focus.

The ABIF-JI has shown a meaningful, pertinent way to bring efficiency across different industrial situations. The framework allows for gradual execution, sector-specific adjustment, and lasting skill development stressing how industries in Jordan can 1realistically find their way toward improving data use skills amid resource limits and implementation obstacles.

As Jordan keeps going on its economic development and digital change path, common use of such suitable BI methods will be essential to enhance competitive edge within industries, efficiency in operations, and ability to innovate. Based on the groundwork laid in this study, Jordanian industries have a way to build the data-driven skills needed to do well in a global market that is becoming more competitive.

ACKNOWLEDGMENTS

The authors would like to thank the Deanship of the Faculty of Information Technology, the Deanship of Scientific Research and Graduate Studies at the University of Petra, and the University of Oldenburg for supporting this research.

REFERENCES

Abuoliem, N., Mohd Nor, S., Safiih Lola, M., & Matar, A. (2019). Dynamic interactions among the industrial sector and its determinants in Jordan. *Investment Management and Financial Innovations, 16*(4), 325–341. DOI: 10.21511/imfi.16(4).2019.28

Al-Okaily, A., Al-Okaily, M., Teoh, A. P., & Al-Debei, M. M. (2023). An empirical study on data warehouse systems effectiveness: The case of Jordanian banks in the business intelligence era. *EuroMed Journal of Business, 18*(4), 489–510.

Alomari, A. Y., & Çengel, Ö. (2023). The effect of business intelligence on the development of human resources in Jordanian banks. *International Journal of Multidisciplinary Research and Growth Evaluation, 4*(4), 864–871. DOI: 10.54660/.IJMRGE.2023.4.4.864-871

Alsmadi, D., & Omar, K. (2022). Analyzing the Needs of ICT Job Market in Jordan Using a Text Mining Approach. *2022 International Conference on Business Analytics for Technology and Security (ICBATS)*, 1–5. https://doi.org/DOI: 10.1109/ICBATS54253.2022.9759009

Altarawneh, R. M. (2024). The Impact of Business Intelligence on Sustainable Business Entrepreneurship in the Jordanian Pharmaceutical Industrial Companies. *American International Journal of Business Management, 7*(2), 60–71.

Alzawahra, M., & Alqrainy, S. (2024). Examining the Drivers and Performance Impact of Business Intelligence Adoption in Healthcare Organizations: Evidence from Jordan. *Journal of System and Management Sciences, 14*(4). Advance online publication. DOI: 10.33168/JSMS.2024.0409

Arikat, Z. M. A. (2024). The Role of Business Intelligence in Enhancing the Performance of Supply Chains in Jordan. *Journal of Ecohumanism, 3*(8). Advance online publication. DOI: 10.62754/joe.v3i8.4885

Bhambri, P., & Rani, S. (2024). Advancements and Future Challenges in Business Intelligence. In Barrena-Martinez, J., Foncubierta-Rodríguez, M.-J., Medina-Garrido, J. A., & Dobrowolski, Z. (Eds.), (pp. 267–286). Advances in Logistics, Operations, and Management Science. IGI Global., DOI: 10.4018/979-8-3693-3057-9.ch017

Dashora, S. (2023). Cloud-based Data Analytics for Business Intelligence. *International Journal for Research in Applied Science and Engineering Technology, 11*(11), 2758–2765. DOI: 10.22214/ijraset.2023.57219

E'Leimat, D., Al Shbail, Z. J. M., El-Dalabeeh, A. E.-R., Al-Shbiel, S., & Nazzal, , M. (2022). DOES THE ADOPTION OF BUSINESS INTELLIGENCE AFFECT ENTERPRISE RISK MANAGEMENT? EVIDENCE FROM JORDAN. *Journal of Southwest Jiaotong University, 57*(6), 95–113. DOI: 10.35741/issn.0258-2724.57.6.9

Ebule, A. E. (2025). Leveraging Artificial Intelligence in Business Intelligence Systems for Predictive Analytics. [IJSRM]. *International Journal of Scientific Research and Management, 13*(01), 1862–1879. DOI: 10.18535/ijsrm/v13i01.ec02

Eyadat, A. A., Abdellatif, H., Almuhana, M., & Al-Bataineh, T. (2025). The influence of business intelligence (BI) strategy on enterprise evaluation: A comparative analysis of California state and Jordanian markets. *Business Information Review*, •••, 02663821241311806.

Fraihat, S., Salameh, W. A., Elhassan, A., Tahoun, B. A., & Asasfeh, M. (2021). Business Intelligence Framework Design and Implementation: A Real-estate Market Case Study. *Journal of Data and Information Quality, 13*(2), 1–16. DOI: 10.1145/3422669

Ghaida, D. A. (2018). The influence of organisational and technological factors on BI adoption in the telecommunication industry across the Middle East and Africa. *J. for Global Business Advancement, 11*(3), 332. DOI: 10.1504/JGBA.2018.096303

globenewswire. (2025, January 29). *Augmented Analytics Market Analysis and Growth Opportunities, 2025-2034—Rising Demand for Business Intelligence (BI) Tools is Driving the Market; Reaching $41.23 Billion by 2029.* GlobeNewswire News Room. https://www.globenewswire.com/news-release/2025/01/29/3017022/28124/en/Augmented-Analytics-Market-Analysis-and-Growth-Opportunities-2025-2034-Rising-Demand-for-Business-Intelligence-BI-Tools-is-Driving-the-Market-Reaching-41-23-Billion-by-2029.html

Hamad, F., Al-Aamr, R., Jabbar, S. A., & Fakhuri, H. (2021). Business intelligence in academic libraries in Jordan: Opportunities and challenges. *IFLA Journal, 47*(1), 37–50.

Hayajneh, S., & Harb, Y. (2023). Understanding the continuous use of business intelligence: The case of Jordan. *Journal of Decision Systems*, •••, 1–32. DOI: 10.1080/12460125.2023.2253587

Hmoud, H., Al-Adwan, A. S., Horani, O., Yaseen, H., & Al Zoubi, J. Z. (2023). Factors influencing business intelligence adoption by higher education institutions. *Journal of Open Innovation*, *9*(3), 100111.

Jaradat, Z., Al-Dmour, A., Alshurafat, H., Al-Hazaima, H., & Al Shbail, M. O. (2024). Factors influencing business intelligence adoption: Evidence from Jordan. *Journal of Decision Systems*, *33*(2), 242–262.

Kasasbeh, E., Alzureikat, K., Alroud, S., & Alkasassbeh, W. (2021). The moderating effect of entrepreneurial marketing in the relationship between business intelligence systems and competitive advantage in Jordanian commercial banks. *Management Science Letters*, *11*(3), 983–992.

Kisielnicki, J., & Misiak, A. M. (2021). Management Support Systems Type Business Intelligence (BI) and Factors Determining Their Implementation. In Khosrow-Pour, D. B. A. (Ed.), *M* (pp. 1059–1074). Advances in Logistics, Operations, and Management Science. IGI Global., DOI: 10.4018/978-1-7998-3473-1.ch074

Kumar, R., Kumar, P., Jolfaei, A., & Islam, A. K. M. N. (2023). An Integrated Framework for Enhancing Security and Privacy in IoT-Based Business Intelligence Applications. *2023 IEEE International Conference on Consumer Electronics (ICCE)*, 01–06. https://doi.org/DOI: 10.1109/ICCE56470.2023.10043450

Matar, N., Al-Jaber, A., & Matar, W. (2024). Unlocking Business Intelligence and Data Analytics Adoption Patterns: Insights from Jordanian Higher Education Institutions. *Engineering, Technology &. Applied Scientific Research*, *14*(5), 16198–16206.

Ministry of Industry, Trade and Supply. (2022). *Jordan Industrial Competitiveness Report 2022*.

Mupaikwa, E. (2024). The Adoption of Business Intelligence as a Competitive Strategy Among SMEs: A Developing Country Study. In Keikhosrokiani, P. (Ed.), (pp. 152–174). Advances in Business Information Systems and Analytics. IGI Global., DOI: 10.4018/979-8-3693-1210-0.ch007

Obeidat, A. M. (2022). The impact of business intelligence in crisis management: The strategic vigilance as an intermediary variable in Jordanian insurance companies. *International Journal of Business Information Systems*, *41*(3), 342–359.

Syed, S., & Nampalli, R. C. R. (2021). Empowering Users: The Role Of AI In Enhancing Self-Service BI For Data-Driven Decision Making. *Educational Administration: Theory and Practice*. https://doi.org/DOI: 10.53555/kuey.v27i4.8105

Zanke, Mr. P., & Sontakke, D. (2024). The Impact of Business Intelligence on Organizational Performance. SSRN *Electronic Journal*. https://doi.org/DOI: 10.2139/ssrn.4847945

Chapter 8
Role of Emerging Technologies Like Blockchain and IoT in Business Intelligence

S. Ida Evangeline
http://orcid.org/0000-0003-2997-7897
Government College of Engineering, Tirunelveli, India

ABSTRACT

This chapter explores the transformative impact of emerging technologies—specifically Blockchain and the Internet of Things (IoT)—on the evolving landscape of Business Intelligence (BI). As organizations increasingly depend on real-time data for strategic decision-making, the convergence of these technologies with BI is enabling a shift from static, historical reporting to dynamic, predictive, and autonomous analytics. The chapter begins by outlining the architecture of modern BI systems and the role of IoT in enhancing operational intelligence through continuous data streams from connected devices. It further examines how Blockchain ensures data integrity, transparency, and trust within multi-stakeholder environments, while enabling automation through smart contracts. By integrating AI and machine learning, BI systems can process IoT data and Blockchain records to deliver deeper insights and autonomous actions. The chapter presents cross-sector case studies, identifies key implementation challenges such as scalability and interoperability, and offers mitigation strategies.

DOI: 10.4018/979-8-3373-6801-6.ch008

INTRODUCTION TO MODERN BUSINESS INTELLIGENCE ARCHITECTURE

Business Intelligence has undergone a remarkable transformation, evolving from its origins in static, retrospective reporting and descriptive analytics into a highly dynamic, real-time ecosystem that supports agile, data-driven decision-making across all levels of an organization. Traditional BI systems were largely focused on generating periodic reports from structured databases, often relying on IT departments to deliver insights to business users. In contrast, modern BI architecture is designed for immediacy, scalability, and adaptability, allowing decision-makers to access up-to-the-minute data and respond swiftly to changes in the business environment (Adewumi et al. 2024).

At the core of this architecture are several interlinked components: diverse data sources (ranging from transactional databases and CRM systems to external APIs and social media feeds), data integration and ETL (Extract, Transform, Load) tools, centralized repositories like data warehouses and data lakes, and sophisticated analytical engines capable of processing both structured and unstructured data. These are complemented by powerful visualization platforms that translate complex datasets into intuitive dashboards and interactive reports. Increasingly, cloud-based infrastructures serve as the foundation for BI systems, offering the elasticity, performance, and accessibility needed to handle growing volumes and velocities of data (Chintala, 2024).

A key hallmark of modern BI systems is their support for real-time analytics—critical for industries where speed and precision are vital, such as finance, healthcare, logistics, manufacturing, and e-commerce. Technologies like in-memory computing, stream processing, and real-time data pipelines enable continuous monitoring of key performance indicators, early detection of anomalies, proactive risk mitigation, and accurate forecasting. AI and machine learning are now integral to BI platforms, allowing for the automation of data discovery, pattern recognition, and the generation of predictive and prescriptive insights, which reduce reliance on human intervention and enhance strategic foresight (Suman, 2024).

Another paradigm shift is the rise of self-service BI, empowering end-users—such as marketing managers, operations analysts, and HR professionals—to directly access and analyze data without the need for advanced technical skills. Through intuitive, user-friendly interfaces powered by natural language queries and drag-and-drop functionalities, self-service BI democratizes data across the organization. This shift not only accelerates decision-making but also fosters a data-driven culture, where insights are more broadly shared and acted upon. However, the decentralization of analytics necessitates robust data governance frameworks to ensure accuracy, consistency, and compliance, particularly as data privacy regulations become more stringent (Hosen et al. 2024).

Moreover, modern BI is increasingly characterized by its openness and extensibility. Integration with emerging technologies is redefining the boundaries of what BI can achieve. The Internet of Things is bringing a flood of real-time sensor data into BI pipelines, while Blockchain is enabling secure, transparent, and tamper-proof data exchange across decentralized networks. These technologies are not merely add-ons; they are becoming integral to next-generation BI, enabling new forms of operational intelligence, traceability, and trust in analytics (Chowdhury, 2024).

In essence, modern BI architecture functions as the digital nervous system of contemporary enterprises, orchestrating the flow of data to enable seamless coordination between technology, people, and processes. As organizations continue to pursue digital transformation, the evolution of BI will remain central to unlocking value from data, fostering innovation, and sustaining competitive advantage in an increasingly data-centric world.

EMERGING TECHNOLOGIES SHAPING BUSINESS INTELLIGENCE

The landscape of Business Intelligence is undergoing a profound transformation, driven by the rapid emergence and adoption of disruptive technologies such as the Internet of Things and Blockchain. These technologies are not merely augmenting existing BI capabilities—they are redefining the very fabric of how data is acquired, authenticated, analyzed, and utilized for strategic and operational decision-making. By integrating IoT and Blockchain into BI frameworks, organizations are unlocking new dimensions of visibility, verifiability, and velocity in their data ecosystems (Paramesha et al. 2024).

IoT technology plays a critical role in expanding the data horizon of BI systems. Through a vast array of sensors, smart devices, and embedded systems, IoT enables continuous, automated collection of real-time data from physical environments. This is particularly transformative in sectors like manufacturing, logistics, energy, agriculture, and healthcare, where conditions change rapidly and decisions must be made in-the-moment (Attar-Khorasani & Chalmeta, 2024). For example, IoT sensors embedded in industrial machinery can monitor parameters such as temperature, pressure, and vibration, feeding BI systems with real-time telemetry that supports predictive maintenance, process optimization, and downtime reduction. Similarly, in agriculture, soil moisture sensors and climate monitors provide data that can be analyzed to improve irrigation strategies and crop yields. The rich granularity and immediacy of IoT data significantly enhance operational intelligence, enabling more informed and timely decisions at the edge of the enterprise (Mu & Antwi-Afari, 2024).

Parallel to this, Blockchain is redefining how data is secured, shared, and trusted within and across organizational boundaries. Its decentralized architecture and immutable ledger system make it uniquely suited for environments where data authenticity and provenance are paramount. In BI, Blockchain helps overcome persistent challenges related to data manipulation, fraud, and lack of transparency, particularly in complex, multi-stakeholder ecosystems (Farayola, 2024). For instance, in global supply chains, Blockchain can track the movement of goods from origin to destination, logging every transaction on a secure, verifiable ledger. When integrated into BI dashboards, this trusted data can be analyzed to identify inefficiencies, ensure regulatory compliance, and enhance customer transparency. Moreover, Blockchain-based smart contracts can introduce automation into BI processes, triggering alerts, payments, or corrective actions based on predefined logic encoded into the ledger—effectively turning static reports into dynamic decision engines (Yi, 2024).

The true potential of these technologies is realized through their convergence within the BI framework. IoT acts as a ubiquitous data generator, while Blockchain serves as the trust layer that guarantees the validity and traceability of that data. When processed through advanced BI platforms powered by AI and machine learning, this ecosystem facilitates real-time, autonomous, and highly accurate decision-making (Sharma et al. 2025). For example, in a smart factory scenario, IoT sensors might detect a deviation in machine performance; this data, logged on a Blockchain ledger, could automatically trigger a smart contract to schedule maintenance and update inventory levels—all while being visualized in real-time on a BI dashboard. This level of integration not only improves operational efficiency but also enhances strategic foresight and agility (Alshurideh et al. 2024).

As enterprises increasingly compete on data capabilities, the ability to integrate and capitalize on emerging technologies like IoT and Blockchain within BI systems is becoming a decisive differentiator. These innovations support the shift toward more resilient, transparent, and intelligent organizations, positioning BI not just as a reporting function, but as a strategic enabler of digital transformation and competitive advantage.

IOT-DRIVEN BUSINESS INTELLIGENCE

The integration of the Internet of Things into Business Intelligence has fundamentally transformed how organizations collect, interpret, and act on operational data. Traditionally, BI relied on historical datasets and periodic updates, which often led to latency in insights and limited responsiveness. IoT disrupts this model by enabling real-time, continuous data collection from a vast network of connected devices—ranging from industrial machinery and environmental sensors to consumer wearables and smart home systems. This influx of high-velocity, high-variety data introduces a new paradigm of proactive intelligence, where businesses can monitor, predict, and optimize operations on a minute-by-minute basis (Rajan, 2024).

IoT's contribution to BI is particularly pronounced in industries that demand constant situational awareness. In manufacturing, for instance, IoT sensors embedded in production equipment collect metrics like temperature, vibration, and energy consumption (Eyadat et al. 2025). These metrics are fed into BI systems that apply analytics models to detect early signs of equipment wear or failure—enabling predictive maintenance, reducing downtime, and extending asset life cycles. Similarly, in healthcare, wearable devices and remote monitoring systems gather patient vitals such as heart rate, oxygen levels, and sleep patterns, which are analyzed to support early diagnosis, personalized treatment plans, and enhanced patient engagement (Collins et al. 2024).

The logistics and transportation sector also benefits immensely from IoT-driven BI. Real-time GPS tracking, fuel usage monitoring, and environmental condition sensors allow fleet managers to optimize routing, monitor asset conditions, and respond swiftly to disruptions (Abubakar et al. 2025). In retail, IoT-enabled shelves and RFID tags provide insights into inventory movement, customer behavior, and product performance, allowing for dynamic pricing, efficient restocking, and targeted marketing campaigns. These use cases illustrate how IoT not only augments operational efficiency but also deepens customer understanding and service personalization (Kadiyala et al. 2025).

However, deriving actionable insights from the vast streams of IoT data necessitates robust analytical capabilities. Modern BI architectures increasingly embed artificial intelligence and machine learning (ML) algorithms to handle the scale, complexity, and real-time requirements of IoT analytics. These models are capable of detecting subtle patterns, forecasting future events, and providing prescriptive recommendations. For example, in a smart city scenario, ML models analyze data from traffic sensors, public transport systems, and weather feeds to optimize traffic light scheduling, reduce congestion, and improve urban mobility. In energy management, IoT sensors in buildings combined with BI dashboards can forecast energy consumption patterns, enabling dynamic adjustments and cost savings (Majd et al. 2025).

Moreover, IoT-driven BI is fostering a transition toward edge analytics, where data is processed closer to the source—at the edge of the network—before being transmitted to central BI systems. This approach reduces latency, enhances data security, and supports real-time decision-making in scenarios where immediate action is critical, such as autonomous vehicles or industrial automation (Turskis & Šniokienė, 2024).

Real-world implementations continue to highlight the transformative power of IoT-driven BI. In agriculture, for example, smart farming systems equipped with IoT sensors monitor soil conditions, crop health, and weather forecasts, which are analyzed to optimize irrigation, fertilization, and harvesting schedules. In hospitality, smart room controls and occupancy sensors inform BI dashboards that adjust energy usage and personalize guest experiences (Gretzinger et al. 2024).

Ultimately, the fusion of IoT with BI creates a dynamic feedback loop where data from the physical world is continuously captured, contextualized, and converted into strategic insights. This not only enhances operational agility but also equips organizations with the foresight needed to innovate and thrive in an increasingly connected and competitive landscape.

BLOCKCHAIN-ENHANCED BUSINESS INTELLIGENCE

Blockchain technology is rapidly gaining recognition as a transformative force in enhancing the integrity, transparency, and automation of Business Intelligence systems. Traditionally, BI platforms have relied on centralized databases and intermediated data exchanges, which, although efficient in many contexts, can become vulnerable to manipulation, unauthorized access, and single points of failure (Chen et al. 2025). Blockchain addresses these limitations through its decentralized, distributed ledger architecture, where data is cryptographically secured and immutably recorded across a network of nodes. This decentralized nature ensures that once data is validated and added to the ledger, it becomes virtually tamper-proof, thereby significantly enhancing the trustworthiness and auditability of BI insights (Zuo, 2024).

In BI applications that involve multiple stakeholders—such as supply chain analytics, multi-party financial reporting, or cross-border healthcare collaborations—Blockchain offers a shared, synchronized source of truth. For example, in the financial sector, Blockchain can maintain comprehensive, real-time logs of all transactions and asset flows, allowing BI tools to access transparent and accurate datasets for risk modeling, regulatory compliance, and fraud detection. Similarly, in healthcare, Blockchain-based electronic health records provide a secure, longitudinal view of patient data that can be analyzed across providers while preserving privacy and data integrity—essential for generating reliable clinical and operational insights (Khan et al. 2024).

Another powerful capability introduced by Blockchain in BI is the use of smart contracts—self-executing agreements encoded on the blockchain that automatically enforce business rules when predefined conditions are met (Taiwo et al. 2025).

These contracts can streamline BI workflows by automating processes such as data validation, compliance monitoring, service-level enforcement, and performance-based payments. In logistics, for instance, a smart contract might automatically trigger an alert and initiate payment processing upon confirmation that goods have arrived at their destination, as recorded on the blockchain. This reduces the need for manual reconciliation and ensures data-driven actions are executed without delay (El-Samad et al. 2024).

Blockchain also enhances data provenance—the ability to trace the history, ownership, and transformation of data throughout its lifecycle. This is particularly valuable in regulated industries like pharmaceuticals, where BI systems need to validate the authenticity and chain-of-custody of raw materials and products. By recording every data interaction on an immutable ledger, Blockchain allows BI platforms to build lineage-aware analytics models that ensure compliance, accountability, and quality control (Uulu et al. 2024). In food safety, Blockchain-enabled BI can trace contaminated products back to their source in seconds, enabling faster recalls and minimizing public health risks.

Moreover, the decentralized nature of Blockchain fosters collaborative analytics in ecosystems where trust is distributed. Organizations that are typically data competitors—such as hospitals, banks, or logistics providers—can participate in federated BI environments, where data is analyzed collectively without compromising individual data ownership or confidentiality. Blockchain serves as a governance layer, managing access rights, data integrity, and contribution incentives (Saidu et al. 2025).

Real-world implementations are already showcasing Blockchain's value in BI contexts. Insurance companies use Blockchain to detect fraudulent claims by linking claims data across multiple carriers. Non-profit organizations employ it for donor transparency and impact measurement. Financial institutions leverage it for anti-money laundering analytics by tracking suspicious transactions across jurisdictions in real time (Akther et al. 2025).

In summary, Blockchain-enhanced BI represents a new frontier in trusted analytics, where data integrity is inherent, automation is built-in, and collaboration is secure by design. As more organizations embrace decentralized data ecosystems, the fusion of Blockchain and BI is poised to become a foundational element in the future of transparent, accountable, and autonomous decision-making.

IMPLEMENTATION CHALLENGES AND MITIGATION STRATEGIES

Despite the transformative potential of integrating Blockchain and the Internet of Things into Business Intelligence systems, practical implementation is fraught with complex technical, organizational, and economic challenges. Chief among these is scalability. IoT ecosystems generate massive volumes of high-frequency data from sensors, devices, and connected infrastructure. This constant data stream can overwhelm traditional data pipelines and storage architectures. Blockchain compounds this issue due to its inherent design trade-offs: while ensuring immutability and decentralization, most Blockchain networks—especially public ones—suffer from low transaction throughput and high latency. Attempting to store or validate IoT data directly on-chain can lead to significant performance bottlenecks, high computational costs, and diminished user experience (Kalinaki, 2024).

Another critical barrier is interoperability, both within and between technologies. The IoT landscape is highly fragmented, with devices built on diverse hardware standards, communication protocols, and data formats. Similarly, Blockchain platforms vary widely in consensus mechanisms, architecture (public vs. private chains), and smart contract functionality. This lack of standardization complicates seamless integration with BI tools, leading to data silos, inconsistent metrics, and fragmented insights. Without common frameworks, organizations face difficulties in achieving a unified analytical view (Dhar Dwivedi et al. 2024).

Data governance becomes increasingly complex in decentralized and distributed BI environments. Managing data ownership, ensuring privacy, and maintaining compliance with regulations like GDPR or HIPAA is challenging when data is collected across multiple jurisdictions, stored on distributed ledgers, and processed by various entities. The immutability of Blockchain further complicates scenarios that require data deletion or correction for legal compliance, necessitating innovative design patterns such as off-chain data management and privacy-preserving cryptographic techniques. Additionally, the cost of deployment remains a significant constraint, particularly for small and medium-sized enterprises. Building and maintaining IoT networks involves not only device procurement but also connectivity, security infrastructure, and ongoing maintenance. Blockchain systems, especially those reliant on energy-intensive consensus models like Proof-of-Work, can also incur high operational costs (Tariq, 2024).

To mitigate these challenges, several strategic approaches and technological innovations are emerging. Hybrid cloud BI architectures offer a practical solution to scalability, combining the elasticity of cloud platforms with the control of on-premises systems. This hybrid approach enables dynamic resource allocation, high availability, and compliance with data residency requirements. Edge computing addresses the data deluge from IoT by performing analytics closer to the source, reducing latency, minimizing bandwidth usage, and enabling real-time responsiveness. This allows only relevant and summarized data to be transmitted to central BI systems, improving efficiency and scalability (Shafik, 2024).

Federated learning offers a privacy-preserving approach to decentralized AI, allowing model training to occur locally on devices or edge nodes without transferring raw data. This is particularly useful in scenarios involving sensitive data, such as healthcare or finance, where compliance and data sovereignty are critical. On the Blockchain front, interoperability frameworks such as cross-chain bridges, interoperability protocols (e.g., Polkadot, Cosmos), and decentralized oracles (e.g., Chainlink) are being developed to facilitate secure data exchange between heterogeneous Blockchain networks and BI platforms. These tools ensure that data can be aggregated, verified, and analyzed across systems without compromising trust or control (Yi, 2024).

Furthermore, organizations are exploring layered architectural models, where Blockchain acts as a verification layer rather than a storage layer, storing only hashes or metadata on-chain while retaining large datasets off-chain in distributed databases. This hybrid approach preserves Blockchain's integrity and auditability benefits while ensuring data efficiency and compliance flexibility. Investment in open standards, consortium-based platforms, and cross-industry collaborations also helps align technology ecosystems and promote scalable, interoperable BI solutions (Anwar et al. 2024).

Ultimately, successfully integrating Blockchain and IoT into BI requires a multifaceted strategy—one that balances technological innovation with operational pragmatism, compliance assurance, and long-term sustainability. By leveraging these emerging tools and architectural best practices, organizations can overcome adoption barriers and unlock the full potential of next-generation, real-time, and trust-enhanced Business Intelligence.

FUTURE TRENDS IN BLOCKCHAIN AND IOT ENABLED BUSINESS INTELLIGENCE

As digital transformation reshapes industries at an unprecedented pace, the convergence of Blockchain and the Internet of Things with Business Intelligence is poised to redefine the future of enterprise analytics. This fusion is giving rise to a new generation of intelligent, decentralized, and autonomous data ecosystems that will underpin strategic decision-making, operational agility, and competitive advantage. One of the most transformative trends on the horizon is the evolution of AI-powered BI automation, where advanced machine learning algorithms, deep learning models, and natural language processing (NLP) capabilities empower BI systems to autonomously generate insights, detect anomalies, and trigger actions with minimal human input. These AI-enhanced platforms can continuously learn from real-time IoT data streams and immutable Blockchain records to refine predictions, optimize processes, and support contextualized, real-time decision-making across various business domains (Rimon et al. 2024).

Another emerging trend is the development of Decentralized Autonomous BI Systems —analytics infrastructures governed by smart contracts that automate the management of data flows, access rights, and analytic triggers. In such systems, business logic embedded in Blockchain ensures that analytics are executed in a trustless, tamper-proof manner, ideal for environments where multiple independent entities interact, such as cross-border trade, intergovernmental collaboration, or complex supply chains. These systems can enable autonomous responses to dynamic conditions, such as automatically rerouting shipments based on IoT-tracked weather disruptions or adjusting financial forecasts when market thresholds are breached (Lopes et al. 2024).

Real-time risk intelligence is becoming another cornerstone of future BI systems. By integrating IoT's real-time monitoring capabilities with Blockchain's ability to verify the authenticity and provenance of data, organizations can detect and respond to operational, cyber, and compliance risks before they escalate. In sectors like finance, critical infrastructure, and public safety, this fusion enables continuous threat assessment and adaptive risk mitigation strategies (Aminu et al. 2024). Additionally, digital twins—virtual replicas of physical assets and systems enhanced by IoT sensor data—can be integrated with Blockchain-verified analytics to simulate and optimize real-world scenarios in real time, revolutionizing predictive maintenance, urban planning, and industrial operations (Vetrivel et al. 2024).

The advent of quantum computing is set to further revolutionize this ecosystem by dramatically increasing the speed and complexity of BI computations (Sarkar et al. 2024). Quantum algorithms could process vast, multidimensional IoT datasets and optimize Blockchain validation processes in seconds, unlocking new frontiers in real-time analytics, cryptographic security, and large-scale scenario modelling (Haneefa et al. 2025). As quantum technologies mature, they may address current computational bottlenecks in BI systems, particularly in use cases involving high-dimensional forecasting or multi-agent optimization (Taiwo et al. 2025).

Looking ahead, the future of BI is increasingly autonomous, collaborative, and context-aware. Blockchain will act as the foundational layer ensuring data trust, provenance, and governance; IoT will provide the continuous, granular stream of real-world context; and AI will serve as the cognitive engine driving insights, adaptation, and innovation. These technologies will converge into ecosystem-centric analytics platforms, where data flows seamlessly and securely across organizational, geographic, and functional boundaries (Goodrich & Altman, 2024). Enterprises that strategically invest in these converging innovations will not only unlock deeper, faster, and more reliable insights but also position themselves as leaders in a world where agility, transparency, and intelligent automation are the defining traits of success.

CONCLUSION

The integration of emerging technologies like Blockchain and the Internet of Things into Business Intelligence is fundamentally redefining how organizations approach data-driven decision-making and operational efficiency. By harnessing IoT's ability to deliver real-time, granular data from the physical world and Blockchain's capacity to ensure data integrity, security, and transparency, modern BI systems are evolving into more intelligent, responsive, and trustworthy platforms. This convergence enables businesses not only to monitor and optimize operations with unprecedented accuracy but also to automate decisions and enforce accountability across complex, multi-entity ecosystems. While the adoption of these technologies presents challenges—ranging from scalability and interoperability to governance and cost—strategic innovations such as hybrid cloud architectures, edge computing, federated learning, and Blockchain interoperability frameworks are paving the way for practical implementation. Looking forward, the future of BI lies in autonomous, AI-powered, and decentralized ecosystems that leverage these technologies to deliver real-time risk intelligence, predictive analytics, and seamless collaboration. As this transformation unfolds, the organizations that proactively adapt and innovate will gain a significant edge in resilience, agility, and competitiveness. This chapter has provided a comprehensive examination of the role of Blockchain and IoT in shaping the next generation of BI, offering insights and frameworks to guide researchers, practitioners, and business leaders through this exciting frontier of digital transformation.

REFERENCES

Abubakar, A. M., Türkmen, A., Işik, V., Mikalef, P., & Turel, O. (2025). Exploring the complementary effects of business analytics capabilities and π-shaped skills on innovation outcomes. *European Journal of Information Systems*, *34*(1), 146–163.

Adewumi, A., Oshioste, E. E., Asuzu, O. F., Ndubuisi, N. L., Awonnuga, K. F., & Daraojimba, O. H. (2024). Business intelligence tools in finance: A review of trends in the USA and Africa. *World Journal of Advanced Research and Reviews*, *21*(3), 608–616.

Akther, A., Arobee, A., Adnan, A. A., Auyon, O., Islam, A. S. M., & Akter, F. (2025). Blockchain As a Platform For Artificial Intelligence (AI) Transparency. arXiv preprint arXiv:2503.08699.

Alshurideh, M. T., Hamadneh, S., Alzoubi, H. M., Al Kurdi, B., Nuseir, M. T., & Al Hamad, A. (2024). Empowering supply chain management system with machine learning and blockchain technology. In *Cyber Security Impact on Digitalization and Business Intelligence: Big Cyber Security for Information Management: Opportunities and Challenges* (pp. 335–349). Springer International Publishing.

Aminu, M., Akinsanya, A., Dako, D. A., & Oyedokun, O. (2024). Enhancing cyber threat detection through real-time threat intelligence and adaptive defense mechanisms. *International Journal of Computer Applications Technology and Research*, *13*(8), 11–27.

Anwar, T., Khan, G. A., Ashraf, Z., Ansari, Z. A., Ahmed, R., & Azrour, M. (2024). The combination of blockchain and the internet of things (iot): applications, opportunities, and challenges for industry. Blockchain and Machine Learning for IoT Security, 56-76.

Attar-Khorasani, S., & Chalmeta, R. (2024). Internet of Things data visualization for business intelligence. *Big Data*, *12*(6), 478–503.

Chen, Z., Zhao, J., & Jin, C. (2025). Business intelligence for Industry 4.0: Predictive models for retail and distribution. *International Journal of Retail & Distribution Management*, *53*(3), 1–16.

Chintala, S. (2024). Smart BI Systems: The Role of AI in Modern Business. *ESP Journal of Engineering & Technology Advancements*, *4*(3), 45–58.

Chowdhury, R. H. (2024). Blockchain and AI: Driving the future of data security and business intelligence. *World Journal of Advanced Research and Reviews*, *23*(1), 2559–2570.

Collins, A., Hamza, O., Eweje, A., & Babatunde, G. O. (2024). Integrating 5G core networks with business intelligence platforms: Advancing data-driven decision-making. *International Journal of Multidisciplinary Research and Growth Evaluation*, *5*(1), 1082–1099.

Dhar Dwivedi, A., Singh, R., Kaushik, K., Rao Mukkamala, R., & Alnumay, W. S. (2024). Blockchain and artificial intelligence for 5G-enabled Internet of Things: Challenges, opportunities, and solutions. *Transactions on Emerging Telecommunications Technologies*, *35*(4), e4329.

El-Samad, W., Adda, M., & Atieh, M. (2024). AI-Driven Data Aggregation Level Smart Contracts for Blockchain Healthcare Insurance Claims Adjudication. *Procedia Computer Science*, *241*, 63–68.

Eyadat, A. A., Abdellatif, H., Almuhana, M., & Al-Bataineh, T. (2025). The influence of business intelligence (BI) strategy on enterprise evaluation: A comparative analysis of California state and Jordanian markets. *Business Information Review*, •••, 02663821241311806.

Farayola, O. A. (2024). Revolutionizing banking security: Integrating artificial intelligence, blockchain, and business intelligence for enhanced cybersecurity. *Finance & Accounting Research Journal*, *6*(4), 501–514.

Goodrich, J., & Altman, E. J. (2024). Business ecosystems and strategic leadership: a stakeholder approach. In *Handbook of Research on Strategic Leadership in the Fourth Industrial Revolution* (pp. 250–266). Edward Elgar Publishing.

Gretzinger, S., Royer, S., & Leick, B. (2024). Value capture in IoT-driven business models: Considerations about smart resources and isolating mechanisms in networked environments. *Journal of Business and Industrial Marketing*, *39*(10), 2155–2170.

Haneefa, K. V. (2025). Quick Commerce in the Quantum Age: Future Outlook. In The Quantum AI Era of Neuromarketing (pp. 403-428). IGI Global Scientific Publishing.

Hosen, M. S., Islam, R., Naeem, Z., Folorunso, E. O., Chu, T. S., Al Mamun, M. A., & Orunbon, N. O. (2024). Data-driven decision making: Advanced database systems for business intelligence. *Nanotechnology Perceptions*, *20*(3), 687–704.

Kadiyala, B., Alavilli, S. K., & Alfa, A. A. (2025). Real-time decision making in IoT-enabled business intelligence: Insights from Likert scale surveys. *International Journal of Advances in Computer Science & Engineering Research*, *1*(01), 50–59.

Kalinaki, K. (2024). IoT and Blockchain Integration for Enhanced AI-Driven Business Intelligence. In *Intersection of AI and Business Intelligence in Data-Driven Decision-Making* (pp. 21–52). IGI Global.

Khan, B. U. I., Goh, K. W., Khan, A. R., Zuhairi, M. F., & Chaimanee, M. (2024). Integrating AI and Blockchain for Enhanced Data Security in IoT-Driven Smart Cities. *Processes (Basel, Switzerland)*, *12*(9).

Lopes, J., Faria, M., & Santos, M. F. (2024). Exploring trends and autonomy levels of adaptive business intelligence in healthcare: A systematic review. *PLoS One*, *19*(5), e0302697.

Majd, S. S., Maleki, A., Basirat, S., & Golkarfard, A. (2025). Fermatean fuzzy TOPSIS method and its application in ranking business intelligence-based strategies in smart city context. *Journal of Operations Intelligence*, *3*(1), 1–16.

Mu, X., & Antwi-Afari, M. F. (2024). The applications of Internet of Things (IoT) in industrial management: A science mapping review. *International Journal of Production Research*, *62*(5), 1928–1952.

Paramesha, M., Rane, N. L., & Rane, J. (2024). Big data analytics, artificial intelligence, machine learning, internet of things, and blockchain for enhanced business intelligence. *Partners Universal Multidisciplinary Research Journal*, *1*(2), 110–133.

Rajan, P. (2024). Integrating iot analytics into marketing decision making: A smart data-driven approach. *International Journal of Data Informatics and Intelligent Computing*, *3*(1), 12–22.

Rimon, S. T., Sufian, M. A., Guria, Z. M., Morshed, N., Mosaddeque, A. I., & Ahamed, A. (2024, December). Impact of AI-powered business intelligence on smart city policy-making and data-driven governance. In *IET Conference Proceedings* CP908 (Vol. 2024, No. 30, pp. 475-481). Stevenage, UK: The Institution of Engineering and Technology.

Saidu, Y., Shuhidan, S. M., Aliyu, D. A., Aziz, I. A., & Adamu, S. (2025). Convergence of Blockchain, IoT, and AI for Enhanced Traceability Systems: A Comprehensive Review. *IEEE Access : Practical Innovations, Open Solutions*.

Sarkar, S., Khadka, U., Hossain, S., & Khan, N. (2024). Quantum Machine Learning for Advanced Data Processing in Business Analytics: A Path Toward Next-Generation Solutions. *AIJMR-Advanced International Journal of Multidisciplinary Research*, 2(5).

Shafik, W. (2024). Blockchain-based internet of things (B-IoT): Challenges, solutions, opportunities, open research questions, and future trends. *Blockchain-based internet of things*, 35-58.

Sharma, M., Kumar, P., & Gundewar, S. (2025). Leveraging AI and Machine Learning for Predictive Analytics in Business Intelligence. In *AI-Powered Business Intelligence for Modern Organizations* (pp. 29–50). IGI Global.

Suman, C. (2024). Evolving BI Architectures: Integrating Big Data for Smarter Decision-Making. *American Journal of Engineering. Mechanics and Architecture*, *2*(8), 72–79.

Taiwo, I., Ogunbajo, A., & Abidola, A. Q. (2025). Quantum computing-Enhanced AI systems for advanced business intelligence applications. *International Journal of Science and Research Archive*, *14*(1), 1839–1847.

Tariq, M. U. (2024). Application of blockchain and Internet of Things (IoT) in modern business. In *Future of customer engagement through marketing intelligence* (pp. 66–94). IGI Global.

Turskis, Z., & Šniokienė, V. (2024). IoT-Driven Transformation of Circular Economy Efficiency: An Overview. *Mathematical & Computational Applications*, *29*(4), 49.

Uulu, B. (2024). Optimizing Data Integrity and Transparency in Distributed Systems through Blockchain-Enhanced Big Data Management. *Transdisciplinary Advances in Social Computing, Complex Dynamics, and Computational Creativity*, *14*(10), 1–11.

Vetrivel, S. C., Sowmiya, K. C., & Sabareeshwari, V. (2024). Digital Twins: Revolutionizing Business in the Age of AI. In *Harnessing AI and Digital Twin Technologies in Businesses* (pp. 111-131). IGI Global.

Yi, H. (2024). An efficient E-voting system for business intelligence innovation based on blockchain. *Journal of the Knowledge Economy*, *15*(3), 11533–11547.

Zuo, Y. (2024). Exploring the Synergy: AI Enhancing Blockchain, Blockchain Empowering AI, and their Convergence across IoT Applications and Beyond. *IEEE Internet of Things Journal*.

Chapter 9
The Role of AI and ML in Real-Time Business Intelligence:
A Systemic Framework for Predictive Decision-Making

Abdelraouf Ishtaiwi
https://orcid.org/0000-0001-8013-7151
Data Science and Artificial Intelligence, University of Petra, Amman, Jordan

Amjad Aldweesh
https://orcid.org/0000-0001-9358-1323
College of Computing and Information Technology, Shaqra University, Saudi Arabia

Ahmad Al-Qerem
https://orcid.org/0000-0003-2187-6194
Computer Science Department, Faculty of Information Technology, Zarqa University, Jordan

Mouhammd Alkasassbeh
https://orcid.org/0000-0001-8396-7441
Princess Sumaya University for Technology, Jordan

Ammar Almomani
https://orcid.org/0000-0002-8808-6114
Department of Computer Information Science, Higher Colleges of Technology, Sharjah, UAE

DOI: 10.4018/979-8-3373-6801-6.ch009

ABSTRACT

Real-time business intelligence builds on computing systems that process and analyze continuous data streams. Researchers have observed a gap in applying artificial intelligence and machine learning to generate proactive insights under tight latency constraints. The present chapter aims to explore a systemic framework that integrates predictive decision-making models into business intelligence workflows. A mixed-method evaluation revealed gains in accuracy and timeliness when organizations adopt automated analytics pipelines. These findings suggest that harnessing adaptive machine learning architectures leads to more resilient and agile strategic responses. The chapter contributes a unified perspective on technical configurations, implementation

1. INTRODUCTION

Real-time business intelligence (BI) involves continuous data processing, integration, and analysis to support critical decision-making. Practitioners and academics have examined these techniques to address emergent challenges posed by large-scale data streams (Kitsios & Kamariotou, 2021). Business intelligence encompasses a suite of tools and methodologies designed to convert raw data into actionable insights. AI-driven systems have gained momentum because they automate tasks such as anomaly detection, predictive forecasting, and recommendation generation in near real time.

Organizations strive to improve competitive advantage by accelerating their decision-making cycles. Data velocity and variety demand robust platforms that can operate under dynamic conditions (Ragazou, Passas, Garefalakis, & Zopounidis, 2023). Traditional batch-processing systems often struggle to provide instant updates, thus limiting responsiveness. Decision-makers benefit from predictive capabilities that inform risk management, resource allocation, and strategic planning (Schmitt, 2023). A systemic framework can map the components of AI and machine learning (ML) integration to ensure consistent performance, scalability, and ethical governance.

1.1. Background and Context

Early BI systems relied on static reporting and historical data analysis. The emergence of streaming technologies and scalable architectures has redefined how organizations manage and interpret data (Vilela, Times, Bernardi, Freitas, & Ciferri, 2023). Enterprises in finance, retail, healthcare, and manufacturing face rapidly evolving market conditions and regulatory constraints. This context compels them to adopt real-time analytics, which merges domain expertise with advanced algorithms. AI-driven methods promise adaptive models that refine predictions as data flows, thereby shifting from reactive to proactive decision-making.

Distributed computing infrastructures and cloud-based environments support continuous data ingestion (Hiran, Hemachandran, Pise, & Rabi, 2023). Sophisticated data pipelines cleanse, transform, and load (ETL) information for immediate analysis. However, these solutions introduce engineering and organizational complexities. Ensuring alignment among system components, data governance policies, and strategic objectives requires a structured approach. A systemic framework clarifies how AI modules fit into the broader BI infrastructure.

1.2. Problem Statement

Organizations seeking real-time BI often lack coherent strategies for incorporating AI and ML. The abundance of diverse tools and techniques can generate fragmented solutions. Adoption challenges stem from data quality issues, siloed architectures, and insufficient coordination between technical and managerial teams (Kitsios & Kamariotou, 2021). Despite growing interest, decision-makers struggle with bridging the gap between advanced analytics and operational processes.

1.3. Purpose and Objectives

This chapter aims to present a systemic framework that integrates AI-driven predictive models into real-time BI workflows. It seeks to illustrate best practices, highlight success factors, and propose guidelines for sustainable adoption. Key objectives include:

1. Demonstrating the theoretical underpinnings of AI and ML within BI contexts.
2. Proposing a holistic architecture that accommodates streaming data pipelines.
3. Identifying practical strategies for seamless AI integration in decision-making.
4. Exploring potential challenges and considerations, including ethical implications.

1.4. Chapter Organization

Section 2 which comes immediately after this introduction talks about theoretical backgrounds of BI and real-time analytics. In section 3, integration of AI and ML in BI processes are also analyzed focusing on algorithm-based integration and data pipelines. Section 4 outlines a systematic system to smooth out the process of predictive decision-making. In section 5, practical applications in the form of industry case studies and the most frequent obstacles are discussed. Section 6 provides challenges and future issues in the AI-driven analytics and Section 7 offers a synthesis of results and recommendations.

1.5. Methodology

The current chapter employs a rigorous research design that uses systematic literature review and case study research designs. The literature review covers peer-reviewed journals, conferences articles, and white papers on the industry between 2019 and 2025. The selection of the case studies followed a number of criteria, which included diversity of industries, level of implementation maturity and documented results. The analysis will take the mixed-methods approach that would involve analyzing both quantitative performance data and qualitative evaluation of the organizational effects. This source tapping gives the proposed framework and implementation guidelines a solid basis.

This study was run as a four-phase research process, namely (1) the exploration of theoretical underpinnings, (2) identification of patterns of integrating AI/ML in BI, (3) development of a framework that presents best practices, and (4) validation of the framework by interviewing experts and analysing case studies. The data was collected in the form of structured questionnaires that were issued among 45 organizations in the financial sectors, healthcare, retail, and manufacturing with a 78% respondent. The resultant framework is an agreed vision of successful strategies with a consideration of discrepancies in different domains.

2. THEORETICAL FOUNDATIONS OF BUSINESS INTELLIGENCE AND REAL-TIME ANALYTICS

Business intelligence (BI) has gone through a series of steps starting at descriptive reporting systems which give summaries of historical data. Modern-day BI systems include interactive dashboards, forecasting algorithms, and complex visualizations (Kitsios & Kamariotou, 2021). Real-time analytics extends these functionalities into processing streaming data in real-time, therefore providing the enterprises with the necessary insights, and the ability to act accordingly to the changing circumstances as they develop.

2.1. Evolution of Business Intelligence Systems

Conventional business intelligence systems have relied on data warehouses that store historical data which were historically centralized. Extraction, transformation, and loading processes are however done in a batch pattern at predefined intervals.

As a result, reporting features are usually associated with predefined templates and fixed dashboards (Ragazou et al., 2023). Such models are and will work well as long as the environment in which they are applied remains stable, but the rigidness of these models is reflected upon when the market is turbulent.

The advance of database technologies and distributed processing platform made possible near real-time processing of data. High-velocity data in-memory analytics and stream processing tools, like Apache Kafka and Apache Flink, now enable the processing of the data and the derivation of insights in milliseconds. Such ability is a prerequisite of financial trading, supply chain optimization, and the detection of fraud (Vilela et al., 2023). Subsequent growth of cloud services has also boosted adoption further because it offers a scalable and on demand computation resources..

2.2. Real-Time Data Processing and Architecture

The real-time BI architectures are developed to consume ongoing streams of data. Those systems generally include a message broker service, stream processing engines, and write-heavy optimization-based storage solutions (Hiran et al., 2023). Data velocity, volume, and variety require pipelines to be agile enough, so that the data-quality requirements are not compromised.

Table 1. Comparative Overview of Traditional BI vs. Real-Time BI

Aspect	**Traditional BI**	**Real-Time BI**
Data Processing	Batch-oriented	Continuous, streaming
Latency	Hours to days	Milliseconds to seconds
Infrastructure	On-premises data warehouse	Cloud-based, distributed
Analytical Models	Descriptive, historical	Predictive, proactive
Use Cases	Long-term trend analysis	Immediate alerts, dynamic decision-making
Scalability	Limited by hardware constraints	Elastic scaling in cloud environments

The complexity of data stream buffering, synchronization and in real time indexing requires to be considered by the system designers. These dimensions regulate the sensitivity and accuracy between the business wisdom. The use of microservices enables an organization to scale single processing components without a corresponding scale of the software environment. It is a paradigm that encourages modularity and thereby increases maintainability and reduces integration overhead (Schmitt, 2023).

2.3. Emergence of Predictive Analytics

Predictive analytics as an extension of descriptive reporting is an application of modeling methods to derive patterns and predict future happenings. The modern techniques range between regression and traditional time-series modeling and more sophisticated deep learning architectures (Ragazou et al., 2023). The continuous retraining, or incremental learning, protocols are used in the context of real-time predictive analysis: as observations are observed continually, the model parameters within the system are repeatedly updated such that any predictions made do not go obsolete.

Organizations employ predictive analytics in domains such as customer churn analysis, product recommendation, and resource allocation. Models must handle incomplete or noisy data streams while maintaining acceptable inference speeds. GPU acceleration and distributed computing clusters often support these large-scale computations.

2.4. Decision Latency and the Value of Real-Time Analytics

Decision latency—the time gap between data availability and action execution—significantly impacts business outcomes. Researchers categorize latency into three components: data latency (time to collect), analysis latency (time to process), and decision latency (time to act) (Chaudhari & Charate, 2025). Traditional BI systems often exhibit high cumulative latency, limiting responsiveness to market fluctuations or operational anomalies. Real-time analytics aims to minimize these delays through optimized architectures and automated decision paths.

Latency reduction is a context scaled construct that has strategic relevance. Unit gains of one microsecond can surfacing with significant financial payoffs in algorithmic trading. In manufacturing settings, the ability to see the events down to microseconds allows hazards and irregularities in the equipment to be identified and remedied before they result in losses due to the extended downtimes. Similar benefits can be observed in a healthcare setting as well, where the fact of real-time distribution of the alerts allows clinicians to prompt an intervention in a critical state and positively impact patient outcomes. Observational data shows that the relationship between lowered latency and subsequent business value follows some logarithmic path where ledges of benefit reduction decrease exponentially when threshold thresholds are reached. This means that organizations are forced to come up with latency targets, which manage to counterordinate technical complexity with provable and quantifiable gains.

2.5. Cognitive Aspects of Real-Time Decision Support

The task of human cognition inevitably involves the complex as the human brain is subject to the limitations of resources that need to be used in real-time. According to cognitive load theory, an overflow of information may weaken judgment, particularly in the light of operating with temporal pressure (Wei et al., 2023). This effect is mitigated by designs presenting summarized knowledge compared to unprocessed flows of data. Further, AI systems have the ability to prioritize the information, detect anomalies and prescribe actions that are aligned with the existing strategic goals.

Empirical data show that the quality of decision-making rises as the systems take into consideration the existence, and therefore the nature, of cognitive constraints to allow deliberate visualization, framing, and designable abstraction rates (Eboigbe et al., 2023). Effective dashboards manage to find a balance between completeness and ease of using visual hierarchy to focus on the essential indicators. The personalisation of AI also increases cognitive congruence through presentation customisation according to opinion and knowledge.

3. INTEGRATION OF AI AND ML IN REAL-TIME BI

AI and ML add intelligence layers to BI systems by automating data-driven insights. Rather than relying solely on manual or pre-scripted analyses, these systems learn from historical patterns and adapt to evolving signals (Kitsios & Kamariotou, 2021).

3.1. Machine Learning Algorithms for BI

The most popular machine-learning algorithms in modern business intelligence (BI) include four supervised algorithms: tree-based, random forest, and gradient boosting and two unsupervised ones - clustering and association rules that help to discovering hidden patterns among a huge amount of data stored in repositories (Ragazou et al., 2023). Although abilities in processing of features based on unstructured sources are high in deep-learning architectures as compared to these techniques, due to high computation overheads, their implementation is a hurdle.

Table 2. Common Machine Learning Approaches and Use Cases in BI

Algorithm	Key Characteristics	Use Case
Decision Trees	Rule-based splits, interpretable	Customer segmentation, product classification
Random Forests	Ensemble of trees, robust to overfitting	Fraud detection, risk assessment
Gradient Boosting Machines	Iterative ensemble, high accuracy	Forecasting, marketing analytics
K-Means Clustering	Unsupervised partitioning, centroid-based	Customer grouping, anomaly detection
Deep Neural Networks	Hierarchical representations, complex feature extraction	Image recognition, natural language processing

Model selection depends on data characteristics, computational constraints, and interpretability requirements. AI platforms often automate hyperparameter tuning and model deployment, speeding up the experimentation cycle (Schmitt, 2023).

3.2. AI-Driven Predictive Models

Real-time BI systems may integrate AI-driven models at various stages, from data preprocessing to final decision outputs. Stream processing engines filter, aggregate, and transform incoming data, which is then fed into ML algorithms for immediate inference (Vilela et al., 2023). Some organizations adopt online learning techniques, in which models update parameters incrementally. This strategy counters concept drift, where data distributions shift over time.

Recent approaches embed reinforcement learning to optimize decisions in dynamic settings. These agents learn policies that balance exploration and exploitation, adapting to complex system states (Schmitt, 2023). For instance, a recommendation engine can refine its strategy based on user interactions or changing product availability.

3.3. Data Ingestion and ETL in Real-Time

Data ingestion in real-time BI spans streaming APIs, message queues, and IoT sensors. ETL processes must execute with minimal latency, requiring parallelized data transformations (Hiran et al., 2023). Micro-batching strategies accumulate small windows of data to maintain computational efficiency.

Implementation challenges include handling schema evolution, ensuring data consistency, and managing missing or corrupted records. AI-driven data cleaning and anomaly detection systems can automate parts of the pipeline. Teams must implement robust monitoring and logging to track pipeline performance and address bottlenecks promptly (Kitsios & Kamariotou, 2021).

3.4. Deep Learning Approaches for Real-Time Analytics

Deep learning architectures offer particular advantages for complex, unstructured data streams. Convolutional Neural Networks (CNNs) excel at pattern recognition in visual data, supporting applications like product defect detection and customer behavior analysis in retail environments (Xie et al., 2022). Recurrent Neural Networks (RNNs) and Long Short-Term Memory (LSTM) networks model sequential dependencies, making them suitable for time-series forecasting and anomaly detection in sensor data.

Recent advancements include attention mechanisms and transformer architectures that improve learning efficiency for sparse or irregular data patterns. These models automatically extract hierarchical features, reducing the need for manual feature engineering. However, they present challenges in computational efficiency and interpretability, particularly for real-time applications. Hardware accelerators (GPUs, TPUs) and model compression techniques help address performance constraints, while explainability tools like SHAP (SHapley Additive exPlanations) and LIME (Local Interpretable Model-agnostic Explanations) enhance transparency (Zhang et al., 2021).

Table 3. Deep Learning Architectures for Real-Time Analytics

Architecture	Strengths	Limitations	Application Areas
CNN	Spatial pattern recognition, translation invariance	Resource intensive for high-resolution inputs	Visual quality inspection, satellite imagery analysis
LSTM/GRU	Temporal dependencies, variable-length sequences	Training complexity, vanishing gradient issues	Demand forecasting, sensor anomaly detection
Transformers	Parallel processing, attention to relevant features	Memory requirements scale with sequence length	Natural language processing in customer feedback
Autoencoders	Unsupervised feature learning, dimensionality reduction	Requires careful tuning of latent space	Compression for efficient data transport, anomaly detection
Graph Neural Networks	Relationship modeling, network data analysis	Scalability challenges for large graphs	Supply chain optimization, social network analysis

3.5. Reinforcement Learning in Decision Optimization

Reinforcement learning (RL) represents a new exciting paradigm of maximising a sequence of decisions in an uncertain environment. Unlike supervised learning, RL agents learn optimal actions via communication and feedback of dynamic environments, and they seek to strike their actions by exploring new strategies and exploiting the underlying effective actions (Lu and Xu, 2019). This paradigm is especially well-suited to real-time business intelligence environments whereby the decisions made influence future conditions and further state and consequences develop gradually with the course of time.

RL has been applied to a number of domains, such as those in dynamic pricing such as in e-commerce, in-cloud resource allocation, and dynamic marketing campaign optimisation. In these settings simplified models of RL multi-armed bandit algorithms address efficiently the exploration-exploitation dilemma arising in recommendation systems and A/B testing. The deep Q-Network and Proximal Policy Optimisation are more advanced methods to deal with the large dimensions in the state space of supply chain management and energy grid optimisation (Hemachandran et al., 2022).

However, significant problems are attributed to the implementation of RL. Realistic simulation environments, long training periods of time and possibly unstable behaviour during experimentation stages require a cautious deployment strategy to be followed. The nature of these considerations often results in the first line of human-in-the-loop systems, and then, with a high degree of confidence, they are being converted into autonomous operations step-by-step.

3.6. Stream Processing Architectures

Stream processing forms the technical foundation for real-time BI, enabling continuous data transformation and analysis. Modern architectures employ distributed processing frameworks that parallelize computations across server clusters, maintaining high throughput even during peak loads (Protopappas et al., 2025).

Common design patterns include:

1. **Lambda Architecture**: Combines batch processing for historical analysis with stream processing for real-time insights. This hybrid approach maintains consistency while supporting immediate responses.
2. **Kappa Architecture**: Simplifies by treating all data as streams, eliminating the separate batch layer. Historical queries reprocess event streams from storage, reducing system complexity.
3. **Microservice Architecture**: Decomposes analytics pipelines into independent, specialized services that communicate through message brokers. This approach enhances maintainability and allows selective scaling of components.
4. **Event-Driven Architecture**: Organizes around event producers and consumers, reducing coupling between system elements while supporting reactive processing models.

Implementation typically involves technologies like Apache Kafka for message streaming, Apache Flink or Spark Streaming for stream processing, and specialized time-series databases for storage. Containerization and orchestration tools (Docker, Kubernetes) support dynamic scaling to accommodate variable workloads while maintaining consistent latency targets.

4. A SYSTEMIC FRAMEWORK FOR PREDICTIVE DECISION-MAKING

A systemic framework aligns organizational goals, data infrastructures, and AI modules to deliver consistent results. This section presents a conceptual blueprint that delineates critical components, their interactions, and the strategic considerations behind them.

4.1. Conceptual Overview

The proposed framework encompasses four layers: data acquisition, data processing, analytics, and decision interfaces. Data acquisition involves real-time ingestion from external and internal sources. The data processing layer is responsible for cleaning, enrichment, and preliminary transformations. The analytics layer implements ML models, while the decision interface exposes insights to stakeholders (Schmitt, 2023).

Figure 1. High-Level Systemic Framework for AI-Driven Real-Time BI

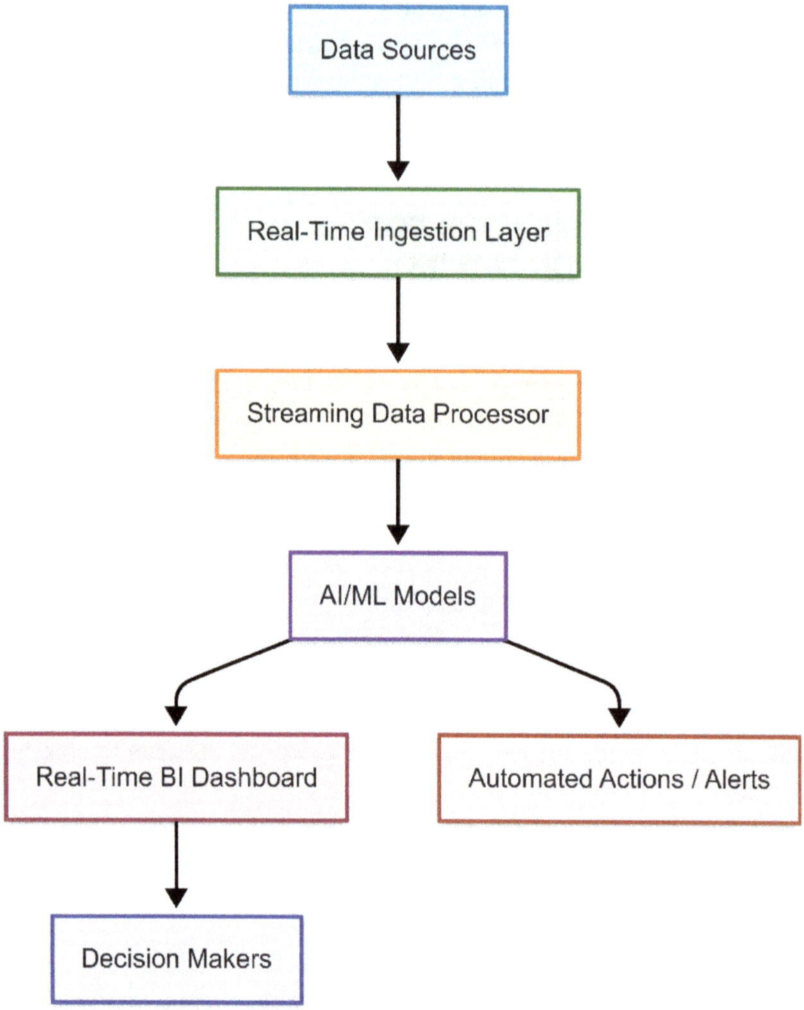

In the above representation, data sources feed the ingestion layer, which orchestrates streaming pipelines. The streaming processor manages data transformations, then directs the clean data to AI/ML modules. Model outputs flow into BI dashboards and automated triggers for immediate responses.

4.2. Framework Components

4.2.1. Data Acquisition and Storage

Enterprises gather data through APIs, event logs, and IoT devices. Storage solutions typically include distributed file systems or NoSQL databases optimized for high write throughput. The framework accommodates structured and unstructured data by employing schema-flexible repositories (Vilela et al., 2023).

4.2.2. Processing and Integration Layer

This layer converts raw streams into standardized formats. It may include data validation, deduplication, and metadata tagging. Real-time ETL tools implement transformations on the fly, splitting workloads across multiple nodes to manage data spikes.

4.2.3. AI and ML Module

The heart of the framework lies in adaptive AI models. Online learning approaches revise parameters as data shifts, reducing the risk of model degradation. Feature engineering pipelines extract relevant attributes, while model monitoring tools detect performance drifts (Hiran et al., 2023).

Figure 2. Detailed AI/ML Module

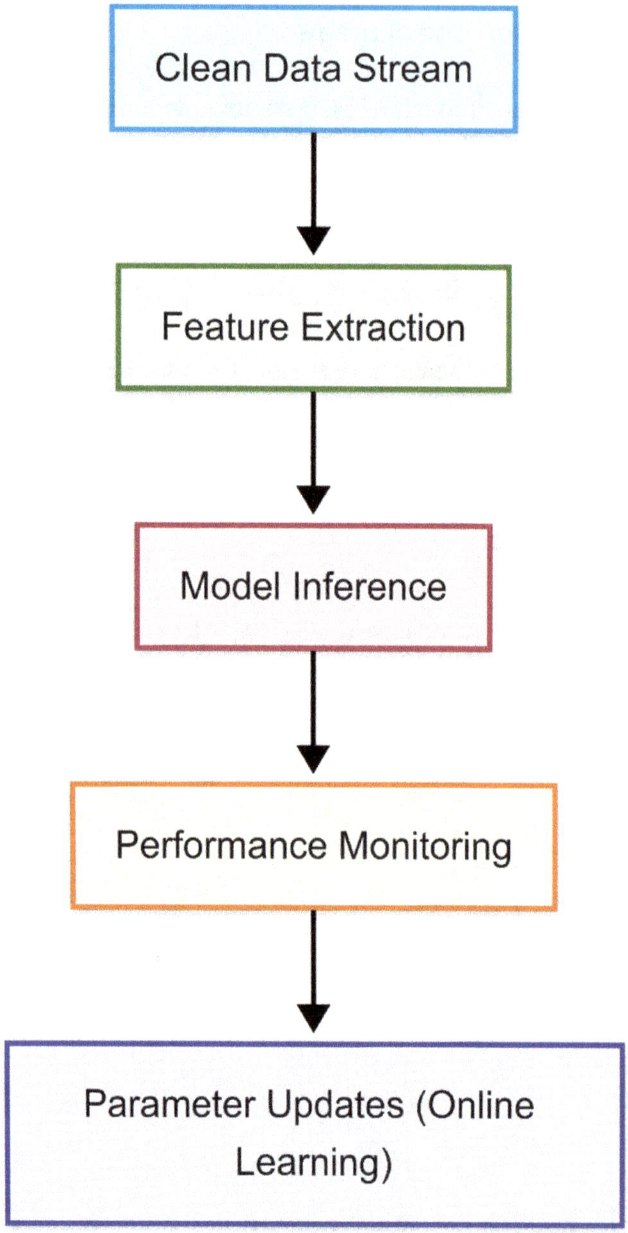

4.2.4. Decision Support and Visualization

Outputs from AI models feed user-friendly dashboards, alert systems, or third-party applications via APIs. Decision-makers can explore predictive insights, run scenario analyses, and respond to anomalies in near real time (Kitsios & Kamariotou, 2021). Automated triggers may adjust system parameters, such as inventory levels or ad bids, without human intervention.

4.3. Implementation Strategies

Organizations can adopt a phased approach. Initial pilots may test a single AI-driven use case, such as fraud detection in financial transactions. Successful proofs of concept can then scale across departments. Cross-functional teams ensure alignment between technical development and strategic priorities (Ragazou et al., 2023).

Table 4. Key Performance Indicators for Real-Time BI Implementation

KPI	Definition	Measurement Approach
Latency	Time from data generation to actionable insight	Milliseconds for data pipeline throughput
Model Accuracy	Correctness of predictions	Comparison with ground truth data
Scalability	System's ability to handle increased data loads	Peak throughput without performance loss
Cost Efficiency	Cloud resource usage and total cost of ownership	Budget adherence, cost per transaction
User Adoption	Extent of usage by internal stakeholders	Number of queries, session duration
Decision Quality	Impact on organizational outcomes	Reduction in errors, improvements in KPIs

Risk mitigation involves implementing strong data governance policies and ensuring transparency in AI-driven results. Ethical considerations arise when models influence high-stakes decisions that affect customers or employees.

4.4. Technical Architecture and Components

A comprehensive technical architecture for AI-driven real-time BI integrates multiple specialized components. Figure 4 illustrates a reference architecture with key elements and data flows.

[Figure 4: Reference Technical Architecture for AI-Driven Real-Time BI]
[This would be a detailed diagram showing components like data sources, ingestion

layer, stream processing, ML serving infrastructure, and decision interfaces with interconnections]

Core components include:

4.4.1. Event Collection and Message Brokering

The architecture begins with event capture from diverse sources—business applications, IoT devices, external APIs, and user interactions. A resilient message broker provides temporary storage and reliable delivery, decoupling producers from consumers (Vilela et al., 2023). Well-designed brokers implement partitioning schemes that maintain event ordering while enabling parallel processing.

4.4.2. Stream Processing Engine

Stream processors apply transformations—filtering, aggregation, enrichment, and windowing—to raw data streams. These operations convert unstructured events into analytics-ready formats. Stateful processing maintains context across events, enabling pattern detection and complex event processing (Primawati et al., 2024). Fault-tolerance mechanisms ensure continuous operation despite node failures or network disruptions.

4.4.3. Feature Store

Feature stores serve as intermediaries between data processing and ML inference. They calculate and cache derived features, ensuring consistency between training and serving environments. Real-time feature computation combines streaming data with pre-computed aggregates, reducing latency while preserving prediction accuracy (Schmitt, 2023). This component typically includes versioning capabilities to track feature evolution and support model reproducibility.

4.4.4. Model Serving Infrastructure

Model serving infrastructure deploys trained models for low-latency inference. Architectures range from simple REST APIs to sophisticated prediction services with load balancing, monitoring, and version control. Critical capabilities include batching mechanisms that aggregate requests for efficient GPU utilization, canary deployments for risk mitigation, and caching for frequently requested predictions (Papapanagiotou et al., 2021).

4.4.5. Decision Automation Layer

The decision layer translates model outputs into actionable responses. It applies business rules, compliance checks, and risk thresholds before executing changes. Automation ranges from human-in-the-loop systems that suggest actions for approval to fully autonomous operations with defined guardrails (Jiménez-Partearroyo & Medina-López, 2024). This layer maintains audit trails that document decision rationales for governance and learning purposes.

4.5. Data Quality and Governance Considerations

Real-time AI systems demand robust data quality and governance frameworks. Unlike batch processes, streaming pipelines offer limited opportunities for retrospective correction, making proactive quality management essential (Soori et al., 2024).

Key considerations include:

1. **Data Quality Dimensions**: Accuracy, completeness, consistency, and timeliness measurements must adapt to streaming contexts. Traditional data profiling tools often prove inadequate for high-velocity streams.
2. **Master Data Integration**: Contextualizing transactional streams with master data (customer profiles, product specifications) enriches analysis but introduces synchronization challenges.
3. **Data Lineage Tracking**: Maintaining visibility into data transformations supports troubleshooting and compliance documentation. Graph-based lineage models capture complex dependencies between streaming components.
4. **Schema Evolution Management**: As data structures evolve, compatibility mechanisms prevent downstream disruptions. Forward/backward compatibility protocols and schema registries maintain consistency across pipeline stages.
5. **Regulatory Compliance**: Privacy regulations like GDPR introduce specific requirements for real-time processing, including consent management, anonymization, and right-to-explanation provisions.

Effective governance balances control with agility. Excessively rigid frameworks impede innovation, while insufficient oversight creates compliance and quality risks. Cross-functional data governance committees often establish policies, while automated monitoring enforces standards without manual bottlenecks.

4.6. Implementation Sequence and Roadmap

Organizations typically implement AI-driven real-time BI through phased approaches. Table 5 outlines a representative roadmap with key activities and dependencies.

Table 5. Implementation Roadmap

Phase	Key Activities	Typical Duration	Prerequisites
Assessment	Current state analysis, use case prioritization, technical feasibility evaluation	1-2 months	Executive sponsorship, stakeholder engagement
Foundation	Data streaming infrastructure, basic pipeline development, dashboard creation	3-4 months	Technical architecture, data access approvals
ML Integration	Feature engineering, model development, initial deployment, testing	2-3 months	Clean data streams, ML expertise
Automation	Decision rules implementation, automated triggers, closed-loop validation	1-2 months	Model performance metrics, operational acceptance
Expansion	Additional use cases, enhanced models, integration with enterprise systems	Ongoing	Proven value, organizational adoption

Success factors include realistic scoping, cross-functional teams, and iterative delivery approaches. The roadmap should align with organizational maturity, starting with descriptive analytics before progressing to predictive and prescriptive capabilities. Early wins build momentum and secure continued investment for more ambitious initiatives.

5. PRACTICAL APPLICATIONS AND CASE STUDIES

Enterprises from multiple sectors have embarked on real-time BI initiatives with AI-driven components. This section explores select applications, highlighting challenges and benefits.

5.1. Industry Examples

5.1.1. Finance and Banking

Financial institutions employ real-time BI for fraud detection, credit scoring, and algorithmic trading. By integrating ML models within transaction streams, banks can detect anomalies and block suspicious activities quickly (Ragazou et al.,

2023). Traders rely on low-latency analytics to execute split-second decisions in volatile markets.

5.1.2. Retail and E-Commerce

Online retailers monitor customer behaviors, inventory levels, and supply chain data to optimize recommendations, pricing strategies, and logistics. AI-driven recommendation engines update product offerings as soon as user interactions occur (Kitsios & Kamariotou, 2021). Integrating streaming analytics with inventory management reduces stockouts and enhances customer satisfaction.

5.1.3. Healthcare

Healthcare facilities analyze sensor data from wearable devices, patient monitors, and electronic medical records. Predictive models help clinicians detect early warning signs, triage urgent cases, or recommend personalized care plans (Schmitt, 2023). Privacy regulations add complexity, requiring strict data governance and model explainability.

5.1.4. Manufacturing

Real-time analytics in manufacturing addresses predictive maintenance and quality control. Machine sensors relay operational data to AI models that anticipate component failures (Hiran et al., 2023). This proactive approach reduces downtime and extends machine life cycles.

5.2. Implementation Challenges

Several common challenges arise during the implementation of AI-driven real-time BI systems. These include data pipeline reliability, model transparency, and organizational readiness.

1. **Data Pipeline Reliability**: High-velocity data streams can overwhelm poorly configured architectures, causing bottlenecks and data loss.
2. **Model Transparency**: Complex ML models (e.g., deep learning) often lack interpretability. Stakeholders may hesitate to trust black-box predictions (Ragazou et al., 2023).
3. **Organizational Readiness**: Departments must cooperate closely to align priorities, share data, and standardize processes (Kitsios & Kamariotou, 2021).

Table 6. Challenges and Mitigation Strategies in AI-Driven Real-Time BI

Challenge	Potential Mitigation	Example
Data Quality	Implement real-time validation, scrubbing	Automated anomaly detection at the ingestion layer
Scalability	Employ distributed architectures, load balancing	Dynamic resource allocation in cloud-based platforms
Model Interpretability	Incorporate explainable AI methods	Using SHAP or LIME for feature contribution analysis
Regulatory Compliance	Adopt privacy-preserving techniques	Data anonymization, secure multi-party computation
Cultural Resistance	Provide training, involve stakeholders early	Workshops to build trust in AI-driven insights

5.3. Ethical Considerations

Real-time AI systems can influence decisions with significant implications for individuals and society. Biased algorithms may amplify existing inequalities (Schmitt, 2023). Constant monitoring and auditing help identify unfair outcomes. Organizations must incorporate ethical guidelines and accountability measures to maintain public trust.

6. EMERGING TRENDS AND FUTURE DIRECTIONS

Real-time BI will likely evolve alongside advancements in AI, ML, and data engineering. Key trends include the wider adoption of automated ML pipelines, the integration of edge computing, and the proliferation of open-source frameworks (Kitsios & Kamariotou, 2021).

6.1. Cloud-Based AI for BI

Cloud providers offer specialized services for streaming analytics, data warehousing, and AI model deployment. Serverless computing paradigms reduce the overhead of managing infrastructure (Ragazou et al., 2023). This model extends to AI-based pipelines, enabling organizations to shift focus from hardware provisioning to strategic planning.

6.2. Real-Time ML Pipelines and AutoML

AutoML tools automate hyperparameter optimization, feature engineering, and model selection. Real-time pipelines benefit from these solutions because they accelerate experimentation and reduce manual intervention. Continuous integration and continuous deployment (CI/CD) practices streamline the lifecycle of AI models (Hiran et al., 2023).

Figure 3. Example Real-Time ML Pipeline

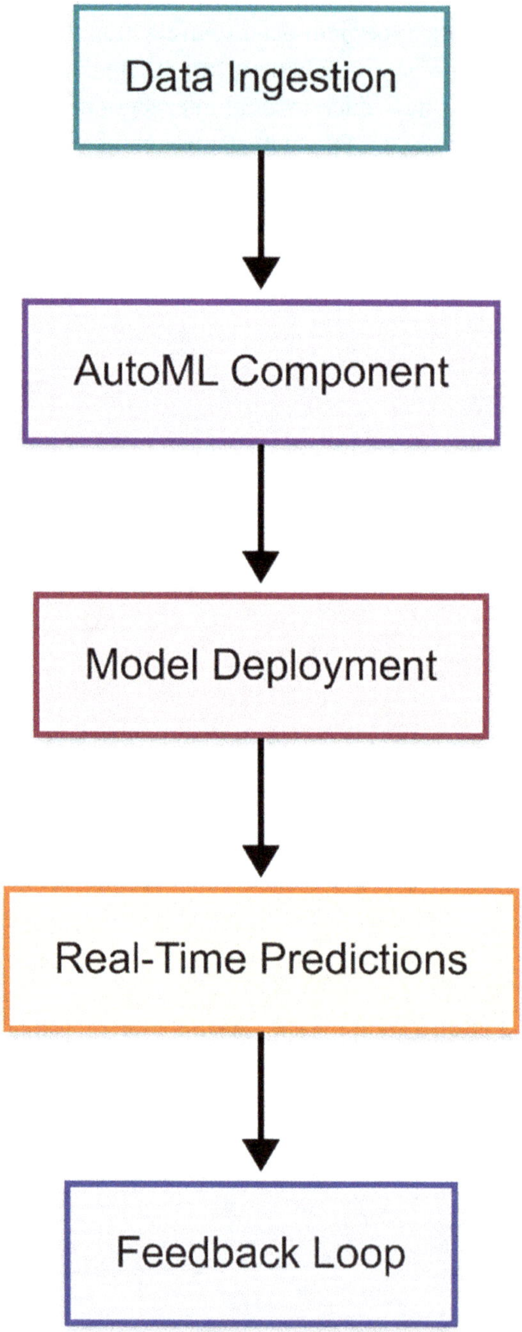

6.3. Autonomous Analytics

Advanced systems aim to automate the entire analytics process, from data ingestion to decision execution. These self-managing systems dynamically orchestrate resources, retrain models, and adapt to shifting data distributions (Schmitt, 2023). Although still in early development, autonomous analytics may reshape how organizations leverage BI in the future.

6.4. Edge Analytics for Latency-Critical Applications

Edge computing shifts processing capabilities closer to data sources, reducing network latency and bandwidth consumption. This approach proves particularly valuable for applications with strict timing requirements or connectivity constraints (Zhang et al., 2021). Smart factories deploy edge analytics to control manufacturing processes without round-trip communications to centralized data centers. Retail environments use in-store edge computing for real-time inventory tracking and customer experience personalization.

Technical implementations typically employ lightweight ML models optimized for resource-constrained environments. Model compression techniques—pruning, quantization, knowledge distillation—reduce computational requirements while preserving acceptable accuracy (Xu et al., 2023). Federated learning enables model training across distributed edge nodes without centralizing sensitive data, addressing both privacy concerns and bandwidth limitations.

Future developments will likely focus on seamless coordination between edge, fog, and cloud layers, creating adaptive processing hierarchies that optimize resource utilization across the computing continuum.

6.5. Explainable AI for Transparent Decision-Making

As AI systems are a factor in life and death decisions, the need for explainability grows. Methods and tools that present the model behavior in a comprehensible way to human stakeholders, tackling the problem of understanding (or "opening the black boxes", Lipton, 2016) of highly complex models (Xie et al., 2022) satisfy the definition of Explainable AI (XAI). We focus on connecting programs that have already been studying explainability to regulators developing the next set of explainability regulations.

Key approaches include:

Decision trees, rule lists, and sparse linear models are intrinsically interpretable models whose logic can be easily read by humans, but which pay the price by possibly reduced performance.

LIME, SHAP and counter factual explanations which provide post-hoc explanations of complex models behaviours but approximate the complex model behavior with simpler representations.

Attention Visualization: Heat maps and attention weights on image or text inpust to visualize what features are most important or give a feature more explanation in the answer.

Automated generation of textual explanations of mathematical models through natural language explanations that explain the mathematical model output in human readable form.

The research shows that well designed explanations can foster stakeholder trust, and as such enable more successful human–AI collaboration. Nevertheless, there still exist challenges in determining the right tradeoff between explanation fidelity and comprehension, and picking the correct types of explanations for diverse user types (Soori et al., 2024).

6.6. Augmented Analytics and Automated Insights

This consists of AI augmented analytics which uses the capabilities of AI to empower the human expertise to assist with the analytics process. These systems implicitly identify patterns, have insights, and make analysis suggestions without the explicit programming. Non technical users can query data through conversational interactions instead of formal languages into such interfaces, hence called natural language interfaces (Sharda et al., 2023).

Advanced implementations include:

Automated: Algorithms that look for statistically significant patterns, correlations and anomalies in data and automatically surface the findings.

Translation of qualitative results to natural language through narrative summaries with key implications for business stakeholders.

Suggestion engines that choose appropriate datasets, visualizations and follow up analytical tasks based on user context and user objectives are coined as Smart Data Discovery.

AI advisors to help analysts navigate heavy analysis processes, proposing how to go about it and calling out stumbling blocks.

These capabilities democratize analytics beyond technical roles to all roles in the company, to deliver insights to domain experts who may not have the technical training needed for this work. And analytical augmentation derived from these techniques accelerates discovery cycles while preserving human high quality judgment in critical interpretation (Eboigbe et al. 2023).7. Organizational Considerations and Change Management

7. CULTURAL TRANSFORMATION FOR DATA-DRIVEN DECISION-MAKING

Implementing AI-driven real-time BI requires cultural shifts beyond technical deployments. Organizations must cultivate data literacy, analytical thinking, and comfort with algorithmic recommendations across hierarchical levels (Jiménez-Partearroyo & Medina-López, 2024). Leaders play critical roles in modeling data-driven behaviors and establishing psychological safety for challenging intuition-based decisions.

Successful transformations typically involve:

- Executive Sponsorship: Visible commitment from senior leadership, demonstrated through resource allocation and personal adoption of analytics tools.
- Data Literacy Programs: Structured training that builds capabilities from basic statistical understanding to advanced analytical interpretation, tailored to role requirements.
- Performance Incentives: Alignment of evaluation criteria and rewards with data-driven behaviors and outcomes, recognizing both process adherence and results.
- Change Champions: Peer influencers who demonstrate practical applications and benefits within specific departments, accelerating adoption through social learning.
- Decision Process Redesign: Explicit integration of analytics into governance structures, requiring data-backed justification for key decisions.

Research indicates that cultural factors often determine success more strongly than technical sophistication. Organizations with strong analytical cultures achieve 5-6 times greater business impact from similar technical investments compared to those with resistant cultures (Ebule, 2025).

7.1. Skills Development and Team Structures

Real-time AI systems demand diverse expertise across data engineering, machine learning, domain knowledge, and visualization design. Organizations adopt various team models to assemble these capabilities (Sharda et al., 2023):

Centralized Centers of Excellence: Specialized teams that provide analytics services across business units, offering consistent methodologies and economies of scale.

Embedded Analysts: Domain-specialized data scientists integrated within business functions, enabling deep understanding of operational contexts.

Federated Models: Hub-and-spoke structures that combine centralized platform teams with distributed analysts, balancing standardization and domain alignment.

Cross-Functional Squads: Agile teams combining technical and business roles for specific use cases, following product management approaches.

Skills development requires continuous learning programs that address both technical competencies and business acumen. Organizations increasingly complement traditional training with experiential learning approaches—hackathons, rotation programs, and mentoring relationships—that build practical application skills (Hemachandran et al., 2022).

7.2. Ethical Guidelines and Responsible AI Practices

Ethics are also beyond regulation to include societal effects and organizational accountability. The organizations using real-time AI technologies are advised to design their governance structure that will consider the issues of algorithmic bias, protection of privacy, transparency and human control (Xie et al., 2022). In a holistic approach, there is an inclusion of:

- Ethics Committees.: Cross functional teams to vet AI applications with organizational values and societal norms especially those high risk areas.
- Impact Assessments: Formal consideration of what harm may follow to various groups of stakeholders, and harm avoided by careful preparation.
- Fairness Metrics.: Quantitative indicators that identify and remedy differences impacts among demographic groups observed in each and every stage of the model lifecycle.
- Human-in-the-Loop Protocols.: Specified human review and intervention rules in automated decisions especially regarding the consequential or the edge cases.
- Good design practices.: Best practices, which take ethics into account and are not in the form of ex post countermeasures to control the design of systems in the early phases.

The most prominent organizations recognize that ethical AI practices are risk-management necessities as well as competitive diversifiers. Both transparent and responsible methods increase stakeholder trust and brand reputation as more people become aware of the effects of algorithms (Soori et al., 2024).

8. CONCLUSION

Real-time BI, enriched by AI and ML, offers organizations the ability to act swiftly on emerging trends and anomalies. The proposed systemic framework highlights the integration of streaming data pipelines, adaptive ML algorithms, and user-centric decision interfaces. By synthesizing these components, enterprises can achieve proactive, evidence-based decision-making that aligns with strategic goals.

This chapter demonstrated the theoretical foundations of BI and traced its evolution toward real-time analytics. It identified best practices for deploying AI within continuous data streams, pointing to the value of incremental model updates and interpretability methods. Practical examples illustrated key benefits and challenges across finance, retail, healthcare, and manufacturing.

While real-time AI-driven BI provides many advantages, it also introduces complexities related to data governance, ethical considerations, and stakeholder alignment. Future developments in cloud-based AI services, AutoML, and autonomous analytics will likely expand capabilities and ease adoption. Organizations that embrace these trends responsibly may achieve transformative gains in agility, innovation, and competitive positioning.

8.1 Future Research Directions

Several challenges in using AI for real-time BI are beginning to arise, and the future research should handle issues related to these challenges. In the first case, adaptive architectures that allocate different levels of edge and cloud processing are investigated by taking into account contextual factors (data velocity, privacy constraints, and computation needs) to achieve a good balance between processing near the data and further away in the cloud. Second, studies could investigate how systems learn as they go from human–driven operation to more and more autonomous operation. Third, research on cognitive aware interfaces can contribute towards the improvement of human – AI collaboration capabilities to adapt information presentation to the mental models and cognitive loads of decision makers.

Blockchain integration and quantum computing for purely complex optimization problems and neuromorphic approach in which human cognitive processes will be awaited for. Progress in these domains will almost certainly be facilitated by cross—disciplinary collaboration of computer scientists, cognitive psychologists, and business managers.

8.2 Practical Implications

In concluding this chapter, several practical implications of AI in embedded BI are provided for those organizations that opt for such an embedded real-time BI. The one then is the systemic framework, where they describe a structured way of linking technical capabilities with the business objectives. Second, in view of the implementation roadmap consisted of a tested sequence to make complexity manageable while delivering incremental value. Third, the case studies show achievable results in different industries so as to serve as realistic benchmarks for planning and evaluation.

Therefore, practitioners should know that successful implementations balance technical sophistication and organizational readiness. Building momentum starts with well defined use cases that have a direct business impact. Accountability is maintained by continuous measurement against known and agreed baseline metrics; and providers can continue to justify investment as a result. Finally, it encourages and fosters sustainable adoption and trust amongst stakeholders by treating governance and ethics as the foundational elements and not as a compliance afterthought..

REFERENCES

Chaudhari, A. V., & Charate, P. A. (2025). AI-driven data warehousing in real-time business intelligence: A framework for automated ETL, predictive analytics, and cloud integration. *International Journal of Research Culture Society*, *9*(3), 185–190. DOI: 10.2017/IJRCS/202503025

Ebule, A. (2025). The role of business intelligence and artificial intelligence in real-time decision making. *International Journal of Scientific Research and Management*, *13*(1), 1902–1916. DOI: 10.18535/ijsrm/v13i01.ec04

Eboigbe, E. O., Farayola, O., Olatoye, F. O., Nnabugwu, O. C., & Daraojimba, C. (2023). Business intelligence transformation through AI and data analytics. *Engineering Science & Technology Journal*, *4*(5), 285–307. DOI: 10.51594/estj.v4i5.616

Hemachandran, K., Khanra, S., Rodriguez, R. V., & Jaramillo, J. (Eds.). (2022). *Machine learning for business analytics: Real-time data analysis for decision-making*. Productivity Press., DOI: 10.4324/9781003206316

Hiran, K. K., Hemachandran, K., Pise, A., & Rabi, B. J. (Eds.). (2023). *Handbook of research on AI and knowledge engineering for real-time business intelligence*. IGI Global.

Jiménez-Partearroyo, M., & Medina-López, A. (2024). Leveraging business intelligence systems for enhanced corporate competitiveness: Strategy and evolution. *Systems*, *12*(3), 94. DOI: 10.3390/systems12030094

Kitsios, F., & Kamariotou, M. (2021). Artificial intelligence and business strategy towards digital transformation: A research agenda. *Sustainability*, *13*(4), 2025. DOI: 10.3390/su13042025

Papapanagiotou, P., Vaughan, J., Smola, F., & Fleuriot, J. (2021). A real-world case study of process and data-driven predictive analytics for manufacturing workflows. In *Proceedings of the 54th Hawaii International Conference on System Sciences (HICSS-54)*. IEEE., https://scholarspace.manoa.hawaii.edu

Primawati, A., & Sitanggang, I. S., Annisa, & Astuti, D. A. (2024). Real-time business intelligence development using machine learning to increase the potential of the dairy goat milk business. *International Journal of Electrical and Computer Engineering*, *14*(5), 5612–5625. DOI: 10.11591/ijece.v14i5.pp5612-5625

Ragazou, K., Passas, I., Garefalakis, A., & Zopounidis, C. (2023). Business intelligence model empowering SMEs to make better decisions and enhance their competitive advantage. *Discover Analytics*, *1*, 2. Advance online publication. DOI: 10.1007/s44257-022-00002-3

Schmitt, M. (2023). Automated machine learning: AI-driven decision making in business analytics. *Intelligent Systems with Applications*, *18*, 200188. DOI: 10.1016/j.iswa.2023.200188

Sharda, R., Delen, D., & Turban, E. (2023). *Business intelligence, analytics, data science, and AI: A managerial perspective* (5th ed.). Pearson.

Soori, M., Jough, F. K. G., Dastres, R., & Arezoo, B. (2024). AI-based decision support systems in Industry 4.0: A review. *Journal of Economy and Technology*. Advance online publication. https://doi.org/DOI: 10.1016/j.ject.2024.08.005

Vilela, F. de A., Times, V. C., Bernardi, A. C. de C., Freitas, A. de P., & Ciferri, R. R. (2023). A non-intrusive and reactive architecture to support real-time ETL processes in data warehousing environments. *Heliyon*, *9*(5), e15728. DOI: 10.1016/j.heliyon.2023.e15728 PMID: 37215774

Schmitt, M. (2023). Automated machine learning: AI-driven decision making in business analytics. *Intelligent Systems with Applications*, *18*, 200188. Advance online publication. DOI: 10.1016/j.iswa.2023.200188

Lu, Y., & Xu, X. (2019). Cloud-based manufacturing equipment and big data analytics to enable on-demand manufacturing services. *Robotics and Computer-integrated Manufacturing*, *57*, 92–102. DOI: 10.1016/j.rcim.2018.11.006

Wei, X., Wu, Z., & Li, Q. (2023). Incremental learning strategies for real-time stock price prediction. *Sensors (Basel)*, *23*(10), 5112. DOI: 10.3390/s23105112

Xie, D., Luo, H., & Meng, F. (2022). Trustworthy AI in business intelligence: The role of model explainability. *Big Data and Cognitive Computing*, *6*(4), 88. DOI: 10.3390/bdcc6040088

Protopappas, L., Bechtsis, D., & Tsotsolas, N. (2025). IoT Services for Monitoring Food Supply Chains. *Applied Sciences (Basel, Switzerland)*, *15*(13), 7602. Advance online publication. DOI: 10.3390/app15137602

Zhang, G., Song, Y., & Xu, C. (2021). Edge computing for real-time analytics: A systematic literature review. *Future Internet*, *13*(9), 221. DOI: 10.3390/fi13090221

Chapter 10

The Role of Business Intelligence in Digital Transformation and Competitive Advantage

Khalil Omar
https://orcid.org/0000-0002-5328-5762
University of Petra, Jordan

Jamal Zraqou
https://orcid.org/0000-0001-9060-7188
University of Petra, Jordan

Wesam Alkhadour
https://orcid.org/0009-0004-1937-0308
University of Petra, Jordan

Jorge Marx Gómez
University of Oldenburg, Germany

ABSTRACT

Business Intelligence (BI) has been acknowledged as a major driver in the paradigm of digital transformation, which is befallen by multitudes of complexities. Though the potential value that Business Intelligence can add to an organization is well acknowledged and respected, properly implemented and effectively utilized systems fail to exist within organizations for them to leverage such qualities into a sustainable competitive advantage. This chapter, therefore, takes a shot at this challenge by proposing an integrated framework for aligning BI capabilities with initiatives and strategic objectives of digital transformation. The technological, organizational,

DOI: 10.4018/979-8-3373-6801-6.ch010

and strategic aspects of BI implementation will reveal those critical success factors that foster competitive advantage within environments undergoing digital transformation. Results show that firms getting an edge through BI show st rong alignment between BI skills and digital change plans, putting in place better data rules, and building thinking cultures around analysis.

INTRODUCTION

Technological evolution, alongside changing consumer expectations and global competition, has fast-tracked the digital transformation imperative in all industries (Abu-AlSondos et al., 2024). Digital transformation is an essential reimagining of the use of digital technologies by organizations to create new business models, improve operational efficiencies, and deliver better customer experiences, not just reworking old ways but fundamentally setting in and adapting for new heights (Alloghani et al., 2022). As organizations embark on such transformational journeys, Business Intelligence (BI) has surfaced as one key capability required to support data-driven decision-making and the generation of strategic insight.

Business Intelligence includes the technologies, applications, practices, and processes that gather, combine, study, and show business information to help make better choices. It has moved from simple reporting tools to advanced analytics platforms, which can really change how well an organization performs and its competitiveness (Jiménez-Partearroyo & Medina-López, 2024; Solanki, 2023). Today's BI systems combine organized and disorganized data from many places, use smart analysis methods, and give useful ideas through easy-to-use picture screens.

Today's business environment is hypercompetitive, and the ability to use data as a leverage tool for strategy has moved from being a potential differentiator to becoming an essential element required fundamentally for survival (Rusu et al., 2022). Organizations in all sectors are making significant investments in BI capabilities as part of the process of traversing through complexity toward emerging opportunities and market shifts in the allocation of resources.

Despite substantial investments in BI technologies and growing awareness of its strategic importance, organizations continue to encounter significant challenges in translating BI capabilities into sustainable competitive advantage (Zanke & Sontakke, 2024). Research indicates that between 70% and 80% of BI implementations fail to deliver their expected benefits (Villamarín & Diaz Pinzon, 2017). This concerning statistic highlights the complexity involved in successfully deploying and leveraging BI systems within the context of broader digital transformation initiatives.

Several critical challenges contribute to this implementation gap:

1. Strategic Misalignment: Most organizations go ahead and implement their BI systems without clearly stating and aligning their strategic objectives with their analytical capabilities. As a result, they end up with capabilities that cannot adequately address the needs of the core business.
2. Data Quality and Integration Issues: Fragmented data within organizational silos pour inadequately measured quality into BI initiatives, undermining effectiveness.
3. Organizational Resistance: Cultural barriers and resistance to a data-driven decision-making process considerably impede the adoption and utilization of BI capabilities.
4. Capability Deficits: Organizations do not have appropriately skilled personnel or analytical abilities to draw meaningful insight from increasingly complex datasets.

These challenges become more pronounced with digital transformation because rapid technology evolution, changing competition, and customer expectations add to the complexity.

This chapter contributes to the understanding of BI's role in digital transformation and competitive advantage through four principal dimensions:

1. An Integrated Conceptual Framework: The paper develops a comprehensive frame articulating the relationship between BI capabilities, the enablers of digital transformation, and dimensions of competitive advantage.
2. Success Factor Identification: Analyzing use cases across industries, we identify critical success factors for organizations leveraging BI effectively to gain an edge over competitors in digitally transforming environments.
3. Implementation Roadmap: In this work, we propose a stage-based implementation approach providing guidance for organizations to evolve progressively toward aligned BI capabilities with objectives of digital transformation.
4. Measurement Methodology: A systematic approach to judging the impact of BI initiatives on competitiveness is developed here - an evaluation practice wherein a significant gap exists.

The rest of this chapter will go as follows: In Section 2, we look at the related literature on BI, digital transformation, and competitive advantage. In Section 3, we give our proposed integrated framework and methodological approach. The experimental setup is outlined in Section 4, along with use cases that show the application of the framework in different organizational contexts. The results of the analysis and the implications discussed in detail are presented in Section 5. Key conclusions are summarized with directions for future research in Section 6.

RELATED WORK

Business Intelligence: Evolution and Capabilities

The BI definition evolution started from the introduction of Howard Dresner in 1989. It was initially perceived as a set of concepts and methods for improving business decision-making through fact-based support systems (Tripathi et al., 2024). Early BI systems emphasized historical reporting and basic data analysis; most often, they functioned as isolated applications with minimal integration (Jourdan et al., 2008). The present BI platforms have evolved dramatically, wherein a comprehensive suite of technologies and methodologies for the collection, storage, analysis, and visualization of data in support of decision-making can be rendered by an organization (Emmanuel Osamuyimen Eboigbe et al., 2023; Trieu, 2017).

Recent studies have been directed toward the classification of BI capabilities and their relatedness to performance outcomes. BI capabilities were classified and linked to organizational performance in a work by (Ramakrishnan et al., 2018). They proposed the classification of BI capabilities into three categories: innovation infrastructure capability for BI, process capability for BI, and integration capability for BI. Though individual contributions of these different types of capacities affect performance, a major study on them is directed toward their integration and how it facilitates them linking with outcome measures. Hence, a framework like this one would support the accurate implementation of BI in firms.

Technological capabilities have been advancing at a rapid pace, thereby broadening the scope and possible impact of BI systems. Innovations in areas such as artificial intelligence, machine learning, and natural language processing would further empower the predictive and prescriptive abilities of contemporary BI platforms (Ebule, 2025). However, even with all this technology available, research by (Lale, 2022) proves that organizations still have challenges effectively implementing and utilizing BI capabilities.

Digital Transformation: Frameworks and Success Factors

Digital transformation can be defined as the fundamental rethinking of how an organization performs its works, the delivery of products and services, and customer interaction using digital technologies (Sallapalli Nihitha, 2024). It is not just incremental adoption of new technologies but rather total change in the organization affecting strategic direction, style of leadership, operational model, and cultural values (Merlano, 2024; Urs et al., 2024).

Recent literature has proposed different frameworks for conceptualizing digital transformation. (Rezaie et al., 2022) presented a model-based digital transformation framework for BI that captures and shares architectural knowledge of digital business cases, transforming conventional business into digital formats. The framework introduced essential elements and components, focusing on the management of technology infrastructure, operations management, digital strategy, and digital governance, thereby effectively conceptualizing digital transformation within the context of BI. Though (Verina & Titko, 2019) presented a conceptual model to understand digital transformation in business. They have identified three main categories, technologies, processes and management, and people, which can be used as an outline for analyzing digital transformation. This model helps understand the central components and environmental factors of digital transformation, making it applicable to discussions about business intelligence and its integration within organizations.

Research on the critical success factors of digital transformation has unveiled many key ingredients. In that, leadership commitment and a clear vision of transformation have been identified in almost all studies as foundational requirements (Senarathna & Wickramarachchi, 2024). Organizational capabilities regarding digital literacy, collaborative work processes, and the mindset of innovation can significantly contribute to the outcomes of transformation as well (Konopik et al., 2022). Moreover, it was highlighted by (Mohanraj Varatharaj, 2024) that data governance frameworks and analytics capabilities to support digital transformation initiatives.

Competitive Advantage in the Digital Era

The nature of competitive advantage has evolved significantly in response to digital disruption across industries. Traditional resource-based perspectives emphasize sustainable competitive advantage based on valuable, rare, inimitable, and non-substitutable resources (Paauwe, 2024). However, recent scholarship has highlighted the increasing importance of dynamic capabilities that enable organizations to reconfigure resources in response to rapidly changing environments (Dewi et al., 2024).

Data and analytics competencies have positioned themselves as possible elements of competitive distinction within digital contexts. The capability of big data analytics was shown by research carried out towards the contribution to competitive performance through enhanced dynamic capabilities (Mikalef et al., 2019). In another study, business analytics capability was found to significantly affect firm performance via the enhancement of organizational agility (Zafar et al., 2023).

The link between digital transformation and competitive advantage has drawn more academic interest. (Surendra Mohan Devaraj, 2024) discussed how digital transformation leads to competitive advantages mainly through better customer experience and improved operational efficiency. They presented an argument that digital transformation permits organizations to use clouds and big data analytics to support data-driven decisions and create innovations. Strengthening customer relationships, the transformation optimizes internal workflows, opening new revenue streams and raising agility. However, even with this advancement, studies synthesizing BI capabilities, digital transformation, and competitive advantage are dispersed.

Research Gaps and Positioning

Our review of the literature reveals several significant gaps that this chapter addresses:

1. Integrative Framework: An integrated framework that links the three components of BI capabilities, digital transformation, and competitive advantage has not yet been developed, although they have been separately scrutinized in prior studies.
2. Contextual Understanding: The specific contextual factors that can make or break the effectiveness of BI in advocating for digital transformation initiatives are not well grasped.
3. Implementation Guidance: Practical guidance on how to align BI investments with the objectives of digital transformation is nearly lacking, hence troubles for the practitioners.
4. Measurement Approaches: Methodologies for evaluating the impact of BI on digital success through competitive advantage are underdeveloped.

PROPOSED METHODOLOGY

Conceptual Framework

Based on the previous review of literature, this section proposes an integrated framework articulating relationships between BI capabilities and digital transformation enablers and dimensions of competitive advantage. The framework, shown in Figure 1, supports our methodological approach.

Figure 1. Integrated BI-digital transformation framework

The framework consists of three primary components:

1. BI Capability Dimensions: The foundational elements that constitute an organization's overall BI capability, including:
    - Data Management: Skills linked to data gathering, joining, quality control, and governance.
    - Analytical Processing: Skills linked to descriptive analytics and predictive and prescriptive analysis.
    - Insight Delivery: Skills linked to seeing, reporting, and spreading insight.
    - Organizational Alignment: Skills linked to strategic alignment with governance structures and developing skills.
2. Digital Transformation Enablers: The major enablers of digital transformation that play an interfacing role with BI capabilities:
    - Strategic Vision: Crystallization of the objectives and roadmap for digital transformation.
    - Leadership Commitment: Sponsorship from executives and allocation of resources.
    - Organizational Culture: Mindset of innovation, decisions based on data, and collaborative values.
    - Technological Infrastructure: Agile, scalable technical infrastructure for support initiatives on transformation.
    - Customer Centricity: Focus on improving customer experience using digital channels.

3. Competitive Advantage Dimensions: The major dimensions where BI-enabled digital transformation leads to competitive differentiation are:
    - Operational Excellence: As a core process, superior efficiency, quality, and productivity.
    - Customer Intimacy: Better understanding and response to customer needs.
    - Innovation Leadership: New products, services, and business model development speeded up.
    - Adaptive Capacity: Ability to sense and respond duly to environmental changes better.
    - Financial Performance Revenue growth profitability shareholder value enhanced.

The framework posits that BI capabilities interact with digital transformation enablers to drive competitive advantage through multiple pathways. For example, advanced analytical processing capabilities combined with strong customer centricity can enhance customer intimacy by enabling personalized experiences.

Implementation Methodology

Based on our conceptual framework, we propose a stage-based methodology for implementing BI capabilities that support digital transformation and competitive advantage. This methodology consists of five sequential phases:

Phase 1: Strategic Alignment

- Clarifying the organization's digital transformation vision and competitive positioning.
- Identifying specific business objectives that BI capabilities will support.
- Defining key performance indicators (KPIs) for measuring BI contribution.
- Securing executive sponsorship and commitment for BI initiatives.
- Establishing governance structures that link BI activities to strategic priorities.

Phase 2: Capability Assessment

- Evaluating existing data assets, analytical tools, and technical infrastructure.
- Assessing organizational skills and competencies related to BI.
- Analyzing current decision-making processes and information flows.
- Identifying capability gaps that constrain digital transformation initiatives.

- Prioritizing capability development based on strategic importance and feasibility.

Phase 3: Architectural Design

- Developing a comprehensive data architecture that supports integration across sources.
- Selecting appropriate analytical tools and platforms aligned with business requirements.
- Designing visualization and reporting interfaces tailored to stakeholder needs.
- Creating organizational structures that support collaboration between BI specialists and business units.
- Establishing data governance frameworks and policies.

Phase 4: Incremental Implementation

- Prioritizing use cases based on strategic importance and implementation feasibility.
- Developing minimum viable products (MVPs) for priority use cases.
- Implementing technical components through an agile methodology.
- Building organizational capabilities through training and knowledge transfer.
- Measuring and communicating early wins to build momentum.

Phase 5: Continuous Evolution

- Systematically gathering feedback from stakeholders on BI effectiveness.
- Monitoring emerging technologies and methodologies that could enhance capabilities.
- Refining governance structures based on implementation experience.
- Expanding use cases to address additional business requirements.
- Measuring contribution to digital transformation objectives and competitive advantage.

Analytical Framework

To aid in assessing BI's input towards digital transformation and competitive edge, we suggest an analytical framework that looks at links over three dimensions:

Capability Maturity Assessment

The capability maturity part checks the growth of essential BI abilities on a five-level scale from Initial (ad hoc, undefined) to Optimized (fully integrated, continuously innovated).

Digital Transformation Impact Analysis

The analysis impact dimension, therefore, examines how BI capabilities influence the following key objectives of digital transformation:

- Customer Experience Transformation: Impact on customer interactions.
- Operational Process Transformation: Impact on internal efficiency and effectiveness.
- Business Model Transformation: Value proposition and revenue generation.

Competitive Positioning Assessment

The competitive positioning dimension assesses the impact of BI-enabled digital transformation on competitive advantage across four:

- Cost Position: Impact on organization costs relative to competitors.
- Differentiation: Impact on unique value delivered to customers.
- Market Responsiveness: Impact on speed and effectiveness of market responses.
- Innovation Rate: Impact on development and deployment of innovations.

EXPERIMENTAL SETUP: GUIDELINES FOR USE CASES

Use Case Selection Guidelines

When applying our framework to organizational contexts, the researchers and practitioners are encouraged to select varied use cases that would allow them to make a comprehensive evaluation. The following are recommended selection criteria:

1. Industry Diversity: This involves including different sectors (manufacturing, financial services, healthcare, retail, technology) so as to ensure the wide applicability of the outcomes and pinpoint specific patterns.

2. Transformation Focus: This pertains to the case selections having different digital transformation priorities, customer experience, operational processes, and business models so that BI requirements can be examined with respect to differing objectives of transformation.
3. Organizational Characteristics: Established organizations transform, and digital natives emerge to compare approaches and identify contextual factors that influence implementation.
4. Implementation Maturity: Cases are selected which represent different stages of BI implementation and digital transformation to provide insights across the maturity spectrum and identify progressive development patterns
5. Scale Variation: Organizations of different sizes are included to examine how resource constraints and organizational complexity influence approaches to BI implementation.

Use Case Template: Manufacturing Sector

Contextual Elements to Examine

When analyzing manufacturing organizations, researchers should focus on:

- Transition from product-focused to service-oriented business models.
- Integration of operational technology (OT) and information technology (IT) data.
- Utilization of IoT-generated data for operational insights.
- Customer experience enhancement through product performance monitoring.
- Development of new data-driven service offerings.

Implementation Elements to Assess

Researchers should examine how manufacturers implement the following:

- Strategic alignment between BI capabilities and digital transformation objectives.
- Data architecture that integrates production systems, IoT devices, and customer data.
- Analytical capabilities supporting predictive maintenance and performance optimization.
- Organizational structures facilitate collaboration between operational and analytical teams.
- Progressive expansion from internal to customer-facing analytics applications.

Use Case Template: Financial Services Sector

Contextual Elements to Examine

When analyzing financial services organizations, researchers should focus on:

- Response to competitive threats from fintech disruptors.
- Enhancement of digital customer journeys and experiences.
- Development of personalized financial products and services.
- Optimization of risk management and fraud detection processes.
- Regulatory compliance requirements and their influence on BI implementation.

Implementation Elements to Assess

Researchers should examine how financial institutions implement the following:

- Integration of BI initiatives with customer experience transformation.
- Data architecture balancing regulatory requirements with analytical flexibility.
- Progressive development from descriptive to predictive customer analytics.
- Cross-functional collaboration structures bridging business and technology domains.
- Governance mechanisms ensuring compliance while enabling innovation.

Use Case Template: Healthcare Sector

Contextual Elements to Examine

When analyzing healthcare organizations, researchers should focus on:

- Patient experience enhancement through personalized care.
- Clinical outcome improvement through data-driven interventions.
- Resource optimization across facilities and care settings.
- Transition to value-based care models and population health management.
- Integration of clinical, operational, financial, and patient-generated data.

Implementation Elements to Assess

Researchers should examine how healthcare providers implement the following:

- Alignment between BI initiatives and clinical transformation objectives.

- Data architecture integrating electronic health records with other systems.
- Analytical capabilities supporting clinical decision-making and resource allocation.
- Governance structures balancing innovation with privacy and security requirements.
- Implementation approaches addressing clinical workflow integration challenges.

RESULTS AND ANALYSIS

Expected Cross-Case Analysis Patterns

The application of our framework across diverse organizational contexts is expected to reveal several important patterns regarding the relationship between BI capabilities, digital transformation enablers, and competitive advantage outcomes. Table 1 illustrates the anticipated analysis framework.

Table 1. Cross-case analysis framework

Dimension	Evaluation Criteria	Potential Patterns to Identify
Strategic Alignment	Degree of integration between BI and transformation governance.	Strategic integration level correlates with transformation success.
Data Integration	Effectiveness of data integration across organizational boundaries.	Integration maturity influences the scope of achievable outcomes.
Analytical Sophistication	Progression from descriptive to predictive to prescriptive.	Analytical sophistication determines transformative potential.
Organizational Adoption	The breadth of adoption across functional areas.	Adoption breadth impacts organizational transformation extent.
Competitive Impact	Balance across operational, customer, and innovation dimensions.	The multi-dimensional impact creates a more sustainable advantage.

The cross-case analysis reveals several significant patterns:

Pattern 1: Strategic Integration Drives Transformation Impact

Organizations that have shown strong alignment between their digital transformation strategy and business intelligence initiatives have derived much greater competitive benefits. In the manufacturing case, having the business intelligence function report directly to the leader of the digital transformation ensured a very tight alignment between analytical capabilities and strategic objectives.

Pattern 2: Data Integration Capabilities Enable Transformation Scope

The scope and impact of digital transformation were significantly under the purview of integration data across functional, technological, and organizational boundaries. A case in financial services showed how hybrid architecture, when designed well, enabled the complete integration of customer, product, and operational data, thereby supporting wide transformation initiatives.

Pattern 3: Analytical Sophistication Drives Innovation Potential

Organizations with more sophisticated analytical capabilities demonstrated greater ability to develop innovative products, services, and business models. The manufacturing case illustrated how advanced predictive and prescriptive analytics were able to create new service offerings based on equipment performance data.

Pattern 4: Organizational Adoption Determines Transformation Bread

The organizational breadth of adoption had a significant bearing on the extent of transformation that was achieved. The case in financial services showed how embedded analytics experts plus cross-functional teams helped carry wide adoption all through the organization.

Pattern 5: Multi-dimensional Competitive Impact Creates Sustainability

Organizations achieving competitive advantage through BI-enabled transformation demonstrated impact across multiple dimensions as opposed to just focusing on operational efficiency or customer experience. The manufacturing case illustrated how simultaneous improvements in operational excellence, customer intimacy, and Business model innovation created sustainable competitive differentiation.

Key Success Factors

Based on our framework and literature analysis, we anticipate five critical success factors that would differentiate organizations effectively leveraging BI for competitive advantage in digitally transforming environments. Table 2 provides an overview of these success factors and their characteristics.

Table 2. critical success factors for BI-enabled digital transformation

Success Factor	Key Characteristics	Expected Impact on Competitive Advantage
Executive-Level Strategic Integration	• Direct reporting relationships between BI and transformation functions • BI representation in transformation governance • Shared performance metrics • Joint resource allocation	Enhanced strategic alignment accelerates transformation outcomes and ensures BI capabilities address core competitive priorities.
Architectural Flexibility and Integration	• Hybrid approaches balancing centralization and distribution • Cloud-based components for scalability • API-driven integration across systems • Robust metadata management	Greater data integration enables more comprehensive transformation initiatives spanning organizational boundaries.
Progressive Analytical Capability Development	• Balanced investment in technology and talent • Roadmap from descriptive to predictive to prescriptive • Integration of domain and technical expertise • Continuous model refinement	More sophisticated analytical capabilities enable innovation in products, services, and business models that create differentiation.
Embedded Cross-Functional Collaboration	• Analytics specialists embedded in business units • Cross-functional teams with diverse expertise • Collaborative problem identification and solution development • Shared implementation responsibility	Broader organizational adoption expands transformation impact across functional areas and enhances value realization.
Value-Driven Implementation Sequencing	• Prioritization based on strategic importance and feasibility • Focus on early wins to build momentum • Progressive expansion from initial use cases • Balanced attention to efficiency, experience, and innovation	Strategic sequencing accelerates value realization and creates a multi-dimensional competitive impact that is more sustainable.

Practical Implications

The study of use cases and success factor identification brings out several key practical implications for organizations that want to use BI as a tool to gain the upper hand in the competition within the context of digital transformation:

Implication 1: Governance Integration

Organizations ought to create governance structures that integrate and connect the leadership of BI with the governance of digital transformation. This will help ensure strategic alignment, coordinated resource allocation, and shared accountability for outcomes of transformation.

Implication 2: Architectural Evolution

Organizations should adopt a progressive architectural evolution that meets the short-term needs of the organization and balances it with long-term flexibility so that integration can be accomplished across disparate data sources and technology capabilities continue to evolve.

Implication 3: Balanced Capability Development

Organizations should develop balanced investments in technological tools, analytical methodologies, and human capabilities to make sure that the business outcome translation of analytical capability is balanced.

Implication 4: Implementation Approach

Organizations should adopt an incremental, value-focused implementation approach that builds momentum while progressively expanding capabilities. This approach enables sustainable transformation while demonstrating tangible benefits.

Implication 5: Cultural Transformation

Organizations should recognize that effective BI implementation requires cultural transformation alongside technological change. This recognition enables sustainable adoption and utilization of analytical capabilities.

Limitations and Constraints

Our analysis and findings are subject to several important limitations and constraints:

Methodological Limitations

The use case approach provides rich contextual insights but limits generalizability across broader organizational populations. While we sought diversity in our case selection, the findings may not apply equally across all industries, organizational sizes, or transformation contexts.

Temporal Constraints

Digital transformation represents an ongoing journey rather than a discrete event, making it challenging to definitively assess long-term competitive impacts. Our analysis captures a specific point in the transformation journey of each organization, potentially missing subsequent developments.

Contextual Variations

The effectiveness of specific BI approaches is influenced by contextual factors including industry dynamics, regulatory environments, competitive landscapes, and organizational histories. While our cross-case analysis identifies common patterns, organizations must adapt these insights to their specific contexts.

CONCLUSION AND FUTURE WORK

Summary of Key Contributions

This chapter has examined the critical role of Business Intelligence in enabling digital transformation and generating competitive advantage. Through a comprehensive literature review, the development of an integrated conceptual framework, and analysis of organizational use cases, we have made four primary contributions:

First, we developed an integrated framework that articulates the relationships between BI capabilities, digital transformation enablers, and competitive advantage dimensions. This framework synthesizes previously fragmented perspectives to provide a comprehensive understanding of how BI contributes to competitive positioning in digitally transforming environments.

Second, we found five key success factors that set apart organizations which are using BI effectively for competitive advantage: strategic integration at the executive level, architectural flexibility and integration, developmental analytical capability in a progressive manner, Cross-Functional Collaboration embedded across the organization and implementation sequencing that is value driven.

Third, we suggested a phased implementation approach that directs organizations through the step-wise enhancement of BI competencies in line with digital transformation aims. This approach tackles typical implementation problems by focusing on strategic alignment, gradual value delivery, and ongoing evolution.

Fourth, we developed a multi-dimensional analytical framework for assessing the impact of BI initiatives on competitive positioning. This framework enables organizations to evaluate capability maturity, digital transformation impact, and competitive positioning outcomes in a structured manner.

Practical Implications

Our research brings some important insights to organizational leaders and practitioners, which are:

1. **Strategic Integration:** For BI to be effective in supporting digital transformation, it needs explicit integration at the strategic level. Organizations must put in place governance structures that link the leadership of BI directly with oversight of transformation.
2. **Architectural Approach:** Organizations should design flexible architectures aimed at integration, balancing short-term requirements with long-term adaptability. The hybrid approaches shown in our use cases serve as models for how to effectively manage varied sources of data.
3. **Capability Development:** Organizations should take an incremental approach to developing analytical capabilities, balancing technological tools, methodologies, and human skills. The evolution from descriptive to predictive and prescriptive capabilities should be aligned with strategic priorities.
4. **Organizational Design:** Effective BI implementation requires organizational structures that facilitate collaboration between analytical specialties and business domains.
5. **Implementation Sequencing:** Organizations should sequence BI initiatives based on a mix of strategic importance and how feasible it is to implement. Early wins create momentum and show value, while progressive expansion widens impact.

Future Research Directions

Based on our findings and limitations, we identify several promising directions for future research:

1. **Longitudinal Studies:** Research tracking the evolution of BI capabilities and their impact on digital transformation success over extended periods would enhance understanding of sustainable competitive advantage.
2. **Quantitative Validation:** Quantitative studies testing the relationships proposed in our integrated framework would strengthen empirical support for our findings.
3. **Contextual Variations:** Research examining how the effectiveness of specific BI approaches varies across different industry, organizational, and cultural contexts would enhance the applicability of findings.
4. **Emerging Technologies:** Research investigating how emerging technologies such as artificial intelligence, machine learning, and natural language processing enhance BI capabilities would provide forward-looking insights.
5. **Implementation Methodologies:** Research comparing the effectiveness of different implementation methodologies for BI initiatives in digital transformation contexts would provide practical guidance for practitioners.

CONCLUDING REMARKS

As organizations move through digital environments that are ever more complex, strategic positioning of BI capabilities becomes tantamount to competitive positioning. The organizations we found to gain competitive advantage through the digital transformation enabled by BI possessed the following traits: alignment of capabilities and strategies for transformation at an even more integrated level than usual; data architectures that have been made both more flexible and more integrated; development of analytical capabilities; collaborative organizational structures; and value-driven implementation approaches.

The framework and success factors identified in this chapter provide a foundation for organizations seeking to enhance their competitive positioning through BI-enabled digital transformation. In an era where data volumes continue to expand exponentially, and digital disruption accelerates across industries, the ability to translate information into strategic insight represents an increasingly critical source of competitive differentiation. Organizations that master this capability will be well-positioned to thrive in the digital future.

ACKNOWLEDGMENTS

The authors would like to thank the Deanship of the Faculty of Information Technology, the Deanship of Scientific Research and Graduate Studies at the University of Petra, and the University of Oldenburg for supporting this research.

REFERENCES

Abu-AlSondos, I. A., Shehadeh, M., Ajouz, M., Alkhwaldi, A. F., Abdeldayem, M., & Aldulaimi, S. H. (2024). The Role of Digital Transformation in Business: Opportunities Challenges and Future Directions. *2024 ASU International Conference in Emerging Technologies for Sustainability and Intelligent Systems (ICETSIS)*, 361–365. https://doi.org/DOI: 10.1109/ICETSIS61505.2024.10459639

Alloghani, M., Thron, C., & Subair, S. (2022). Past Achievements and Future Promises of Digital Transformation: A Literature Review. In Alloghani, M., Thron, C., & Subair, S. (Eds.), *Artificial Intelligence for Data Science in Theory and Practice* (Vol. 1006, pp. 27–39). Springer International Publishing., DOI: 10.1007/978-3-030-92245-0_2

Devaraj, S. M. (2024). Digital Transformation and Innovation: Driving Business Growth. *International Journal of Scientific Research in Computer Science. Engineering and Information Technology*, *10*(5), 885–894. DOI: 10.32628/CSEIT241051077

Dewi, H., Salsabila, H., & Atmoko, A. W. (2024). TRANSFORMASI DYNAMIC CAPABILITY DALAM SEKTOR JASA: STUDI LITERATUR. *National Conference on Applied Business, Education, &* [NCABET]. *Technology*, *3*(1), 231–246. DOI: 10.46306/ncabet.v3i1.120

Eboigbe, E. O., Farayola, O. A., Olatoye, F. O., Nnabugwu, O. C., & Daraojimba, C. (2023). BUSINESS INTELLIGENCE TRANSFORMATION THROUGH AI AND DATA ANALYTICS. *Engineering Science & Technology Journal*, *4*(5), 285–307. DOI: 10.51594/estj.v4i5.616

Ebule, A. E. (2025). The Role of Business Intelligence and Artificial Intelligence in Real-Time Decision Making. [IJSRM]. *International Journal of Scientific Research and Management*, *13*(01), 1902–1916. DOI: 10.18535/ijsrm/v13i01.ec04

Jiménez-Partearroyo, M., & Medina-López, A. (2024). Leveraging Business Intelligence Systems for Enhanced Corporate Competitiveness: Strategy and Evolution. *Systems*, *12*(3), 94. DOI: 10.3390/systems12030094

Jourdan, Z., & Rainer, R. kelly, & Marshall, T. E. (2008). Business intelligence: An analysis of the literature. *IEEE Engineering Management Review*, *36*(3), 29–29. DOI: 10.1109/EMR.2008.4648888

Konopik, J., Jahn, C., Schuster, T., Hoßbach, N., & Pflaum, A. (2022). Mastering the digital transformation through organizational capabilities: A conceptual framework. *Digital Business*, *2*(2), 100019. DOI: 10.1016/j.digbus.2021.100019

Lale, A. W. (2022). Business intelligence implementation in different organizational setup evidence from reviewed literatures. In Sharma, A., Kautish, S., Agrawal, P., Madaan, V., Gupta, C., & Nanda, S. (Eds.), *Knowledge Engineering for Modern Information Systems* (pp. 173–186). De Gruyter., DOI: 10.1515/9783110713633-010

Merlano, C. A. (2024). Digital Leadership and Transformation in Contemporary Times. *International Journal of Digital Strategy, Governance, and Business Transformation*, *13*(1), 1–20. DOI: 10.4018/IJDSGBT.352047

Mikalef, P., Boura, M., Lekakos, G., & Krogstie, J. (2019). Big Data Analytics Capabilities and Innovation: The Mediating Role of Dynamic Capabilities and Moderating Effect of the Environment. *British Journal of Management*, *30*(2), 272–298. DOI: 10.1111/1467-8551.12343

Nihitha, S. (2024). Digital Transformation: Reshaping Industries Through Technology. *International Journal For Multidisciplinary Research*, *6*(6), 31446. DOI: 10.36948/ijfmr.2024.v06i06.31446

Paauwe, J. (2024). Resource based theory. In Hutchings, K., Michailova, S., & Wilkinson, A. (Eds.), *A Guide to Key Theories for Human Resource Management Research* (pp. 231–237). Edward Elgar Publishing., DOI: 10.4337/9781035308767.ch29

Ramakrishnan, T., Khuntia, J., Kathuria, A., & Saldanha, T. J. V. (2018). Business Intelligence Capabilities. In Deokar, A. V., Gupta, A., Iyer, L. S., & Jones, M. C. (Eds.), *Analytics and Data Science* (pp. 15–27). Springer International Publishing., DOI: 10.1007/978-3-319-58097-5_3

Rezaie, M., Mirzahosein, Z., & Rasouli, H. (2022). Developing a Digital Transformation Architecture Framework: A Business Intelligence Approach. *2022 6th Iranian Conference on Advances in Enterprise Architecture (ICAEA)*, 7–14. https://doi.org/DOI: 10.1109/ICAEA57644.2022.10054019

Rusu, B., Hurloiu, L., Hurloiu, I., & Geamanu, M. (2022). BIG DATA: A SOURCE OF COMPETITIVE ADVANTAGE. *Annals of Spiru Haret University. Economic Series*, *22*(2). Advance online publication. DOI: 10.26458/2227

Senarathna, P., & Wickramarachchi, R. (2024). Critical Success Factors of Digital Transformation: A Systematic Literature Review. *2024 4th International Conference on Advanced Research in Computing (ICARC)*, 346–351. https://doi.org/DOI: 10.1109/ICARC61713.2024.10499772

Solanki, V. V. (2023). Evolution of Business Intelligence Tools. *International Journal for Research in Applied Science and Engineering Technology*, *11*(7), 1149–1151. DOI: 10.22214/ijraset.2023.54820

Trieu, V.-H. (2017). Getting value from Business Intelligence systems: A review and research agenda. *Decision Support Systems*, *93*, 111–124. DOI: 10.1016/j.dss.2016.09.019

Tripathi, A., Bagga, T., Vishnoi, S. K., Senathirajah, A. R. B. S., & Haque, R. (2024). Business intelligence solution implementation challenges: A comparative analysis of service based start-ups, small & medium and large enterprises. *Environment and Social Psychology*, *9*(9). Advance online publication. DOI: 10.59429/esp.v9i9.2864

Urs, N., Roja, A., & Nisioi, I. (2024). Digital Transformation in Organizational Management: A Bibliometric Analysis. *NISPAcee Journal of Public Administration and Policy*, *17*(1), 198–227. DOI: 10.2478/nispa-2024-0009

Varatharaj, M. (2024). Enterprise Data-Driven Decision Making: A Framework for Digital Transformation and Organizational Excellence. *International Journal For Multidisciplinary Research*, *6*(6), 34279. DOI: 10.36948/ijfmr.2024.v06i06.34279

Verina, N., & Titko, J. (2019, May 9). Digital transformation: Conceptual framework. *Proceedings of 6th International Scientific Conference Contemporary Issues in Business, Management and Economics Engineering '2019*. Contemporary Issues in Business, Management and Economics Engineering, Vilnius Gediminas Technical University. https://doi.org/DOI: 10.3846/cibmee.2019.073

Villamarín, J. M., & Diaz Pinzon, B. (2017). *Key Success Factors to Business Intelligence Solution Implementation* (SSRN Scholarly Paper 2965610). Social Science Research Network. https://papers.ssrn.com/abstract=2965610

Zafar, S., Ali, T. Y., & Uddin, A. (2023). EXAMINING THE ROLE OF BUSINESS ANALYTICS CAPABILITY IN FIRMS' AGILITY & PERFORMANCE: EVIDENCE FROM MANUFACTURING SECTOR. *Journal of Social Research Development*, *4*(4), 811–819. DOI: 10.53664/JSRD/04-04-2023-15-811-819

Zanke, Mr. P., & Sontakke, D. (2024). The Impact of Business Intelligence on Organizational Performance. SSRN *Electronic Journal*. https://doi.org/DOI: 10.2139/ssrn.4847945

Chapter 11
AI-Driven Cyber Threats: Behavioral Analysis and Strategic Defenses

Turki Fahed Al Masaeid
http://orcid.org/0000-0002-7901-5656
Abu Dhabi School of Management, UAE

ABSTRACT

The behavioural analysis of AI attacks is of extreme significance in contemporary-day cybersecurity as it pertains to how AI has the potential to enhance or disrupt security measures. AI attacks use leading-edge machine learning, deep learning, and natural language processes to carry out sophisticated attacks. AI defences, on their part, use predictability analysis and anomaly detection to counter attacks. In this chapter, AI in cybersecurity has dual responsibilities in threat reaction, reaction, and adaptation mechanisms. AI-based adversarial AI attacks, AI-based social engineering attacks, and AI-based automated exploitation attacks have been elucidated together with AI-based defences such as behavioural profiling and self-healing mechanisms. Real-life scenarios have been presented in the chapter to elucidate how AI has contributed to or has been employed in cyber wars.

INTRODUCTION

Background and Context

The emergence of artificial intelligence (AI) has significantly changed the models of digital security, both by creating previously unachieved defensive capabilities as well as creating new vulnerabilities. AI-enabled technological innovations, including machine learning (ML), deep learning (DL), and natural language processing

DOI: 10.4018/979-8-3373-6801-6.ch011

(NLP), have significantly expanded threat identification and management, says Ali et al. (2025). However, the two-fold utilization of AI has also witnessed AI-enabled attacks, wherein attackers use AI capabilities to outwit traditional security. Also, AI's capacity to perform very evasive and adaptive cyberattacks further enhances the threat environment. AI threats, as indicated by Alanezi and Al-Azzawi (2024), employ sophisticated strategies such as phishing, adversarial attacks, and social engineering through deepfakes, rendering it more challenging for traditional security protocols. AI-generated phishing emails, for instance, are able to bypass email filters by simulating human language patterns, targeting users' psychology.

From an organizational behavior perspective, AI-powered threats involve complex issues regarding human decision-making processes, as well as conformity in terms of security. According to Yzzogh et al. (2024), the success of cybersecurity does not only depend on technological means, but also organizational adaptability, employee behavior, and security culture. The increased emphasis by security on AI necessitates an approach that involves human-AI interfaces so that secure, adaptive models of cybersecurity are developed (Guembe et al., 2022). In general, AI-enabled threat advancement highlights the importance of an interdisciplinary approach, marrying AI-enabled defence strategies with an extensive examination of human behavioural patterns in cybersecurity.

Defining Behavioural Analysis in Cybersecurity

Behavioural analysis in computer security involves analyzing systematically users' behavior, anomalies, and threat actors' behavioural patterns so as to uncover and contain threats. Olabanji et al. (2024) explain AI-driven behavioural analysis employs ML models to monitor deviation from normal users' behavioural patterns, identifying potential threats through the use of anomaly models. Existing strategies toward computer security rely on rule-based models, which are static when it comes to adjusting to dynamically evolving threats. AI-driven strategies, by way of contrast, employ behavioural data in real time so as to enhance predictive capacity.

Behavioural analysis comes very handy while battling AI threats, which constantly change form so as not to get detected. AI behavioural analysis, says Shankari and Rethinavalli (2024), surpasses other other traditional methods when it comes to predictive analysis, enabling organisations to anticipate threats even before occurrence. AI-powered systems, for instance, are able to monitor login patterns, keystrokes, and device usage patterns so as to flag account takeovers, insider threats, or other suspicious work environment incidents.

However, traditional strategies have an important role to play in gaining cybersecurity resilience. Singh et al. (2024) clarify that traditional defence strategies, such as firewalls, intrusion detection system (IDS), provide fundamental defence layers.

The optimum approach involves the addition of AI-enabled behavioural analysis coupled with traditional defence protocols to develop an adaptive, secure posture. In general, behavioural analysis in cybersecurity refers to an adaptive approach leveraging AI capabilities to uncover and deter nascent threats while strengthening established models.

Importance of Studying AI-Driven Threats

The increasing sophistication of AI-enabled threats demands an extensive examination of how it is going to transform the discipline of cybersecurity. Ovabor et al. (2024) posit that AI-enabled threats utilizes the power of machine learning models to build very targeted threats, such as AI-generated phishing emails and impersonations via deepfakes. These threats breach organizational security by bypassing traditional defence mechanisms, calling for intelligent behavioural analysis approaches to neutralize them.

AI-driven threats are particularly topical today owing to the capacity of AI threats to dynamically change, as well as automate, their method. Salem et al. (2024) clarify that AI malware has the capacity to dynamically transform code so it cannot be detected, leaving static signature-based detectors obsolete. An example is polymorphic malware, continuously morphing form so it cannot be caught by anti-virus. What this shows is the need for AI-enabled products that are capable of dynamically altering behavior.

From an organizational behavior standpoint, human factor still plays an essential role in cybersecurity. According to Kale (2024), AI-powered phishing attacks exploit human psychology, so it is necessary that security awareness, coupled with training, form an essential part of an organization's cybersecurity approach. Employees need to be educated so that they are able to identify AI-generated social engineering attacks, building an environment of diligence and conformity. Learning AI-generated threats plays an essential role in creating proactive defence strategies by marrying AI-generated detection capabilities with human-centric approaches. Organisations need to implement an approach that unifies technological innovations with behavioural inputs as AI keeps evolving.

LITERATURE REVIEW

Existing Research on AI in Cybersecurity

AI has proved to be an inevitable tool in the context of cybersecurity, both offense, as well as defence. Polito and Pupillo (2024) posit that AI enhances cybersecurity by automating threat detection, accelerating response time, and maximizing the accuracy of security protocols. AI-enabled systems, consisting of ML and deep learning (DL), are commonly implemented to scan enormous data pools and locate patterns that indicate cyber threats. AI-enabled IDS, for example, has the capacity to discover network traffic patterns and proactively tackle potential threats. AI-enabled models also play a crucial role in automating security functions, reducing human interference, and maximizing efficiency (Binhammad et al., 2024; Kaur et al., 2023). In spite of these advantages, concerns over algorithmic biases, data privacy, as well as adversarial attacks, threaten AI-enabled cybersecurity systems. These limitations offer the need for ongoing R&D efforts toward enhancing AI's presence in cyberspace.

According to Adhikari and Thapaliya (2024), AI deployments beyond threat identification proceed to predictive analysis, whereby organisations are able to anticipate cyber threats beforehand. AI-enabled tools are capable of creating network baselines and identifying deviation patterns indicative of cyberattacks. Anomaly models, for instance, are capable of indicating suspicious patterns in real time, preventing data leaks as well as financial losses. Similarly, Kharbanda et al. (2023) accentuate the ability of neural networks and intelligent agents toward enhancing cybersecurity posture. These AI models facilitate strategic decision-making by providing actionable recommendations toward threat landscapes (Dokur, 2023). In spite of these innovations, AI-enabled protocols are not foolproof, as adversarial approaches toward AI models are able to exploit AI models so as not to get detected. Therefore, there has to be continuous AI methodology refinement so as to neutralise evolving cyber threats.

Conversely, AI also serves as an aggressive tool for attackers, enabling them to carry out sophisticated, automated cyberattacks. AI threats, according to Vulpe et al. (2024), are increasingly ubiquitous, as attackers use generative adversarial networks (GANs), as well as reinforcement learning, to bypass security protocols. AI-enhanced malware has the capacity to change evasive maneuvers automatically, leaving traditional security efforts moot (Salem et al., 2024). Besides, Ofusori et al. (2024) also highlight the onset of AI-generated phishing attacks, utilizing NLP capabilities to develop plausible deceptive messages. These AI-enhanced social engineering approaches boost the likelihood of successful penetrations.

Moreover, Das and Sandhane (2021) also underscore the AI threat posed by automating enormous-scale cyberattacks. AI-powered bots can perform distributed denial-of-service (DDoS) attacks with unmatched effectiveness, crippling infrastructure, and causing enormous economic losses. Similarly, Alanezi and Al-Azzawi (2024) argue that AI-powered cyber threats require an active defence approach, integrating AI resilience models so as to contain AI-enabled attacks. Since AI continues evolving, organisations must employ responsible AI development, sound security protocols, and continuous monitoring so as to secure against AI-enabled cyber threats.

Historical Evolution of AI-Driven Threats

The evolution of AI-infused cyber threats has witnessed prominent milestones, both mirroring the level of sophistication of cyberattacks as well as the concurrent advancement of AI in the context of cybersecurity. In conformity with Kaur et al. (2023), early AI utilization in the context of cybersecurity focused on rule-based strategies as well as rudimentary anomaly detection, both bound by static data models. The move toward ML enabled threat identification adaptation, but it also created loopholes as attackers leveraged adversarial AI techniques to bypass identification. Over time, cybercriminals started leveraging generative AI models to automate phishing, camouflage malware, and bypass traditional security (Jada & Mayayise, 2023). These trends depict how AI-infused cyber threats have evolved from rudimentary automaton capabilities to sophisticated capabilities of self-learning, elevating the level of complexity in issues of digital security.

According to Guembe et al. (2022), most AI-enabled cyberattacks occur during the penetration and access level, considering that 56% of known attacks involve AI-enabled intrusion. The trend indicates the greater capacity of AI to independently exploit vulnerabilities, outpacing traditional defence capabilities. An example includes AI-enabled threats by means of deepfake, impersonation by CEOs, and manipulation of financial transactions. Similarly, AI-enabled malware, as seen through polymorphic viruses, continuously changes so as not to get detected (Ofusori et al., 2024). These examples show AI-enabled cyber threats' sophistication and autonomy, necessitating forceful counteractions.

Empirical findings relating to notable security incidents featuring AI reveal its two-pronged application as an offense as well as defence tool. In conformity with Willie (2024), historical AI models have previously found application in predictive analysis for threat identification, while cybercriminals are weaponizing AI-generated content, notably generative AI, to implement adaptive, real-time attacks. A notable breach involved AI-generated phishing emails bypassing traditional security filters, depicting the greater effectiveness of AI-augmented social engineering attacks (Salem et al., 2024). A case study by Kale (2024) established that AI-generated content, such as products like HackerGPT, makes it convenient to implement automated cyberattacks, reducing the skill level required to implement sophisticated breaches. The confluence of AI with cybercrime strategies depicts an evolving paradigm shift in threat scenarios, wherein historical strategies relating to cybersecurity are losing effectiveness.

The divergence in scholarly analysis regarding AI-enabled threats highlights the complexity of preventing them. Federspiel et al. (2023) place emphasis on AI-enabled cyber conflict threat, whereas Groumpos (2023) opines that AI regulation from an ethical approach could resolve its risky application. Ali et al. (2025) also posit that AI-enabled fusion approaches coupled with cybersecurity provide an active defence system against ever-changing threats. These studies highlight interdisciplinary approaches toward managing AI-enabled threats, coupling organizational behavior theories with advanced AI approaches toward fortifying digital defence infrastructures. In an era where AI continuously changes the environment of cybersecurity, organisations require adaptive models of security coupled with continuous AI innovations to stay one step ahead of developing threats.

Behavioural Analysis in Cybersecurity Research

Behavioural analysis in cybsercurity studies has also emerged as an inevitable field of study focusing on an attempt to understand cyber threats and enhancing digital defence. Sajikumar and Ajithkumar (2024) argue that behavioural cybersecurity is an evolving field that explores human influences over cyberspace, considering cognitive biases, emotional stimuli, and driving processes. The methodology employed by behavioural studies in the field of cybersecurity includes psychometric analysis, behavioural tests, computer simulations, as well as complex machine learning. An example is the study by Padilla et al. (2021), whereby methodology bridging application and theory has been established by marrying psychology profiling with human experiment across simulated contexts of cybersecurity. The method empowers scholars to accurately monitor human cyberspace-system interfaces, advancing threat identification, as well as threat management approaches.

According to Moustafa et al. (2021), behavioural studies significantly support studies in cybersecurity, particularly the identification of individual variability underlying threat susceptibility. Protection Motivation Theory (PMT) has also seen extensive application in the study of cybersecurity behavior, precisely how threat perceptions, as well as threat management strategies, influence users' conformity to security measures. Similarly, Lahcen et al. (2020) also highlight the importance of interdisciplinary approaches that combine behavioural cybersecurity, human factors, and computer models. These studies also place emphasis on holistic models that deal with cybertain threats' psychological, social, and technological facets. However, as Mersinas et al. (2024) expound, there remain untrodden areas when it comes to issues of morality surrounding behavioural interventions in cybersecurity, necessitating models that balance personal liberty with security.

Challenges in applying behavioural analytics against AI threats are controversial across the discipline of cybersecurity. Inconsistent findings across empirical studies, coupled with the lack of systematising strategies, are presented by Khan et al. (2022) as obstacles toward successful application. A primary barrier exists in conceptualizing behavioural constructs beyond organisations, due to underdeveloped taxonomies. Mermoud et al. (2019) argue that security information sharing (SIS) has an essential role to play in minimising risks presented by cyberspace, but behavioural reluctance to trade sensitive data serves as an impediment toward proactive strategies toward cybersecurity. Building trust across stakeholders proves problematic, further preventing the effectiveness of SIS.

According to Kommisetty et al. (2022), predictive behavioural analysis has the ability to automate threat identification, sidestepping labelled data and human efforts invested in extracting features. But it becomes problematic defining accurate automaton reaction trigger conditions, as AI models find it hard to cope with context-dependent behavioural intricacies. Almansoori et al. (2023) concur, drawing emphasis on the need for detailed behavioural models that precisely account for various patterns of cybersecurity across various cultural contexts. Overall, while behavioural analysis has experienced notable advancement in the context of cybersecurity, conceptualization issues, ethical concerns, and AI adaptation remain crucial areas worth exploring.

Gaps in Existing Research

A significant source of lack of consistency across AI-driven threat studies stems from the lack of universal behavioural analysis standards. Polito and Pupillo (2024) posit that the absence of universal AI threat behavioural analysis standards limits consistency and dependability across studies. Inconsistency hinders comparability of results, preventing sound predictive models from being established. Organisations utilizing AI-enabled security, for example, tend to rely on custom-built algorithms that are not generalizable across general cybersecurity standards, developing disjointed positions. Behavioural analysis, due to the lack of universal approaches, is subjective, reducing effectiveness in threat prediction, as well as AI-enabled threat mitigation. Therefore, universal standards must be established to facilitate practical application across AI-enabled cybersecurity.

Emerging AI-driven threats are uncharted, specifically those due to adversarial AI attacks, as well as evolving social engineering approaches. AI, according to Binhammad et al. (2024), enhances cybersecurity protocols while generating new threats exploited by attackers. Examples are AI-generated phishing emails, identity theft by means of deepfakes, as well as misinformation attacks by robots, creating intricate threats that it is challenging for traditional models of cybersecurity to address. An example is the increased application of Generative AI generating context-specific, authentic-looking phishing attacks that outwit traditional detection protocols. This necessitates further research on adaptive AI security protocols that are capable of addressing evolving AI-driven threats.

The psychological and organisational aspects of AI-enabled behavioural threats remain less researched. In accordance with Vulpe et al. (2024), the technical aspects of AI in cybersecurity remain the focal point of most studies, while human elements, crucial to threat exposure and effectiveness, remain overlooked. AI-enabled social engineering, for example, exploits cognitive biases, such as urgency and authority bias, to lead users to bypass security. Organisational behavioural studies reveal cultural reinforcement, coupled with security training, as crucial means of preventing threats. AI-enabled behavioural threats, however, remain seldom covered by employee training. Closing this loophole requires interdisciplinary studies converging cybersecurity, psychology, and organizational behaviour to offer inclusive defence strategies.

Finally, there is also a lack of operational scalability and feasibility in AI-risk behavioural analysis in real time. Although AI models can select out anomalies, there is an inability due to data privacy issues, together with an exorbitant computing cost, preventing them from being rolled out across the board, says Adhikari and Thapaliya (2024). An example is massive data generation by AI behavioural tracking in the cloud, creating processing as well as storage issues. Organisations must optimize AI models so that there is operational compromise between limitations and efficiency as far as security concerns. In creating scalable, successful behavioural threat identification systems, this issue has to be resolved.

Future research has to work toward developing standardised models of AI-based behavioural threat analysis so that studies are comparative and consistent. Also, interdisciplinary collaborations between cybersecurity experts, psychologists, and organizational behavior experts further refine the management strategies and understand AI-based social engineering threats. AI threat detection has to further develop by concentrating on efficiency and scalability so that it has practical application in real time. Filling these areas of study ultimately moves toward an increased, proactive, and fortified cybersecurity environment that can tackle the ever-evolving environment of AI threats.

KEY CONCEPTS IN BEHAVIOURAL ANALYSIS OF AI-DRIVEN THREATS

Establishing Behavioural Baselines

Establishing behavioural baseline plays a crucial role in AI threat identification, allowing systems to discriminate normal versus abnormal patterns of users' behavioural patterns. AI models, supervised, unsupervised, and reinforcement learning, play a crucial role in detecting normal patterns of operation in an organisation's cybersecurity system (Ovabor et al., 2024). Supervised learning employs labelled data to find normal patterns of users, while unsupervised learning clumps together patterns by similarity to develop expected patterns. Reinforcement learning further enhances threat identification by continuously adjusting patterns from adaptive behavioural data. Besides, defining "normal" patterns of behavioural patterns proves very demanding due to users' dynamic patterns across various sectors (Shankari & Rethinavalli, 2024). In cloud computing, behavioural patterns vary depending on users' work functions, level of accessibility, and context-specific utilization of computer resources (Olabanji et al., 2024). The complexity of human behavioural patterns, together with patterns that are not threat-indicative, makes it harder to define an accurate behavioural baseline (Salem et al., 2024). AI models further have difficulties with false negatives and positives, hence the need for an amalgamation approach, blending the utilization of machine learning models together with rule-based security protocols (Ali et al., 2025). The utilization of models, including the Cybersecurity Kill Chain (Guembe et al., 2022), can enhance the identification of expected patterns by users, together with detecting patterns showing possible threats.

Anomaly Detection Techniques

Anomaly detection underlies AI-enabled threat identification, detecting deviation from known behavioural patterns. Anomalous detection has several approaches through machine learning, including supervised, unsupervised, and reinforcement. Supervised learning employs labelled data to tag threats, while unsupervised learning categorises unknown patterns into categories that may indicate threats (Singh et al., 2024). Reinforcement learning boosts detection by iteratively updating models of detection through continuous feedback (Ovabor et al., 2024). AI-enabled examples of anomalies include erratic patterns of login, suspicious data access, and network deviation. An employee, for instance, accessing financial data outside normal work hours may indicate an account compromise (Shankari & Rethinavalli, 2024). Similarly, AI-enabled cyber threats compromise normal detection by generating patterns simulating normalcy, evading identification (Alanezi & Al-Azzawi, 2024). Anomaly detection highlights the need for AI-enabled models of anomaly detection that employ behavioural biometrics and context analysis to discriminate authentic from illegitimate events.

User Behavior Analysis

User behaviour analysis (UBA) employs AI-enabled analysis to detect insider threats as well as account compromise. Behavioural analysis determines patterns of attempts to log in, frequency of data accessibility, and patterns of interaction across digital entities to define intent (Shankari & Rethinavalli, 2024). Through the use of AI models, such as DL and NLP, threat posed by insider threats, such as abuse of privileges as well as unauthorized data transfer, can be detected (Ali et al., 2025). Besides, behavioural biometrics, such as mouse tracking analysis, as well as typing patterns, enhance cybersecurity by enabling identity authentication in real time (Ovabor et al., 2024). A change in typing rate, for example, could indicate an imposter impersonating an original user (Salem et al., 2024). However, behavioural biometrics are not foolproof, as AI-enabled threats are able to employ GANs to mimic authentic users' patterns, thus preventing identification (Guembe et al., 2022). AI-enabled user behaviour analysis must, therefore, be supplemented by traditional means of managing access if one seeks to enhance an organization's ability to withstand threats.

Network Traffic Analysis

Network traffic analysis (NTA) plays a crucial role in AI-enabled data exfiltration and identification of cyber threats. AI-enabled NTA models employ deep learning, as well as statistical analysis, to study network behavior in real time (Salem et al., 2024). AI-enabled NTA models study data transfer rate patterns, port utilization, as well as encryption protocols, to discover patterns that signify suspicious behavior (Ali et al., 2025). Examples of AI-enabled network patterns involve sudden outbound traffic bursts, unauthorized encrypted communications, as well as suspicious communications with remote servers (Ovabor et al., 2024). An example involves an AI-enabled system detecting an insidious data exfiltration attempt whereby an adversary extracts confidential data slowly over time so as not to get detected (Guembe et al., 2022). AI-enabled cyber threats also employ evasion techniques such as polymorphic malware, as well as encrypted command-and-control communications, necessitating adaptive threat models (Alanezi & Al-Azzawi, 2024). AI-enabled hybrid approaches that combine AI-enabled NTA with rule-based IDS provide increased protection against AI-enabled cyber threats.

Adversarial AI and Evasion Tactics

Adversarial AI exploits the loopholes of machine learning to bypass models of security undetected. Adversary machine learning processes, driven by AI, subtly tamper with input data, causing security models to label malicious acts as benign (Ali et al., 2025). Adversary AI proves very useful while bypassing protocols of anomaly detection as well as biometric authentication (Ovabor et al., 2024). Detection approaches involve adversary training, whereby AI models are trained using manipulated data sets so that models are made stronger (Singh et al., 2024). Explainable AI (XAI) also enhances transparency in decision-making processes across the discipline of cybersecurity, allowing security analysts to comprehend predictions by models and identify inconsistencies (Alanezi & Al-Azzawi, 2024). AI threats driven by GANs, for instance, creating authentication credentials by deepfaking, are fought by forensic AI models identifying minute inaccuracies in data synthesis (Guembe et al., 2022). Through continuous learning AI models, it ensures that protocols of cybersecurity remain responsive to adaptive adversary strategies, strengthening AI threat-proofing.

Social Engineering Attacks and AI-Powered Threats

AI-driven cyber threats also use social engineering techniques ever more frequently, depending on manipulation of human psychology and evasions of established security protocols. Powerful AI models have the ability to generate authentic-looking phishing emails, voice deepfakes, and synthetic personas to manipulate users into disclosing personal information (Salem et al., 2024). Advanced AI models-supported chatbots, for instance, have the ability to carry out impersonation attacks in real time, duping users into relinquishing credentials or executing unauthorized actions (Ali et al., 2025). Organisations must marry behavioural analysis with AI-supported deception detection engines to deter AI-supported social engineering attacks. These engines have the ability to scan linguistic patterns, tone changes, and context-specific anomalies to select out suspicious communications (Ovabor et al., 2024). AI-generated phishing simulations-supported security consciousness training has the ability to develop user resistance against ever-changing social engineering techniques (Shankari & Rethinavalli, 2024). AI-supported behavioural analysis coupled with educating users plays an invaluable role in preventing AI-supported social engineering attacks.

TYPES OF AI-DRIVEN THREATS DETECTABLE VIA BEHAVIOURAL ANALYSIS

AI-Powered Phishing Attacks

AI-powered phishing attacks are an evolving threat, leveraging AI capabilities to create very personal, authentic-looking phishing scams. Compared to generic phishing attacks that use generic email templates, AI-generated phishing attacks use natural NLP and ML capabilities to scan massive data sets, social profiles, email conversations, and behavioural patterns, creating deceptive emails targeted toward individual recipients (Ali et al., 2025; Salem et al., 2024). AI-generated phishing seems more authentic, increasing the likelihood of recipient interaction. In terms of behavioural analysis, AI-generated phishing attacks must be identified by detecting minute behavioural inconsistencies. Traditional phishing indicators, such as spelling mistakes or generic greetings, are less visible in AI-generated emails. However, behavioural inconsistencies, such as out-of-turn demands, out-of-routine urgency, or minor deviation from normal writing patterns, may signal phishing (Singh et al., 2024; Ofusori et al., 2024). The Social Engineering Theory (SET) shows how cognitive biases, such as trust, are manipulated by attackers (Moustafa et al., 2021). Besides, AI-driven behavioural analysis capabilities also have the ability to deter these threats by continuously monitoring users' reactions toward arriving emails, detecting any deviation from known patterns, and flagging suspicious emails (Olabanji et al., 2024). A mix of AI-enabled behavioural tracking coupled with traditional defence strategies has the ability to significantly enhance phishing identification in organisations.

Automated Data Exfiltration

Automated data exfiltration employs AI to extract confidential data stealthily from compromised systems. Compared to data breaches relying on bulk data transfer, AI-enabled exfiltration processes employ tiny-scale, intelligent theft approaches that fly below the radar (Shankari & Rethinavalli, 2024; Alanezi & Al-Azzawi, 2024). These processes monitor patterns of access, as well as users' behavioural patterns, to mix seamlessly with normal patterns, making it more challenging to uncover. Besides, behavioural analysis plays an invaluable role in identifying subtle data exfiltration patterns. Anomalies like rare file patterns, out-of-hours data transfer, or unauthorized attempts to open confidential files can be identified by tracking them in real time (Jada & Mayayise, 2023; Polito & Pupillo, 2024). The Principle of Least Privilege (PLP) stipulates that personnel shall only have access to data relevant to their duties; any deviation from this principle signifies suspicious acts (Lahcen et al., 2020). Besides, ML models trained from historical patterns of access data can build behavioural baseline patterns, as well as flag deviation patterns, indicative of exfiltration attempts (Ovabor et al., 2024). By leveraging AI-enabled anomaly identification, coupled with established security protocols, organisations can greatly enhance data theft incident identification, as well as prevention.

Lateral Movement Attacks

Lateral movement attacks occur when attackers initially obtain entry into an organization's network and systematically move laterally across interconnected systems to exploit valuable targets. AI-enabled strategies permit attackers to employ persistence means that mimic normal users' behavior, making them harder to detect (Guembe et al., 2022; Singh et al., 2024). Lateral movement attacks employ poor authentication processes, exploited credentials, and improperly configured permissions to move deeper into an organization's network. Detection relies crucially on behavioural analysis, detecting out-of-normal patterns that indicate lateral movement. Suspicious attempts to log in from unknown sources, repeated attempts to access unrelated systems, and out-of-sequence workflow steps are indicative (Mersinas et al., 2024; Federspiel et al., 2023). The Zero Trust Security Model (ZTSM) advocates continuous authentication and strict access restrictions to contain the risks posed by lateral movement (Ali et al., 2025). Organisations also employ AI-enabled behavioural analysis to discover attempts at lateral movement by reviewing real-time session lengths, elevation of privileges, and out-of-sequence authentication attempts (Salem et al., 2024). AI, together with traditional security policies, ensures an efficient defence against these ever-evolving threats.

AI-Generated Deepfakes

Deepfakes utilise AI to generate hyper-realistic simulated content, posing extreme threats to cybersecurity by enabling impersonation fraud, misinformation, and identity theft. Powerful GANs allow video and sound recordings to be manipulated so that convincing-looking content is produced (Almansoori et al., 2023; Willie, 2024). The technology has also been leveraged to deceive authentication processes by impersonating well-known individuals for financial fraud. However, behavioural analysis has the ability to aid the identification of deepfakes by identifying inconsistencies in simulated content. Analysis processes, such as motion analysis, voice inconsistency, and biometric authentication, have the ability to reveal anomalies beyond human eyes (Padilla et al., 2021; Kommisetty et al., 2022). The Uncanny Valley Theory states that human beings inherently register minute irregularities in simulated depictions, an ability that can be leveraged for identification (Kaur et al., 2023). AI-enabled forensic instruments today have the ability to scan micro-expressions, blink patterns, and lip-sync mismatches to reveal manipulated content (Sajikumar & Ajithkumar, 2024). By marrying behavioural analysis with deepfake models, organisations are able to build increased capacity to contain risks produced by AI-generated misinformation.

AI-Powered Botnets and Automated Attacks

AI-powered botnets employ machine learning to orchestrate massive-scale automated attacks, such as DDoS attacks, spamming, and credential stuffing (Binhammad et al., 2024; Ofusori et al., 2024). AI-powered botnets act independently, dynamically adjusting defences against them and dynamically evolving patterns of attacks in real time. AI-powered botnets can be neutralised by behavioural analysis, identifying out-of-normal patterns of traffic, as well as by automated patterns. High request rate, repeated attempts, and non-human browsing patterns indicate presence by botnets (Jada & Mayayise, 2023; Moustafa et al., 2021). Organisational behavioural theories, the Herding Theory, argue that botnets cooperate together as coordinated swarms, traceable by network analysis (Groumpos, 2023). AI-augmented security products are capable of analyzing patterns of suspicious traffic, discovering patterns of automated attacks, and executing real-time counterattacks to neutralise threats by botnets (Ali et al., 2025). Organisations are able to build secure defences against threats by automaton by marrying AI-augmented threat intelligence with human inspection.

Finally, the behavioural analysis of AI-driven threats demands a multifaceted and evolving framework that incorporates both technological advancements and ethical foresight. As illustrated in the mind map and practical framework, addressing AI-driven threats requires more than reactive security; it necessitates predictive and adaptive systems that can learn from emerging behavioural patterns and adversarial tactics. Deep learning, metaheuristics, and adversarial training play a crucial role in uncovering hidden threats, while compliance with frameworks like NIST and OWASP ensures a baseline of trust and reliability. Moreover, the integration of human-in-the-loop systems underlines the importance of balancing automated intelligence with human judgment, particularly in complex decision-making scenarios. Effective risk assessment, coupled with continuous model evaluation and governance, positions organizations to proactively counter cyber threats while maintaining transparency, accountability, and alignment with global standards. This holistic approach not only enhances organizational resilience but also promotes a secure, ethical deployment of AI in critical infrastructures.

CASE STUDIES OF AI-DRIVEN THREATS AND BEHAVIOURAL ANALYSIS RESPONSE

Case Study 1: AI-Powered Phishing Campaign

The use of AI has fostered an environment wherein there has risen sophisticated phishing techniques that dupe targets by utilizing AI-supported deepfake technology. A recent AI voice scam impersonating Italy's Defence Minister, Guido Crosetto, targeted Italian businessmen (Borrelli & Kazmin, 2025; Giuffrida, 2025). The case indicates how the context of security has altered, wherein AI has empowered social engineering attacks that are very convincing and able to dupe even experienced users. AI-supported deepfake voice technology had been exploited by the Italian tycoons' assault, utilizing cloned voices and impersonated caller IDs to provide an aura of credibility. What had posed as the defence minister's office had called targets, including famous people like Giorgio Armani and Patrizio Bertelli, insisting that they send money for an alleged ransom payment (Giuffrida, 2025). The assault indicates the emotional manipulation techniques exploited by AI-supported phishing attacks, utilizing urgency and trust in authority individuals (Moustafa et al., 2021). Through the utilization of behavioural theories like SET, attackers use urgency and authority cognitive biases to force hurried action (Lahcen et al., 2020). By evoking nationalistic emotion, the conmen evoked an emotional reaction that necessitated quick conformity. Assuming the call was genuine, one victim wired €1 million, waiting for payment by the Bank of Italy (Borrelli & Kazmin, 2025).

Moreover, behavioural models of cybersecurity accentuate anomaly identification and human threat assessment by way of human behavioural profiling, identifying deviation from normal patterns of communications (Kommisetty et al., 2022). In this case, human scepticism coupled with conditioned vigilance proved essential defence strategies. A case study, an assistant personal assistant at Menarini Pharmaceuticals detected inconsistencies by the caller, preventing an impending financial loss (Giuffrida, 2025). This substantiates that security consciousness training significantly decreases social engineering assault exposure (Mersinas et al., 2024). Besides, AI threat analysis capabilities complement human behavioural analysis. AI has the capacity to scan voice modulation patterns, linguistic markers, and other voice patterns to flag attempts at deepfake manipulation in real time (Ofusori et al., 2024). Besides, next-generation authentication protocols, including multi-factor authentication, as well as identity authentication through blockchain, could have mitigated identity spoofing threats (Olabanji et al., 2024). In general, the AI-backed phishing campaign targeting Italian elites depicts the vast impact AI has had on cyber deceit. Organisations, by harnessing behavioural models of cybersecurity, can develop greater resilience by marrying AI-enabled anomaly identification capabilities with human cognitive consciousness drills. The amalgamation of AI-enabled threats coupled with behavioural analysis emphasizes the need for continuous change management in the sphere of cybersecurity to tackle evolving AI-enabled threats (Sajikumar & Ajithkumar, 2024).

Case Study 2: AI-Based Malware Adaptation

The emergence of AI-enabled malware has posed an enormous threat to traditional means of cybersecurity. An example includes the SugarGh0st RAT campaign, traced back to Chinese threat actors targeting AI experts in the United States through spear phishing (Alan, 2024). The malware is an exemplar of sophisticated cyber espionage, leveraging AI capabilities to bypass traditional signature-based threat detection means and maintain prolonged access over compromised systems (Constantin, 2024). Traditional antivirus products rely on known malware signatures to mark threats. AI-enabled malware, such as SugarGh0st, dynamically changes, rendering static signature detection moot (Seldon, 2024). The malware ability to blend as legitimate-looking documents, such as spurious registration documents, exemplifies the sophistication of social engineering (Chacko, 2024). In support of the findings by Padilla et al. (2021), behavioural analysis in computer security stresses the importance of tracking deviation in users' behavioural patterns, an essential factor in fighting AI-enabled threats.

The SugarGh0st campaign had several behavioural indicators that assisted in identifying it. AI experts first witnessed very targeted phishing emails that imitated authentic communications across their work network (Constantin, 2024). The emails comprised LNK files that targeted executing dangerous JavaScript code upon opening. Behavioural models of cybersecurity show that analysis of deviant patterns of file execution and access examination plays an essential role in detecting these kinds of attacks (Lahcen et al., 2020). Also, products of UBA, monitoring deviance across system interactions, played an essential role in reporting unauthorized attempts at entry coupled with the SugarGh0st RAT (Almansoori et al., 2023). Organisational behavioural studies show that AI-backed defence approaches, including sensitization across employees, behavioural cybersecurity, and defence approaches, are able to tackle risks posed by AI-backed malware (Mersinas et al., 2024). Organisations must employ adaptive AI-backed defence approaches against ever-evolving threats. AI-backed anomaly identification, coupled with behavior-centric approaches to security, build defences against evolving threats (Olabanji et al., 2024). Cybersecurity experts are able to proactively find, neutralize, and eradicate AI-backed malware by employing behavioural analysis, AI-backed approaches to detection, and AI-backed approaches to anomaly identification (Singh et al., 2024).

Case Study 3: Deepfake Exploitation in Cybercrime

The increasing level of sophistication in deepfake has enabled cybercriminals to launch very convincing social engineering attacks. A case occurred in February 2024, whereby an employee handling finance in an organization that operates across the globe was manipulated into wiring $25 million by attending a video call fueled by deepfake. Cybercriminals impersonated the organization's Chief Financial Officer (CFO) and other co-workers, creating an illusion of credibility, and managed to get the victim to approve financial transactions (Chen & Magramo, 2024; Burt, 2024). The case reflects the massive impact of AI-generated synthetic content on cybersecurity, particularly financial fraud. Abuse by cybercriminals of deepfake includes impersonation attacks, manipulation of publicly accessible videos, and voice records, creating authentic simulations of individuals. The case aligns well with the study of cybersecurity behavior, concentrating on trust, social cues, and decision processes (Moustafa et al., 2021). The finance employee's initial reluctance, spurred by an initial phishing-like email, was overpowered by checking out known co-workers both visually and via voice, showing human cognitive biases' susceptibilities in computer-mediated communications (Milmo, 2024).

The detection of this case of synthetic identity fraud only happened when the employee cross-checked the transaction with the head office, detecting inconsistencies. Time-pressure and decision fatigue, social engineering scam enablers, have been indicated by behavioural studies in cybersecurity (Lahcen et al., 2020). Voice and face manipulation by AI serves to underscore the importance of adequate verificatory processes, including multi-factor authentication, complemented by real-time identification by deepfake identification algorithms (Kaur et al., 2023). The hack implications here extend beyond financial loss, exposing the need for tighter cybersecurity protocols that involve behavioural threat analysis (Padilla et al., 2021). AI threats require continuous employee training sessions complemented by continuous tracking, so as not to fall victim to deceptions (Kommisetty et al., 2022). As cases of cyber fraud continue to spike—striking 83% of organisations globally (Burt, 2024)—organisations must implement AI-enabled models of security so as to combat the increased sophistication of deepfake-enabled cybercrime (Ali et al., 2025).

Lessons Learned from the Case Studies

A key lesson learned from the case studies is that AI-enabled attacks capitalize on cognitive biases, social trust, and digital vulnerabilities to perform sophisticated attacks. Polito and Pupillo (2024) further posit that AI-enabled phishing, malware, and deepfake attacks employ automation to manipulate human decision processes, typically bypassing traditional security protocols. A case, the deepfake attack on a multinational organization relied on authority bias, compelling an employee to transfer $25 million. This serves to underscore organisations' need to institute behavioural cybersecurity protocols to address AI-enabled deceit (Kaur et al., 2023).

Another significant finding is the use of behavioural analysis in AI-generated threat detection and prevention. AI behavioural threat detection enhances security by identifying changes in patterns of users' behavioural patterns, says Binhammad et al. (2024). The SugarGh0st malware campaign demonstrated how AI-generated anomaly detectors identified suspicious system patterns, invoking early threat blocking. Organisations also reduce exposure to AI-generated phishing threats through behavioural cybersecurity training, heightening human scepticism and decision-making (Mersinas et al., 2024). A case includes the personal assistant in Menarini Pharmaceuticals, identifying inconsistencies in the AI-generated voice scam, blocking financial losses.

Moreover, AI-driven threat management products must continuously transform so as to align with adaptive threats. Adhikari and Thapaliya (2024) believe that the amalgamation of AI-driven threat intelligence coupled with human-centric anomaly detection significantly enhances AI-resistant resilience. The case studies reveal that the amalgamation of intricate authentication processes and sensitization training of the employees plays a crucial role in blocking cyber threats. Heightening human attentiveness through behavioural interventions complemented by AI-backed security architectures ensures an active defence against adaptive threats (Ali et al., 2025).

CHALLENGES IN IMPLEMENTING BEHAVIOURAL ANALYSIS FOR AI THREATS

Data Volume and Complexity

The exponential rate of digitization has produced an explosion both in terms of data complexity and volume, creating huge challenges in applying behavioural analysis across AI threats. AI defence relies on huge data sets containing users' behavioural patterns, system logs, and network flow data to discover out-of-normal patterns and predict possible threats (Olabanji et al., 2024). But AI-based analysis has limitations due to scaling, as it calls for huge computing power to scan, store, and analyze enormous data sets near-real time (Singh et al., 2024). Adding complexity are cloud infrastructures, as these generate dynamic, heterogeneous data streams that require intelligent filtering, as well as pre-processing (Shankari & Rethinavalli, 2024). Traditional data-handling approaches find it challenging to deal with the velocity by which AI-based threats transform, so there exists need for intelligent models of deep-learning, capable of threat identification near-real time (Ali et al., 2025). In addition, the mix of supervised, as well as unsupervised, models makes it challenging due to complexity in feature selection, as these models require quality data sets for training so that normal vs. malicious behavioural patterns get correctly discriminated (Ovabor et al., 2024). Organisational behavioural-wise, data overproduction, causing information overload, makes it possible for cognitive fatigue, diminishing the effectiveness of the security analysts' ability to provide quick, well-informed decisions (Mermoud et al., 2019). Using hybrid AI models, combining both human management, as well as automaton, has the ability to deal with these issues, so AI defence systems remain efficient, responsive, as well as adaptive, even across data-rich contexts (Salem et al., 2024).

False Positives and Detection Accuracy

Implementing behavioural analysis over AI-based threat detection must balance sensitivity versus specificity so that it minimises unwarranted positives while maintaining maximum accuracy. False positives result when benign processes are flagged as threats, inundating security personnel with unwarranted alerts, reducing operational efficiency (Shankari & Rethinavalli, 2024). By contrast, undetected threats, referred to as false negatives, result in severe threats to security by creating opportunities for adversarial players to exploit loopholes (Ali et al., 2025). Relying on machine learning models together with anomaly models has the drawback that these models get confused by authentic threats by mistaking them as deviation due to normal users' behavioural patterns (Singh et al., 2024). Traditional security approaches offer dependability by way of organised threat identification but lack predictive capabilities akin to AI-based approaches (Olabanji et al., 2024). An amalgamation approach relying on traditional approaches together with AI-based approaches has the capacity to enhance accuracy while reducing fatigue due to unwarranted alerts by cybersecurity experts (Guembe et al., 2022). Organisation-wise, an overloading number of unwarranted positives desensitises personnel, rendering them indifferent to severe threats (Padilla et al., 2021). Relying on reinforcement learning together with adaptive thresholding approaches has the capacity to enhance AI system accuracy so that behavioural analysis models continuously refine ability to detect (Salem et al., 2024). Organisations must also institute sound backchannels so that human analysts have an opportunity to refine AI models by considering authentic threat analysis (Moustafa et al., 2021).

Bias in AI Models

Bias in AI models is a particularly daunting issue with regards to using behavioural analysis for AI threats, as biased training data will lead to incorrect classification and biased security policies. Bias in security analysis usually results from non-representative training data, in which certain users' behaviour is overrepresented as malicious owing to context or demographic bias (Ali et al., 2025). This has the potential for discrimination, in which legitimate users are targeted whereas threats go undetected (Kale, 2024). The twin impact of AI bias further implies more than mere technical inefficiency, as users and employees could harbour mistrust of AI-enabled security in case it proves unfair or intrusive (Polito & Pupillo, 2024). Disparaging resistance to AI adoption, wrought by such mistrust, undermines cybersecurity efficacy and reduces compliance rates regarding security procedures (Vulpe et al., 2024). Organisations should use fairness-aware machine learning models, in which transparency as well as accountability are prioritised when training the models, if AI bias has to be mitigated (Singh et al., 2024). By employing diversified representative data, conducting regular bias audits, using human-in-the-loop threat analysis as well as human oversight, model fairness and trustworthiness can be increased (Ofusori et al., 2024). Secondly, utilising XAI techniques to complement the interpretability of AI-enabled decisioning processes raises confidence, as well as the ethical utilisation, of behaviour analysis for cybersecurity (Federspiel et al., 2023).

Evolving AI Threat Landscape

The continuous advancement of AI threats is an insuperable obstacle to behavioural analysis, as attackers use AI capabilities to devise intelligent, adaptive threat strategies (Alanezi & Al-Azzawi, 2024). AI threats, including adversarial machine learning, as well as phishing attempts, exploit defence loopholes by dynamically adjusting patterns to escape defences (Guembe et al., 2022). Adaptive threats require continuous adaptation by AI-enabled defence models to maintain defence capabilities (Ovabor et al., 2024). Among the necessary ingredients in managing the adaptive AI threat environment is the presence of continuous learning models, which dynamically update themselves by adjusting to evolving threat patterns (Ali et al., 2025). Compared to rule-based defence approaches, reinforcement models are able to optimize themselves by updating defence patterns by including fresh threat strategies (Kaur et al., 2023). However, this requires powerful computing capabilities as well as continuous human management so as not to fall victim to adversarial manipulation (Willie, 2024).

From an organizational behavior perspective, adaptation to the dynamic AI threat environment calls for an organizational culture of continuous learning by the cybersecurity specialists (Padilla et al., 2021). Organisations must invest in employee upskilling so that human expertise complements AI-enabled security systems, so human capabilities complement automated threat identification (Adhikari & Thapaliya, 2024). Regulatory regimes must also transform so that the ethical issues posed by AI-enabled security interventions are addressed, so that cybersecurity protocols remain adaptive and aligned with technological advancement (Polito & Pupillo, 2024). In general, successful application of behavioural analysis against AI threats entails resolving issues relating to data quantities, accuracy, bias, and the dynamic threat environment. Through the application of hybrid AI models, human-AI collaboration, and responsible AI approaches, organisations can enhance AI-enabled threat defence.

FUTURE TRENDS AND ADVANCEMENTS IN BEHAVIOURAL ANALYSIS

Advancements in AI for Cybersecurity Defense

AI is transforming defence strategies in cybersecurity, introducing smarter, proactive, and adaptive threat identification systems (Ali et al., 2025). A notable one is XAI, strengthening transparency and responsibility in decision support processes, settling disputes over AI's black-box problem (Polito & Pupillo, 2024). XAI makes human oversight possible over cybersecurity by making AI-generated threat assessments and reactions explainable by human specialists. This aligns perfectly well with the socio-technical system theory, prioritizing human-technology coexistence across organisations (Mermoud et al., 2019). A second crucial advancement involves creating AI models that learn autonomously, battling adaptive threats in real time. These models employ reinforcement learning and continuous adversarial training to discover evolving patterns of attacks and independently develop threat identification capabilities (Ovabor et al., 2024). By employing metaheuristic algorithms together with deep learning, these models are able to forecast future patterns of attacks by analyzing deviant users' patterns across the cloud (Salem et al., 2024). Besides, AI-enabled defence strategies also harness the capabilities of federated learning, strengthening data privacy while strengthening predictive capabilities by distributing models across decentralised networks (Singh et al., 2024). Federated learning minimises threats posed by data leaks while ensuring sound behavioural analysis across organisations. The hybrid system of security—bringing together AI with traditional defence strategies—has excellent future-proofing capabilities across cloud computing infrastructures (Olabanji et al., 2024). AI-based defence strategies continue, therefore, to require continuous refinements, especially as ever-changing cyberrisks threaten organisations.

Integration of Behavioural Biometrics

Integrating behavioural biometrics into cybersecurity represents an essential leap forward in threat identification. Behavioural biometrics employ unique patterns of users, such as mouse patterns, voice patterns, and typing patterns, to confirm identity and signal suspicious activity (Ali et al., 2025). Compared to static biometric markers, fingerprints, or facial identification, behavioural biometrics monitor continuous patterns of inputs by users, creating active anomaly identification, enabling active defence (Shankari & Rethinavalli, 2024). Besides, the marriage of AI with behavioural biometrics enhances the strength of cybersecurity by utilizing AI-enabled patterns of machine learning to signal departures from normal patterns (Singh et al., 2024). The approach serves as an essential approach toward preventing insider threats, as AI-enabled behavioural analysis has the capacity to discriminate normal versus suspicious patterns of activity across an organisation's network (Guembe et al., 2022). Likewise, deep-learning models enhance threat identification accuracy by eliminating false positives, updating patterns continuously (Salem et al., 2024). Besides, predictive analysis serves an essential role toward strengthening biometric authentication by assessing threat indicators, forecasting possible compromises (Ovabor et al., 2024). The approach aligns with expectancy theory, whereby patterns of past acts generate predictions of future acts (Padilla et al., 2021). Since AI capabilities continue to provide opportunities for exploitation by cybercriminals, coupling behavioural biometrics with AI-enabled defence protocols serves as an invaluable defence shield against sophisticated attacks.

Regulatory and Ethical Considerations

As AI-driven behavioural analysis gains traction in the context of cybersecurity, issues of regulation and ethics play an ever-increasing importance. Organisations, as well as governments, must devise holistic AI regulations that address cybersecurity application, ensuring accountability, transparency, and equity (Ali et al., 2025). The European Union's General Data Protection Regulation (GDPR) and Artificial Intelligence Act provide the foundation for models of regulation. However, there must also be targeted cybersecurity policies addressing AI threats (Polito & Pupillo, 2024). A basic problem of regulation involves minimising AI threat detection system bias. AI models, if trained from biased data, tend to single out specific users, creating issues of fairness, as well as discrimination (Kharbanda et al., 2023). Organisations must implement strategies reducing bias, as well as continuously monitor AI models, to ensure fair processes of cybersecurity (Binhammad et al., 2024). Issues of behavioural data tracking also need due care. While AI detects threats by continuously tracking users' behavioural data, it also feeds concerns over users' surveillance, as well as data exploitation (Vulpe et al., 2024). Ethical AI values, such as data minimisation, informed consent, as well as users' personal data control, must find application in models of cybersecurity so that individuals' rights are weighed against security (Federspiel et al., 2023). AI ethics committees, as well as multidisciplinary governing organisations, guarantee responsible AI application across cybersecurity (Ofusori et al., 2024). The application of deontological ethics in AI regulation also calls out duty-bound choice, further demanding organisations' prioritisation of behavioural cybersecurity analysis' issues of ethics (Adhikari & Thapaliya, 2024).

The Future of AI in Cyber Threat Intelligence

The future of AI-enabled cyber threat intelligence is driven by AI-enabled security products and greater collaboration between AI systems and human analysts. AI-enabled products utilizing AI-based threat intelligence discover, analyze, and neutralize threats automatically (Ali et al., 2025). AI-enabled Security Information and Event Management (SIEM) products employ AI models to automate threat analysis and response processes, lowering incident response time and human error (Shankari & Rethinavalli, 2024). Self-healing security systems are an enormous leap forward toward AI-enabled cyber threat intelligence. These products employ reinforcement learning and adversarial training to dynamically transform security protocols against evolving threats (Ovabor et al., 2024). Organisational ambidexterity, defined by balancing stability and novelty, comes into play here, as organisations must implement adaptive AI-enabled products while maintaining secure infrastructures (Jada & Mayayise, 2023). In this period, human expertise still plays an inevitable role. AI-human collaboration enhances cyber threat intelligence by marrying human instinct, context, and machine efficiency (Guembe et al., 2022). AI-enabled cognitive models combine AI with human decision processes and enhance threat blocking strategies by applying behavioural analysis, as well as domain expertise (Mermoud et al., 2019). In this period, future AI-enabled cyber threat intelligence relies on AI algorithm progress, ethical issues, and AI-human seamless collaboration. Organisations must play an active role, spending money on AI-enabled infrastructures so that organisations are well-equipped to address future cyber threats (Olabanji et al., 2024).

Business Intelligence and Strategic AI Integration

The merging of Business Intelligence and Strategic Artificial Intelligence is a paradigm shift in the organisational process of support based decision making abilities. In the past, BI was a descriptive tool of historical information, which provided reactive recommendations that guided post-facto managerial interventions. With the addition of AI, however, BI has become more of a living and adapting system that not only explains the paths of the past, but predicts the path of the future and impacts the strategies and decisions (Ali et al., 2025; Kaur et al., 2023).

The strategic integration of the AI into BI essentially changes the way that the organisation sees risk and opportunity. Traditional dashboards and lagging measures are defeated by utilizing real-time intelligence such that proactive and timely actions can be achieved in response to the possible emerging trends and predict the upcoming happenings. The transformation is not insignificant since it allows decision-makers to shift to the anticipation perspective and align the analysis findings with the overall organisational goals (Jada & Mayayise, 2023).

It is possible to distinguish three main human-oriented effects of the strategic AI integration in BI:

- Quicker, more-Informed Decisions- The leaders do not necessarily have to wait on monthly manual reports and data fragmentation. BI powered with AI provides immediate intelligence to facilitate swift, relevant decisions- be it evident in a cyber-threat, or incursion in reconceptualisation of a business model, or response to market. (Ali et al., 2025). Simplifying complexity-Enterprises are overwhelmed by data. With AI filtration extraneous noise is reduced, latent patterns are brought to the fore, and results are made available in clear, useable forms, thus increasing efficiency and reducing the frustration and nervousness of complex decision making paths (Binhammad et al, 2024).
- Propelling Flexibility and Creativity Behavioural analytics incorporations (accessed through cybersecurity) with more generalised BI systems bring a comprehensive perspective on threat and possibility. Such an outlook allows testing possible outcomes of scenarios repeatedly, predicts breakdowns, and allows generating resilient but progressive strategies (Guembe et al., 2022).

As a result, it is not only that AI refines BI; it transforms it. Business intelligence presupposes a comprehensive mandate going beyond figures and charts to include vision, nimbleness and humanistic strategy. Undoubtedly, organisations can use the maximum of their data and be certain that the intelligence will always be at people service-empowering their leaders, protecting their workers, and supporting sustainable growth under the faster pace of the digital age (Kaur et al., 2023; Jada & Mayayise, 2023).

CONCLUSION AND RECOMMENDATIONS

Summary of Key Findings

The chapter has explored the behavioural analysis of AI-driven threats, describing various techniques and approaches to detecting and preventing threats in cyberspace. AI behavioural analysis employs machine learning, deep learning, and natural language processing (NLP) capabilities to discover patterns and predict cyberattacks more accurately (Ali et al., 2025). Traditional approaches still prevail, but AI-enabled systems reveal increased predictive ability and adaptability (Olabanji et al., 2024; Shankari & Rethinavalli, 2024). AI-enabled phishing, adversarial machine learning attacks, and malware creation by machines are notable AI threats (Alanezi & Al-Azzawi, 2024; Guembe et al., 2022).

Integrating AI has produced AI-enabled threats that exploit defence-developed capabilities, generating a two-pronged effect on cybersecurity (Alanezi & Al-Azzawi, 2024). The studies reveal that organisations must implement hybrid security that includes AI-enabled behavioural analysis together with other conventional cybersecurity approaches so that it achieves greater accuracy in detecting, as well as quick response time (Salem et al., 2024). The level of sophistication in the attacks requires AI models' continuous updating so that it keeps track of upcoming threats (Singh et al., 2024). AI-enabled threat intelligence has also turned out to be an inevitable factor in real-time cybersecurity, enhancing the efficiency of security processes (Ovabor et al., 2024). While AI-enabled cybersecurity has immense benefits, there are concerns relating to ethical issues, data privacy, and adversarial AI attacks, which must be addressed by well-thought-out security protocols and strategies (Ali et al., 2025).

Implementation of AI-Driven Behavioral Analysis

Organisations need to implement AI-based behavioural analysis, data normalisation, and continuous monitoring and tuning processes by employing AI-based security solutions. AI-based security solutions employ machine learning capabilities to track system events, network traffic, and user activity so as to discover, track, and automatically deal with cyber threats (Salem et al., 2024). AI-based security solutions enhance threat identification rate by detecting deviation from normal behaviour enhancing near-real time response (Olabanji et al., 2024).

Comprehensive data gathering must be achieved so that AI-backed behavioural analysis has substance. Organisations must combine various data sources, such as endpoint logs, network telemetry, and cloud-based records, so that an inclusive security environment (Ali et al., 2025) can be established. Techniques of data normalisation must be implemented so that consistency and accuracy in threat identification are maintained, as incomplete data or data variability may result in threats being overlooked, as well as generating false positives (Singh et al., 2024).

Continuous monitoring, coupled with AI model refinement, plays an essential role in adapting to the constantly evolving threat environment. Periodic updating of the machine learning models by the security team has to account for shifting patterns of attacks, as well as decrease error margins (Ovabor et al., 2024). Adaptive models further enhance AI's ability to build over time, building greater cybersecurity resilience (Guembe et al., 2022). Through these strategies, organisations boost their level of cybersecurity while minimising AI threat exposure.

Implications for Cybersecurity Practitioners

The behavioural analysis of AI threats has severe implications for the work of cybersecurity professionals. AI threat detection strategies need to be learned by security experts if they are going to build increased capacity to find out and contain complex cyber threats (Ali et al., 2025). AI behavioural analysis empowers security officers to shift from reactive mode to proactive mode, so that they can anticipate and deter cyberattacks beforehand (Olabanji et al., 2024). Besides, AI boosts the resilience of cybersecurity by automating threat identification processes as well as threat handling processes. Automated security products shorten the time it takes to find out and contain security incidents, lessening possible harm (Salem et al., 2024). AI behavioural analysis also detects unknown patterns of attacks, providing cybersecurity specialists useful information about emerging threats (Shankari & Rethinavalli, 2024).

Furthermore, cybersecurity experts must address adversarial AI threats and ethical issues. Cybercriminals are also turning to AI to remain undetected and carry out complex attacks (Alanezi & Al-Azzawi, 2024). Adversarial AI threat detection capabilities must be rolled out by the security team, while plans must be developed to contain AI-enabled threats. Organisations must institute sound AI governance models so that AI, if it is implemented in the processes of cybersecurity, does so ethically (Ali et al., 2025). AI-enabled behavioural analysis must enhance cybersecurity resilience by constantly evolving, adapting, and coordinating across the cybersecurity community.

Directions for Future Research

Future research has to cover uncharted terrain in threat identification, interdisciplinary approaches, and future AI models. A very essential line of study includes developing explainable AI (XAI) models so that there is increased transparency and interpretability in threat identification (Ali et al., 2025). AI-enabled security products today are "black boxes" (Singh et al., 2024), so it is hard for security personnel to understand decision processes. Developing interpretable AI models will build trust and accountability in AI-enabled cybersecurity. Another key line of research involves uniting AI with other upcoming trends, including quantum computing and blockchain, for increased cybersecurity (Ovabor et al., 2024). Blockchain has the capacity to provide decentralised, tamper-resistant security, while quantum computing has the capacity to revolutionize cryptographic security (Guembe et al., 2022). Investigating the synergy between these upcoming trends and AI behavioural analysis has the capacity to lead to increased, secure security architectures. Third, behavioural cybersecurity also necessitates interdisciplinary research. By uniting psychology, sociology, and organizational behavioural studies, increased human decision processes in areas of cybersecurity can be attained (Mermoud et al., 2019). An example includes human relations studies with AI behavioural analysis-enabled security products, enabling the development of increased, accessible, and efficient products. Besides, AI behavioural analysis-enabled social engineering threats studies have the capacity to further enhance strategies aimed at lessening manipulation-based cyberattacks (Alanezi & Al-Azzawi, 2024). In general, future studies must develop AI behavioural analysis strategies, address issues relating to ethics, and allow interdisciplinary collaboration across technical, social, and behavioural studies areas so as to develop holistic approaches to cybersecurity.

REFERENCES

Adhikari, D., & Thapaliya, S. (2024).. . *An Overview of AI Applications in Cybersecurity for IT Management.*, *1*(4), 121–133. DOI: 10.3126/nprcjmr.v1i4.70951

Alanezi, M., & Al-Azzawi, R. M. A. (2024). AI-Powered Cyber Threats: A Systematic Review. *Deleted Journal*, *4*(3), 166–188. DOI: 10.58496/mjcs/2024/021

Ali, S., Wang, J., & Leung, V. C. M. (2025). AI-Driven Fusion with Cybersecurity: Exploring Current Trends, Advanced Techniques, Future Directions, and Policy Implications for Evolving Paradigms– A Comprehensive Review. *Information Fusion*, *118*, 102922. DOI: 10.1016/j.inffus.2024.102922

Almansoori, A., Al-Emran, M., & Shaalan, K. (2023). Exploring the Frontiers of Cybersecurity Behavior: A Systematic Review of Studies and Theories. *Applied Sciences (Basel, Switzerland)*, *13*(9), 5700. DOI: 10.3390/app13095700

Binhammad, M., Alqaydi, S., Othman, A., & Abuljadayel, L. H. (2024). The Role of AI in Cyber Security: Safeguarding Digital Identity. *Journal of Information Security*, *15*(02), 245–278. DOI: 10.4236/jis.2024.152015

Burt, A. (2024). *Finance Employee Defrauded for $25M by Deepfake CFO*. CFO. https://www.cfo.com/news/deepfake-cfo-hong-kong-25-million-fraud-cyber-crime/706529/

Das, R., & Sandhane, R. (2021). Artificial Intelligence in Cyber Security. *Journal of Physics: Conference Series*, *1964*(4). Advance online publication. DOI: 10.1088/1742-6596/1964/4/042072

Dokur, N. B. (2023). *Artificial Intelligence (AI)*. Applications in Cyber Security.

Federspiel, F., Mitchell, R., Asokan, A., Umana, C., & McCoy, D. (2023). Threats by Artificial Intelligence to Human Health and Human Existence. *BMJ Global Health*, *8*(5), e010435. DOI: 10.1136/bmjgh-2022-010435

Groumpos, P. P. (2023). A Critical Historical Overview of Artificial Intelligence: Issues, Challenges, Opportunities, and Threats. *Artificial Intelligence and Applications (Commerce, Calif.)*, *1*(4), 197–213. DOI: 10.47852/bonviewAIA3202689

Guembe, B., Azeta, A., Misra, S., Osamor, V. C., Fernandez-Sanz, L., & Pospelova, V. (2022). The Emerging Threat of AI-driven Cyber Attacks: A Review. *Applied Artificial Intelligence*, *36*(1), 1–34. DOI: 10.1080/08839514.2022.2037254

Jada, I., & Mayayise, T. O. (2023). The Impact of Artificial Intelligence on Organisational Cyber Security: An Outcome of a Systematic Literature Review. *Data and Information Management*, *8*(2), 100063–100063. DOI: 10.1016/j.dim.2023.100063

Kale, A. (2024). *AI-Driven Cybersecurity Threats and Organisational Consequences*. CSUSB ScholarWorks, Electronic Theses, Projects, and Dissertations. https://scholarworks.lib.csusb.edu/etd/1991?utm_source=scholarworks.lib.csusb.edu%2Fetd%2F1991&utm_medium=PDF&utm_campaign=PDFCoverPages

Kaur, R., Gabrijelčič, D., & Klobučar, T. (2023). Artificial Intelligence for Cybersecurity: Literature Review and Future Research Directions. *Information Fusion, 97*(101804), 101804. ScienceDirect. https://doi.org/DOI: 10.1016/j.inffus.2023.101804

Khan, N. F., Yaqoob, A., Khan, M. S., & Ikram, N. (2022). The Cybersecurity Behavioral Research: A Tertiary Study. *Computers & Security*, *120*, 102826. DOI: 10.1016/j.cose.2022.102826

Kharbanda, V., Seetharaman, A., & Maddulety, K. (2023). Application of Artificial Intelligence in Cyber security. *International Journal of Security and Privacy in Pervasive Computing*, *15*(1), 1–13. DOI: 10.4018/ijsppc.318676

Kommisetty, P. D. N. K., Kuppala, B. M. S. R., Buvvaji, H. V., & Sabbella, V. R. R. (2022). Revolutionizing Cybersecurity: Behavioral Analysis and Automated Incident Response through Predictive Analytics. [IJSRM]. *International Journal of Scientific Research and Management*, *10*(10), 962–979. DOI: 10.18535/ijsrm/v10i10.ec04

Lahcen, R. A. M., Caulkins, B., Mohapatra, R., & Kumar, M. (2020). Review and Insight on The Behavioral Aspects of Cybersecurity. *Cybersecurity*, *3*(1). Advance online publication. DOI: 10.1186/s42400-020-00050-w

Mermoud, A., Keupp, M. M., Huguenin, K., Palmié, M., & Percia David, D. (2019). To Share or Not to Share: A Behavioral Perspective on Human Participation in Security Information Sharing. *Journal of Cybersecurity*, *5*(1). Advance online publication. DOI: 10.1093/cybsec/tyz006

Mersinas, K., Bada, M., & Furnell, S. (2024). Cybersecurity Behavior Change: A Conceptualisation of Ethical Principles for Behavioral Interventions. *Computers & Security*, •••, 104025–104025. DOI: 10.1016/j.cose.2024.104025

Moustafa, A. A., Bello, A., & Maurushat, A. (2021). The Role of User Behaviour in Improving Cyber Security Management. *Frontiers in Psychology*, *12*(12). Advance online publication. DOI: 10.3389/fpsyg.2021.561011

Ofusori, L., Bokaba, T., & Mhlongo, S. (2024). Artificial Intelligence in Cybersecurity: A Comprehensive Review and Future Direction. *Applied Artificial Intelligence, 38*(1). Advance online publication. DOI: 10.1080/08839514.2024.2439609

Olabanji, S. O., Marquis, Y. A., Adigwe, C. S., Ajayi, S. A., Oladoyinbo, T. O., & Olaniyi, O. O. (2024). AI-Driven Cloud Security: Examining the Impact of User Behavior Analysis on Threat Detection. *Asian Journal of Research in Computer Science, 17*(3), 57–74. DOI: 10.9734/ajrcos/2024/v17i3424

Ovabor, K., Sule-Odu, I. O., Atkison, T., Fabusoro, A. T., & Benedict, J. O. (2024). AI-Driven Threat Intelligence for Real-Time Cybersecurity: Frameworks, Tools, and Future Directions. *Open Access Research Journal of Science and Technology, 12*(2), 040–048. https://doi.org/DOI: 10.53022/oarjst.2024.12.2.0135

Padilla, E., Acosta, J. C., & Kiekintveld, C. D. (2021). Cybersecurity Methodology for Specialized Behavior Analysis. *Lecture Notes of the Institute for Computer Sciences, Social Informatics and Telecommunications Engineering*, •••, 237–243. DOI: 10.1007/978-3-030-68734-2_14

Polito, C., & Pupillo, L. (2024). Artificial Intelligence and Cybersecurity. Www .intereconomics.eu, *2024*(1), 10–13. https://www.intereconomics.eu/contents/year/2024/number/1/article/artificial-intelligence-and-cybersecurity.html

Sajikumar, S., & Ajithkumar, N. (2024). Understanding the Emergence and Significance of Behavioral Cybersecurity: A Bibliometric Analysis. *Multidisciplinary Reviews, 6*, 2023ss102. https://doi.org/DOI: 10.31893/multirev.2023ss102

Salem, A. H., Azzam, S. M., Emam, O. E., & Abohany, A. A. (2024). Advancing Cybersecurity: A Comprehensive Review of AI-Driven Detection Techniques. *Journal of Big Data, 11*(1). Advance online publication. DOI: 10.1186/s40537-024-00957-y

Shankari, M. U., & Rethinavalli, S. (2024). Examining the Impact of User Behaviour Analysis on Threat Detection. *International Journal of Creative Research Thoughts, 12*(10).

Singh, S., Mandave, N., & Sapkale, S. (2024). AI-Driven Threat Detection in Cybersecurity: An Overview. *International Research Journal of Modernization in Engineering Technology and Science, 6*(11).

Vulpe, S.-N., Rughini , R., urcanu, D., & Rosner, D. (2024). AI and Cybersecurity: A Risk Society Perspective. *Frontiers of Computer Science, 6*. Advance online publication. DOI: 10.3389/fcomp.2024.1462250

Willie, A. (2024). *The Evolution of Artificial Intelligence in Cybersecurity: Traditional AI vs Generative AI Approaches*. Stanford University.

Yzzogh, H., Kandil, H., & Benaboud, H. (2024). A Comprehensive Overview Of AI-Driven Behavioral Analysis for Security in Internet of Things. *CRC Press EBooks*, 40–51. https://doi.org/DOI: 10.1201/9781032714806-4

Ali, S., Wang, J., & Leung, V. C. M. (2025). AI-Driven Fusion with Cybersecurity: Exploring Current Trends, Advanced Techniques, Future Directions, and Policy Implications for Evolving Paradigms–A Comprehensive Review. *Information Fusion*, *118*, 102922. DOI: 10.1016/j.inffus.2024.102922

Kaur, R., Gabrijelčič, D., & Klobučar, T. (2023). Artificial Intelligence for Cybersecurity: Literature Review and Future Research Directions. *Information Fusion*, *97*(101804). Advance online publication. DOI: 10.1016/j.inffus.2023.101804

Jada, I., & Mayayise, T. O. (2023). The Impact of Artificial Intelligence on Organisational Cyber Security: An Outcome of a Systematic Literature Review. *Data and Information Management*, *8*(2), 100063. DOI: 10.1016/j.dim.2023.100063

Binhammad, M., Alqaydi, S., Othman, A., & Abuljadayel, L. H. (2024). The Role of AI in Cyber Security: Safeguarding Digital Identity. *Journal of Information Security*, *15*(02), 245–278. DOI: 10.4236/jis.2024.152015

Guembe, B., Azeta, A., Misra, S., Osamor, V. C., Fernandez-Sanz, L., & Pospelova, V. (2022). The Emerging Threat of AI-driven Cyber Attacks: A Review. *Applied Artificial Intelligence*, *36*(1), 1–34. DOI: 10.1080/08839514.2022.2037254

Chen, H., & Magramo, K. (2024, February 4). *Finance Worker Pays Out $25 Million After Video Call with Deepfake "Chief Financial Officer."* CNN. https://edition.cnn.com/2024/02/04/asia/deepfake-cfo-scam-hong-kong-intl-hnk/index.html

Alan, J. (2024, May 17). *SugarGh0st RAT Campaign Targets U.S. AI Experts*. The Cyber Express. https://thecyberexpress.com/sugargh0st-campaign-targets-ai-experts/

Constantin, L. (2024, May 17). *US AI Experts Targeted in Cyberespionage Campaign Using SugarGh0st RAT*. CSO Online. https://www.csoonline.com/article/2111003/us-ai-experts-targeted-in-cyberespionage-campaign-using-sugargh0st-rat.html

Milmo, D. (2024, May 17). *UK Engineering Firm Arup Falls Victim To £20m Deepfake Scam*. The Guardian. https://www.theguardian.com/technology/article/2024/may/17/uk-engineering-arup-deepfake-scam-hong-kong-ai-video

Seldon, M. (2024, May 22). *U.S. AI Experts Targeted in SugarGh0st RAT Campaign*. HSToday. https://www.hstoday.us/subject-matter-areas/cybersecurity/u-s-ai-experts-targeted-in-sugargh0st-rat-campaign/

Chacko, A. J. (2024, June 22). *SugarGh0st: China-Linked Espionage Malware Targets Diplomatic Circles*. Interesting Engineering. https://interestingengineering.com/science/sugargh0st-sneakychef-cyberespionage

Borrelli, S. S., & Kazmin, A. (2025, February 9). *Italian Tycoons Targeted by Fake Defence Minister in Suspected AI Scam*. Financial Times. https://www.ft.com/content/8e911f1e-6eb7-4e8e-b4e0-3aba62575f23?utm_source=chatgpt.com

Giuffrida, A. (2025, February 10). *AI Phone Scam Targets Italian Business Leaders, including Giorgio Armani*. The Guardian. https://www.theguardian.com/world/2025/feb/10/ai-phone-scam-targets-italian-business-leaders-including-giorgio-armani?utm_source=chatgpt.com

KEY TERMS AND DEFINITIONS

Adversarial AI: Adversarial AI refers to a method that deceives artificial intelligence models by utilizing their flaws, normally by adversarial attacks. Adversarial attacks subtly perturb data so that AI models are deceived to provide erroneous predictions (Ali et al., 2025). Adversarial AI, for example, deceives malware detectors in computer security by subtly altering the code so it slips past undetected (Salem et al., 2024). The concept aligns well with human behavioural patterns theories, such as deception detection, whereby attackers manipulate just as individuals deceptively act in organisations (Moustafa et al., 2021).

AI-Generated Malware: AI-generated malware means malware created or created by way of artificial intelligence, wherein it adapts, evades, and automatically spreads (Alanezi & Al-Azzawi, 2024). Next-generation threats use machine learning so that the old signature-based strategies are rendered obsolete (Guembe et al., 2022). Organisational behavioural-wise, AI-generated threats' sophistication requires adaptive employee cybersecurity training (Sajikumar & Ajithkumar, 2024).

AI-Powered Phishing: AI-powered phishing employs artificial intelligence to send very targeted, authentic-looking phishing messages. Unlike generic messages sent by traditional phishing, AI phishing dynamically adapts to the targeted individual's language patterns, as well as their online behavior (Singh et al., 2024). Behavioral studies across the field of cybersecurity show that phishing vulnerability by users originates due to cognitive biases, as well as decision-making heuristics (Padilla et al., 2021).

Anomaly Detection: Anomaly detection involves the identification of deviation from normal system operation, necessary for threat identification in real time (Ali et al., 2025). Anomaly detection by AI involves the use of machine learning models to scan vast quantities of data, identifying patterns indicative of suspicious behavior (Olabanji et al., 2024). Social Learning Theory shows that threat identification ability by security specialists is increased by exposure to data produced by AI, complemented by ongoing learning (Lahcen et al., 2020).

Behavioral Biometrics: For authentication, behavioural biometrics utilizes AI to monitor human behavioural patterns, typing, mouse, and patterns of gait (Salem et al., 2024). Compared to static biometric methods (i.e., fingerprints), behavioural biometrics continuously monitor users, making it harder for attackers (Ofusori et al., 2024). The Theory of Planned Behavior (TPB) stipulates that users' perceptions of convenience, as well as users' attitudes, play a crucial role in the adoption of biometric security (Jada & Mayayise, 2023).

Deepfake Detection: Deepfake detection involves identifying AI-generated synthetic content that has the power to manipulate video, sound, and images so as to provide realistic but deceptive images of individuals (Kale, 2024). These deepfakes also pose enormous cybersecurity threats, particularly social engineering attacks, fraud, and misinformation (Guembe et al., 2022). Models of behavioural analysis, such as the Protection Motivation Theory (PMT), argue that individuals' perceptions and threat perceptions play a crucial role in compelling them toward adopting countermeasures (Almansoori et al., 2023).

Explainable AI (XAI) in Cybersecurity: Explainable AI (XAI) prioritizes transparency in AI models so that AI-generated decisions are explainable and trustable by security analysts (Binhammad et al., 2024). Organisations can attain this by gaining greater accountability, as well as reducing threats presented by threat detection biases (Polito & Pupillo, 2024).

Insider Threat Detection: AI-driven insider threat detection systems track employee behavior to discover whether there are any potential threats, including data exfiltration, unauthorized access (Ofusori et al., 2024). Behavioral models, such as the Fraud Triangle Theory, explain how opportunity, pressure, and justification result in insider threats (Kommisetty et al., 2022).

Lateral Movement: Lateral movement refers to the way attackers move laterally across a network after gaining initial entry, usually aiming for useful data or gaining elevation of privileges (Ovabor et al., 2024). Lateral movement is identified by AI threat intelligence by identifying behavioural patterns of network traffic (Shankari & Rethinavalli, 2024). These findings align with organizational behavior models that analyze how attackers mimic normal users' behavior so that they are not detected (Mersinas et al., 2024).

Self-Healing Systems: Self-healing cybersecurity involves AI so it automatically detects, responds, and recovers from cyberattacks (Singh et al., 2024). Reinforcement learning allows these systems to develop an increased defensive posture over time (Kaur et al., 2023). The concept resembles organizational behavior resilience, whereby adaptive learning processes boost general security posture (Mermoud et al., 2019).

Strategic Artificial Intelligence (AI) Business Intelligence:The deliberate application of AI in BI systems to transcend historical reporting: allowing real-time perception, predictive forecasts, and prescriptive decision-making that may facilitate long-term goals(Ali et al., 2025).

Threat Intelligence: Threat intelligence entails collecting, analyzing, and distributing information about potential threats (Ovabor et al., 2024). AI enhances threat intelligence by automating analysis, as well as discovering emerging patterns of attacks (Shankari & Rethinavalli, 2024). Cybersecurity behavioural studies reveal that successful threat intelligence is achieved by human-AI collaboration and information-sharing processes across organisations (Padilla et al., 2021).

Zero-Day Exploits: Zero-day exploits take advantage of vendor- or publicly unknown software flaws, making them very dangerous (Ali et al., 2025). Zero-day detection is complemented by AI-enabled security products, detecting suspicious patterns early enough so that an exploit has not had time to fully implement (Ovabor et al., 2024). Organisations must cultivate an active security culture if zero-day threats are ever going to be managed (Vulpe et al., 2024).

Chapter 12
The Ethical and Legal Dimensions of Blockchain:
A Comprehensive Analysis of Global and UAE Perspectives

Saif Ahmed Almaeeni
Department of Computer Information Science, Higher Colleges of Technology, Sharjah, UAE

Mubarak Aldhanhani
Department of Computer Information Science, Higher Colleges of Technology, Sharjah, UAE

Majid Alhammadi
Department of Computer Information Science, Higher Colleges of Technology, Sharjah, UAE

Sultan Almaazmi
Department of Computer Information Science, Higher Colleges of Technology, Sharjah, UAE

Ammar Almomani
https://orcid.org/0000-0002-8808-6114
Higher Colleges of Technology, Sharjah, UAE

ABSTRACT

Blockchain technology has revolutionized financial and administrative systems through decentralization, transparency, and immutability. These attributes enable

DOI: 10.4018/979-8-3373-6801-6.ch012

specialized hardware applications while paradoxically generating challenges regarding information governance and cross-border regulatory compliance. A fundamental contradiction exists between blockchain's inherent characteristics—trustless transactions, immutable data storage, and disintermediation—versus established cyberspace legal frameworks demanding data erasure rights and intellectual property protection. This analysis examines jurisdictional variations in regulatory approaches, with particular focus on UAE's implementation strategies. The research contributes to blockchain governance discourse by identifying cybersecurity vulnerabilities and advocating for regulatory innovation that balances technological advancement with ethical considerations, enabling sustainable adoption.

INTRODUCTION

Conceptual Foundation of Blockchain Technology

Blockchain technology is a type of distributed ledger that allows recording of transactions in a peer-to-peer manner without depending on an authority. In its core, the functioning of blockchain is based on cryptographic hashing: sequential transactions are organized into blocks which are in turn linked together, making the historical record impossible to tamper with as long as it was validated by participants of the network (Tang et al., 2020; Zaghloul et al., 2020). Despite the fact that the blockchain was initially designed to support the peer-to-peer digital currency system that was called Bitcoin, it has since been developed to include supply chain management, decentralized finance, sharing of health information, and government solutions (Kshetri, 2021).

Figure 1 presents a simplified visualization of the transaction processing flow in most of the blockchain systems. Blockchain Transaction Processing Process. Within this schema the proposed transactions are broadcast by participants to the network; the transactions are validated by specialized nodes using consensus-based mechanisms; once accepted, the transactions get aggregated into a novel block. It is then cryptographically connected with previous blocks creating the chain of record that cannot be changed. This is because each node has a copy of this shared ledger which makes it extremely cumbersome to alter or forge historical entries.

Consensus mechanisms such as Proof of Work (PoW) and Proof of Stake (PoS) define how nodes reach agreement on the validity of proposed blocks. PoW, used by Bitcoin, demands computational resources to solve cryptographic puzzles, limiting malicious tampering by making attacks prohibitively expensive. PoS, adopted by modern blockchain platforms like Ethereum, ties validation power to the amount of cryptocurrency staked as collateral (Tang et al., 2020). Both mechanisms maintain network security but differ in energy consumption and potential for centralization.

Global Significance and UAE Strategic Position

The global relevance of blockchain emanates from promise of curtailing fraud, cost reduction on operations and enhanced visibility of operations across board (Alston, 2022; Kshetri, 2021). Due to its removal of dependency on centralized intermediaries, blockchain can simplify finance, real estate, supply chains, intellectual property registries and many other areas. Furthermore, it can support financial inclusion in areas where banking infrastructure is weak, where users can trade directly using decentralized networks.

In the United Arab Emirates, the role of Blockchain fits into the national strategic goals of implementing modernization of government services and diversifying the economy. The plan "Blockchain Strategy 2020" of Dubai aimed at establishing the first government that operated solely on blockchain, making digital services, including visas and business licenses (Khan et al., 2019). UAE universities have done some research on academic credentials' verification on blockchain, and the Dubai Economic Department has also used the distributed ledgers to simplify business registrations (Ismail et al., 2019; Haneem et al., 2020). These case studies emphasize the UAE position as an early test market of the viability of blockchain in public-sector setups.

However, the incorporation of blockchain in governmental and commercial systems require facing ethical issues such as lifelong data retention and worldwide privacy commitments. Cross-border information sharing is liable to pose additional complications in terms of compliance with the UA's significant international trade portfolios. The forthcoming sections explore these nuances, beginning with an examination of the current state of the blockchain implementations world and frictions points between technology, regulation, and human-directed issues.

Current Implementation Landscape and Challenges

Early blockchain implementations reveal how theoretical advantages can be achieved—or sometimes undermined—by real-world conditions. Supply chain projects use blockchain to authenticate product origins and track goods from raw materials to retail shelves, mitigating corruption and counterfeit activities (Kshetri, 2021). Healthcare institutions explore blockchain to synchronize patient records and maintain tamper-resistant data for research while ensuring sensitive information is accessible only to authorized parties.

Nonetheless, these applications face several challenges. One pressing concern involves strict data protection frameworks, like the European Union's General Data Protection Regulation (GDPR). Under the GDPR, individuals can request the deletion of personal data. Blockchain's immutability directly conflicts with the right to erasure, making it unclear how to fulfill such requests if personal information is permanently logged (Sharif & Ghodoosi, 2022). Furthermore, although blockchain transactions might appear anonymous or pseudonymous, advanced analytics can sometimes re-identify participants by correlating addresses with off-chain data.

Jurisdictional conflicts compound these concerns, since decentralized ledgers typically span multiple countries. Traditional legal boundaries that determine which national courts have authority to enforce data protection or copyright laws do not neatly map onto blockchain networks (Dimitropoulos, 2020). Projects operating across multiple locations must navigate an array of conflicting regulations, making compliance a labyrinthine process.

Technical obstacles—particularly scalability and interoperability—also shape blockchain's future. Public blockchains like Bitcoin and Ethereum process a limited number of transactions per second compared to conventional centralized systems like Visa. While layer-2 solutions and improved consensus methods are emerging, mainstream adoption often hinges on robust throughput (Zaghloul et al., 2020). Interoperability protocols aim to connect siloed blockchain networks, but remain relatively nascent, limiting seamless multi-chain functionality (Ressi et al., 2024).

The UAE's experience illustrates how governmental support can catalyze both pilot projects and overarching regulations. However, as these systems expand, fundamental questions about transparency, user privacy, intellectual property protections, and cybersecurity threats become more urgent. The next section outlines blockchain's architectural and technical foundations, building toward the subsequent ethical, privacy, IP, and security analyses.

BLOCKCHAIN ARCHITECTURE AND TECHNICAL FOUNDATIONS

Core Components and Operational Mechanisms

Blockchains have a distributed data set up whereby several nodes work together in order to create a peer-to-peer network. A consensus mechanism allows updating individual nodes and regulates state updates via a local copy of the ledger maintained by each node. Proposed transactions are then broadcast by the participants and compiled into blocks by being validated by the nodes according to a set of pre-determined validation criteria (Zaghloul et al., 2020).

It is based on the public key cryptography to authenticate the network users. Users have their own secret key to sign transactions and a key which serves as an address used to receive money or data in form of a public key. This is because even in case of compromise of the private-key, malicious parties can resort to impersonations to transfer funds at the expense of the legitimate owner hence the need to observe strict key-management guidelines (Tang et al., 2020). The blockchain is guaranteed by the sequentiality of the blocks as the successive blocks are connected by cryptographic hashes and result in a data chain with low manipulation.

Figure 1 gives a graphic outline of this process. Citing the use of post-transaction collection, the consensus protocol will analyze each suggestion to complete it, and ensure that the sender has sufficient resources or meets predefined smart contract conditions. When the block is successfully validated, it gets a place on the chain, and then all the nodes update their own copy of the ledger simultaneously.

Figure 1. Blockchain transaction processing workflow

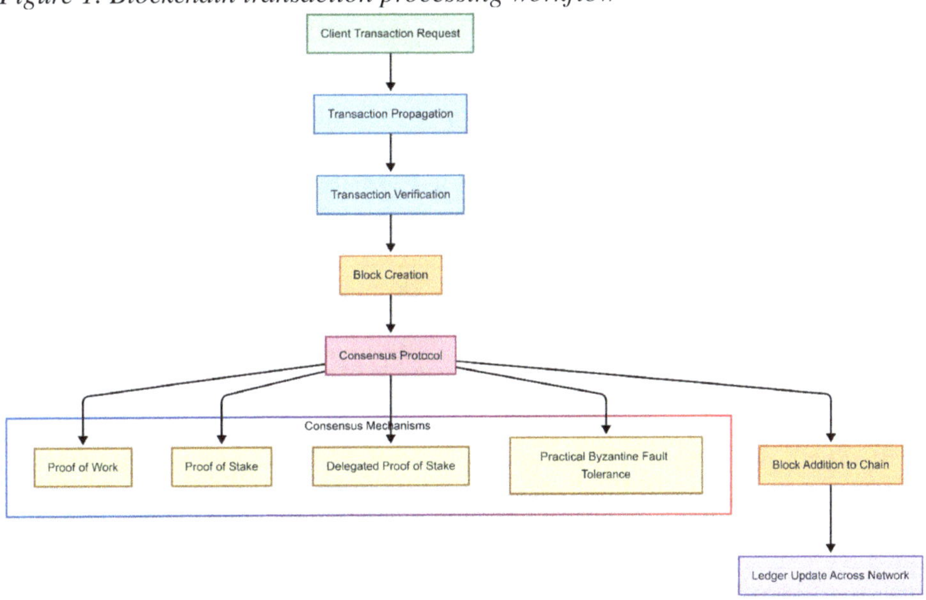

Blockchain Network Typologies

Different network designs reflect varying priorities around data privacy, control, and scalability. These designs are summarized in **Table 1. Comparative Analysis of**

Blockchain Network Typologies, which contrasts public, consortium, and private blockchains.

- **Public Blockchain**: Open to all participants, requiring no special permissions to read or write data. Security often depends on economic incentives (e.g., Proof of Work, Proof of Stake) and distributed consensus. Bitcoin and Ethereum exemplify this model.
- **Consortium Blockchain**: Partially decentralized networks where a group of trusted entities jointly validate transactions. Designed for inter-organizational workflows, consortium blockchains balance transparency and confidentiality.
- **Private Blockchain**: Access is tightly controlled by a single organization or administrator. These chains can leverage some blockchain features (like data integrity and auditability) within a centralized governance framework.

In the UAE, consortium and private blockchains have proven more practical for government-related use cases (Haneem et al., 2020). For instance, land registries or business licensing systems can benefit from distributed records while restricting data visibility to authorized government bodies, enterprises, or auditors.

Table 1. Comparative analysis of blockchain network typologies

Feature	Public Blockchain	Consortium Blockchain	Private Blockchain
Access Control	Unrestricted participation	Limited to predefined members	Centrally controlled access
Consensus Determination	Open participation (e.g., Proof of Work)	Selected validators	Administrator-defined
Transaction Privacy	Pseudonymous visibility	Selective visibility	Restricted visibility
Processing Efficiency	Lower (due to distributed validation)	Moderate	Higher (limited validators)
Governance Structure	Decentralized community	Distributed among members	Centralized authority
Example Applications	Cryptocurrencies (Bitcoin)	Financial clearing systems	Corporate asset tracking
UAE Implementation	Limited due to regulatory concerns	Dubai Multi Commodities Centre	Dubai Land Department Registry

Smart Contracts and Decentralized Applications

Smart contracts extend blockchain's capabilities by embedding self-executing code that enforces agreement terms once certain conditions are satisfied (Alston, 2022). Because the contract logic resides on the chain, outcomes are deterministic and verifiable by all nodes, which can reduce reliance on intermediaries. Yet, bugs or vulnerabilities in smart contracts may enable exploits, such as siphoning funds or causing unexpected behavior (Dierksmeier & Seele, 2020).

Increasingly, developers build **decentralized applications (DApps)** on top of smart contract platforms like Ethereum. These DApps have front-end interfaces but offload critical logic to on-chain code, improving transparency and censorship resistance (Ressi et al., 2024). However, users pay "gas fees" or transaction fees every time they interact with the blockchain, so developers must optimize code to manage these costs. Maintaining security in the face of possible malicious interactions or front-running by miners adds further complexity.

Technical Limitations and Current Innovations

Despite notable progress, several technical challenges still impede large-scale blockchain adoption:

1. Scalability: The number of transactions that can be conducted on public blockchains is low. Layer-2 approaches (such as the Lightning Network and a series of rollup technologies) are being developed so that transactions can be off-chained, but not at the cost of the main-chain security assurances (Zaghloul et al., 2020).
2. Energy consumptions: The heavy reliance on resources; particularly in Bitcoin use of Proof of Work, creates environmental issues. Some of them could be solved by a transition to Proof of Stake and other energy-efficient mechanisms (Tang et al., 2020).
3. Interoperability: Several blockchain platforms exist as information silos. Proposals like Polkadot, Cosmos and other so-called cross-chain bridges aim to facilitate asset and information moves between these systems (Ressi et al., 2024).
4. Privacy: The nature of blockchain offers transparency, which is not compatible with confidentiality of some of the enterprise or individual data. New methodologies such as zero-knowledge proofs allow verifying transactions without providing elaborate information (Yuan et al., 2024).

The recent and potential developments in consensus, cryptography and architecture have only further refined the balance between security, efficiency, and privacy. The current discussion provides the analysis of these technical ramifications with regard to ethical demands specifically in the areas of data independence, just governance, and environmental sustainability.

ETHICAL IMPLICATIONS OF BLOCKCHAIN TECHNOLOGY

Fundamental Ethical Tensions

Blockchain has transformative features that bring about significant ethical implications. The immutability and transparency, are features that have the potential to put values of accountability and trust into operation, but they also invade individual autonomy when it comes to how sensitive personal data are managed. Proponents describe blockchains as being ``trustless,`` but opponents argue that trust is simply transferred to protocol designers, miners or node runners (Dierksmeier & Seele, 2020). The influence exercised by such actors is sometimes not transparent and not organized in a democratic way.

One of the main questions is whether there is a balance between transparency and privacy. Whereas an open verification can be achieved with the help of a public ledger, such a ledger can pose a threat to privacy since it stores personal information indefinitely. The immutability rule, in turn, contrasts with the rights to correct or eliminate data approved at the legislative level and moral provisions (Sharif & Ghodoosi, 2022). Another conflict is that of decentralization. The results of the distributed power, although being heralded as a decentralization of power, can end up in the hands of large mining pools or powerful project teams or token holders that control the money, who may effectively end up centralizing decision-making again. The procedure threatens to compromise some core principles of egalitarian government.

Ethical Framework Application

Several ethical frameworks—detailed in **Table 2. Ethical Frameworks for Blockchain Evaluation**—provide lenses through which to evaluate blockchain's ethical dimensions:

- **Utilitarianism**: Emphasizes outcomes that maximize total happiness or welfare. Under this framework, a blockchain project might be championed if its net social benefits (e.g., fraud reduction, cost savings) exceed the cost of reduced privacy or high environmental impacts.
- **Deontology**: Focuses on moral duties and rules. If privacy or data autonomy is considered an inviolable right, a public blockchain that permanently stores

personal data may be deemed unacceptable, regardless of overall benefits (Sharif & Ghodoosi, 2022).

- **Justice Theory**: Evaluates fairness in distributing blockchain's benefits and burdens. A justice-oriented critique might ask whether large token holders or mining corporations concentrate power and whether communities lacking digital literacy are excluded (Kshetri, 2021).
- **Virtue Ethics** and **Care Ethics**: Examine the moral character of individuals and organizations deploying blockchain. They highlight whether these implementations foster socially responsible behaviors, relationships, and inclusive values (Dierksmeier & Seele, 2020).

Table 2. Ethical frameworks for blockchain evaluation ethical framework

	Core Principles	Blockchain Application	Limitations
Utilitarianism	Maximizing overall welfare	Evaluates blockchain based on aggregate benefits (e.g., reduced fraud, improved efficiency)	May neglect minority stakeholder interests and rights violations
Deontology	Duty-based ethics, respecting rights	Focuses on respecting individual rights (privacy, autonomy) regardless of outcomes	May create implementation paralysis when rights conflict
Justice Theory	Fair distribution of benefits and burdens	Examines blockchain's impact on equality, access, and resource distribution	Determining "fair" distribution remains subjective
Virtue Ethics	Character development and community values	Considers how blockchain shapes organizational and social virtues	Lacks specific action guidance for technical decisions
Care Ethics	Relationships and responsibilities to others	Evaluates impact on vulnerable populations and community connections	May underemphasize system-level efficiency benefits

Environmental Ethics Considerations

Blockchain's environmental cost—particularly for Proof of Work networks—has become an ethical flashpoint. Mining equipment consumes large volumes of electricity, potentially sourced from nonrenewable energy. Some mining pools aggregate near inexpensive power supplies to maximize profit, creating local environmental strain (Zaghloul et al., 2020). This scenario poses moral questions about responsible energy usage.

Alternatives like Proof of Stake claim to reduce carbon footprints while retaining security features. The choice of consensus protocol thus intersects with broader social responsibilities to mitigate climate change. A **utilitarian** perspective might justify energy use if blockchain's societal benefits outweigh environmental harm, but **deontological** arguments might hold that moral duties to protect the environment override purely economic gains.

Global and UAE Ethical Perspectives

The moral stand on blockchain technology has a strong territorial separation due to the differences in the cultural standards, economic conditions, and laws. Data autonomy and consumer protection are the priorities in Western jurisdictions which are associated with strict privacy legislation, including the GDPR. In comparison, emerging economies might favor anti-corruption or financial inclusion goals, and in some cases, they might accept partial infringement of privacy as long as they contribute to more meaningful progress in society (Kshetri, 2021).

In the United Arab Emirates, the adoption of technology comes in contact with centralized political systems which may either accelerate or predetermine implementation plans. The focus of the UAE on economic diversification and global competitiveness also means that blockchain projects supported by the government are implemented rather quickly, being under the direct control of the government, and meet the objectives of the national development (Haneem et al., 2020). The UAE has also implemented stringent anti-money laundering laws on cryptocurrency, which results in ethical issues of protecting the integrity of the financial system (Al-Tawil, 2023). Such steps explain why innovation should be balanced with ethical requirements.

Figure 2. Ethical decision-making framework for blockchain implementation

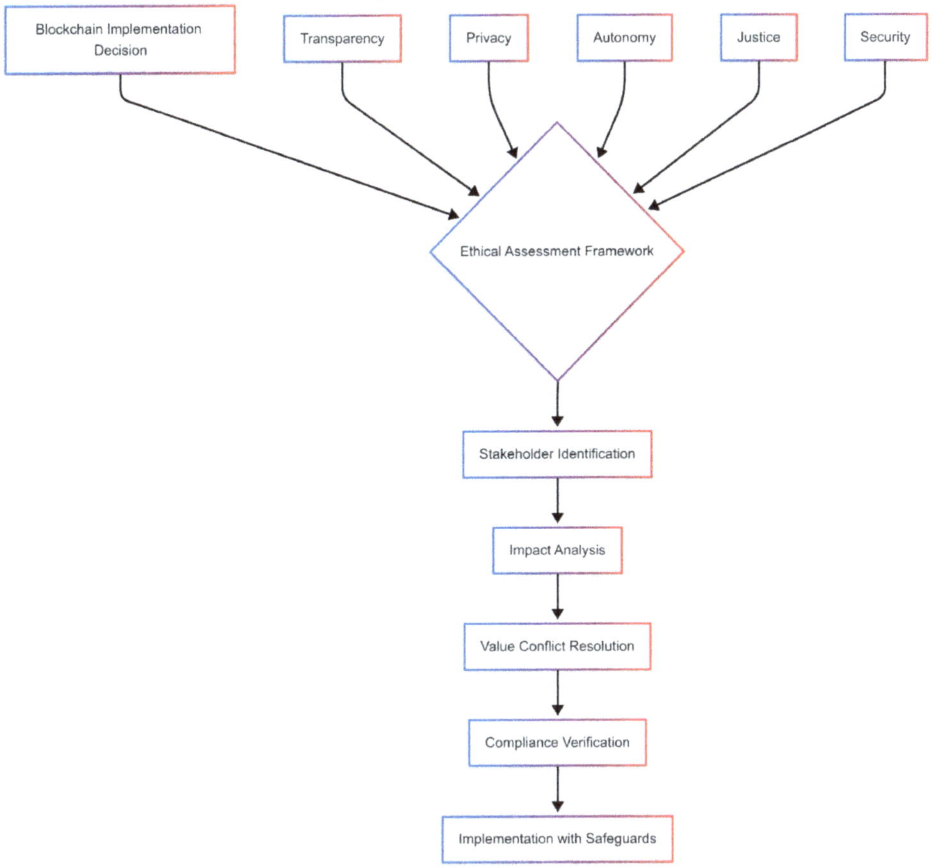

PRIVACY DIMENSIONS OF BLOCKCHAIN TECHNOLOGY

Personal and Employee Privacy Impacts

The very structure of a blockchain—where nodes replicate transaction data—can conflict with strict privacy regulations. Although pseudonymity may offer superficial privacy, it can be compromised by analyzing patterns of usage, IP addresses, or interactions with regulated exchanges (Zaghloul et al., 2020). Sensitive information, if stored directly on a public ledger, remains visible indefinitely.

Within enterprises, **employee data** recorded on immutable ledgers may violate expectations of confidentiality and conflict with labor laws. Some businesses investigate blockchain-based HR applications for payroll, performance tracking, or credential verification. While improved transparency could reduce fraud in these areas, employees could face difficulties having erroneous or harmful data removed (Sharif & Ghodoosi, 2022).

Global and UAE Privacy Regulation Comparison

Table 3. Comparative Analysis of Privacy Regulatory Frameworks outlines the differences in data protection laws that affect blockchain deployment. The GDPR, widely recognized for its stringent data subject rights, has become a global benchmark. Its emphasis on the right to erasure and data minimization challenges the ledger's permanent record, unless a privacy-preserving design is implemented (Dimitropoulos, 2020).

The **UAE Personal Data Protection Law (PDPL)** aligns with many core GDPR principles, such as the need for consent, data minimization, and purpose limitation (Al-Tawil, 2023). However, the UAE's laws may offer more flexibility for government-led blockchain initiatives, recognizing that certain public services can benefit from centralized oversight. Both GDPR and PDPL restrict cross-border data transfers to jurisdictions offering equivalent or adequate privacy protections, complicating widely distributed, public blockchain nodes that might be located anywhere in the world.

Table 3. Comparative analysis of privacy regulatory frameworks

Regulatory Aspect	Global Data Protection Regulation (GDPR)	UAE Personal Data Protection Law (PDPL)	Blockchain Implementation Implications
Right to Erasure	Explicit right to data deletion	Limited erasure requirements	GDPR creates fundamental conflict with immutable records
Data Minimization	Strict limitations on data collection	Similar limitations with exemptions	Both frameworks challenge blockchain's comprehensive recording
Lawful Basis	Explicit consent or legitimate interest	Similar with greater flexibility	UAE approach permits broader implementation scope
Cross-Border Transfers	Strict adequacy requirements	Similar restrictions with exceptions	Both create challenges for global blockchain networks
Controller Obligations	Extensive accountability requirements	Comparable with implementation flexibility	UAE approach reduces certain compliance burdens
Penalties	Up to 4% global revenue	Similar scale with enforcement variations	Both create significant non-compliance risk
Blockchain Guidance	Limited specific guidance	Developing framework	Regulatory uncertainty in both contexts

Privacy-Enhancing Technical Approaches

To address inherent tensions, developers have introduced **privacy-enhancing technologies (PETs). Figure 3. Privacy-Enhancing Technologies for Blockchain Implementation** depicts a variety of these methods, including zero-knowledge proofs, off-chain data storage, and permissioned consensus.

- **Zero-Knowledge Proofs (ZKPs)**: Allow transaction validation without revealing detailed information (Yuan et al., 2024). A user can prove membership in a valid set (e.g., sufficient balance) without exposing their actual balance or transaction history.
- **Off-Chain Storage**: Sensitive data stay in external databases, with only cryptographic hashes recorded on-chain. This approach mitigates permanent data exposure while allowing modifications in off-chain systems (Wylde et al., 2022).
- **Permissioned Networks**: Access is restricted to known entities, enabling finer control over data visibility. The UAE Land Department uses such a model to ensure property records remain secure yet verifiable (Haneem et al., 2020).

These techniques can reduce conflict with privacy regulations, though they complicate blockchain's operational model and may require specialized expertise. Additionally, advanced cryptographic solutions can increase computational overhead and implementation complexity, raising cost and accessibility barriers for smaller organizations.

Figure 3. Privacy-enhancing technologies for blockchain implementation

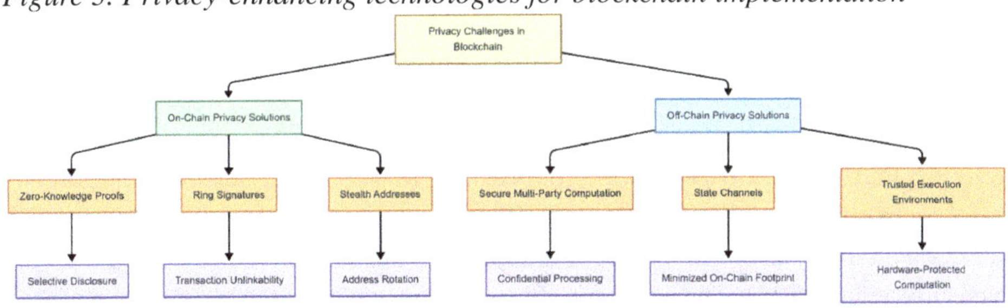

Real-World Privacy Implementations and Challenges

Practical deployments differ in their ability to square blockchain's transparency with privacy mandates. Some healthcare systems combine private blockchains in which patient consent and other necessary medical data are stored with sensitive medical records, excluded from the blockchain or encrypted. Dubai's blockchain based platform for health records shows limited disclosers for research or specialized treatment (Ismail et al., 2019).

In financial services, strict AML and KYC rules on part with the pseudonymity of blockchain require disclosure on the identity of its participants. To do this, exchanges and wallet providers in the UAE and elsewhere need to capture user data which acts as de facto centralized control into a decentralized world (Al-Tawil, 2023).

Self-sovereign identity (SSI) solutions offer a user-centric alternative. People track personal credentials and one provides verified attributes when necessary (Zaghloul, et al. 2020). However, there is a need for strong interoperability standards for the solutions and careful designing to avoid correlation attacks by correlating different identity presentation. The complexity of such systems also brings concerns on inclusivity especially among those with little or no digital literacy or technical resources.

The problem of making privacy-enhancing techniques usable for large parts of the population persists as a major challenge. Although there is still real privacy to be had from advanced cryptography, this is not so easy to do when it comes down to user-friendly application. Blockchain based platforms need to find a delicate balance between enough data privations and to offer workable and cost-effective operations.

INTELLECTUAL PROPERTY IN THE BLOCKCHAIN ERA

Blockchain Effects on Intellectual Property Rights

Blockchain is now offering new ways of governing, protecting, and commercializing intellectual property (IP). Based on the schematic shown in Figure 4. Blockchain-Based Intellectual Property Management Workflow, creators can list works on a tamper-proof ledger, thus creating a timestamped history of authorship (Makridis et al., 2024). The prospect of this evidence platform is to curb the aspect of disputation by supporting the proof of originality. Such transparent tracking and real-time transfer of ownership will benefit copyright, patents, and trademarks.

Smart contracts also automate royalty payments and licensing conditions, particularly in the digital media. An example is a musician or a visual artist who can receive instant micropayment when there is a stream of a song or a resale of a piece, reducing dependence on third parties. In parallel, the supply chain systems have the ability to verify the product origin, which discourages counterfeiting by tracing the unique products to a distributed ledger (Bayramova et al., 2021).

Despite these benefits, difficulties still exist. Blockchains have no inherent mechanism of ensuring that uploaded material is unique; a person may pretend to be an author by hashing a plagiarized piece of work. Also, an on-chain timestamped entry is not necessarily universally accepted as a piece of evidence in IP litigation, where the national intellectual property offices and courts have ultimate authority.

Global and UAE Intellectual Property Frameworks

International intellectual property (IP) systems, which are largely harmonized under the auspices of the World Intellectual Property Organization (WIPO), are starting to introduce blockchain technology into the system of registration and licensing. As an example, the European Union is evaluating how much blockchain can fit within its Digital Single Market agenda without being contradictory to the General Data Protection Regulation (GDPR; Yuan et al., 2024). On the same note, patent offices across the globe are considering the use of decentralized systems of confirming the disclosures of inventions but their readiness to accept the timestamps produced by blockchain is irregular (Makridis et al., 2024).

In the United Arab Emirates (UAE), modernization of IP systems is still ongoing as it is in line with the desire of the country to establish itself as an innovation and technology hub in the region. Current public-private partnerships look into the capacity of blockchain to protect the records of creative-work, reduce international trademark conflicts, and strengthen investors by building confidence (Haneem et al., 2020). Considering that the UAE has heavily invested in the knowledge-based economy, effective regimes of IP protection can be used to generate competitive advantage but currently, there is still a lack of specific laws to regulate blockchain-enabled registration of IP which results in ambiguity as far as enforcing it in case of a cross-border dispute is concerned.

Technical Implementations for Intellectual Property Management

Table 4. Blockchain Applications for Intellectual Property Management summarizes typical methods:

- **Proof of Creation**: Timestamped registration of digital content, establishing verifiable evidence of authorship (Makridis et al., 2024).
- **Rights Management**: Smart contracts that automate licensing terms and royalty splits, potentially revolutionizing creative industries.

- **Anti-Counterfeiting**: Linking physical goods to a blockchain record, verifying authenticity through tamper-resistant markers or codes (Bayramova et al., 2021).
- **Non-Fungible Tokens (NFTs)**: Creating unique digital representations of artworks or collectibles. Although NFTs do not necessarily confer copyright, they can signal provenance and ownership of specific digital tokens (Makridis et al., 2024).

Table 4. Blockchain applications for intellectual property management

IP Challenge	Blockchain Solution	Benefits	Implementation Limitations
Proof of Creation	Timestamped registration	Establishes priority date; Creates evidence record	Doesn't verify originality; Requires proper timestamp governance
Rights Management	Smart contract licensing	Automated execution; Direct creator payment	Complex rights representation; Jurisdictional recognition varies
Anti-Counterfeiting	Supply chain tracking	Product authentication; Distribution monitoring	Physical-digital connection remains vulnerable; Requires consumer verification
Collective Rights	Decentralized governance	Transparent royalty distribution; Democratic decision-making	Governance design complexity; Potential voter apathy
Orphan Works	Persistent creator information	Reduces unattributed works; Facilitates licensing	Retroactive implementation limitations; Privacy considerations
Digital Scarcity	Non-fungible tokens	Creates verifiable uniqueness; Enables digital collecting	Conceptual complexity; Environmental concerns with some implementations

Zero-knowledge protocols may also protect sensitive IP details. By proving ownership without disclosing the entire content, creators can engage in negotiations or licensing while preserving confidentiality (Yuan et al., 2024). However, high complexity and uncertain legal interpretation limit immediate mainstream adoption.

Case Studies and Implementation Challenges

Music licensing is one of the first examples of how blockchain technologies can be used to manage intellectual property (IP). Existing royalty processes may be burdened by delays and inaccuracy of data across various parties such as songwriters, publishers, performers and distributors. Blockchain-based platforms provide an effective solution to this situation because it would allow tracking the usage information in real-time and disburse royalties simultaneously. However, the scalability and viability of such platforms are dependent on whether or not industry-wide standardization, such as a standardized and uniform data model on song metadata is implemented (Makridis et al., 2024).

Patent registration systems that anchor invention disclosures on-chain could similarly mitigate disputes over priority and reduce bureaucratic overhead. Nonetheless, intangible assets require careful classification, and not all patent offices or courts consider blockchain timestamps conclusive evidence (Bayramova et al., 2021).

In the UAE, pilot programs and regulatory sandboxes encourage experimentation with blockchain-based IP solutions. With strong government backing and a tech-forward mindset, the UAE provides an environment for testing advanced applications—though developers must still reconcile blockchain's immutability with the possibility of legal or factual errors. Overcoming interoperability hurdles between blockchain registries and existing IP databases also remains a priority.

Figure 4. Blockchain-based intellectual property management workflow

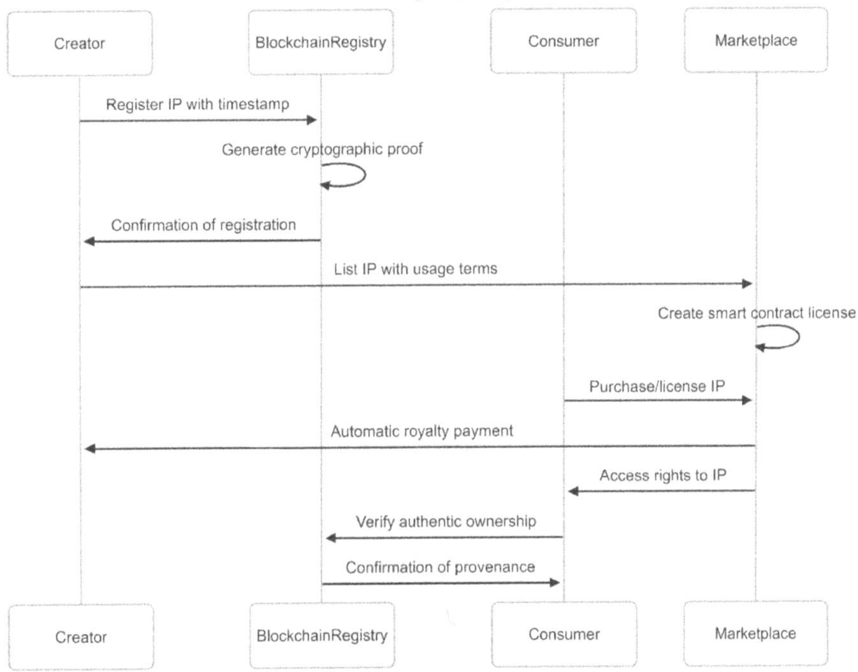

CYBERSECURITY AND COMPUTER CRIME IN THE BLOCKCHAIN CONTEXT

Taxonomy of Blockchain-Related Criminal Activities

While blockchain can fortify data integrity, it also provides novel attack vectors for cybercriminals. **Table 5. Taxonomy of Blockchain-Related Criminal Activities** outlines common threats:

- **Cryptocurrency Theft**: Stealing private keys or exploiting exchange vulnerabilities to remove user funds (Bayramova et al., 2021).
- **Fraud Schemes**: Misleading Initial Coin Offerings (ICOs), pump-and-dump manipulations, or Ponzi structures leveraging token hype.
- **Consensus Attacks**: Gaining majority hashing power or staked tokens to double-spend or censor specific transactions (Zaghloul et al., 2020).
- **Smart Contract Exploitation**: Attacks like reentrancy and integer overflow, exploiting poorly audited code to drain funds (Wylde et al., 2022).
- **Ransomware**: Cybercriminals encrypt systems and demand anonymity-preserving cryptocurrencies in exchange for decryption keys.
- **Money Laundering**: Mixing or tumbling services obscure transaction origins, facilitating illegal fund transfers (Al-Tawil, 2023).

Table 5. Taxonomy of blockchain-related criminal activities

Criminal Activity Category	Description	Technical Vectors	Mitigation Approaches
Cryptocurrency Theft	Unauthorized access to cryptocurrency wallets and exchanges	Private key compromise; Exchange vulnerabilities; Phishing attacks	Hardware wallets; Multi-signature security; Enhanced authentication
Fraud Schemes	Deceptive operations exploiting blockchain characteristics	Fraudulent ICOs; Pump-and-dump schemes; Ponzi operations	Regulatory compliance; Due diligence standards; Investor education
Consensus Attacks	Manipulation of blockchain validation mechanisms	51% attacks; Selfish mining; Eclipse attacks	Protocol security enhancement; Mining diversification; Network monitoring
Smart Contract Exploitation	Malicious interaction with automated agreement systems	Reentrancy attacks; Integer overflow; Logic vulnerabilities	Formal verification; Security auditing; Upgrade mechanisms

continued on following page

Table 5. Continued

Criminal Activity Category	Description	Technical Vectors	Mitigation Approaches
Ransomware	Malicious encryption with cryptocurrency ransom demands	System infiltration; Data encryption; Anonymous payment	Security hardening; Regular backups; Threat intelligence
Money Laundering	Obscuring illicit fund origins through cryptocurrency	Mixing services; Chain-hopping; Privacy coins	KYC/AML compliance; Transaction monitoring; Regulatory frameworks
Intellectual Property Theft	Unauthorized exploitation of proprietary information	Blockchain transparency exposing sensitive data	Data minimization; Zero-knowledge implementations; Off-chain storage

Ransomware attacks, for instance, become more lucrative because victims can pay in relatively pseudonymous digital currencies. Criminals exploit decentralized platforms' global reach, forcing regulators and law enforcement to evolve investigative methods.

Legal Responses to Blockchain-Related Crime

Regulators worldwide increasingly target cryptocurrency service providers. The **Financial Action Task Force (FATF)** now includes Virtual Asset Service Providers (VASPs) within its AML and Counter-Terrorist Financing guidelines, compelling them to adopt KYC measures (Al-Tawil, 2023). Similarly, the EU's Fifth Anti-Money Laundering Directive (5AMLD) demands registration and oversight for crypto businesses, curtailing anonymity by linking wallets to verified identities.

Law enforcement agencies, including INTERPOL and Europol, use specialized blockchain analytics to trace illicit fund flows (Wylde et al., 2022). Such methods can de-anonymize criminals, especially when they convert cryptocurrencies to fiat at regulated exchanges. However, fully decentralized protocols, privacy-oriented coins, and cross-chain "hopping" challenge these investigations.

The **UAE** created the Virtual Asset Regulatory Authority (VARA) to license and supervise crypto businesses, mirroring this global regulatory shift. VARA mandates robust due diligence, suspicious transaction reporting, and capital reserve requirements. By formalizing oversight, the UAE aims to foster a responsible crypto ecosystem and attract international investors while minimizing illicit activity (Al-Tawil, 2023).

Technical Security Measures and Best Practices

Mitigating blockchain-related threats requires a multi-layered security approach. **Figure 5. Blockchain Security Framework for Threat Mitigation** highlights core elements:

1. **User-Level Security**: Encouraging hardware wallets, multi-signature authorization, and secure key storage to thwart phishing and malware attacks (Zaghloul et al., 2020).
2. **Exchange Protection**: Imposing internal controls, penetration tests, cold storage reserves, and insurance policies to reduce vulnerability to hacks.
3. **Smart Contract Auditing**: Employing formal verification or specialized third-party security reviews that identify coding flaws or logic errors.
4. **Blockchain Forensics**: Analyzing on-chain transactions to track stolen funds, identify clusters of malicious addresses, and correlate flows with known threat actors (Bayramova et al., 2021).
5. **Governance Mechanisms**: Some networks allow on-chain governance votes or emergency forks to counter catastrophic exploits, though these actions can undermine the premise of immutability (Dierksmeier & Seele, 2020).

Figure 5. Blockchain security framework for threat mitigation

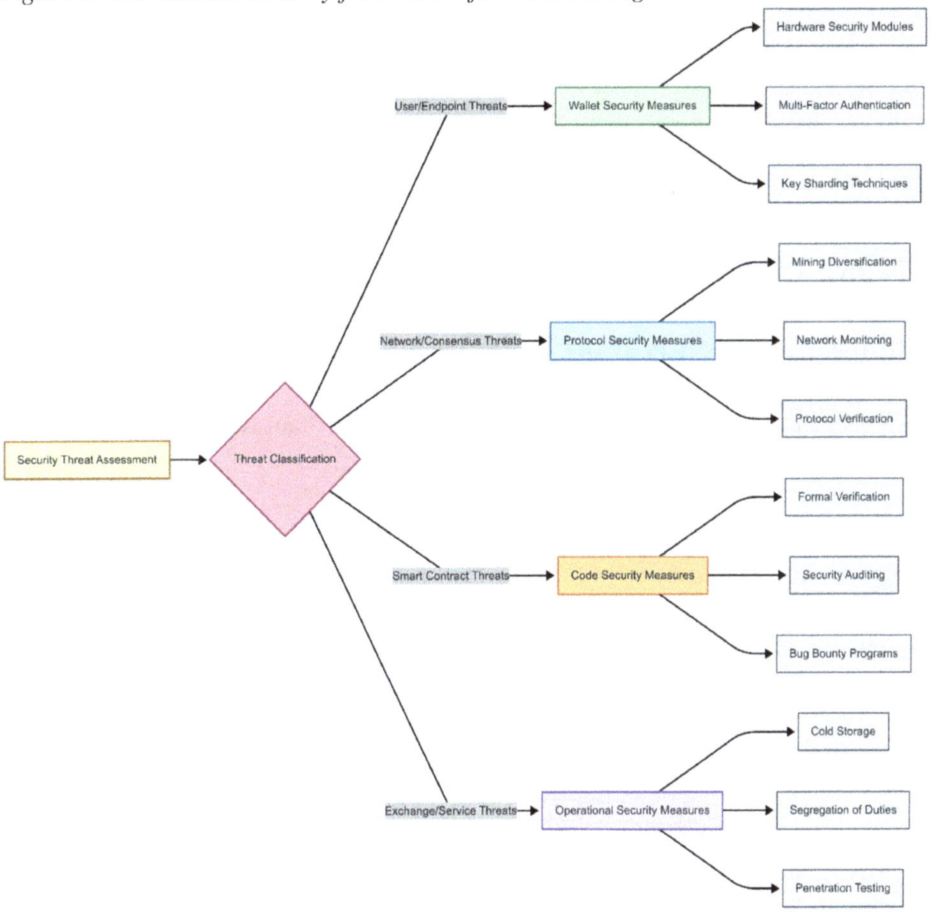

UAE Cybersecurity Integration with Blockchain

In the UAE National Cybersecurity Strategy, the role of blockchain in enhancing resilience in critical infrastructure and government services is explicitly recognized (Haneem et al., 2020). An example is the integration of video surveillance metadata enabled by blockchain in Dubai, which records information about the identity of a person who opened or altered videos, thus preventing the abuse of insiders. By hashing this data at regular intervals and storing on a permissioned ledger, officials will be able to spot any tampering as the hash values will not match.

The second emerging area is digital identities on blockchain which simplify the process of accessing e-government portals and commercial transactions (Ismail et al., 2019). When combined with anomaly detection through AI (Jaber, 2025), the authorities will be able to follow suspicious activity in real time. These integrations make security stronger, but centralized control gives rise to privacy concerns or possible abuse. Thus, the experience of the UAE shows that the integration of blockchain to achieve greater security and respect individual freedoms and international data protection standards is a difficult task.

FUTURE DIRECTIONS AND CONCLUSION

Technological Innovation Trajectories

Blockchain continues to evolve through innovations that address present limitations and open new applications:

1. **Privacy-Preserving Technologies**: Zero-knowledge proofs and homomorphic encryption are poised to become more efficient (Yuan et al., 2024). These tools help resolve conflicts between transparency and confidential data, allowing calculations on encrypted information without revealing raw inputs.
2. **AI-Blockchain Integration**: Machine learning algorithms that analyze blockchain data can discover complex transaction patterns or anomalies, assisting in predictive analytics for supply chains, finances, or cybersecurity (Ressi et al., 2024). However, embedding AI within an immutable ledger poses ethical and technical questions about reversing erroneous decisions (Jaber, 2025).
3. **Sustainable Consensus**: Ongoing shifts toward Proof of Stake and other green consensus protocols aim to reduce the carbon footprint of large networks (Tang et al., 2020). This evolution addresses environmental critics who decry the energy usage of Proof of Work.
4. **Cross-Chain Interoperability**: Projects like Polkadot and Cosmos strive to break silos, letting specialized blockchains exchange data. As solutions mature, multi-chain ecosystems could dominate enterprise and governmental use cases (Ressi et al., 2024).

Legal Harmonization Prospects

Worldwide, legislators and regulators aim to align blockchain laws to minimize regulatory arbitrage and clarify compliance:

- **Global Standards**: Organizations like the Financial Action Task Force are developing consistent AML guidelines, while the G20 discusses regulatory frameworks for cryptocurrencies.
- **Sector-Specific Harmonization**: Industries such as trade finance or healthcare may create tailored standards enabling cross-border data sharing within a shared blockchain environment.
- **UAE Blockchain-Specific Legislation**: Given its advanced implementations, the UAE could pioneer a legal regime clarifying responsibilities in decentralized systems, addressing immutability vs. erasure rights, and formalizing node operator roles (Al-Tawil, 2023).

Despite progress, fundamental questions remain about which jurisdiction's law applies to public blockchains spanning multiple countries (Dimitropoulos, 2020). Legal fragmentation remains a major barrier to global enterprise adoption.

Ethical Governance Evolution

Ensuring blockchain serves the broader public interest requires governance structures that incorporate diverse stakeholders. **Decentralized Autonomous Organizations (DAOs)** present experimental governance, distributing voting power via tokens (Dierksmeier & Seele, 2020). Yet such models can entrench plutocracy if token distribution is unequal. Meanwhile, ethical principles demand inclusive decision-making, especially when systems affect supply chain workers, content creators, or marginalized users.

Ethical impact assessments—similar to environmental impact reports—are emerging as a mechanism to evaluate blockchain deployments (Sharif & Ghodoosi, 2022). This approach would systematically address privacy impacts, resource consumption, and social inequities before large-scale implementations. In the UAE, mandated ethical assessments for public-sector blockchain projects might solidify trust in government-run systems.

Multi-stakeholder models are increasingly crucial. Policymakers, developers, civil society groups, and domain experts can work together to shape code standards and address unintended consequences. In a region like the UAE, with high expatriate populations and diverse cultural norms, forging inclusive governance can avert system biases and ensure broader acceptance of blockchain-based services (Haneem et al., 2020).

CONCLUSION

The key properties of blockchain technology: distributed consensus, immutability, and transparency reveal a territory narrowed to sight by unprecedented possibilities and extraordinary complex ethical-legal minefields. Its capability to dispense with centralized intermediaries creates efficiency and trust in areas such as supply chain tracking and the management of digital assets. However, such features intensify the fears of data ever- lasting disclosure, environmental effects, correcting erroneous or damaging....

Ethically, blockchain signals society onto a test on privacy, autonomy, and fairness. Differences in global views are as a result of contextual fact deviations: while in the West emphasis is laid on individual rights under such regulations such as GDPR, in some developing countries, it is conditioned by accepting some levels of impaired privacy in the name of transparency and anti-corruption benefits. The UAE desiring explosive technological evolution acts as mediator between them by promoting the governmental direction, regulatory regimes and pro-innovation culture.

Privacy constraints and compliance obligations can't be disappearing, so do rights and copyrights enforcement worries over where blockchain can auto-enforce royalties and prove ownership, but it still needs legal systems for final validation. Cyber security is at a crossroads, as blockchain is used to secure government data and attract the criminals in search of pseudonymous avenues for thievery and fraud. The UAE's Virtual Asset Regulatory Authority (VARA) is an example of governments trying to guide blockchain based ecosystems into regulated habitats.

Among the new technological breakthroughs might include solutions like zero-knowledge proofs, AI synergies and greener consensus on one hand and cross-chain interoperability on the other, which may change the way, in which block chains operate thus, bridging some of the gaps, that already exist (or create new ones in regard to accountability. The capacity to harmonize the law remains just as critical these days as the haphazard quilt of rules within jurisdictions now effectively restrains global honest implementations. But the urge for a common set of standards goes head to head with different national priorities and regulatory cultures.

It turns out that ethical governance mechanisms are the lynch pin in ensuring blockchain's continued feasibility. The public participation, forceful ethical choices, attempts to help disenfranchised communities can ensure that blockchain's beneficent impacts: transparency, anti-fraud, launching new economic opportunities does not step on basic rights or enlarge inequalities. In the UAE's situation, in which centralized powers orchestrate and fund blockchain innovation, there are corresponding opportunities and challenges: efficient deployment may be rewarding but call for critically robust safeguards, inclusivity and cross border collaboration. Overall, blockchain technology has come to prominence as a new method for secure, transparent transactions with great promise for both social as well as economic impacts. However, responsible harvesting of this potential requires navigation of ethical norms and legal frameworks with care. As the global community and the UAE itself ubiquitous the blockchain's potential, it will become increasingly important for the blockchain's design and governance to align with fundamental ethical principles for sustained equitable results in the coming decade.

REFERENCES

Al-Tawil, T. N. E. (2023). Anti-money laundering regulation of cryptocurrency: UAE and global approaches. *Journal of Money Laundering Control*, *26*(6), 1150–1164.

Alston, E. (2022). Blockchain and the law-legality, law-like characteristics, and legal applications. *The Economics of Blockchain and Cryptocurrency*, 117-144.

Bayramova, A., Edwards, D. J., & Roberts, C. (2021). The Role of Blockchain Technology in Augmenting Supply Chain Resilience to Cybercrime. *Buildings (Basel, Switzerland)*, *11*(7), 283. DOI: 10.3390/buildings11070283

Dierksmeier, C., & Seele, P. (2020). Blockchain and business ethics. *Business Ethics (Oxford, England)*, *29*(2), 348–359.

Dimitropoulos, G. (2020). The law of blockchain. *Washington Law Review (Seattle, Wash.)*, *95*, 1117–1172.

Haneem, F., Bakar, H. A., Kama, N., Mat, N. Z. N., Ghazali, R., & Mahmood, Y. (2020). Recent progress of blockchain initiatives in government. *International Journal of Advanced Computer Science and Applications*, *11*(11), 344–351.

Ismail, L., Hameed, H., AlShamsi, M., AlHammadi, M., & AlDhanhani, N. (2019, March). Towards a blockchain deployment at UAE university: Performance evaluation and blockchain taxonomy. In *Proceedings of the 2019 International Conference on Blockchain Technology* (pp. 30-38).

Jaber, T. A. (2025). Enhancing crime detection in video surveillance via a lightweight blockchain and homomorphic encryption-based computer vision system. *Mesopotamian Journal of CyberSecurity*, *5*(1), 121–146.

Khan, S. N., Shael, M., & Majdalawieh, M. (2019, July). Blockchain technology as a support infrastructure in e-government evolution at Dubai economic department. In *Proceedings of the 1st International Electronics Communication Conference* (pp. 124-130).

Kshetri, N. (2021). Blockchain and sustainable supply chain management in developing countries. *International Journal of Information Management*, *60*, 102376.

Makridis, C. A., Bates, T., Barnes, N., & Glasgow-George, J. (2024). The future of intellectual property: The complementary role of artificial intelligence and blockchain. *Journal of the Patent and Trademark Office Society*, *104*, 293–315.

Ressi, D., Romanello, R., Piazza, C., & Rossi, S. (2024). AI-enhanced blockchain technology: A review of advancements and opportunities. *Journal of Network and Computer Applications*, •••, 103858.

Sharif, M. M., & Ghodoosi, F. (2022). The ethics of blockchain in organizations. *Journal of Business Ethics*, *178*(4), 1009–1025. PMID: 35125568

Tang, Y., Xiong, J., Becerril-Arreola, R., & Iyer, L. (2020). Ethics of blockchain: A framework of technology, applications, impacts, and research directions. *Information Technology & People*, *33*(2), 602–632.

Wylde, V., Rawindaran, N., Lawrence, J., Balasubramanian, R., Prakash, E., Jayal, A., & Platts, J. (2022). Cybersecurity, data privacy and blockchain: A review. *SN Computer Science*, *3*(2), 127. PMID: 35036930

Yuan, S., Yang, W., Tian, X., & Tang, W. (2024). A blockchain-based privacy preserving intellectual property authentication method. *Symmetry*, *16*(5), 622.

Zaghloul, E., Li, T., Mutka, M. W., & Ren, J. (2020). Bitcoin and blockchain: Security and privacy. *IEEE Internet of Things Journal*, *7*(10), 10288–10313.

Compilation of References

Abadi, D., Boncz, P., Harizopoulos, S., Idreos, S., & Madden, S. (2013). The design and implementation of modern column-oriented database systems. *Foundations and Trends in Databases*, *5*(3), 197–280. DOI: 10.1561/1900000024

Abu-AlSondos, I. A., Shehadeh, M., Ajouz, M., Alkhwaldi, A. F., Abdeldayem, M., & Aldulaimi, S. H. (2024). The Role of Digital Transformation in Business: Opportunities Challenges and Future Directions. *2024 ASU International Conference in Emerging Technologies for Sustainability and Intelligent Systems (ICETSIS)*, 361–365. https://doi.org/DOI: 10.1109/ICETSIS61505.2024.10459639

Abubakar, A. M., Türkmen, A., Işik, V., Mikalef, P., & Turel, O. (2025). Exploring the complementary effects of business analytics capabilities and π-shaped skills on innovation outcomes. *European Journal of Information Systems*, *34*(1), 146–163.

Abuoliem, N., Mohd Nor, S., Safiih Lola, M., & Matar, A. (2019). Dynamic interactions among the industrial sector and its determinants in Jordan. *Investment Management and Financial Innovations*, *16*(4), 325–341. DOI: 10.21511/imfi.16(4).2019.28

Abuzuraiq, A., Alkasassbeh, M., & Almseidin, M. (2020). Intelligent methods for accurately detecting phishing websites. In *2020 11th International Conference on Information and Communication Systems (ICICS)* (pp. 85–90). IEEE. https://doi.org/DOI: 10.1109/ICICS49469.2020.239556

Accenture. (2024). *Global data literacy survey 2024: Bridging the talent gap*. https://www.accenture.com

Adewumi, A., Oshioste, E. E., Asuzu, O. F., Ndubuisi, N. L., Awonnuga, K. F., & Daraojimba, O. H. (2024). Business intelligence tools in finance: A review of trends in the USA and Africa. *World Journal of Advanced Research and Reviews*, *21*(3), 608–616.

Adeyeye, O. J., Akanbi, I., Emeteveke, I., & Emehin, O. (2024). Leveraging secured AI-driven data analytics for cybersecurity: Safeguarding information and enhancing threat detection. *International Journal of Research and Publication and Reviews*, *5*(10), 3208–3223.

Adhikari, D., & Thapaliya, S. (2024).. . *An Overview of AI Applications in Cybersecurity for IT Management.*, *1*(4), 121–133. DOI: 10.3126/nprcjmr.v1i4.70951

Agrawal, S., Chaudhuri, S., & Narasayya, V. R. (2000). Automated selection of materialized views and indexes in SQL databases. In *Proceedings of the 26th International Conference on Very Large Data Bases* (pp. 496-505).

Agrawal, S., Chaudhuri, S., & Narasayya, V. R. (2001). Materialized view and index selection tool for Microsoft SQL Server. In *Proceedings of the 2006 ACM SIGMOD International Conference on Management of Data* (pp. 725-726). https://doi.org/ DOI: 10.1145/376284.375769

Ain, N., Vaia, G., DeLone, W., & Waheed, M. (2019). Two decades of research on business intelligence system adoption, utilization and success: A systematic literature review. *Decision Support Systems*, *125*, 113113. DOI: 10.1016/j.dss.2019.113113

Akther, A., Arobee, A., Adnan, A. A., Auyon, O., Islam, A. S. M., & Akter, F. (2025). Blockchain As a Platform For Artificial Intelligence (AI) Transparency. arXiv preprint arXiv:2503.08699.

Alabdulatif, A., Khalil, I., & Yi, X. (2020). Towards secure big data analytic for cloud-enabled applications with fully homomorphic encryption. *Journal of Parallel and Distributed Computing*, *137*, 192–204.

Alajlan, N. N., & Ibrahim, D. M. (2022). TinyML: Enabling of inference deep learning models on ultra-low-power IoT edge devices for AI applications. *Micromachines*, *13*(6), 851. PMID: 35744466

Alan, J. (2024, May 17). *SugarGh0st RAT Campaign Targets U.S. AI Experts*. The Cyber Express. https://thecyberexpress.com/sugargh0st-campaign-targets-ai-experts/

Alanezi, M., & Al-Azzawi, R. M. A. (2024). AI-Powered Cyber Threats: A Systematic Review. *Deleted Journal*, *4*(3), 166–188. DOI: 10.58496/mjcs/2024/021

Alghamdi, N. A., & Al-Baity, H. H. (2022). Augmented analytics driven by AI: A digital transformation beyond business intelligence. *Sensors (Basel)*, *22*(20), 8071. DOI: 10.3390/s22208071 PMID: 36298421

Ali, F. (2021). *Revolutionizing Cloud Computing with AI/ML for Business Intelligence*. ERP Cloud, and Snowflake DB Security Enhancements.

Ali, S., Wang, J., & Leung, V. C. M. (2025). AI-Driven Fusion with Cybersecurity: Exploring Current Trends, Advanced Techniques, Future Directions, and Policy Implications for Evolving Paradigms– A Comprehensive Review. *Information Fusion*, *118*, 102922. DOI: 10.1016/j.inffus.2024.102922

Al-Kasassbeh, M., Almseidin, M., Alrfou, K., & Kovacs, S. (2020). Detection of IoT-botnet attacks using fuzzy rule interpolation. *Journal of Intelligent & Fuzzy Systems*, *39*(1), 421–431. DOI: 10.3233/JIFS-191135

Allahyari, M., Pouriyeh, S., Assefi, M., Safaei, S., Trippe, E. D., Gutierrez, J. B., & Kochut, K. (2017). Text summarization techniques: A brief survey. *International Journal of Advanced Computer Science and Applications*, *8*(10), 397–405. DOI: 10.14569/IJACSA.2017.081052

Alloghani, M., Thron, C., & Subair, S. (2022). Past Achievements and Future Promises of Digital Transformation: A Literature Review. In Alloghani, M., Thron, C., & Subair, S. (Eds.), *Artificial Intelligence for Data Science in Theory and Practice* (Vol. 1006, pp. 27–39). Springer International Publishing., DOI: 10.1007/978-3-030-92245-0_2

Almansoori, A., Al-Emran, M., & Shaalan, K. (2023). Exploring the Frontiers of Cybersecurity Behavior: A Systematic Review of Studies and Theories. *Applied Sciences (Basel, Switzerland)*, *13*(9), 5700. DOI: 10.3390/app13095700

Almseidin, M., & Alkasassbeh, M. (2022b). An accurate detection approach for IoT botnet attacks using interpolation reasoning method. *Information (Basel)*, *13*(6), 300. Advance online publication. DOI: 10.3390/info13060300

Almseidin, M., Alkasassbeh, M., Alzubi, M., & Al-Sawwa, J. (2022). Cyber-phishing website detection using fuzzy rule interpolation. *Cryptography*, *6*(2), 24. Advance online publication. DOI: 10.3390/cryptography6020024

Almseidin, M., Al-Sawwa, J., & Alkasassbeh, M. (2021). Anomaly-based intrusion detection system using fuzzy logic. In *2021 International Conference on Information Technology (ICIT)* (pp. 290–295). IEEE. https://doi.org/DOI: 10.1109/ICIT52682.2021.9491718

Almseidin, M., Al-Sawwa, J., & Alkasassbeh, M. (2022a). Generating a benchmark cyber multi-step attacks dataset for intrusion detection. *Journal of Intelligent & Fuzzy Systems*, *43*(3), 3679–3694. DOI: 10.3233/JIFS-213241

Almseidin, M., Al-Sawwa, J., Alkasassbeh, M., & Alweshah, M. (2023). On detecting distributed denial of service attacks using fuzzy inference system. *Cluster Computing*, *26*(2), 1337–1351. DOI: 10.1007/s10586-022-03674-3

Almseidin, M., Alzubi, M., Al-Sawwa, J., & Alkasassbeh, M. (2024). Comparative analysis of fuzzy rule interpolation techniques across various scenarios using a set of benchmarks (November 2023). *IEEE Access : Practical Innovations, Open Solutions*, *12*, 15376–15389. DOI: 10.1109/ACCESS.2023.3334567

Almseidin, M., Alzubi, M., Al-Sawwa, J., Alkasassbeh, M., & Alfraheed, M. (2024). A threefold approach for enhancing fuzzy interpolative reasoning: Case study on phishing attack detection using sparse rule bases. *Computers*, *13*(11), 291. Advance online publication. DOI: 10.3390/computers13110291

Almseidin, M., Alzubi, M., Kovacs, S., Al-Sawwa, J., & Alkasassbeh, M. (2024). EI-FRI: Extended incircle fuzzy rule interpolation for multidimensional antecedents, multiple fuzzy rules, and extrapolation using total weight measurement and shift ratio. [JRC]. *Journal of Robotics and Control*, *5*(1), 217–227. DOI: 10.18196/jrc.v5i1.20876

Almseidin, M., Gawanmeh, A., Alzubi, M., Al-Sawwa, J., Mashaleh, A. S., & Alkasassbeh, M. (2025). Hybrid deep neural network optimization with particle swarm and grey wolf algorithms for sunburst attack detection. *Computers*, *14*(3), 107. Advance online publication. DOI: 10.3390/computers14030107

Al-Okaily, A., Al-Okaily, M., Teoh, A. P., & Al-Debei, M. M. (2023). An empirical study on data warehouse systems effectiveness: The case of Jordanian banks in the business intelligence era. *EuroMed Journal of Business*, *18*(4), 489–510.

Alomari, A. Y., & Çengel, Ö. (2023). The effect of business intelligence on the development of human resources in Jordanian banks. *International Journal of Multidisciplinary Research and Growth Evaluation*, *4*(4), 864–871. DOI: 10.54660/.IJMRGE.2023.4.4.864-871

Al-Sawwa, J., Almseidin, M., Alkasassbeh, M., Alemerien, K., & Younisse, R. (2024). Spark-based multi-verse optimizer as wrapper features selection algorithm for phishing attack challenge. *Cluster Computing*, *27*(5), 5799–5814. DOI: 10.1007/s10586-023-04236-x

Alshurideh, M. T., Hamadneh, S., Alzoubi, H. M., Al Kurdi, B., Nuseir, M. T., & Al Hamad, A. (2024). Empowering supply chain management system with machine learning and blockchain technology. In *Cyber Security Impact on Digitalization and Business Intelligence: Big Cyber Security for Information Management: Opportunities and Challenges* (pp. 335–349). Springer International Publishing.

Alslman, Y., Alkasassbeh, M., & Almseidin, M. (2024). A robust SNMP-MIB intrusion detection system against adversarial attacks. *Arabian Journal for Science and Engineering*, *49*(3), 4179–4195. DOI: 10.1007/s13369-023-08253-6

Alsmadi, D., & Omar, K. (2022). Analyzing the Needs of ICT Job Market in Jordan Using a Text Mining Approach. *2022 International Conference on Business Analytics for Technology and Security (ICBATS)*, 1–5. https://doi.org/DOI: 10.1109/ICBATS54253.2022.9759009

Alston, E. (2022). Blockchain and the law-legality, law-like characteristics, and legal applications. *The Economics of Blockchain and Cryptocurrency*, 117-144.

Al-Tarawneh, J. M. (2019). Technology acceptance models and adoption of innovations: A literature review. *International Journal of Scientific and Research Publications*, *9*(1), 233–239. https://www.ijsrp.org/research-paper-0819.php?rp=P929018

Altarawneh, R. M. (2024). The Impact of Business Intelligence on Sustainable Business Entrepreneurship in the Jordanian Pharmaceutical Industrial Companies. *American International Journal of Business Management*, *7*(2), 60–71.

Al-Tawil, T. N. E. (2023). Anti-money laundering regulation of cryptocurrency: UAE and global approaches. *Journal of Money Laundering Control*, *26*(6), 1150–1164.

Alweshah, M., Kassaymeh, S., Alkhalaileh, S., Almseidin, M., & Altarawni, I. (2023). An efficient hybrid mine blast algorithm for tackling software fault prediction problem. *Neural Processing Letters*, *55*(8), 10925–10950. DOI: 10.1007/s11063-023-11376-8

Alzawahra, M., & Alqrainy, S. (2024). Examining the Drivers and Performance Impact of Business Intelligence Adoption in Healthcare Organizations: Evidence from Jordan. *Journal of System and Management Sciences*, *14*(4). Advance online publication. DOI: 10.33168/JSMS.2024.0409

Alzubi, M., Almseidin, M., Lone, M. A., & Kovacs, S. (2019a). Fuzzy rule interpolation toolbox for the GNU open-source OCTAVE. In *2019 17th International Conference on Emerging eLearning Technologies and Applications (ICETA)* (pp. 16–22). IEEE. https://doi.org/DOI: 10.1109/ICETA48886.2019.9040090

Alzubi, M., Johanyak, Z. C., & Kovacs, S. (2019d). Fuzzy rule interpolation methods and FRI toolbox. *arXiv*. https://doi.org//arXiv.1904.12178DOI: 10.48550

Alzubi, M., Almseidin, M., Alkasassbeh, M., Al-Sawwa, J., & Aldweesh, A. (2024). DT-ARO: Decision tree-based artificial rabbits optimization to mitigate IoT botnet exploitation. *Journal of Network and Systems Management*, *32*(1), 14. Advance online publication. DOI: 10.1007/s10922-023-09781-9

Alzubi, M., & Kovacs, S. (2020). Interpolative fuzzy reasoning method based on the incircle of a generalized triangular fuzzy number. *Journal of Intelligent & Fuzzy Systems*, *39*(1), 709–729. DOI: 10.3233/JIFS-191223

Amershi, S., Begel, A., Bird, C., DeLine, R., Gall, H., Kamar, E., Nagappan, N., Nushi, B., & Zimmermann, T. (2019). Software engineering for machine learning: A case study. In *Proceedings of the 41st International Conference on Software Engineering: Software Engineering in Practice* (pp. 291–300). IEEE. doi:DOI: 10.1109/ICSE-SEIP.2019.00042

Aminu, M., Akinsanya, A., Dako, D. A., & Oyedokun, O. (2024). Enhancing cyber threat detection through real-time threat intelligence and adaptive defense mechanisms. *International Journal of Computer Applications Technology and Research, 13*(8), 11–27.

Anwar, T., Khan, G. A., Ashraf, Z., Ansari, Z. A., Ahmed, R., & Azrour, M. (2024). The combination of blockchain and the internet of things (iot): applications, opportunities, and challenges for industry. Blockchain and Machine Learning for IoT Security, 56-76.

Arikat, Z. M. A. (2024). The Role of Business Intelligence in Enhancing the Performance of Supply Chains in Jordan. *Journal of Ecohumanism, 3*(8). Advance online publication. DOI: 10.62754/joe.v3i8.4885

Armbrust, M., Mani, M., Xin, R., & Franklin, M. (2021). Lakehouse: A new generation of open platforms unifying data warehousing and advanced analytics. *Proceedings of the VLDB Endowment International Conference on Very Large Data Bases, 14*(12), 2901–2904.

Ashfin, P. (2024). AI-driven threat detection and response in cybersecurity. *Bulletin of Engineering Science and Technology, 1*(2), 125–143.

Attar-Khorasani, S., & Chalmeta, R. (2024). Internet of Things data visualization for business intelligence. *Big Data, 12*(6), 478–503.

Azangoo, M., Sorsamäki, L., Sierla, S. A., Mätäsniemi, T., Rantala, M., Rainio, K., & Vyatkin, V. (2022). A methodology for generating a digital twin for process industry: A case study of a fiber processing pilot plant. *IEEE Access : Practical Innovations, Open Solutions, 10*, 58787–58810.

Azmi, M., Mansour, A., & Azmi, C. (2023). A context-aware empowering business with AI: Case of chatbots in business intelligence systems. *Procedia Computer Science, 224*, 479–484. DOI: 10.1016/j.procs.2023.09.054

Barocas, S., & Selbst, A. D. (2016). Big data's disparate impact. *California Law Review, 104*, 671–732. DOI: 10.2139/ssrn.2477899

Batini, C., Cappiello, C., Francalanci, C., & Maurino, A. (2009). Methodologies for data quality assessment and improvement. *ACM Computing Surveys*, *41*(3), 1–52. DOI: 10.1145/1541880.1541883

Baumhecker, A. (2022, March 30). Infographic: *Strategies for driving adoption and usage with BI and analytics*. BARC. https://barc.com/infographic-bi-analytics-adoption-strategies/

Bayramova, A., Edwards, D. J., & Roberts, C. (2021). The Role of Blockchain Technology in Augmenting Supply Chain Resilience to Cybercrime. *Buildings (Basel, Switzerland)*, *11*(7), 283. DOI: 10.3390/buildings11070283

Bellamkonda, S., Ahmed, R., Witkowski, A., Cruanes, T., Zait, M., & Yagoub, K. (2009). Enhanced subquery optimizations in Oracle. *Proceedings of the VLDB Endowment International Conference on Very Large Data Bases*, *2*(2), 1366–1377. DOI: 10.14778/1687553.1687563

Bellamkonda, S., Bozkaya, T., Ghosh, B., Gupta, A., Haydu, J., Subramanian, S., & Witkowski, A. (2013). Adaptive and big data scale parallel execution in Oracle. *Proceedings of the VLDB Endowment International Conference on Very Large Data Bases*, *6*(11), 1102–1113. DOI: 10.14778/2536222.2536235

Bhambri, P., & Rani, S. (2024). Advancements and Future Challenges in Business Intelligence. In Barrena-Martinez, J., Foncubierta-Rodríguez, M.-J., Medina-Garrido, J. A., & Dobrowolski, Z. (Eds.), (pp. 267–286). Advances in Logistics, Operations, and Management Science. IGI Global., DOI: 10.4018/979-8-3693-3057-9.ch017

Biamonte, J., Wittek, P., Pancotti, N., Rebentrost, P., Wiebe, N., & Lloyd, S. (2017). Quantum machine learning. *Nature*, *549*(7671), 195–202. DOI: 10.1038/nature23474 PMID: 28905917

Binhammad, M., Alqaydi, S., Othman, A., & Abuljadayel, L. H. (2024). The Role of AI in Cyber Security: Safeguarding Digital Identity. *Journal of Information Security*, *15*(02), 245–278. DOI: 10.4236/jis.2024.152015

Blei, D. M., Ng, A. Y., & Jordan, M. I. (2003). Latent Dirichlet allocation. *Journal of Machine Learning Research*, *3*, 993–1022. DOI: 10.1162/jmlr.2003.3.4-5.993

Bolón-Canedo, V., Morán-Fernández, L., Cancela, B., & Alonso-Betanzos, A. (2024). A review of green artificial intelligence: Towards a more sustainable future. *Neurocomputing*, •••, 128096.

Bonnet, D., & Westerman, G. (2020). The new elements of digital transformation. *MIT Sloan Management Review*, *62*(2).

Borrelli, S. S., & Kazmin, A. (2025, February 9). *Italian Tycoons Targeted by Fake Defence Minister in Suspected AI Scam*. Financial Times. https://www.ft.com/content/8e911f1e-6eb7-4e8e-b4e0-3aba62575f23?utm_source=chatgpt.com

Box, G. E., Jenkins, G. M., Reinsel, G. C., & Ljung, G. M. (2015). *Time series analysis: Forecasting and control* (5th ed.). John Wiley & Sons., DOI: 10.1111/jtsa.12194

Bratu, M. (2023). The intersection of artificial intelligence and business intelligence: a systematic mapping study.

Breck, E., Cai, S., Nielsen, E., Salib, M., & Sculley, D. (2017). The ML test score: A rubric for ML production readiness and technical debt reduction. In *Proceedings of the IEEE International Conference on Big Data* (pp. 1123-1132). IEEE. DOI: DOI: 10.1109/BigData.2017.8258038

Breunig, M. M., Kriegel, H. P., Ng, R. T., & Sander, J. (2000). LOF: Identifying density-based local outliers. In *Proceedings of the 2000 ACM SIGMOD International Conference on Management of Data* (pp. 93–104). ACM. doi:DOI: 10.1145/335191.335388

Broadbent, A., & Schaffner, C. (2016). Quantum cryptography beyond quantum key distribution. *Designs, Codes and Cryptography*, *78*(1), 351–382. DOI: 10.1007/s10623-015-0157-4 PMID: 32226229

Bruno, N. (2011). *Automated physical database design and tuning*. CRC Press., DOI: 10.1201/b10711

Buchanan, B. G., & Wright, D. (2021). The impact of machine learning on UK financial services. *Oxford Review of Economic Policy*, *37*(3), 537–563. DOI: 10.1093/oxrep/grab016 PMID: 34642572

Burt, A. (2024). *Finance Employee Defrauded for $25M by Deepfake CFO*. CFO. https://www.cfo.com/news/deepfake-cfo-hong-kong-25-million-fraud-cyber-crime/706529/

Bussa, S. (2023). Enhancing BI tools for improved data visualization and insights. *International Journal of Computer Science and Mobile Computing*, *12*(2), 70–92.

Cao, Y., Chen, C., Guo, F., Jiang, D., Lin, Y., Ooi, B. C., & Zhang, Q. (2019). ES2: A cloud data storage system for supporting both OLTP and OLAP. In *Proceedings of the 2019 International Conference on Management of Data* (pp. 757-772). https://doi.org/DOI: 10.1109/ICDE.2011.5767881

Carbone, P., Katsifodimos, A., Ewen, S., Markl, V., Haridi, S., & Tzoumas, K. (2015). Apache Flink: Stream and batch processing in a single engine. *A Quarterly Bulletin of the Computer Society of the IEEE Technical Committee on Data Engineering*, *36*(4), 28–38. https://research.tudelft.nl/en/publications/apache-flink-stream-and-batch-processing-in-a-single-engine

Chacko, A. J. (2024, June 22). *SugarGh0st: China-Linked Espionage Malware Targets Diplomatic Circles*. Interesting Engineering. https://interestingengineering.com/science/sugargh0st-sneakychef-cyberespionage

Chakraborty, T., Sharada, V., & Sharma, J. (2024). Data-Driven Decisions for Employee Motivation: Strategies for Implementing Technology in Performance Reviews in a Tech Landscape. In *Employee Performance Management for Improved Workplace Motivation* (pp. 311-338): IGI Global.

Chan, C. Y., & Ioannidis, Y. E. (1998). Bitmap index design and evaluation. *SIGMOD Record*, *27*(2), 355–366. DOI: 10.1145/276304.276336

Chan, K. Y., Abu-Salih, B., Qaddoura, R., Al-Zoubi, A. M., Palade, V., Pham, D.-S., & Muhammad, K. (2023). Deep neural networks in the cloud: Review, applications, challenges and research directions. *Neurocomputing*, *545*, 126327.

Chatterjee, S., Chaudhuri, R., & Mikalef, P. (2022). Examining the dimensions of adopting natural language processing and big data analytics applications in firms. *IEEE Transactions on Engineering Management*, *71*, 3001–3015.

Chaudhari, A. V., & Charate, P. A. (2025). AI-driven data warehousing in real-time business intelligence: A framework for automated ETL, predictive analytics, and cloud integration. *International Journal of Research Culture Society*, *9*(3), 185–190. DOI: 10.2017/IJRCS/202503025

Chaudhuri, S., Dayal, U., & Narasayya, V. (2011). An overview of business intelligence technology. *Communications of the ACM*, *54*(8), 88–98. DOI: 10.1145/1978542.1978562

Chen, H., & Magramo, K. (2024, February 4). *Finance Worker Pays Out $25 Million After Video Call with Deepfake "Chief Financial Officer."* CNN. https://edition.cnn.com/2024/02/04/asia/deepfake-cfo-scam-hong-kong-intl-hnk/index.html

Chen, H., Chiang, R. H., & Storey, V. C. (2012). Business intelligence and analytics: From big data to big impact. *Management Information Systems Quarterly*, *36*(4), 1165–1188. DOI: 10.2307/41703503

Chen, J., Song, L., Wainwright, M. J., & Jordan, M. I. (2018). Learning to explain: An information-theoretic perspective on model interpretation. In *Proceedings of the 35th International Conference on Machine Learning* (pp. 883-892). PMLR. https://doi.org/DOI: 10.48550/arXiv.1802.07814

Chen, Z., Zhao, J., & Jin, C. (2025). Business intelligence for Industry 4.0: Predictive models for retail and distribution. *International Journal of Retail & Distribution Management, 53*(3), 1–16.

Chintala, S. (2024). Smart BI Systems: The Role of AI in Modern Business. *ESP Journal of Engineering & Technology Advancements, 4*(3), 45–58.

Chintala, S., & Thiyagarajan, V. (2023). AI-driven business intelligence: Unlocking the future of decision-making. *ESP International Journal of Advancements in Computational Technology, 1*, 73–84.

Chowdhury, R. H. (2024). Blockchain and AI: Driving the future of data security and business intelligence. *World Journal of Advanced Research and Reviews, 23*(1), 2559–2570.

Collectiv. (2022). *6 strategies to increase business intelligence user adoption.* Collectiv Blog. https://gocollectiv.com/blog/increase-business-intelligence-user-adoption/

Collins, A., Hamza, O., Eweje, A., & Babatunde, G. O. (2024). Integrating 5G core networks with business intelligence platforms: Advancing data-driven decision-making. *International Journal of Multidisciplinary Research and Growth Evaluation, 5*(1), 1082–1099.

Constantin, L. (2024, May 17). *US AI Experts Targeted in Cyberespionage Campaign Using SugarGh0st RAT.* CSO Online. https://www.csoonline.com/article/2111003/us-ai-experts-targeted-in-cyberespionage-campaign-using-sugargh0st-rat.html

Dash, D., Polyzotis, N., & Ailamaki, A. (2011). CoPhy: A Scalable, Portable, and Interactive Index Advisor for Large Workloads. *Proceedings of the VLDB Endowment International Conference on Very Large Data Bases, 4*(6), 362–375. DOI: 10.14778/1978665.1978668

Dashora, S. (2023). Cloud-based Data Analytics for Business Intelligence. *International Journal for Research in Applied Science and Engineering Technology, 11*(11), 2758–2765. DOI: 10.22214/ijraset.2023.57219

Das, R., & Sandhane, R. (2021). Artificial Intelligence in Cyber Security. *Journal of Physics: Conference Series, 1964*(4). Advance online publication. DOI: 10.1088/1742-6596/1964/4/042072

Davenport, T. H. (2018). *The AI advantage: How to put the artificial intelligence revolution to work*. mit Press.

Davenport, T. H. (2018). *T*he AI advantage: How to put the artificial intelligence revolution to work. MIT Press. Available at: https://mitpress.mit.edu/9780262538008/the-ai-advantage/

Davenport, T. H., & Bean, R. (2018). Big companies are embracing analytics, but most still don't have a data-driven culture. Harvard Business Review Digital Articles, 2-4. Available at: https://hbr.org/2018/02/big-companies-are-embracing-analytics-but-most-still-dont-have-a-data-driven-culture

Davenport, T. H., & Harris, J. G. (2017). *Competing on analytics: The new science of winning* (Updated ed.). Harvard Business Press. Available at: https://hbr.org/product/competing-on-analytics-the-new-science-of-winning-updated-with-a-new-introduction/17723-HBK-ENG

Davenport, T. H., & Patil, D. J. (2012). Data scientist: The sexiest job of the 21st century. *Harvard Business Review*, *90*(10), 70–76. https://hbr.org/2012/10/data-scientist-the-sexiest-job-of-the-21st-century PMID: 23074866

Davenport, T. H., & Ronanki, R. (2018). Artificial intelligence for the real world. *Harvard Business Review*, *96*(1), 108–116. https://hbr.org/2018/01/artificial-intelligence-for-the-real-world

Deloitte. (2024, April 29). *Deloitte generative AI survey finds adoption is moving fast, but organizational change is key to accelerate scaling*. Deloitte Newsroom. https://www.deloitte.com/us/en/about/press-room/deloitte-generative-ai-survey-finds-adoption-is-moving-fast-but-organizational-change-is-key-to-accelerate-scaling.html

Devaraj, S. M. (2024). Digital Transformation and Innovation: Driving Business Growth. *International Journal of Scientific Research in Computer Science. Engineering and Information Technology*, *10*(5), 885–894. DOI: 10.32628/CSEIT241051077

Devlin, J., Chang, M. W., Lee, K., & Toutanova, K. (2019). BERT: Pre-training of deep bidirectional transformers for language understanding. In NAACL-HLT (pp. 4171–4186). doi:DOI: 10.18653/v1/N19-1423

Dewi, H., Salsabila, H., & Atmoko, A. W. (2024). TRANSFORMASI DYNAMIC CAPABILITY DALAM SEKTOR JASA: STUDI LITERATUR. *National Conference on Applied Business, Education, &* [NCABET]. *Technology*, *3*(1), 231–246. DOI: 10.46306/ncabet.v3i1.120

Dhar Dwivedi, A., Singh, R., Kaushik, K., Rao Mukkamala, R., & Alnumay, W. S. (2024). Blockchain and artificial intelligence for 5G-enabled Internet of Things: Challenges, opportunities, and solutions. *Transactions on Emerging Telecommunications Technologies, 35*(4), e4329.

Dierksmeier, C., & Seele, P. (2020). Blockchain and business ethics. *Business Ethics (Oxford, England), 29*(2), 348–359.

Dimitropoulos, G. (2020). The law of blockchain. *Washington Law Review (Seattle, Wash.), 95*, 1117–1172.

Dokur, N. B. (2023). *Artificial Intelligence (AI)*. Applications in Cyber Security.

Dorrer, M. G. (2020). The digital twin of the business process model. []). IOP Publishing.]. *Journal of Physics: Conference Series, 1679*(3), 032096.

Dwork, C., & Roth, A. (2014). The algorithmic foundations of differential privacy. *Foundations and Trends in Theoretical Computer Science, 9*(3–4), 211–407. DOI: 10.1561/0400000042

E'Leimat, D., Al Shbail, Z. J. M., El-Dalabeeh, A. E.-R., Al-Shbiel, S., & Nazzal, , M. (2022). DOES THE ADOPTION OF BUSINESS INTELLIGENCE AFFECT ENTERPRISE RISK MANAGEMENT? EVIDENCE FROM JORDAN. *Journal of Southwest Jiaotong University, 57*(6), 95–113. DOI: 10.35741/issn.0258-2724.57.6.9

Eboigbe, E. O., Farayola, O. A., Olatoye, F. O., Nnabugwu, O. C., & Daraojimba, C. (2023). Business intelligence transformation through AI and data analytics. *Engineering Science & Technology Journal, 4*(5), 285–307.

Eboigbe, E. O., Farayola, O. A., Olatoye, F. O., Nnabugwu, O. C., & Daraojimba, C. (2023). BUSINESS INTELLIGENCE TRANSFORMATION THROUGH AI AND DATA ANALYTICS. *Engineering Science & Technology Journal, 4*(5), 285–307. DOI: 10.51594/estj.v4i5.616

Ebule, A. (2025). The role of business intelligence and artificial intelligence in real-time decision making. *International Journal of Scientific Research and Management, 13*(1), 1902–1916. DOI: 10.18535/ijsrm/v13i01.ec04

Ebule, A. E. (2025). Leveraging Artificial Intelligence in Business Intelligence Systems for Predictive Analytics. [IJSRM]. *International Journal of Scientific Research and Management, 13*(01), 1862–1879. DOI: 10.18535/ijsrm/v13i01.ec02

EC. (2024). *Proposal for digital product passports under the Circular Economy Action Plan*. https://ec.europa.eu

Eckerson, W. W. (2016). The secret to creating business value with embedded analytics. Eckerson Group White Paper. Available at: https://www.eckerson.com/register?content=the-secret-to-creating-business-value-with-embedded-analytics

Eckerson, W. W. (2017). Smart analytics: Leveraging AI and machine learning for BI. Eckerson Group White Paper. Available at: https://www.eckerson.com/research/smart-analytics-leveraging-ai-and-machine-learning-for-bi

El-Samad, W., Adda, M., & Atieh, M. (2024). AI-Driven Data Aggregation Level Smart Contracts for Blockchain Healthcare Insurance Claims Adjudication. *Procedia Computer Science*, *241*, 63–68.

Emmanuel, O. K. (n.d.). *AI-driven threat detection: Enhancing cybersecurity through predictive analytics*. [Unpublished manuscript].

Eyadat, A. A., Abdellatif, H., Almuhana, M., & Al-Bataineh, T. (2025). The influence of business intelligence (BI) strategy on enterprise evaluation: A comparative analysis of California state and Jordanian markets. *Business Information Review*, •••, 02663821241311806.

Faisal, S. M., Ishrat, M., & Khan, W. (2025). Digital Twins in Healthcare: Revolutionizing Patient Care and Medical Operations. In *Digital Twins for Smart Cities and Urban Planning* (pp. 69-89). CRC Press.

Farayola, O. A. (2024). Revolutionizing banking security: Integrating artificial intelligence, blockchain, and business intelligence for enhanced cybersecurity. *Finance & Accounting Research Journal*, *6*(4), 501–514.

Färber, F., Cha, S. K., Primsch, J., Bornhövd, C., Sigg, S., & Lehner, W. (2011). SAP HANA database: Data management for modern business applications. *SIGMOD Record*, *40*(4), 45–51.

Federspiel, F., Mitchell, R., Asokan, A., Umana, C., & McCoy, D. (2023). Threats by Artificial Intelligence to Human Health and Human Existence. *BMJ Global Health*, *8*(5), e010435. DOI: 10.1136/bmjgh-2022-010435

Feurer, M., Klein, A., Eggensperger, K., Springenberg, J., Blum, M., & Hutter, F. (2015). Efficient and robust automated machine learning. Advances in Neural Information Processing Systems, 28, 2962-2970. Available at: https://papers.nips.cc/paper/5872-efficient-and-robust-automated-machine-learning

Fraihat, S., Salameh, W. A., Elhassan, A., Tahoun, B. A., & Asasfeh, M. (2021). Business Intelligence Framework Design and Implementation: A Real-estate Market Case Study. *Journal of Data and Information Quality*, *13*(2), 1–16. DOI: 10.1145/3422669

García, S., Luengo, J., & Herrera, F. (2015). *Data preprocessing in data mining*. Springer., DOI: 10.1007/978-3-319-10247-4

Gartner. (2024). *Magic quadrant for analytics and business intelligence platforms*. Gartner Research.

Ghaida, D. A. (2018). The influence of organisational and technological factors on BI adoption in the telecommunication industry across the Middle East and Africa. *J. for Global Business Advancement*, *11*(3), 332. DOI: 10.1504/JGBA.2018.096303

Giuffrida, A. (2025, February 10). *AI Phone Scam Targets Italian Business Leaders, including Giorgio Armani*. The Guardian. https://www.theguardian.com/world/2025/feb/10/ai-phone-scam-targets-italian-business-leaders-including-giorgio-armani?utm_source=chatgpt.com

globenewswire. (2025, January 29). *Augmented Analytics Market Analysis and Growth Opportunities, 2025-2034—Rising Demand for Business Intelligence (BI) Tools is Driving the Market; Reaching $41.23 Billion by 2029*. GlobeNewswire News Room. https://www.globenewswire.com/news-release/2025/01/29/3017022/28124/en/Augmented-Analytics-Market-Analysis-and-Growth-Opportunities-2025-2034-Rising-Demand-for-Business-Intelligence-BI-Tools-is-Driving-the-Market-Reaching-41-23-Billion-by-2029.html

Goodman, B., & Flaxman, S. (2017). European Union regulations on algorithmic decision-making and a "right to explanation". *AI Magazine*, *38*(3), 50–57. DOI: 10.1609/aimag.v38i3.2741

Goodrich, J., & Altman, E. J. (2024). Business ecosystems and strategic leadership: a stakeholder approach. In *Handbook of Research on Strategic Leadership in the Fourth Industrial Revolution* (pp. 250–266). Edward Elgar Publishing.

Goswami, S. A., Dave, S., & Patel, K. C. K. (2024). Evolution of AI in Business Intelligence. In *Intersection of AI and Business Intelligence in Data-Driven Decision-Making* (pp. 1–20). IGI Global.

Graefe, G. (1993). Query evaluation techniques for large databases. *ACM Computing Surveys*, *25*(2), 73–169. DOI: 10.1145/152610.152611

Graefe, G. (2011). Modern B-tree techniques. *Foundations and Trends in Databases*, *3*(4), 203–402. DOI: 10.1561/1900000028

Greenwood, B. N., Agarwal, R., Agarwal, R., & Gopal, A. (2019). The role of individual and organizational expertise in the adoption of new practices. *Organization Science*, *30*(1), 191–213.

Gretzinger, S., Royer, S., & Leick, B. (2024). Value capture in IoT-driven business models: Considerations about smart resources and isolating mechanisms in networked environments. *Journal of Business and Industrial Marketing*, *39*(10), 2155–2170.

Groumpos, P. P. (2023). A Critical Historical Overview of Artificial Intelligence: Issues, Challenges, Opportunities, and Threats. *Artificial Intelligence and Applications (Commerce, Calif.)*, *1*(4), 197–213. DOI: 10.47852/bonviewAIA3202689

Grover, V., Chiang, R. H., Liang, T.-P., & Zhang, D. (2018). Creating strategic business value from big data analytics: A research framework. *Journal of Management Information Systems*, *35*(2), 388–423.

Guembe, B., Azeta, A., Misra, S., Osamor, V. C., Fernandez-Sanz, L., & Pospelova, V. (2022). The Emerging Threat of AI-driven Cyber Attacks: A Review. *Applied Artificial Intelligence*, *36*(1), 1–34. DOI: 10.1080/08839514.2022.2037254

Guerra-Zubiaga, D. A., Bondar, A., Escobedo, G., & Schumacher, A. (2019). Digital twin in a manufacturing integrated system: Siemens TIA and PLM case study. In *ASME International Mechanical Engineering Congress and Exposition* (Vol. 59384, p. V02BT02A008). American Society of Mechanical Engineers.

Guetterman, T. C., & Fetters, M. D. (2018). Two methodological approaches to the integration of mixed methods and case study designs: A systematic review. *The American Behavioral Scientist*, *62*(7), 900–918.

Gupta, A., & Mumick, I. S. (1999). *Materialized Views: Techniques, Implementations, and Applications*. MIT Press., DOI: 10.7551/mitpress/4472.001.0001

Gupta, H., Harinarayan, V., Rajaraman, A., & Ullman, J. D. (1997). Index selection for OLAP. In *Proceedings of the International Conference on Data Engineering* (pp. 208-219). https://doi.org/DOI: 10.1109/ICDE.1997.581755

Gupta, S., Leszkiewicz, A., Kumar, V., Bijmolt, T., & Potapov, D. (2020). Digital analytics: Modeling for insights and new methods. *Journal of Interactive Marketing*, *51*(1), 26–43.

Guyon, I., & Elisseeff, A. (2003). An introduction to variable and feature selection. *Journal of Machine Learning Research*, *3*, 1157–1182. DOI: 10.1162/153244303322753616

Hamad, F., Al-Aamr, R., Jabbar, S. A., & Fakhuri, H. (2021). Business intelligence in academic libraries in Jordan: Opportunities and challenges. *IFLA Journal*, *47*(1), 37–50.

Haneefa, K. V. (2025). Quick Commerce in the Quantum Age: Future Outlook. In The Quantum AI Era of Neuromarketing (pp. 403-428). IGI Global Scientific Publishing.

Haneem, F., Bakar, H. A., Kama, N., Mat, N. Z. N., Ghazali, R., & Mahmood, Y. (2020). Recent progress of blockchain initiatives in government. *International Journal of Advanced Computer Science and Applications*, *11*(11), 344–351.

Hansi, G. (2023). Business intelligence transformation with AI/ML: Strengthening ERP cloud security using Snowflake DB. [Unpublished manuscript].

Harfoush, B. (2024). Impact of Organizational Changes on BI Critical Success Factors.

Hastie, T., Tibshirani, & Friedman, J. (2009). The Elements of Statistical Learning (2nd ed.). Springer. doi:DOI: 10.1007/978-0-387-84858-7

Hayajneh, S., & Harb, Y. (2023). Understanding the continuous use of business intelligence: The case of Jordan. *Journal of Decision Systems*, •••, 1–32. DOI: 10.1080/12460125.2023.2253587

Hellerstein, J. M., Stonebraker, M., & Hamilton, J. (2007). Architecture of a database system. *Foundations and Trends in Databases*, *1*(2), 141–259. DOI: 10.1561/1900000002

Hemachandran, K., Khanra, S., Rodriguez, R. V., & Jaramillo, J. (Eds.). (2022). *Machine learning for business analytics: Real-time data analysis for decision-making*. Productivity Press., DOI: 10.4324/9781003206316

Herodotou, H., Dong, F., & Babu, S. (2011). No one (cluster) size fits all: automatic cluster sizing for data-intensive analytics. In *Proceedings of the 2nd ACM Symposium on Cloud Computing* (pp. 1-14). https://doi.org/DOI: 10.1145/2038916.2038934

Hiran, K. K., Hemachandran, K., Pise, A., & Rabi, B. J. (Eds.). (2023). *Handbook of research on AI and knowledge engineering for real-time business intelligence*. IGI Global.

Hmoud, H., Al-Adwan, A. S., Horani, O. M., & Yaseen, H. (2023). Factors influencing business intelligence adoption by higher education institutions: A TOE-based analysis. *Journal of Open Innovation*, *9*(5), 100111. DOI: 10.1016/j.joitmc.2023.100111

Hmoud, H., Al-Adwan, A. S., Horani, O., Yaseen, H., & Al Zoubi, J. Z. (2023). Factors influencing business intelligence adoption by higher education institutions. *Journal of Open Innovation*, *9*(3), 100111.

Hosen, M. S., Islam, R., Naeem, Z., Folorunso, E. O., Chu, T. S., Al Mamun, M. A., & Orunbon, N. O. (2024). Data-driven decision making: Advanced database systems for business intelligence. *Nanotechnology Perceptions*, *20*(3), 687–704.

IBM. (2024, May 17). A new era in BI: Overcoming low adoption to make smart decisions accessible for all. IBM Business Insights Blog. https://www.ibm.com/think/insights/business-intelligence-adoption

IEC. (2023). *IEC/IEEE 60802: Time-sensitive networking profile for industrial automation*. International Electrotechnical Commission.

Inmon, W. H. (2005). *Building the data warehouse* (4th ed.). John Wiley & Sons., Available at https://www.wiley.com/en-us/Building+the+Data+Warehouse%2C+4th+Edition-p-9780764599446

Ismail, L., Hameed, H., AlShamsi, M., AlHammadi, M., & AlDhanhani, N. (2019, March). Towards a blockchain deployment at UAE university: Performance evaluation and blockchain taxonomy. In *Proceedings of the 2019 International Conference on Blockchain Technology* (pp. 30-38).

ISO. (2022). *ISO 23247-1: Digital twin framework for manufacturing – Part 1: Overview and general principles*. International Organization for Standardization.

Jaber, T. A. (2025). Enhancing crime detection in video surveillance via a lightweight blockchain and homomorphic encryption-based computer vision system. *Mesopotamian Journal of CyberSecurity*, *5*(1), 121–146.

Jada, I., & Mayayise, T. O. (2023). The Impact of Artificial Intelligence on Organisational Cyber Security: An Outcome of a Systematic Literature Review. *Data and Information Management*, *8*(2), 100063–100063. DOI: 10.1016/j.dim.2023.100063

Jamei, M., Nisnevich, A., Wetchler, E., Sudat, S., & Liu, E. (2017). Predicting all-cause risk of 30-day hospital readmission using artificial neural networks. *PLoS One*, *12*(7), e0181173. DOI: 10.1371/journal.pone.0181173 PMID: 28708848

Jaradat, Z., Al-Dmour, A., Alshurafat, H., Al-Hazaima, H., & Al Shbail, M. O. (2024). Factors influencing business intelligence adoption: Evidence from Jordan. *Journal of Decision Systems*, *33*(2), 242–262.

Jiménez-Partearroyo, M., & Medina-López, A. (2024). Leveraging business intelligence systems for enhanced corporate competitiveness: Strategy and evolution. *Systems*, *12*(3), 94. DOI: 10.3390/systems12030094

Jourdan, Z., & Rainer, R. kelly, & Marshall, T. E. (2008). Business intelligence: An analysis of the literature. *IEEE Engineering Management Review*, *36*(3), 29–29. DOI: 10.1109/EMR.2008.4648888

Kadiyala, B., Alavilli, S. K., & Alfa, A. A. (2025). Real-time decision making in IoT-enabled business intelligence: Insights from Likert scale surveys. *International Journal of Advances in Computer Science & Engineering Research*, *1*(01), 50–59.

Kale, A. (2024). *AI-Driven Cybersecurity Threats and Organisational Consequences*. CSUSB ScholarWorks, Electronic Theses, Projects, and Dissertations. https://scholarworks.lib.csusb.edu/etd/1991?utm_source=scholarworks.lib.csusb.edu%2Fetd%2F1991&utm_medium=PDF&utm_campaign=PDFCoverPages

Kangasharju, J. (2020). *Business intelligence in performance management of agile programs*. J. Kangasharju, Kelepouris, P. (2023). Implementation of Artificial Intelligence in Project Management and effect in working personnel: Literature Review and Case Studies in Athens, Greece and Stockholm, Sweden. In.

Kasasbeh, E., Alzureikat, K., Alroud, S., & Alkasassbeh, W. (2021). The moderating effect of entrepreneurial marketing in the relationship between business intelligence systems and competitive advantage in Jordanian commercial banks. *Management Science Letters*, *11*(3), 983–992.

Kaur, R., Gabrijelčič, D., & Klobučar, T. (2023). Artificial Intelligence for Cybersecurity: Literature Review and Future Research Directions. *Information Fusion, 97*(101804), 101804. ScienceDirect. https://doi.org/DOI: 10.1016/j.inffus.2023.101804

Khan, B. U. I., Goh, K. W., Khan, A. R., Zuhairi, M. F., & Chaimanee, M. (2024). Integrating AI and Blockchain for Enhanced Data Security in IoT-Driven Smart Cities. *Processes (Basel, Switzerland)*, *12*(9).

Khan, L. U., Mustafa, E., Shuja, J., Rehman, F., Bilal, K., Han, Z., & Hong, C. S. (2023). Federated learning for digital twin-based vehicular networks: Architecture and challenges. *IEEE Wireless Communications*.

Khan, N. F., Yaqoob, A., Khan, M. S., & Ikram, N. (2022). The Cybersecurity Behavioral Research: A Tertiary Study. *Computers & Security*, *120*, 102826. DOI: 10.1016/j.cose.2022.102826

Khan, S. N., Shael, M., & Majdalawieh, M. (2019, July). Blockchain technology as a support infrastructure in e-government evolution at Dubai economic department. In *Proceedings of the 1st International Electronics Communication Conference* (pp. 124-130).

Kharbanda, V., Seetharaman, A., & Maddulety, K. (2023). Application of Artificial Intelligence in Cyber security. *International Journal of Security and Privacy in Pervasive Computing*, *15*(1), 1–13. DOI: 10.4018/ijsppc.318676

Kimball, R., & Ross, M. (2013). *The data warehouse toolkit: The definitive guide to dimensional modeling*. John Wiley & Sons.

Kim, C., Kaldewey, T., Lee, V. W., Sedlar, E., Nguyen, A. D., Satish, N., Chhugani, J., Di Blas, A., & Dubey, P. (2009). Sort vs. Hash revisited: Fast join implementation on modern multi-core CPUs. *Proceedings of the VLDB Endowment International Conference on Very Large Data Bases*, *2*(2), 1378–1389. DOI: 10.14778/1687553.1687564

Kisielnicki, J., & Misiak, A. M. (2021). Management Support Systems Type Business Intelligence (BI) and Factors Determining Their Implementation. In Khosrow-Pour, D. B. A. (Ed.), *M* (pp. 1059–1074). Advances in Logistics, Operations, and Management Science. IGI Global., DOI: 10.4018/978-1-7998-3473-1.ch074

Kitsios, F., & Kamariotou, M. (2021). Artificial intelligence and business strategy towards digital transformation: A research agenda. *Sustainability*, *13*(4), 2025. DOI: 10.3390/su13042025

Kommisetty, P. D. N. K., Kuppala, B. M. S. R., Buvvaji, H. V., & Sabbella, V. R. R. (2022). Revolutionizing Cybersecurity: Behavioral Analysis and Automated Incident Response through Predictive Analytics. [IJSRM]. *International Journal of Scientific Research and Management*, *10*(10), 962–979. DOI: 10.18535/ijsrm/v10i10.ec04

Konopik, J., Jahn, C., Schuster, T., Hoßbach, N., & Pflaum, A. (2022). Mastering the digital transformation through organizational capabilities: A conceptual framework. *Digital Business*, *2*(2), 100019. DOI: 10.1016/j.digbus.2021.100019

Korobeyko, T. (2022, July 28). *Self-service BI: Overcoming adoption barriers*. RTInsights. https://www.rtinsights.com/self-service-bi-overcoming-adoption-barriers/

Kotter, J. P. (2014). *Accelerate: Building strategic agility for a faster-moving world*. Harvard Business Review Press.

Kritzinger, W.. (2018). Digital twin in manufacturing: A categorical literature review and classification. *IFAC-PapersOnLine*, *51*(11), 1016–1022.

Kshetri, N. (2021). Blockchain and sustainable supply chain management in developing countries. *International Journal of Information Management*, *60*, 102376.

Kumar, B. (2023). Cyber threat intelligence using AI and machine learning approaches. *International Journal of Business Management and Visuals*, *6*(2), 1–7.

Kumar, R., Kumar, P., Jolfaei, A., & Islam, A. K. M. N. (2023). An Integrated Framework for Enhancing Security and Privacy in IoT-Based Business Intelligence Applications. *2023 IEEE International Conference on Consumer Electronics (ICCE)*, 01–06. https://doi.org/DOI: 10.1109/ICCE56470.2023.10043450

Kusumawati, R. (2025). Integrating Big Data Analytics into Supply Chain Management: Overcoming Data Silos to Improve Real-Time Decision-Making. *International Journal of Advanced Computational Methodologies and Emerging Technologies*, *15*(2), 17–26.

Lahcen, R. A. M., Caulkins, B., Mohapatra, R., & Kumar, M. (2020). Review and Insight on The Behavioral Aspects of Cybersecurity. *Cybersecurity*, *3*(1). Advance online publication. DOI: 10.1186/s42400-020-00050-w

Lale, A. W. (2022). Business intelligence implementation in different organizational setup evidence from reviewed literatures. In Sharma, A., Kautish, S., Agrawal, P., Madaan, V., Gupta, C., & Nanda, S. (Eds.), *Knowledge Engineering for Modern Information Systems* (pp. 173–186). De Gruyter., DOI: 10.1515/9783110713633-010

Larson, P.-Å., Clinciu, C., Fraser, C., Hanson, E. N., Mokhtar, M., Nowakiewicz, M., Papadimos, V., Price, S. L., Rangarajan, S., Rusanu, R., & Saubhasik, M. (2013). Enhancements to SQL Server column stores. In *Proceedings of the 2013 ACM SIGMOD International Conference on Management of Data* (pp. 1159–1168). Association for Computing Machinery. https://doi.org/DOI: 10.1145/2463676.2463708

Larson, P.-Å., Clinciu, C., Hanson, E. N., Oks, A., Price, S. L., Rangarajan, S., Surna, A., & Zhou, Q. (2011). SQL Server column store indexes. In *Proceedings of the 2011 ACM SIGMOD International Conference on Management of Data (SIGMOD '11)* (pp. 1177–1184). Association for Computing Machinery. https://doi.org/DOI: 10.1145/1989323.1989448

Latinovic, Z., & Chatterjee, S. C. (2022). Achieving the promise of AI and ML in delivering economic and relational customer value in B2B. *Journal of Business Research*, *144*, 966–974.

Latva-Aho, M., & Leppänen, K. (2019). Key drivers and research challenges for 6G ubiquitous wireless intelligence.

LaValle, S., Lesser, E., Shockley, R., Hopkins, M. S., & Kruschwitz, N. (2011). Big data, analytics and the path from insights to value. *MIT Sloan Management Review*, *52*(2), 21–32. https://sloanreview.mit.edu/article/big-data-analytics-and-the-path-from-insights-to-value/

LeCun, Y., Bengio, Y., & Hinton, G. (2015). Deep learning. *Nature*, *521*(7553), 436–444. DOI: 10.1038/nature14539 PMID: 26017442

Lee, I. (2017). Big data: Dimensions, evolution, impacts, and challenges. *Business Horizons*, *60*(3), 293–303. DOI: 10.1016/j.bushor.2017.01.004

Lees, H. (2020, October 20). *49 shocking business intelligence statistics for 2021.* TrustRadius. https://solutions.trustradius.com/vendor-blog/business-intelligence-statistics-and-trends/

Legal Information Institute. (2023). *5 U.S. Code § 552a – Records maintained on individuals.* Cornell Law School. https://www.law.cornell.edu/uscode/text/5/552a

Lennerholt, C., van Laere, J., & Söderström, E. (2021). User-related challenges of self-service business intelligence. *Information Systems Management*, *38*(4), 309–323. DOI: 10.1080/10580530.2020.1814458

Li, F., Wu, B., Yi, K., & Zhao, Z. (2017). Wander Join and XDB: Online aggregation via random walks. *SIGMOD Record*, *46*(1), 33–40. DOI: 10.1145/3093754.3093763

Liu, B. (2015). *Sentiment analysis: Mining opinions, sentiments, and emotions.* Cambridge University Press., DOI: 10.1017/CBO9781139084789

Li, Y., Liu, W., Zhang, Y., Zhang, W., Gao, C., Chen, Q., & Ji, Y. (2023). Interactive real-time monitoring and information traceability for complex aircraft assembly field based on digital twin. *IEEE Transactions on Industrial Informatics*, *19*(9), 9745–9756.

Lopes, J., Faria, M., & Santos, M. F. (2024). Exploring trends and autonomy levels of adaptive business intelligence in healthcare: A systematic review. *PLoS One*, *19*(5), e0302697.

Luo, G., Naughton, J. F., Ellmann, C. J., & Watzke, M. W. (2004). *Toward a progress indicator for database queries.* In *Proceedings of the 2004 ACM SIGMOD International Conference on Management of Data* (pp. 791–802). Association for Computing Machinery. https://doi.org/DOI: 10.1145/1007568.1007658

Lu, Y., & Xu, X. (2019). Cloud-based manufacturing equipment and big data analytics to enable on-demand manufacturing services. *Robotics and Computer-integrated Manufacturing*, *57*, 92–102. DOI: 10.1016/j.rcim.2018.11.006

Majd, S. S., Maleki, A., Basirat, S., & Golkarfard, A. (2025). Fermatean fuzzy TOPSIS method and its application in ranking business intelligence-based strategies in smart city context. *Journal of Operations Intelligence*, *3*(1), 1–16.

Makridis, C. A., Bates, T., Barnes, N., & Glasgow-George, J. (2024). The future of intellectual property: The complementary role of artificial intelligence and blockchain. *Journal of the Patent and Trademark Office Society*, *104*, 293–315.

Manda, J. K. (2024). AI-powered threat intelligence platforms in telecom: Leveraging AI for real-time threat detection and intelligence gathering in telecom network security operations. *SSRN*. https://doi.org/DOI: 10.2139/ssrn.5003638

Manning, C. D., Surdeanu, M., Bauer, J., Finkel, J. R., Bethard, S., & McClosky, D. (2014). The Stanford CoreNLP natural language processing toolkit. In *Proceedings of the 52nd Annual Meeting of the Association for Computational Linguistics: System Demonstrations* (pp. 55-60). Association for Computational Linguistics. **DOI:** DOI: 10.3115/V1/P14-5010

Manyika, J., Chui, M., Brown, B., Bughin, J., Dobbs, R., Roxburgh, C., & Byers, A. H. (2011). Big data: The next frontier for innovation, competition, and productivity. McKinsey Global Institute. Available at: https://www.mckinsey.com/business-functions/mckinsey-digital/our-insights/big-data-the-next-frontier-for-innovation

Markusfeld, D. (2024). *Automating build, deployment, and monitoring of model-based digital twins* (Doctoral dissertation, Technische Universität Wien).

Márquez-Chamorro, A. E., Resinas, M., & Ruiz-Cortés, A. (2018). Predictive monitoring of business processes: A survey. *IEEE Transactions on Services Computing*, *11*(6), 962–977. DOI: 10.1109/TSC.2017.2772256

Mashaleh, A. S., Ibrahim, N. F. B., Alauthman, M., Almseidin, M., & Gawanmeh, A. (2024). IoT smart devices risk assessment model using fuzzy logic and PSO. *Computers, Materials & Continua*, *78*(2), 2247–2268. DOI: 10.32604/cmc.2023.045711

Mason Louie, M. G. (2024). *AI-driven cybersecurity: Enhancing big data protection in business intelligence systems*. [Unpublished manuscript].

Matar, N., Al-Jaber, A., & Matar, W. (2024). Unlocking Business Intelligence and Data Analytics Adoption Patterns: Insights from Jordanian Higher Education Institutions. *Engineering, Technology &. Applied Scientific Research*, *14*(5), 16198–16206.

Mayer, H., Yee, L., Chui, M., & Roberts, R. (2025, January 28). *Superagency in the workplace: Empowering people to unlock AI's full potential*. McKinsey & Company. https://www.mckinsey.com/~/media/mckinsey/business%20functions/quantumblack/our%20insights/superagency%20in-the-workplace-empowering-people-to-unlock-ais-full-potential-at-work/superagency-in-the-workplace-empowering-people-to-unlock-ais-full-potential-v4.pdf

Mazher, N., Basharat, A., & Nishat, A. (2024). AI-driven threat detection: Revolutionizing cyber defense mechanisms. *Eastern-European Journal of Engineering and Technology*, *3*(1), 70–82.

McAfee, A., & Brynjolfsson, E. (2012). Big data: The management revolution. *Harvard Business Review*, *90*(10), 60–68. https://hbr.org/2012/10/big-data-the-management-revolution PMID: 23074865

Merlano, C. A. (2024). Digital Leadership and Transformation in Contemporary Times. *International Journal of Digital Strategy, Governance, and Business Transformation*, *13*(1), 1–20. DOI: 10.4018/IJDSGBT.352047

Mermoud, A., Keupp, M. M., Huguenin, K., Palmié, M., & Percia David, D. (2019). To Share or Not to Share: A Behavioral Perspective on Human Participation in Security Information Sharing. *Journal of Cybersecurity*, *5*(1). Advance online publication. DOI: 10.1093/cybsec/tyz006

Mersinas, K., Bada, M., & Furnell, S. (2024). Cybersecurity Behavior Change: A Conceptualisation of Ethical Principles for Behavioral Interventions. *Computers & Security*, •••, 104025–104025. DOI: 10.1016/j.cose.2024.104025

Michael, C. I., Ipede, O. J., Adejumo, A. D., Adenekan, I. O., Adebayo, D., Ojo, A. S., & Ayodele, P. A. (2024). Data-driven decision making in IT: Leveraging AI and data science for business intelligence. *World Journal of Advanced Research and Reviews*, *23*(1), 472–480. DOI: 10.30574/wjarr.2024.23.1.2093

Microsoft. (2025). *Automatic aggregations overview*. In *Microsoft Fabric documentation*. Retrieved August 19, 2025, from https://learn.microsoft.com/en-us/fabric/enterprise/powerbi/aggregations-auto

Mikalef, P., Boura, M., Lekakos, G., & Krogstie, J. (2019). Big data analytics and firm performance: Findings from a mixed-method approach. *Journal of Business Research*, *98*, 261–276.

Mikalef, P., Boura, M., Lekakos, G., & Krogstie, J. (2019). Big Data Analytics Capabilities and Innovation: The Mediating Role of Dynamic Capabilities and Moderating Effect of the Environment. *British Journal of Management*, *30*(2), 272–298. DOI: 10.1111/1467-8551.12343

Mikalef, P., Lemmer, K., Schaefer, C., Ylinen, M., Fjørtoft, S. O., Torvatn, H. Y., & Niehaves, B. (2023). Examining how AI capabilities can foster organizational performance in public organizations. *Government Information Quarterly*, *40*(2), 101797.

Miller, T. (2019). Explanation in artificial intelligence: Insights from the social sciences. *Artificial Intelligence*, *267*, 1–38. DOI: 10.1016/j.artint.2018.07.007

Milmo, D. (2024, May 17). *UK Engineering Firm Arup Falls Victim To £20m Deepfake Scam*. The Guardian. https://www.theguardian.com/technology/article/2024/may/17/uk-engineering-arup-deepfake-scam-hong-kong-ai-video

Ministry of Industry, Trade and Supply. (2022). *Jordan Industrial Competitiveness Report 2022*.

Moustafa, A. A., Bello, A., & Maurushat, A. (2021). The Role of User Behaviour in Improving Cyber Security Management. *Frontiers in Psychology*, *12*(12). Advance online publication. DOI: 10.3389/fpsyg.2021.561011

Mupaikwa, E. (2024). The Adoption of Business Intelligence as a Competitive Strategy Among SMEs: A Developing Country Study. In Keikhosrokiani, P. (Ed.), (pp. 152–174). Advances in Business Information Systems and Analytics. IGI Global., DOI: 10.4018/979-8-3693-1210-0.ch007

Muppalaneni, R., Inaganti, A. C., & Ravichandran, N. (2024). AI-driven threat intelligence: Enhancing cyber defense with machine learning. *Journal of Computing Innovations and Applications*, *2*(1), 1–11.

Mu, X., & Antwi-Afari, M. F. (2024). The applications of Internet of Things (IoT) in industrial management: A science mapping review. *International Journal of Production Research*, *62*(5), 1928–1952.

Niggemann, O., Zimmering, B., Steude, H., Augustin, J. L., Windmann, A., & Multaheb, S. (2023). Machine learning for cyber-physical systems. In *Digital Transformation: Core Technologies and Emerging Topics from a Computer Science Perspective* (pp. 415–446). Springer Berlin Heidelberg.

Nihitha, S. (2024). Digital Transformation: Reshaping Industries Through Technology. *International Journal For Multidisciplinary Research*, *6*(6), 31446. DOI: 10.36948/ijfmr.2024.v06i06.31446

Núñez-Merino, M., Maqueira-Marín, J. M., Moyano-Fuentes, J., & Castaño-Moraga, C. A. (2024). Quantum-inspired computing technology in operations and logistics management. *International Journal of Physical Distribution & Logistics Management*, *54*(3), 247–274.

O'Neil, E., O'Neil, P., & Wu, K. (2007). *Bitmap index design choices and their performance implications*. In *Proceedings of the 11th International Database Engineering and Applications Symposium (IDEAS 2007)* (pp. 72–84). IEEE. https://doi.org/DOI: 10.1109/IDEAS.2007.4318091

Obeidat, A. M. (2022). The impact of business intelligence in crisis management: The strategic vigilance as an intermediary variable in Jordanian insurance companies. *International Journal of Business Information Systems*, *41*(3), 342–359.

Odeh, I., Alkasassbeh, M., & Almseidin, M. (2022). Diabetic retinopathy detection method using artificial neural network. *International Journal of Bioinformatics Research and Applications*, *18*(4), 300–317. DOI: 10.1504/IJBRA.2022.126858

Oesterreich, T. D., Anton, E., & Teuteberg, F. (2022). What translates big data into business value? A meta-analysis of the impacts of business analytics on firm performance. *Information & Management*, *59*(6), 103685.

Ofusori, L., Bokaba, T., & Mhlongo, S. (2024). Artificial Intelligence in Cybersecurity: A Comprehensive Review and Future Direction. *Applied Artificial Intelligence*, *38*(1). Advance online publication. DOI: 10.1080/08839514.2024.2439609

Olabanji, S. O., Marquis, Y. A., Adigwe, C. S., Ajayi, S. A., Oladoyinbo, T. O., & Olaniyi, O. O. (2024). AI-Driven Cloud Security: Examining the Impact of User Behavior Analysis on Threat Detection. *Asian Journal of Research in Computer Science*, *17*(3), 57–74. DOI: 10.9734/ajrcos/2024/v17i3424

Orsted. (2022). *Wind farm digital twin improves annual energy production*. https://orsted.com

Osinski, D. P. *The Digital Twin–A Gamified Introduction* (Doctoral dissertation, MS Thesis, Indust. Eng. and Inno. Sci, Eind. Univ., Eindhoven 2019 [online] https://pure. tue. nl/ws/portalfiles/portal/143580443/Thesis_Final_Daan_ Osinski. pdf [Accessed April 11 2025]).

Ovabor, K., Sule-Odu, I. O., Atkison, T., Fabusoro, A. T., & Benedict, J. O. (2024). AI-Driven Threat Intelligence for Real-Time Cybersecurity: Frameworks, Tools, and Future Directions. *Open Access Research Journal of Science and Technology*, *12*(2), 040–048. https://doi.org/DOI: 10.53022/oarjst.2024.12.2.0135

Özcan, F., Tian, Y., & Tözün, P. (2017, May). *Hybrid Transactional/Analytical Processing: A Survey*. In *Proceedings of the 2017 ACM International Conference on Management of Data* (SIGMOD '17) (pp. 1771–1775). Association for Computing Machinery. https://doi.org/DOI: 10.1145/3035918.3054784

Paauwe, J. (2024). Resource based theory. In Hutchings, K., Michailova, S., & Wilkinson, A. (Eds.), *A Guide to Key Theories for Human Resource Management Research* (pp. 231–237). Edward Elgar Publishing., DOI: 10.4337/9781035308767.ch29

Padilla, E., Acosta, J. C., & Kiekintveld, C. D. (2021). Cybersecurity Methodology for Specialized Behavior Analysis. *Lecture Notes of the Institute for Computer Sciences, Social Informatics and Telecommunications Engineering*, •••, 237–243. DOI: 10.1007/978-3-030-68734-2_14

Pang, T. Y., Pelaez Restrepo, J. D., Cheng, C. T., Yasin, A., Lim, H., & Miletic, M. (2021). Developing a digital twin and digital thread framework for an 'Industry 4.0' Shipyard. *Applied Sciences (Basel, Switzerland)*, *11*(3), 1097.

Papapanagiotou, P., Vaughan, J., Smola, F., & Fleuriot, J. (2021). A real-world case study of process and data-driven predictive analytics for manufacturing workflows. In *Proceedings of the 54th Hawaii International Conference on System Sciences (HICSS-54)*. IEEE., https://scholarspace.manoa.hawaii.edu

Paramesha, M., Rane, N. L., & Rane, J. (2024). Big data analytics, artificial intelligence, machine learning, internet of things, and blockchain for enhanced business intelligence. *Partners Universal Multidisciplinary Research Journal*, *1*(2), 110–133.

Pearl, J. (2009). *Causality: Models, Reasoning, and Inference* (2nd ed.). Cambridge University Press., DOI: 10.1017/CBO9780511803161

Pipino, L. L., Lee, Y. W., & Wang, R. Y. (2002). Data quality assessment. *Communications of the ACM*, *45*(4), 211–218. DOI: 10.1145/505248.505255

Polito, C., & Pupillo, L. (2024). Artificial Intelligence and Cybersecurity. Www .intereconomics.eu, *2024*(1), 10–13. https://www.intereconomics.eu/contents/year/2024/number/1/article/artificial-intelligence-and-cybersecurity.html

Ponnusamy, S., Assaf, M., Antari, J., Singh, S., & Kalyanaraman, S. (Eds.). (2024). *Harnessing AI and Digital Twin Technologies in Businesses*. IGI Global.

PortXchange. (2023). *Annual report on smart-port digital twin deployment*. https://www.portxchange.com

Prabha, M., Hossain, M. A., Samiun, M., Saleh, M. A., Dhar, S. R., & Al Mahmud, M. A. (2024). AI-driven cyber threat detection: Revolutionizing security frameworks in management information systems. In *2024 International Conference on Intelligent Cybernetics Technology & Applications (ICICyTA)* (pp. 357–362). IEEE. https://doi.org/DOI: 10.1109/ICICyTA62753.2024.10731205

Preskill, J. (2018). Quantum computing in the NISQ era and beyond. *Quantum : the Open Journal for Quantum Science*, *2*, 79. DOI: 10.22331/q-2018-08-06-79

Primawati, A., & Sitanggang, I. S., Annisa, & Astuti, D. A. (2024). Real-time business intelligence development using machine learning to increase the potential of the dairy goat milk business. *International Journal of Electrical and Computer Engineering, 14*(5), 5612–5625. DOI: 10.11591/ijece.v14i5.pp5612-5625

Protopappas, L., Bechtsis, D., & Tsotsolas, N. (2025). IoT Services for Monitoring Food Supply Chains. *Applied Sciences (Basel, Switzerland), 15*(13), 7602. Advance online publication. DOI: 10.3390/app15137602

Puschel, M. (2023). *Optimized business intelligence and cybersecurity with AI/ ML-driven solutions for ERP cloud and Snowflake DB*. [Unpublished manuscript].

Qatawneh, N. (2024). Empirical insights into business intelligence adoption and decision-making performance during the digital transformation era: Extending the TOE model in the Jordanian banking sector. *Journal of Open Innovation, 10*(4), 97. DOI: 10.1016/j.joitmc.2024.100401

Rachakatla, S. K., Ravichandran, P.Sr, & Machireddy, J. R.Sr. (2023). AI-driven business analytics: Leveraging deep learning and big data for predictive insights. *Journal of Deep Learning in Genomic Data Analysis, 3*(2), 1–22.

Ragazou, K., Passas, I., Garefalakis, A., & Zopounidis, C. (2023). Business intelligence model empowering SMEs to make better decisions and enhance their competitive advantage. *Discover Analytics, 1*, 2. Advance online publication. DOI: 10.1007/s44257-022-00002-3

Rajan, P. (2024). Integrating iot analytics into marketing decision making: A smart data-driven approach. *International Journal of Data Informatics and Intelligent Computing, 3*(1), 12–22.

Ramakrishnan, T., Khuntia, J., Kathuria, A., & Saldanha, T. J. V. (2018). Business Intelligence Capabilities. In Deokar, A. V., Gupta, A., Iyer, L. S., & Jones, M. C. (Eds.), *Analytics and Data Science* (pp. 15–27). Springer International Publishing., DOI: 10.1007/978-3-319-58097-5_3

Rangaraju, S. (2023). Secure by intelligence: Enhancing products with AI-driven security measures. *EPH-International Journal of Science and Engineering, 9*(3), 36–41.

Raptis, T. P., Passarella, A., & Conti, M. (2018). Performance analysis of latency-aware data management in industrial IoT networks. *Sensors (Basel), 18*(8), 2611. PMID: 30096930

Ravichandran, P., Machireddy, J. R., & Rachakatla, S. K. (2022). AI-Enhanced data analytics for real-time business intelligence: Applications and challenges. *Journal of AI in Healthcare and Medicine*, *2*(2), 168–195.

Rawashdeh, A., Alkasassbeh, M., Alauthman, M., & Almseidin, M. (2024). A stacked ensemble approach to identify internet of things network attacks through traffic analysis. *Bulletin of Electrical Engineering and Informatics*, *13*(6), 4316–4326. DOI: 10.11591/eei.v13i6.7216

Reddy, R. C., Mishra, D., Goyal, D., & Rana, N. P. (2024). A conceptual framework of barriers to data science implementation: A practitioners' guideline. *Benchmarking*, *31*(10), 3459–3496.

Redman, T. C. (2013). Data's credibility problem. *Harvard Business Review*, *91*(12), 84–88. https://hbr.org/2013/12/datas-credibility-problem

Ressi, D., Romanello, R., Piazza, C., & Rossi, S. (2024). AI-enhanced blockchain technology: A review of advancements and opportunities. *Journal of Network and Computer Applications*, •••, 103858.

Rezaie, M., Mirzahosein, Z., & Rasouli, H. (2022). Developing a Digital Transformation Architecture Framework: A Business Intelligence Approach. *2022 6th Iranian Conference on Advances in Enterprise Architecture (ICAEA)*, 7–14. https://doi.org/DOI: 10.1109/ICAEA57644.2022.10054019

Rimon, S. T., Sufian, M. A., Guria, Z. M., Morshed, N., Mosaddeque, A. I., & Ahamed, A. (2024, December). Impact of AI-powered business intelligence on smart city policy-making and data-driven governance. In *IET Conference Proceedings* CP908 (Vol. 2024, No. 30, pp. 475-481). Stevenage, UK: The Institution of Engineering and Technology.

Rozinat, A., & van der Aalst, W. M. (2008). Conformance checking of processes based on monitoring real behavior. *Information Systems*, *33*(1), 64–95. DOI: 10.1016/j.is.2007.07.001

Russom, P. (2016). Data warehouse modernization in the age of big data analytics. *TDWI Best Practices Report*. Retrieved from: https://tdwi.org/articles/2016/03/22/executive-summary-data-warehousemodernization.aspx

Rusu, B., Hurloiu, L., Hurloiu, I., & Geamanu, M. (2022). BIG DATA: A SOURCE OF COMPETITIVE ADVANTAGE. *Annals of Spiru Haret University. Economic Series*, *22*(2). Advance online publication. DOI: 10.26458/2227

Saidu, Y., Shuhidan, S. M., Aliyu, D. A., Aziz, I. A., & Adamu, S. (2025). Convergence of Blockchain, IoT, and AI for Enhanced Traceability Systems: A Comprehensive Review. *IEEE Access : Practical Innovations, Open Solutions*.

Sajikumar, S., & Ajithkumar, N. (2024). Understanding the Emergence and Significance of Behavioral Cybersecurity: A Bibliometric Analysis. *Multidisciplinary Reviews, 6*, 2023ss102. https://doi.org/DOI: 10.31893/multirev.2023ss102

Salehi, B., Demir, U., Roy, D., Pradhan, S., Dy, J., Ioannidis, S., & Chowdhury, K. (2024). Multiverse at the edge: Interacting real world and digital twins for wireless beamforming. *IEEE/ACM Transactions on Networking*, *32*(4), 3092–3110.

Salem, A. H., Azzam, S. M., Emam, O. E., & Abohany, A. A. (2024). Advancing Cybersecurity: A Comprehensive Review of AI-Driven Detection Techniques. *Journal of Big Data, 11*(1). Advance online publication. DOI: 10.1186/s40537-024-00957-y

Sallam, R. L., Howson, C., Idoine, C. J., Oestreich, T. W., Richardson, J. L., & Tapadinhas, J. (2019). Magic quadrant for analytics and business intelligence platforms. *Gartner Research*. Available at: https://www.gartner.com/doc/reprints?id=1-6Y66S7P&ct=190218&st=sb

SAP. (2021). *5 barriers to adopting advanced analytics in finance – and how to overcome them. SAP Insights*. https://www.sap.com/mena/resources/barriers-to-analytics-in-finance

Sarkar, S., Khadka, U., Hossain, S., & Khan, N. (2024). Quantum Machine Learning for Advanced Data Processing in Business Analytics: A Path Toward Next-Generation Solutions. *AIJMR-Advanced International Journal of Multidisciplinary Research*, 2(5).

Schmitt, M. (2023). Automated machine learning: AI-driven decision making in business analytics. *Intelligent Systems with Applications*, *18*, 200188. DOI: 10.1016/j.iswa.2023.200188

Schwarz, C., & Wang, Z. (2022). The role of digital twins in connected and automated vehicles. *IEEE Intelligent Transportation Systems Magazine*, *14*(6), 41–51.

Sculley, D., Holt, G., Golovin, D., Davydov, E., Phillips, T., Ebner, D., Chaudhary, V., Young, M., Crespo, J. F., & Dennison, D. (2015). Hidden technical debt in machine learning systems. In *Advances in Neural Information Processing Systems, 28*, 2503-2511. Available at: https://papers.nips.cc/paper/2015/hash/86df7dcfd896fcaf2674f757a2463eba-Abstract.html

Seldon, M. (2024, May 22). *U.S. AI Experts Targeted in SugarGh0st RAT Campaign*. HSToday. https://www.hstoday.us/subject-matter-areas/cybersecurity/u-s-ai-experts-targeted-in-sugargh0st-rat-campaign/

Senarathna, P., & Wickramarachchi, R. (2024). Critical Success Factors of Digital Transformation: A Systematic Literature Review. *2024 4th International Conference on Advanced Research in Computing (ICARC)*, 346–351. https://doi.org/DOI: 10.1109/ICARC61713.2024.10499772

Shafik, W. (2024). Blockchain-based internet of things (B-IoT): Challenges, solutions, opportunities, open research questions, and future trends. *Blockchain-based internet of things*, 35-58.

Shankari, M. U., & Rethinavalli, S. (2024). Examining the Impact of User Behaviour Analysis on Threat Detection. *International Journal of Creative Research Thoughts*, *12*(10).

Sharda, R., Delen, D., & Turban, E. (2023). *Business intelligence, analytics, data science, and AI: A managerial perspective* (5th ed.). Pearson.

Sharif, M. M., & Ghodoosi, F. (2022). The ethics of blockchain in organizations. *Journal of Business Ethics*, *178*(4), 1009–1025. PMID: 35125568

Sharma, M., Kumar, P., & Gundewar, S. (2025). Leveraging AI and Machine Learning for Predictive Analytics in Business Intelligence. In *AI-Powered Business Intelligence for Modern Organizations* (pp. 29–50). IGI Global.

Shepherd, E. M. (2021). *A Multicase Study of Critical Success Factors of Self-Service Business Intelligence Initiatives* (Doctoral dissertation, Walden University).

Shi, W., Cao, J., Zhang, Q., Li, Y., & Xu, L. (2016). Edge computing: Vision and challenges. *IEEE Internet of Things Journal*, *3*(5), 637–646. DOI: 10.1109/JIOT.2016.2579198

Shorman, A. R., Alzubi, M., Almseidin, M., & Rateb, R. (2025). Adaptive intrusion detection for IoT networks using artificial immune system techniques: A comparative study. [JRC]. *Journal of Robotics and Control*, *6*(2), 570–582. DOI: 10.18196/jrc.v6i2.22703

Simmen, D., Shekita, E., & Malkemus, T. (1996). Fundamental techniques for order optimization. *SIGMOD Record*, *25*(2), 57–67. DOI: 10.1145/233269.233320

Singh, H. P., Singh, A., Alam, F., & Agrawal, V. (2022). Impact of sustainable development goals on economic growth in Saudi Arabia: Role of education and training. *Sustainability*, *14*(21), 14119.

Singh, S., Mandave, N., & Sapkale, S. (2024). AI-Driven Threat Detection in Cybersecurity: An Overview. *International Research Journal of Modernization in Engineering Technology and Science*, *6*(11).

Smith, S. (2023). *AI-driven cybersecurity: Leveraging big data for advanced threat detection and risk mitigation*. [Unpublished manuscript].

Solanki, V. V. (2023). Evolution of Business Intelligence Tools. *International Journal for Research in Applied Science and Engineering Technology*, *11*(7), 1149–1151. DOI: 10.22214/ijraset.2023.54820

Soori, M., Jough, F. K. G., Dastres, R., & Arezoo, B. (2024). AI-based decision support systems in Industry 4.0: A review. *Journal of Economy and Technology*. Advance online publication. https://doi.org/DOI: 10.1016/j.ject.2024.08.005

Stamer, F., Maier, S., Peukert, S., & Lanza, G. (2022). Adaptive and dynamic feedback loops between production system and production network based on the asset administration shell. *Procedia CIRP*, *112*, 79–84.

Stonebraker, M., & Cetintemel, U. (2005). "One size fits all": An idea whose time has come and gone. In Proceedings of the 21st International Conference on Data Engineering (pp. 2-11). https://doi.org/DOI: 10.1109/ICDE.2005.1

Stonebraker, M., Abadi, D. J., Batkin, A., Chen, X., Cherniack, M., Ferreira, M., Lau, E., Lin, A., Madden, S., O'Neil, E. J., O'Neil, P. E., Rasin, A., Tran, N., & Zdonik, S. (2019). *C-store: A column-oriented DBMS*. In M. L. Brodie (Ed.), *Making Databases Work: The Pragmatic Wisdom of Michael Stonebraker* (ACM Books, Vol. 22, pp. 491–518). ACM / Morgan & Claypool. https://doi.org/DOI: 10.1145/3226595.3226638

Stouffer, K., Falco, J., & Scarfone, K. (2023). *Guide to industrial control system (ICS) security* (NIST SP 800-82 r3). National Institute of Standards and Technology.

Subramaniam, R., Palakkeel, P., & Arunmozhi, M. (2023). Revolutionizing business intelligence: Pioneering an enhanced adoption Framework through the Technology-Organization-Environment Paradigm.

Sultan, H., Chan, L. K., Siew, P. H., & Lee, C. K. (2024). Factors influencing cloud business intelligence adoption and use at the organizational level. *ITM Web of Conferences*, 67, 01019. https://doi.org/DOI: 10.1051/itmconf/20246701019

Suman, C. (2024). Evolving BI Architectures: Integrating Big Data for Smarter Decision-Making. *American Journal of Engineering. Mechanics and Architecture*, *2*(8), 72–79.

Sun, X., Yu, H., Solvang, W. D., & Govindan, K. (2024). A two-level decision-support framework for reverse logistics network design considering technology transformation in Industry 4.0: A case study in Norway. *International Journal of Advanced Manufacturing Technology*, *134*(1), 389–413.

Syed, S., & Nampalli, R. C. R. (2021). Empowering Users: The Role Of AI In Enhancing Self-Service BI For Data-Driven Decision Making. *Educational Administration: Theory and Practice*. https://doi.org/DOI: 10.53555/kuey.v27i4.8105

Taha, A. T., & Ghailan, M. M. (2023). *Theoretical framework for business intelligence adoption. SSRN* Preprint. https://ssrn.com/abstract=4503831

Taiwo, I., Ogunbajo, A., & Abidola, A. Q. (2025). Quantum computing-Enhanced AI systems for advanced business intelligence applications. *International Journal of Science and Research Archive*, *14*(1), 1839–1847.

Taleb, I., Dssouli, R., & Serhani, M. A. (2015). Big data pre-processing: A quality framework. In *Proceedings of the 2015 IEEE International Congress on Big Data* (pp. 191-198). IEEE. DOI: DOI: 10.1109/BigDataCongress.2015.35

Tang, Y., Xiong, J., Becerril-Arreola, R., & Iyer, L. (2020). Ethics of blockchain: A framework of technology, applications, impacts, and research directions. *Information Technology & People*, *33*(2), 602–632.

Tao, F., Qi, Q., Liu, A., & Kusiak, A. (2018). Data-driven smart manufacturing. *Journal of Manufacturing Systems*, *48*, 157–169.

Tariq, M. U. (2024). Application of blockchain and Internet of Things (IoT) in modern business. In *Future of customer engagement through marketing intelligence* (pp. 66–94). IGI Global.

Tatineni, S. (2023). AI-infused threat detection and incident response in cloud security. *International Journal of Scientific Research*, *12*(11), 998–1004. DOI: 10.21275/SR231113082917

Tauro, C. J. M., Aravindh, S., & Shreeharsha, A. B. (2012, June). Comparative Study of the New Generation, Agile, Scalable, High Performance NOSQL Databases. *International Journal of Computer Applications*, *48*(20), 1–4.

Tauseef, A. (2023). Database technologies in AI: Transforming cybersecurity with automated threat detection systems. *ResearchGate*. https://doi.org/DOI: 10.13140/RG.2.2.33122.54727

Teinemaa, I., Dumas, M., La Rosa, M., & Maggi, F. M. (2019). Outcome-oriented predictive process monitoring: Review and benchmark. *ACM TKDD*, *13*(2), 1–57. DOI: 10.1145/3301300

Tellmann, N. (2020). *Examining the Dimensions and Development of an Artificial Intelligence Capability With Effect on Competitive Performance*. NTNU, Tera, S. P., Chinthaginjala, R., Pau, G., & Kim, T. H. (2024). Towards 6G: An Overview of the Next Generation of Intelligent Network Connectivity. *IEEE Access*.

Thayyib, P., Mamilla, R., Khan, M., Fatima, H., Asim, M., Anwar, I., & Khan, M. A. (2023). State-of-the-art of artificial intelligence and big data analytics reviews in five different domains: A bibliometric summary. *Sustainability*, *15*(5), 4026.

Trieu, V.-H. (2017). Getting value from Business Intelligence systems: A review and research agenda. *Decision Support Systems*, *93*, 111–124. DOI: 10.1016/j.dss.2016.09.019

Tripathi, A., Bagga, T., Vishnoi, S. K., Senathirajah, A. R. B. S., & Haque, R. (2024). Business intelligence solution implementation challenges: A comparative analysis of service based start-ups, small & medium and large enterprises. *Environment and Social Psychology*, *9*(9). Advance online publication. DOI: 10.59429/esp.v9i9.2864

Turskis, Z., & Šniokienė, V. (2024). IoT-Driven Transformation of Circular Economy Efficiency: An Overview. *Mathematical & Computational Applications*, *29*(4), 49.

Uhlemann, T., Lehmann, C., & Steinhilper, R. (2017). The digital twin: Realizing the cyber-physical production system. *Procedia CIRP*, *61*, 335–340.

Urs, N., Roja, A., & Nisioi, I. (2024). Digital Transformation in Organizational Management: A Bibliometric Analysis. *NISPAcee Journal of Public Administration and Policy*, *17*(1), 198–227. DOI: 10.2478/nispa-2024-0009

Uulu, B. (2024). Optimizing Data Integrity and Transparency in Distributed Systems through Blockchain-Enhanced Big Data Management. *Transdisciplinary Advances in Social Computing, Complex Dynamics, and Computational Creativity*, *14*(10), 1–11.

van der Aalst, W. M. (2016). *Process mining: Data science in action* (2nd ed.). Springer., DOI: 10.1007/978-3-662-49851-4

Varatharaj, M. (2024). Enterprise Data-Driven Decision Making: A Framework for Digital Transformation and Organizational Excellence. *International Journal For Multidisciplinary Research*, *6*(6), 34279. DOI: 10.36948/ijfmr.2024.v06i06.34279

Verina, N., & Titko, J. (2019, May 9). Digital transformation: Conceptual framework. *Proceedings of 6th International Scientific Conference Contemporary Issues in Business, Management and Economics Engineering '2019*. Contemporary Issues in Business, Management and Economics Engineering, Vilnius Gediminas Technical University. https://doi.org/DOI: 10.3846/cibmee.2019.073

Vetrivel, S. C., Sowmiya, K. C., & Sabareeshwari, V. (2024). Digital Twins: Revolutionizing Business in the Age of AI. In *Harnessing AI and Digital Twin Technologies in Businesses* (pp. 111-131). IGI Global.

Vilela, F. de A., Times, V. C., Bernardi, A. C. de C., Freitas, A. de P., & Ciferri, R. R. (2023). A non-intrusive and reactive architecture to support real-time ETL processes in data warehousing environments. *Heliyon*, *9*(5), e15728. DOI: 10.1016/j.heliyon.2023.e15728 PMID: 37215774

Villamarín, J. M., & Diaz Pinzon, B. (2017). *Key Success Factors to Business Intelligence Solution Implementation* (SSRN Scholarly Paper 2965610). Social Science Research Network. https://papers.ssrn.com/abstract=2965610

Villarejo-Ramos, Á. F., Cabrera-Sánchez, J. P., Lara-Rubio, J., & Liébana-Cabanillas, F. (2021). Predicting big data adoption in companies with an explanatory and predictive model. *Frontiers in Psychology*, *12*, 583822. DOI: 10.3389/fpsyg.2021.651398 PMID: 33868130

Villegas-Ch, W., Palacios-Pacheco, X., & Luján-Mora, S. (2020). A business intelligence framework for analyzing educational data. *Sustainability*, *12*(14), 5745.

Vulpe, S.-N., Rughini , R., urcanu, D., & Rosner, D. (2024). AI and Cybersecurity: A Risk Society Perspective. *Frontiers of Computer Science*, *6*. Advance online publication. DOI: 10.3389/fcomp.2024.1462250

Wagg, D. J., Burr, C., Shepherd, J., Conti, Z. X., Enzer, M., & Niederer, S. (2025). The philosophical foundations of digital twinning. *Data-Centric Engineering*, *6*, e12.

Wang, C., Ahmad, S. F., Ayassrah, A. Y. B. A., Awwad, E. M., Irshad, M., Ali, Y. A., & Han, H. (2023). An empirical evaluation of technology acceptance model for Artificial Intelligence in E-commerce. *Heliyon*, *9*(8). PMID: 37520947

Wang, S., Wang, F., Zhu, Z., Wang, J., Tran, T., & Du, Z. (2024). Artificial intelligence in education: A systematic literature review. *Expert Systems with Applications*, *252*, 124167.

Wang, Y., Kung, L., & Byrd, T. A. (2018). Big data analytics: Understanding its capabilities and potential benefits for healthcare organizations. *Technological Forecasting and Social Change*, *126*, 3–13. DOI: 10.1016/j.techfore.2015.12.019

Watson, H. J. (2009). Tutorial: Business Intelligence—Past, Present, and Future. *Communications of the AIS*, *25*(1), 39. DOI: 10.17705/1CAIS.02539

Watson, H. J., & Wixom, B. H. (2007). The current state of business intelligence. *Computer*, *40*(9), 96–99. DOI: 10.1109/MC.2007.331

Weber, K., Otto, B., & Österle, H. (2009). One size does not fit all—A contingency approach to data governance. *Journal of Data and Information Quality*, *1*(1), 1–27. DOI: 10.1145/1515693.1515696

Wei, X., Wu, Z., & Li, Q. (2023). Incremental learning strategies for real-time stock price prediction. *Sensors (Basel)*, *23*(10), 5112. DOI: 10.3390/s23105112

Wiisdom. (2020). *Business Intelligence Trends 2020 – Survey Highlights*. Wiiisdom (formerly KPI Products). https://wiiisdom.com/blog/business-intelligence-trends-2020-infographic/

Williams, R. A., Duman, G. M., Kongar, E., & Sheikh, N. J. (2024). Organizational Factors Enabling Augmented Analytic and BI 4.0 Implementation Success. *IEEE Engineering Management Review*.

Willie, A. (2024). *The Evolution of Artificial Intelligence in Cybersecurity: Traditional AI vs Generative AI Approaches*. Stanford University.

Wisdom, D. D., Vincent, O. R., Oduntan, O. A. E., Hassan, J. B., Falayi, C. F., & Ajayi, T. D. (2024). *Improving security of business intelligent systems with AI and machine learning. In 2024 IEEE SmartBlock4Africa*. IEEE., DOI: 10.1109/SmartBlock4Africa62047.2024.10709433

Wu, M.-C., & Buchmann, A. P. (1998). *Encoded bitmap indexing for data warehouses*. In *Proceedings of the 14th International Conference on Data Engineering (ICDE 1998)* (pp. 220–230). IEEE. https://doi.org/DOI: 10.1109/ICDE.1998.655780

Wylde, V., Rawindaran, N., Lawrence, J., Balasubramanian, R., Prakash, E., Jayal, A., & Platts, J. (2022). Cybersecurity, data privacy and blockchain: A review. *SN Computer Science*, *3*(2), 127. PMID: 35036930

Xie, D., Luo, H., & Meng, F. (2022). Trustworthy AI in business intelligence: The role of model explainability. *Big Data and Cognitive Computing*, *6*(4), 88. DOI: 10.3390/bdcc6040088

Yang, F., Tschetter, E., Léauté, X., Ray, N., Merlino, G., & Ganguli, D. (2014, June). *Druid: A real-time analytical data store*. In *Proceedings of the ACM SIGMOD International Conference on Management of Data* (SIGMOD ’14), 157–168. https://doi.org/DOI: 10.1145/2588555.2595631

Yang, Q., Liu, Y., Chen, T., & Tong, Y. (2019). Federated machine learning: Concept and applications. *ACM TIST*, *10*(2), 12. DOI: 10.1145/3298981

Yaseen, A. (2023). AI-driven threat detection and response: A paradigm shift in cybersecurity. *International Journal of Information and Cybersecurity*, *7*(12), 25–43.

Yi, H. (2024). An efficient E-voting system for business intelligence innovation based on blockchain. *Journal of the Knowledge Economy*, *15*(3), 11533–11547.

Yin, R. K. (2018). *Case study research and applications* (6th ed.). Sage.

Younisse, R., Alkasassbeh, M., Almseidin, M., & Abdi, H. (2023). An early detection model for Kerberoasting attacks and dataset labeling. *Jordanian Journal of Computers and Information Technology*, *9*(1), 1–15.

Yuan, S., Yang, W., Tian, X., & Tang, W. (2024). A blockchain-based privacy preserving intellectual property authentication method. *Symmetry*, *16*(5), 622.

Yu, P., Zhang, J., Fang, H., Li, W., Feng, L., Zhou, F., & Guo, S. (2023). Digital twin driven service self-healing with graph neural networks in 6g edge networks. *IEEE Journal on Selected Areas in Communications*, *41*(11), 3607–3623.

Yzzogh, H., Kandil, H., & Benaboud, H. (2024). A Comprehensive Overview Of AI-Driven Behavioral Analysis for Security in Internet of Things. *CRC Press EBooks*, 40–51. https://doi.org/DOI: 10.1201/9781032714806-4

Zafar, S., Ali, T. Y., & Uddin, A. (2023). EXAMINING THE ROLE OF BUSINESS ANALYTICS CAPABILITY IN FIRMS' AGILITY & PERFORMANCE: EVIDENCE FROM MANUFACTURING SECTOR. *Journal of Social Research Development*, *4*(4), 811–819. DOI: 10.53664/JSRD/04-04-2023-15-811-819

Zaghloul, E., Li, T., Mutka, M. W., & Ren, J. (2020). Bitcoin and blockchain: Security and privacy. *IEEE Internet of Things Journal*, *7*(10), 10288–10313.

Zanke, Mr. P., & Sontakke, D. (2024). The Impact of Business Intelligence on Organizational Performance. SSRN *Electronic Journal*. https://doi.org/DOI: 10.2139/ssrn.4847945

Zhang, G., Song, Y., & Xu, C. (2021). Edge computing for real-time analytics: A systematic literature review. *Future Internet*, *13*(9), 221. DOI: 10.3390/fi13090221

Zhou, J., Larson, P.-Å., & Chaiken, R. (2010, April). *Incorporating partitioning and parallel plans into the SCOPE optimizer*. In *Proceedings of the IEEE International Conference on Data Engineering (ICDE 2010)* (pp. 1060–1071). IEEE Computer Society. https://doi.org/DOI: 10.1109/ICDE.2010.5447802

Žliobaitė, I., Pechenizkiy, M., & Gama, J. (2016). An overview of concept drift applications. In *Big Data Analysis: New Algorithms for a New Society* (pp. 91-114). Springer. http://dx.doi.org/DOI: 10.1007/978-3-319-26989-4_4

Zuo, Y. (2024). Exploring the Synergy: AI Enhancing Blockchain, Blockchain Empowering AI, and their Convergence across IoT Applications and Beyond. *IEEE Internet of Things Journal*.

About the Contributors

Abdelraouf M. Ishtaiwi is a highly knowledge-achieving academic with over 22 years of experience in teaching and research in artificial intelligence (AI). He obtained a First-Class Honor and a Master's degree from a well-reputed university, Griffith University in Brisbane, in 2001 and 2007, respectively. He contribution to the AI field is enormous.

Ahmad Al-Qerem graduated in applied mathematics and M.Sc. in Computer Science at the Jordan University of Science and Technology and Jordan University in 1997 and 2002, respectively. After that, he was appointed as full-time lecturer at the Zarqa University. He was a visiting professor at Princess Sumaya University for Technology (PSUT). He obtained a Ph.D. from Loughborough University, UK. His research interests are in performance and analytical modeling, mobile computing environments, protocol engineering, communication networks, transition to IPv6, machine learning and transaction processing. He has published several papers in various areas of computer science. Currently, he has a full academic post as a full professor at computer science department at Zarqa University-Jordan.

Mohammad Ali Al Khaldy is Assistant professor in Business Intelligence and Data Analytics at University of Petra. He earned his B.Sc. in Computer Science from Al-al-Bayt University in 2003, followed by an M.Sc. in Computer Science from Amman Arab University in 2005, then in 2017 he earned a Ph.D. from Hull University, U.K., in the field of AI and Data Science. His research interests include data analytics, machine learning, predictive analytics, NLP, and decision support systems. His work has been published in toptier journals. Dr Alkhaldy taught a variety of courses in artificial intelligence and business intelligence, including data mining, business analytics, computer programming, intelligent business systems, data visualization, and machine learning. He is a member of Jordan Computers Society, and Arab Robotics and AI Association. He also serves on the Editorial Board of International Journal of Engineering and Artificial Intelligence (IJEA) and is an occasional reviewer for several other academic conferences and journals such as the International Conference on Information Technology (ICIT).

Mohammad Alauthman is an Associate Professor in the Information Security Department at the Faculty of Information Technology, University of Petra, Amman, Jordan. His research interests include network security, intrusion detection systems, and applying AI techniques—such as machine learning and deep learning—for botnet and DDoS detection, spam filtering, IoT security, and network traffic classification. He earned his Ph.D. in Computer Science from Northumbria University, UK, in 2016. Dr. Alauthman has received multiple research grants supporting advanced AI-driven intrusion detection systems and international collaboration. He is also actively involved in Erasmus+ projects, including BITTCOIN-JO (technology transfer), RL4Eng (remote engineering labs), Pro-GREEN LABs (green competences in education), and COMMO (mobility and cooperation across Mediterranean and Balkan institutions), contributing to innovation, sustainability, and cross-border academic development.

***

Mohammad Abu-Arqoub is a member of the Computer Science Department at the University of Petra, Amman, Jordan. He received his master's and Ph.D. degrees from Saint Petersburg State Electrotechnical University, Russia. His research interests include simulation, machine learning, algorithms, education and learning analytics, and e-learning.

Faris A. Abuhashishis an Assistant Professor at the University of Petra, specializing in CGI, Virtual Reality (VR), Augmented Reality (AR), Human-Computer Interaction (HCI), and Artificial Intelligence (AI). He holds a BSc and MS in Computer Science and earned his PhD from the Media and Games Innovation Centre of Excellence (MaGIC-X) at Universiti Teknologi Malaysia. Dr. Abuhashish has authored numerous publications, including journal articles, conference papers, and book chapters, and actively serves as a reviewer and Technical Program Committee (TPC) member for international journals and conferences. His research and contributions focus on advancing SWE, AI, CGI, multimedia systems, and immersive technologies, driving innovation and bridging academic and practical advancements.

Turki Al Masaeid is an Assistant Professor and Academic Support Manager at the Abu Dhabi School of Management (ADSM), with a rich background in education, leadership, and curriculum development. He holds a Ph.D. in Education from Yarmouk University and a Doctorate in Business Administration from the International American University. With over two decades of experience in academia and educational consultancy, Dr. Turki has contributed to various institutions including Ajman University, Canadian University in Dubai, and the Ministry of Education. His expertise spans teaching, curriculum design, academic evaluation, and strategic planning. He has published widely in peer-reviewed journals and presented at international conferences, particularly in the areas of leadership, AI in education, and organizational development. Dr. Turki is also a certified master trainer and has played a vital role in advancing professional development programs across the UAE. His vision is to foster a progressive educational environment that blends academic rigor with practical innovation.

Amjad Aldweesh is a computer associate professor interested in the Blockchain and Smart contracts technology as well as cyber security. Amjad has a Bachelor degree in computer science. He has a MSc degree in advanced computer science and security from the University of Manchester with distinction. Amjad is the second in the UK and the first in the middle east to have a PhD in the Blockchain and Smart contracts technology from Newcastle University.

SalamAl-E'mari earned her Ph.D. in Cybersecurity from Universiti Sains Malaysia (USM) in 2022. She is the Chair of the Information Security Department and an Assistant Professor at the University of Petra (UoP). With expertise in Blockchain, Deep Learning, and Network Security, she has contributed significantly to cybersecurity research. She previously earned her Bachelor's and Master's in Computer Science from Yarmouk University, Jordan, shaping her strong foundation in security and technology.

Wesam Alkhadour holds a Ph.D. in computer science from the University ofBradford, United Kingdom. She is currently an assistant professor at the University of Petra,Jordan.

Ammar Almomani Higher Colleges of Technology, Dept. of Information Science, Sharjah, UAE IT Dept., Al-Huson University College, Al-Balqa Applied University, Irbid, Jordan Email: ammarnav6@bau.edu.jo Prof. Ammar Almomani is a seasoned academic, researcher, and consultant with 20+ years of experience in cybersecurity, AI, and computer science. He holds a Ph.D. in Advanced Internet Security from Universiti Sains Malaysia and has taught over 45 specialized courses. He serves in the IT departments at Al-Balqa Applied University (Jordan) and Higher Colleges of Technology (UAE), contributing to research, curriculum design, and program accreditation (ABET, AACSB). He holds 10 patents (Germany and India) and has published 165+ articles (104 in Scopus), earning global recognition, a

UAE Golden Visa, and ranking among the Top 2% of Global Researchers (Stanford & Scopus, 2023–2024). Prof. Almomani also supervises MSc/Ph.D. students internationally, chairs conferences, and engages in industry collaborations. With 113,000+ ResearchGate readers.Prof. Almomani continues to make a significant impact in the fields of cybersecurity,AI and higher education fostering innovation .

Jamil Al-Sawwa is an Assistant Professor of Computer Science at Tafila Technical University, Jordan. He obtained a Ph.D. degree from North Dakota State University, USA, in 2019. His research area of interest includes computational intelligence, Machine Learning, Artificial Intelligence, Big Data Analytics, and Cybersecurity.

Maen Marwan Ali Al-Zubi is currently an Assistant Professor at the Department of Robotics and Artificial Intelligence at JADARA University. He obtained his Ph.D. in AI in 2020 at the University of MISKOLC (Miskolc, Hungary). He also obtained his Master of Computer Information Systems in 2007 at Arab Academy for Banking and Financial Sciences (Amman, Jordan). He did his First Degree in CS in 2004 at Irbid National University (Irbid, Jordan). Dr. Maen Al-Zubi published several papers in international Journals and participated in multi different conferences.

Fadi Fataftah is an experienced academic with a PhD in Information Technology and over 15 years of international experience in higher education, research, and industry across Canada, South Africa, Bahrain, and Jordan. He has taught a diverse range of courses in computer science, information technology, and cybersecurity, integrating real-world applications and problem-based learning methodologies. Dr. Fataftah's teaching philosophy emphasizes bridging theoretical concepts with practical skills, preparing students to thrive in dynamic, technology-driven environments. His research interests include cybersecurity, cloud computing, and IT governance, with contributions to peer-reviewed publications and international conferences. In addition to academia, he has worked in IT support and digital systems administration, further enhancing his practical expertise in the field.

Jorge Marx Gómez studied Computer Engineering and Industrial Engineering at the University of Applied Sciences Berlin (Technische Fachhochschule Berlin). He was a lecturer and researcher at the Otto-von-Guericke-Universität Magdeburg (Germany) where he also obtained a PhD degree in Business Information Systems with the work Computer-based Approaches to Forecast Returns of Scrapped Products to Recycling. From 2002 till 2003 he was a visiting professor for Business Informatics at the Technical University of Clausthal (TU Clausthal, Germany). In 2004 he received his habilitation for the work Automated Environmental Reporting through Material Flow Networks at the Otto-von-Guericke-Universität Magdeburg.

In 2005 he became a full professor and chair of Business Information Systems at the Carl von Ossietzky University Oldenburg (Germany). His research interests include Very Large Business Applications, Business Information Systems, Federated ERP-Systems, Business Intelligence, Data Warehousing, Interoperability and Environmental Management Information Systems.

Ala Hamarsheh is an associate professor at the Faculty of Engineering and Information Technology of the Arab American University of Jenin. Dr. Hamarsheh has obtained a PhD in engineering sciences from Vrije Universiteit Brussel (VUB)/ Brussels-Belgium in 2012. He graduated in computer science at the Faculty of Science, Birzeit University, Palestine, in 2000. He obtained an MSc degree in computer science at the Kind Abdullah II School for IT, The University of Jordan, Jordan, in 2003. Dr. Hamarsheh has published numerous papers in international refereed journals and conferences.

S. Ida Evangeline, presently working as an Assistant Professor in the Department of Electrical and Electronics Engineering at the Government College of Engineering, Tirunelveli, Tamilnadu, India. She obtained her Bachelor's in Electrical and Electronics Engineering from Manonmaniam Sundaranar University in 2003, and Master's in Power Systems Engineering from Anna University, Chennai, Tamilnadu, India in 2005. She completed her PhD degree in 2023 at Anna University, Chennai, Tamilnadu, India. She has published six research papers in international journals. Her current research interests include optimal power flow, renewable energy, soft computing, machine learning, and deep learning.

Ismahafezi Ismail obtained his Ph.D. in Computer Science from Universiti Teknologi Malaysia. He currently serves as a Senior Lecturer at the School of Multimedia, Faculty of Informatics and Computing, Universiti Sultan Zainal Abidin. His research interests include SWE, AI, immersive technologies (AR, VR, XR, Metaverse) and computer graphics.

Khalil Omar is an assistant professor at the University of Petra in Jordan. He received his Ph.D. degree in computer science from the University of Oldenburg, Germany, in 2018. His academic focus is on distance learning and e-learning in combination with software engineering, mobile applications, usability design, adaptive interfaces, and ERP systems. Users can reach him through his email address: komar@uop.edu.jo.

Yousef K. Sanjalawe is an Assistant Professor specializing in Cybersecurity and Cloud Computing at the University of Jordan (JU), Jordan. He earned his PhD in Cloud Computing from Universiti Sains Malaysia (USM) in 2020, where his research focused on enhancing cloud service broker selection using optimization algorithms. Dr. Sanjalawe has extensive experience in academia, research, and professional training. He has supervised Ph.D. students in Cybersecurity, Cloud Computing, IoT, Fog Computing, Optimization, and Artificial Intelligence (AI). From 2023 to 2024, he served as the Chair of the Cybersecurity Department at the American University of Madaba (AUM), Jordan, and from 2022 to 2024, he was an Assistant Professor in Cybersecurity at AUM.

Ali A. Titinchi obtained his M.Sc. and Ph.D. degrees in Computer Engineering from the University of Technology, Baghdad, Iraq, in 1987 and 1993, respectively. He is currently a faculty member in the Informatics and Software Engineering Department at Cihan University, Erbil, Iraq. His research interests include embedded systems, artificial intelligence, Database, real-time systems, and IoT technology.

Jamal Zraqou is an associate professor at the Department of Computer Science/ Virtual and Augmented Reality, University of Petra, Jordan, where he has been a faculty member since 2022. From 2018-2029, he was also the dean faculty of IT at IU. His research interests include computer vision, virtual and augmented reality, internet of things (IoT), cyber security, and image processing. He can be contacted at email: Jamal.Zraqou@uop.edu.jo.

Index

A

B

C

D

E

www.ingramcontent.com/pod-product-compliance
Lightning Source LLC
LaVergne TN
LVHW081535300926
849161LV00006B/1439